Innovating at the Edge

Innovating at the Edge

How organizations evolve and embed
innovation capability

Tim Jones

OXFORD AMSTERDAM BOSTON LONDON NEW YORK PARIS
SAN DIEGO SAN FRANCISCO SINGAPORE SYDNEY TOKYO

Butterworth-Heinemann
An imprint of Elsevier Science
Linacre House, Jordan Hill, Oxford OX2 8DP
225 Wildwood Avenue, Woburn MA 01801-2041

First published 2002

British Library Cataloguing in Publication Data
A catalogue record for this book is available from the British Library

Library of Congress Cataloguing in Publication Data
A catalogue record for this book is available from the Library of Congress

ISBN 0 7506 5519 4

For information on all Butterworth-Heinemann publications
visit our website at www.bh.com

Composition by Genesis Typesetting, Rochester, Kent
Printed and bound in Great Britain by Biddles Ltd.www.biddles.co.uk

Contents

Foreword

In *Innovating at the Edge*, Tim Jones gives us a very practical guide to what may have been seen historically as the preserve of R&D departments in large corporations. He brings innovation out of the shadowy confines of 'technology driven' companies and into the mainstream of corporate performance. No longer can companies hide behind the age-old reasoning that the tangible benefit of innovation may be 'difficult to define accurately', or 'not appropriate for a company of our size/in our industry'. The book demonstrates how innovation should now be viewed not only as a highly effective weapon on the battlefield of shareholder value and overall financial performance, but also as a raw ingredient in creating value. The weapon is not new, having effectively been available to all companies for some time. However it should not be confined by scale or culture, but embraced as a core strategic process across the whole spectrum of industrial endeavour.

This book is unique in effectively providing a 'How to . . .' for the business capabilities that drive innovation, a complete picture. In particular the case studies Tim Jones chooses bring to life as practical illustrations the embodiment of his message; the need to constantly improve a company's effectiveness by identifying the right approach.

Innovating at the Edge stresses to the reader the idea of a leading edge developing for innovation practice, and shows how things are constantly evolving. Companies are now taking an ever-expanding approach to reviewing and improving their performance. There has been a shift from companies perceiving innovation as an 'add-on', to a perception of it being a core means of long-term survival. Companies in today's competitive environment cannot afford to stand still, particularly those who are under pressure from investors looking for a particular return within a specified timeframe. But which way is forward? New products and new services will be developed, and if your company does not develop them then someone else will. That is an unavoidable truth. But these developments, be they product or service, cannot be attained without a coherent understanding of how and why innovation is necessary, coupled with a concerted approach to integrating that as a core business process.

Being aware of the potential for developing a competitive edge through innovation is one thing, taking advantage of that potential, and integrating that development into a company's strategic approach is an altogether larger and more significant step. Innovation is meaningless and ultimately worthless unless there is an increase in the perception of the 'value' to the customer, and it is this 'value' that differentiates between otherwise similar suppliers, not the actual products or the services offered. *Innovating at the Edge* goes a long way towards illustrating how best practice can be developed. The 'bottom line' is that the bottom line can be improved, with the right approach.

Richard James
Director
Reuters Business Insight

Preface

Through the class-leading successes of firms such as Amazon, Dow, Egg, Honda, Nokia, Samsung, Virgin and 3M, innovation has been brought to the front of the corporate psyche and is now viewed as the key differentiator in company performance. It fuels growth, engages customers, inspires teams, rewards investors and motivates the whole organization. Innovation is a fundamental driver of business success and, as such, requires informed, insightful and enthusiastic pioneers to take it to the next level. This book has been written for tomorrow's leaders. It is, at heart, about three issues – how companies have innovated in the past, the leading edge of innovation practice today, and how organizations embed innovation across their business activities. It is aimed at those who want to learn from others, and understand the context of where we have come from and where we are today in order that they can help to make the next advance. It has been written to inform, enthuse and guide those who will lead the next wave of innovation practice.

In writing *Innovating at the Edge* I have sought to address the three key questions:

1. How did we get here and what has worked in the past?
2. What are the latest ideas and approaches emerging today?
3. How can organizations best improve their innovation performance?

This book is therefore split into three core sections, each of which focuses on answering one of the above questions.

Part 1, Evolution of Innovation Capability, provides an overview of all of the major developments that have taken place to date. It describes the key steps that have occurred in the evolution of innovation capability over the past twenty years. Using a common set of themes and the most relevant examples of lead companies, it outlines the core strategic, operational and organizational approaches that have been introduced, adopted, adapted, refined and integrated within organizations during this period, and groups these into three distinct temporal phases:

1 1980–1986: Putting the basics in place
2 1987–1993: Globalization and acceleration
3 1994–1999: Focus and integration.

Part 2, Innovating at the Edge, details the latest leading edge innovation approaches that are being increasingly adopted today. Using examples of companies both large and small, it explains how organizations are now making the next steps forward in evolving how they innovate through redefining markets, recognizing customer values, sharing intellectual property to drive market penetration, integrating external investment, collaborating through networks and creating and leveraging value partnerships with brand equity. Although not all present in any one organization at the moment, these practices are all having an impact and are delivering results. As such, they can be seen to be the foundations of this, the latest phase of innovation evolution.

Part 3, Embedding Innovation, discusses how to position innovation successfully at the heart of the organization and reap the associated benefits. It focuses on the five critical steps in introducing sustainable improvement:

1 *Evaluation* – understanding current company and industry performance, identifying opportunities and assessing benefits
2 *Focus* – prioritizing action against corporate reality and defining the scope of the desired improvements and associated targets
3 *Design* – defining the most appropriate paths forward in the key enabling areas of strategy, process and organization
4 *Implementation* –providing clarity of responsibility for integration, introducing metrics to drive behaviour and measure progress, and raising awareness and understanding of the improvements being made, and
5 *Review* – ensuring assessment of progress, identifying areas for attention, re-evaluating performance, capability and culture and then planning the next phase of continued improvement.

Using several case studies throughout, this section highlights some of the varied techniques that are being used to embed innovation in organizations and, also identifies some of the pitfalls that are encountered along the way.

These three core sections have been written so that they can be read individually as separate entities. However, to gain the full insight of context and implication and to achieve the greatest benefit, it is recommended that all three be followed in order.

Innovation is driven by the desire and the ability to take on the next challenge, raise your game and make the next move forward. I hope that, as both a provocation and a guide, *Innovating at the Edge* will prove to be of value in helping your organization advance.

Tim Jones
London, 2002

Acknowledgements

This book has grown from several years of searching for a reasoned yet insightful overview of successful innovation practice as it has evolved. As I have worked with a wide range of differing organizations across multiple sectors, many new issues and potential problems in successfully innovating have been raised. In many cases the solutions have already existed, albeit elsewhere, in another industry. More often than not, the answer to any major concern has already been developed and proven by another organization. It may require adaptation to suit the individual circumstances present in the new application but, in essence, the core approach has already been defined. The challenge therefore is not in reinventing the wheel but in tweaking it so that it meets the new needs at hand. By adding an extra spoke to strengthen the methodology, increasing the tyre width to broaden scope or better lubricating the axle to aid implementation, adopting the insights from the learning achieved by one company can aid the improving of innovation performance that can be achieved by another. The secret is in working out which elements are the most appropriate and which are not. This book addresses my search by bringing together such insights within an overall framework that provides context and understanding of benefit.

Like any new idea, *Innovating at the Edge* is a product not just of one mind but of many. Although I have led the creation of the concept and have been responsible for the delivery of the text, in preparing it I have drawn on input from past and current colleagues and friends who have been very much part of an extended development team. Within and outside Innovaro, there are several key people that I would therefore like to thank:

Sue Austin for the days spent proof reading the draft text; Bob Brentin for pointing the way to the appropriate information at Dow; David Coates for the discussions on the role of the brand in innovation; Janette Dobson for the feedback on Qualcomm and Bluetooth; Chris Fitzsimmons for his insights on intellectual property and investment processes; Lisa Fretwell for her perspectives from experience in enabling virtual collaboration; David Humphries for the Clarks case material; Max Khan for the fan's point of view on Manchester United; Neil Kirby for his comments on the development of WAP; Simon Kirby for his input on ABB, eBay and Skandia; Ben Luckett for his insights on web site development; Gary McCloskey for the detailed overview of digital TV; Stuart McGregor for the MSN perspective; Tobias Rooney for the updates on the pharmaceutical industry; and Anna Soisalo for the contributions on Zara and continuous development.

In particular I would like to thank Anna Soisalo for the extensive editing over numerous Sunday afternoons and weekday evenings and the encouragement in driving the project to timely completion. Finally I would like to thank Ailsa Marks, my editor at Butterworth-Heinemann, and her team for the continued support in moving the concept from design into reality.

Author profile

Tim Jones is a Principal with Innovaro, a firm focused exclusively on enabling improved innovation performance within organizations. For nearly twenty years he has been active in the conception, development and introduction of a wide range of both evolutionary and revolutionary products and services across multiple sectors. He has gained an extensive understanding of the consumer products, telecommunications and pharmaceuticals sectors, and has also worked in the aerospace, automotive and financial services industries.

With experience obtained from a variety of design, research, consultancy and line management roles, Tim has worked with many of the world's leading innovation companies, creating and developing new ideas, leading development teams, defining new strategies and processes, designing new organizational structures and creating innovation-centric cultures to build new and improved innovation capability.

Tim is also involved with several professional organizations, including the Product Development and Management Association, which he led in the UK from 2000 to 2002. He has Masters degrees from Cambridge and the Royal College of Art, and a PhD in conflict within multidisciplinary teams. Having spent time over the years in the UK, the USA and the Netherlands, Tim now lives and works in London.

Introduction

Ten innovation myths

Organizations fearing the impact of innovation or believing that innovation does not apply to their arenas of activity frequently cite a number of justifications for not embracing it. They create excuses and do this, not from the perspective of what it is about their company that is preventing innovation, but as opinions about innovation itself. These views are used to refuse investment in new ideas, maintain a conservative *status quo* and dispel arguments supporting organic growth, and, in effect, become one of the primary barriers to innovation and progress. These innovation myths are killers of creativity, diluters of organizational capability development and often obstructions to substantial progress. Before addressing how organizations have and continue to successfully innovate, it is therefore pertinent first to dispel these myths for what they are – myths.

Myth 1: Innovation does not impact the bottom line

Yes it does. Companies that use innovation as a core part of their strategy and as a key driver of new product and service development have been proven to be more successful than those that don't. Study after study has shown that firms that use innovation to differentiate their products are more successful, that innovative companies grow faster, and that the most innovative firms provide returns, in such hard measurable areas as shareholder value, many times those of non-innovators. Innovation, whether focused on new technologies, new products, new business models or new customer relationships, not only fuels top line growth but also has a direct and positive impact on the bottom line. Companies as diverse as American Express, Ford and eBay all use innovation as a key part of their business strategies, not because it sounds good and will make the CEO stand out from his or her peers, but because it has a direct, positive effect on profitability.

Myth 2: Innovation only applies to products, not services

Federal Express, UPS, Cantor and Sprint are all US-based organizations that are continually developing and offering new innovations into the marketplace. First Direct, Egg, Rentokil and Direct Line are similarly innovative companies in the UK. Likewise, across the rest of the world – from News International and AMP in Australia, HSBC and Hutchinson in Asia to Deutsche Post and Swiss Re in the heart of Europe and Skandia in Scandinavia – leading companies are using innovation as a core element to drive growth. Although innovation is often associated in the media and hence the business mind with product-based firms such as Sony, the companies above are innovating in services across the board from financial and delivery services to telecommunication services. Moreover, there is an increasing array of firms from Amazon and Dell to Shell and Zara that are using innovation in both products and services to sustain growth, increase market share and improve margins.

Myth 3: Innovation is only relevant to a few industries

Because of the noise that is generated whenever new products are released in some arenas, it is easy to believe that innovation is only applicable in, say, the consumer products, retailing, banking, aerospace, pharmaceutical and telecommunications industries. However, innovation is certainly not restricted to these sectors. It is just as relevant in the chemicals, education, insurance, real estate, distribution and construction industries. Companies as varied as BOC, Dow, EF, Lloyds, CGNU, Pilkington and Amec are all keen innovators in their own fields. They and their innovations, from new chemical solutions to on-line house selling and fast-track construction techniques, may not be as famous in the consumer mindset, but they are all testament to the power of innovation across all industries. In fact, in these sectors where innovation is not as expected, the ability to use it and apply it as a key source of gaining competitive advantage has, in many ways, more impact.

Myth 4: Innovation requires high investment in new technology

If a laundry is improving service quality by introducing a slimmed-down order intake process or doubling home deliveries, it is innovating. Where is the new technology here? Innovation can be enabled by new technology, but it is not a prerequisite. For many industries, innovation is technology independent. Quicker production processes, more accurate customer targeting, reduction in component cost, faster order turnaround and improved brand awareness are all components and consequences of innovation, and can all be achieved without investment in technology. Although technology has to be used to enable innovations resulting in improved microchip manufacture or automated voice recognition software, these are actually in the minority. Less than 20 per cent of innovation involves technology investment, for the majority is focused on improving the processes, strategies and organizational structures delivering new products and services, none of which are implicitly linked to technology investment.

Myth 5: Innovation only occurs in R&D and marketing

Within the organization, two functional areas have emerged in the minds of many as the primary sources of innovation. Research and development, with a focus on inventing and developing new technologies, and marketing, with a corresponding focus on understanding and identifying new and emerging opportunities in the marketplace, are both seen as the centres of innovation in many companies. Whilst it is clearly true that both play a vital role in many firms, it is wrong to assume that they are the sole sources of corporate innovation. Externally, suppliers, customer and distributors are all major sources of innovation, and inside the organization, operations, sales and customer support are frequently the areas where new ideas first emerge. As well as proactively coming up with such elements as improvements in process efficiency, these disciplines are able to use their immediate participation in the delivery of products and services to the actual customers to spot new issues. Recent enhancements in air travel for Continental came not from R&D or marketing, but from the baggage handlers and stewardesses whose day-to-day interaction with the business gave them the necessary insights to identify opportunities for innovation. Likewise, and somewhat more famously, it was a salesman and not a researcher at 3M who first identified the need for a tape that could easily peel off painted surfaces – an insight that resulted in the development of Scotch tape.

Myth 6: Innovation is a talent that a few people are born with, and cannot be learnt

Creativity, invention and the ability to innovate are in us all. As children we are constantly questioning everything around us, encountering new objects and having new experiences that prompt us to come up with new ideas – sometimes similar to others, but sometimes also quite bizarre. For the majority of us our education forces us, both by stimulus and reward, to be more 'left-brained' – to analyse and think logically. Both in the majority of subjects that we follow and often the means by which we are taught, the desire for academic rigour kills creativity. With the exception of a few subjects and educational establishments, for most of us the ages between five and twenty are when we learn how not to be innovative. Those that escape this either through focusing on the arts or by becoming outsiders are not necessarily the candidates that many businesses recruit. They are not your typical company people. However, the latent talent for innovation still exists within everyone. It may well be hidden under a mass of procedure and logical thinking, but it can be re-ignited. Many firms, from Microsoft to Safeway, are using a host of techniques from the environmental to the attitudinal to help their employees rediscover creativity, break down the barriers between work and play and learn how to be innovative again.

Myth 7: Only small companies can innovate

This is an understandable but again false perspective, for innovation is a capability that can be and is successfully utilized across organizations large and small alike. This is often more evident in the success of a small company entering into a new market or developing a new technology, specifically because the success of the firm itself is probably highly dependent on how successful and therefore how well promoted the associated innovation is. However, innovation is just as prominent in large companies as in small ones; it is because large companies already have an established market position, product portfolio and customer base on which a good proportion of the organization and revenue generation is focused that innovation is sometimes less apparent, although not always. There are many large companies that can indeed be characterized by successful innovation. Nokia, 3M, Canon, Sony, DuPont and GE are clearly some of the exemplars in their respective sectors, but other, less innovation-renowned companies such as Exxon, Corus, Nestlé and Bank of America all have active new product and service development activities driving and supporting corporate growth. Innovation is not unique to any size of company; it is a capability that applies and can be adopted by all.

Myth 8: Innovation disrupts the organization

Particularly in established companies with mature processes and long-term customers, it is understandable why some fear that innovation will be a disruption. Overprotection of existing steady state production, delivery and customer management activities frequently causes the prospect of, and the opportunities to be gained from, innovation to be rejected. Some firms are scared that the introduction of innovation, something that is clearly different and likely to challenge the *status quo*, is better off kept in check, most likely outside the organization. Letting it in would mean change, and nobody wants that. For those with such a closed perspective there are clearly many hurdles to be overcome, but for the vast majority of companies, innovation is not disruptive but instead rejuvenating. Stagnation and complacency are barriers to growth and killers of creating value. Innovation can disrupt the organization if you want it to be used to bring about fundamental change, as has happened with GE. However, if introduced in a controlled manner to only one area, as it was by Prudential when it established Egg, the UK online financial services operator, then the impact on existing businesses (in this case door-to-door selling of insurance) can be mitigated. Innovation can disrupt the organization, but only if you want it to, and certainly not always.

Myth 9: Innovation cannot be managed

Creativity may well be unpredictable, but it is not uncertain. It will happen. The challenge is in focusing it and capturing the outputs. Managing creativity within the innovation process is not easy, but, just as with the rest of the more predictable development and realization innovation activities, it can be managed. From providing the initial stimulus for new ideas and a means of collating and evaluating them through to determining the most appropriate exploitation approaches and selecting delivery partners, innovation is a process and can therefore be managed. Moreover, it is a process that is largely generic and hence similar from one sector to another. Innovation in financial services follows the same path as innovation in consumer goods. The detail may vary, but the approach is frequently identical. As a consequence, managing innovation is also a generic skill that can be learnt in one arena and applied to another.

Myth 10: Innovation cannot be measured

Although not an assembly line where efficiency can be measured by tolerance or rejection rates, and not itself a service where activation time or number of customer complaints can be tracked to indicate effectiveness, innovation can be measured. Innovative companies do not encourage innovation without paying careful attention to the success of their innovations. Just as the quality of output from any production process can be measured in terms of both overall performance and individual stage efficiency, so can innovation. Whether using high-level metrics such as revenue from new products, or component elements such as ideas generated, patents granted, time to market, number of products launched or payback times, any organization can create its own series of innovation indicators. Either as part of a cascaded balanced scorecard or as a stand-alone performance metric, innovation can be and is successfully measured and monitored in many leading firms.

2

Why innovate?

Innovation has moved from a good idea to an imperative.
Paul Saffo, Director, Institute for the Future, Palo Alto, California

An individual innovation has value, but it doesn't make or break a company anymore. That's why you need the culture of Innovation.
Tom Kelley, IDEO, San Francisico

Innovation is the pirate ship sailing into the yacht club.
John Jordan, Principal, CGEY Centre for Business Innovation, Boston

These three varied *Business Week* quotations (Cortese, 2001) are all good sound bites, but what do they really mean? This thing called innovation is clearly something that many firms are paying more attention to, and it sounds good, but what is the real impact? Is it here to stay, or is it just another business school fad? Is this not just another convenient buzzword for improved efficiency and effectiveness? Should you, as say a manager busy with meeting the needs of the day-to-day survival and growth of your business, concern yourself with this innovation thing? Does it really apply? Isn't there something else that can have more immediate influence on company performance? If innovation is relevant, than how and where can it be applied? What does it involve? What are the benefits? Basically, why innovate?

Corporate performance

Throughout the 1980s and 1990s, a wide range of panaceas for the problem of becoming more competitive and improving business performance were proposed. However, although a number of practices such as Total Quality Management and Business Process Re-engineering provided some improvement, not all delivered consistent benefit. Whilst the original predictions for the value of these techniques was strong, with failure rates of TQM programmes running as high as 80 per cent one year after inception and BPR projects being abandoned, many companies reaped little benefit. It is not that the original concepts were flawed, but rather that many organizations assumed that they could simply be copied, without the need to adapt them to suit individual circumstances (Tidd *et al.*, 1997).

Over the same period, some of the companies that have shown repeatedly above-average growth in both performance and shareholder value have used innovation as a core strategic means of developing their businesses. Indeed, financial markets reward innovation. A recent study found that the top 20 per cent of the most innovative firms deliver almost four times the total shareholder returns of the bottom 20 per cent of innovators (Jones and Kirby, 2001). Share price includes an element of implied growth, be it organic or by merger and acquisition (M&A). The M&A route is perilous – most studies have found that around three-quarters of M&A activity fails to create value for shareholders, and, of the mergers that fail, 70 per cent do so due to cultural and people issues. Organic growth is the alternative to M&A, and for this, innovation is almost always necessary. Even a decade ago, innovative organizations – those that are able to use innovation to differentiate their products and services from competitors – were, on average, twice as profitable as other firms (Pavitt, 1991). Companies as varied as 3M, Xerox, Nike, DuPont, First Direct and Sony have all since continued to use innovation to meet such challenges as exploiting discontinuities, accelerating activities, encouraging growth and developing new businesses. Moreover, as new opportunities have been identified, new companies have been created to exploit them. Innovation has been at the forefront of the growth and development of new products and services for a host of new arrivals, from Amazon, eBay and Egg in the Internet space to Smint, Dyson and Orange in the 'real' world. Each of these successful companies continues to position innovation at the heart of their business strategy to challenge convention and redefine the competitive landscapes within which they operate.

The development of new products and services that can successfully compete in local, national and global markets has now become a key concern for organizations, regardless of the sector in which they operate. Across industries, effective innovation performance has overtaken production efficiency as the key industrial battleground as companies all seek to reduce time-to-market and to access new technologies in their bid to develop more and better products and services. This is occurring not just in the core manufacturing sectors, but also in service sectors as varied as insurance, waste management and education. In all fields, the benefits to be attained range from better resource utilization and sustained competitiveness to increased revenue generation and improved shareholder return. Whether involved in the manufacture of discrete products such as consumer goods, medical devices and industrial machinery, in the production of consumables such as chemicals, paper and cereals, or in the provision of services such as banking, IT support and tourism, most forward looking organizations are today continuously looking for new opportunities to develop and exploit new or improved products and services.

'Innovate or die' has been the mantra for many leading companies over the past twenty years as they have sought to drive the whole ethos of innovation and continuous improvement throughout their organizations. Firms worldwide have adopted an increasing variety of techniques and approaches to improve their innovation performance and to benefit more from new ideas. Some of these have addressed strategic issues and some the varied processes in use across the company and its network of suppliers and customers, whilst others have focused on core organizational issues such as motivation, reward and structure.

For many, innovation is about small changes to existing products or services. This incremental innovation keeps products and services in tune with customer needs, but never surprises them. It is responsible for the introduction of a new feature in the Word software or the Sony laptop that is being used to write this book. It is incremental innovation that drives the introduction of a new flavour of toothpaste, a new DVD player fascia, or quicker pizza delivery. Incremental innovation is a key component of the innovation toolbox, but in itself is not the be all and end all.

Especially in a world where such incremental innovation is increasingly the norm, coming up with the next step advance is something that is becoming all too easy and, in turn, is rarely enough to guarantee success. Often it is not the first idea that makes it, nor is it the second or the third. These are usually the obvious solutions that many may come up with to a given problem. It is the 'non-obvious', the 'left-field' concept that is 'out of the box', that is needed. Whatever the expression you choose, to be successful today you are not after small step, incremental improvements, but the big leap forwards. You are after your equivalent of the Walkman, the Post-it or Viagra.

Real innovation is more fundamental than incremental innovation. It goes deeper. Real innovation concerns new ideas, and not updated versions of old ones. It stimulates new thoughts, defines new processes, builds new organizational structures and enables new and exciting strategies to be realized. Real innovation can at its most extreme change markets. Innovation can disrupt industries. Napster, Dyson, Smint, Egg and eBay have all redefined their respective marketplaces. They have fundamentally changed the *status quo*.

However, one brilliant idea is not, by itself, sufficient to bring success to a company. Nor does the adoption of an experimental creative environment ensure any lasting value. An organization focused on innovation and on efficiently developing ideas and launching them into the marketplace does not guarantee profitable revenue streams either. In fact, the successful exploitation of new ideas is not solely concerned with any of the following:

- Being creative
- Seeing a promising opportunity
- Having the resources available to develop an idea
- Efficiently launching a new product into a market
- Copying what others have done before.

It is all of these. These are some of the essential components of the capability that many organizations aspire to but only a select few truly possess. Each of these form only part of the means by which leading companies deliver exciting new products and services to their customers.

It is the orchestrated interplay between the creation, selection and delivery of new ideas that allows companies like Sony, GE and Nokia consistently to outperform their competitors by being the quickest and the smartest as they grasp new technological opportunities, create new and unique propositions, and continuously deliver compelling and competitive new products and services. Companies that do not achieve this are increasingly unlikely to be able to enjoy any significant level of sustained performance in this area. While these capabilities may not necessarily reside in any one group or even one company, it is their bringing together in a synergistic manner that allows leading organizations successfully to deliver new ideas into their chosen markets time after time after time.

Innovation in good times

In times of fast economic growth or accelerated corporate expansion, innovation is the fuel of new business development. New ideas, new products and new services are the lifeblood of sustained increases in both revenue and profitability. When times are good, the opportunity for enhanced margins through providing the latest and the most exciting propositions is something that many firms can take advantage of. As ever more companies seek to exploit emerging opportunities and provide similar services targeted on new markets, innovation is a key differentiator. When all and sundry are releasing new products, innovation is a main driver of many purchase decisions. As organizations vie with one another to be the first to market with new technology, product innovation is an added benefit for the customer that will often influence product selection. When price is secondary to value, innovation in such arenas as new technology or improved customer interaction is key to providing companies with the all-important competitive advantage. Furthermore, as firms seek to diversify activities into new arenas, innovative value-sharing partnerships are a key mechanism to providing extended corporate reach and exploitation of brand and customer bases.

Throughout the 1990s boom, companies across the board from GE, Intel and IBM to Amazon, eBay and even MP3 and Napster all used new ways of doing business to change the rules; firms from Apple to Zanussi all used leadership in product innovation to move to the fore and regain market share; organizations such as American Express, FedEx and HSBC all used innovative enhancements in customer service to provide that little bit extra that grew their market shares. There is little doubt that when businesses and consumers alike have money to spend, innovation is a key desirable for all, and creating new revenues is more effective than reducing costs. Increased margins can be far more effectively delivered through the development and introduction of value-providing new products than by the slimming down of operations. Efficient delivery is a key component of profitable products and services, but, if there is a choice of focus in any period of economic boom, using innovation to exploit the opportunities that are made available is by far a better route for corporate growth and improved profitability.

Innovation in a downturn

In the more challenging times of recession, innovation is no longer an option to add value and deliver extra competitive advantage. When costs are reduced to the minimum, budgets are cut and growth subsides, innovation becomes a core means of survival. This is when, more than ever, it really is a case of innovate or die! As prices fall to a common base and margins are cut to secure turnover, the market becomes more selective, and products and services are often pitched at the same level, it is innovation that again provides the critical differentiator. Additional performance, increased functionality or improved customer service for the same price all provide focus and become the main drivers in defining customer preferences. In good times and bad, innovation is the core means of driving growth, as it affects both the top and bottom lines.

As firms are prompted to adopt best practice quickly to reduce costs and improve efficiency, competitive advantages are lost and, in the provision of products and services, if it is to survive, one company has to become as good as another. In such circumstances value and not just price becomes a differentiator, and companies who leverage innovation in new ways come out on top. Dyson's vacuum cleaners continued to sell well in the 2001/2002 downturn in consumer confidence, even though the company maintained its higher price points. Likewise, sales of Sony's Playstation, Apple's iBook and Daimler-Chrysler's Smart car all outpaced rivals despite a general consumer slowdown. Innovation sells products and services no matter what the economic conditions.

Organizational effects

As well as having an impact on financial performance, innovation also affects the organization itself. A successful innovation exploiter requires and acquires a creative culture. This in turn stimulates a motivated workforce and, as a reputation for innovation grows, so more people seek to join in. Innovative companies attract the best people, and so the benefits multiply. In the parlance of *Funky Business*, innovative companies become the 'organizations worth working for' and so attract the 'people worth employing' (Nordstom and Ridderstrale, 1999). In contrast to the cost-cutting culture of much of the financial services sector, innovative companies like Egg, Virgin Money and First Direct in the UK attract the leaders. As such, innovation supports and drives the development of a new culture.

In addition, an innovative organization promotes a positive message to the outside world. Companies such as 3M, Canon, BMW, Lexus and numerous other emulators use the fact that they are innovative as a key message in much of their corporate advertising. Innovation thus supports the brand. IBM, Intel and Nokia are three of the world's top five brands, not because they spend a fortune on advertising like fellow brand value leaders Coca Cola and Marlboro, but because they are known as the innovation leaders (Interbrand, 2001). Moreover, the perception of an innovative organization helps to maintain leadership. Sony has, through its long-term track record in continued product innovation, created an aura of innovation to such an extent that for many it has become the brand of choice. Even when faced with two nearly identical products at a similar price point, it is the one with a Sony label on it that is more likely to sell.

Outside the organization

Innovation success also influences the external environment of the firm. Through the positive impact on customers, suppliers and subcontractors, innovation success within the firm in turn promotes and encourages more innovation outside. As one company flourishes or one source of innovation prospers, so others are either created or moved into close proximity. Whether through the founding of new companies by leaving employees, the spinning out of new ventures or the relocation of partner or supplier operations into the local area, once sufficient inertia is achieved, innovation in one company quickly creates a cluster of other innovative firms. As such, a hot bed of innovation can be the driver of economic growth in a whole region. Frequently linked to either a leading university or a major company, innovation clusters pushing regional growth have become an increasingly common phenomenon. Either by accident or design, innovation clusters have become predominant in the expansion and success of a number of identifiable regions:

- Cambridge University and MIT have both facilitated the establishment and growth of major technology-driven innovation firms in the surrounding areas. Just as Polaroid, Gillette, Genzyme and a host of organizations including Innovation Associates, Akamai and Cap Gemini Ernst & Young's Centre for Business Innovation have grown up in the Boston area, so have companies such as PA Technology, Generics Group, The Technology Partnership, Zeus, ARM and Autonomy all been outcomes of England's Silicon Fen around Cambridge.
- Nokia's growth throughout the 1990s stimulated a massive increase in the creation of innovative companies in and around Helsinki. The continued presence of a developing major multinational demanded not only a host of suppliers and subcontractors able to provide and partner on new innovations in the mobile telecommunications area, but also encouraged the development of south-west Finland as one of Europe's innovation powerhouses. Especially in the high-tech arena, and largely on the back of Nokia, Finland has moved to top position

in Europe for high-tech patent filings per capita, and number two in the EU Innovation Scoreboard (EU Innovation Scoreboard, 2001).

- Similarly, areas such as North Carolina's Research Triangle, Silicon Valley and, more recently, the Sophia Antipolis park in Southern France have all grown into major global innovation centres from the consequence of the co-location of a combination of leading universities and the corporate research activities of such organizations as Lucent, Intel and IBM.

At its greatest extent, innovation has also shown itself capable of driving a whole country's development and fuelling national economies. Innovation is now a major issue for every developed and developing economy; it is vital to business and wider economic growth. Firms that are successful in innovation increase exports and so secure competitive advantage in rapidly changing world markets, and the economies that generate and support such firms prosper (HM Treasury, 1998). Innovation is therefore seen as fundamental to stimulating and supporting economic growth, and in enabling wealth generation in many industrialized nations. Just as the Industrial Revolution was responsible for the accelerated growth of the British economy in the eighteenth and nineteenth centuries, in the more recent past a number of other countries have also been able to use innovation as a key component of economic growth. As well as Finland, the most prominent in this have been Ireland, Taiwan and Korea, each of which has adopted different approaches for attracting investment and leveraging the benefits of innovation.

- For Ireland, a combination of low corporation tax and a highly skilled English-speaking workforce was the driver for the location of leading R&D and production facilities for many US-based pharmaceutical, computing and telecommunications companies, including Merck, Dell and Nortel. The consequential growth from local innovation resulted in Ireland becoming Europe's leading generator of added value from technology throughout the 1990s (EU Innovation Scoreboard, 2001).
- Taiwan used its global 'Innovalue' campaign to promote the whole country as a source of innovation and high quality production, to raise itself from being a low-cost manufacturing site for Japanese and US companies and to move home-grown companies to the forefront. Giant, now the world's leading bicycle producer is Taiwanese, as is top ten PC manufacturer Acer.
- Korea's five major *chaebol*, led by Samsung, Hyundai and Lucky-Goldstar, have collectively made a significant and

world-leading shift from followers to leaders in the introduction of innovative new products which through the 1990s simultaneously lifted the whole country's GDP per capita to European levels, exhibiting average growth of 7.3 per cent (Economist Intelligence Unit, 1998).

Innovation today

As firms have developed across industry, so the portfolio of approaches to taking new ideas to market has itself evolved. As the new economy is brought into line with the old, and the increasing fragmentation of a global economy drives change across multiple sectors, firms operating at the leading edge of the innovation paradigm are adopting a whole new set of approaches to help them redefine the present and build the future. No longer shackled with traditional asset-based economics, companies are increasingly seeing the value of exploiting their intellectual property across multiple sectors, collaboratively working across networks, matching equity to brand value, and introducing a continuous stream of ever-evolving new products and services.

As the demands of escalating globalization, greater market variation, faster product introduction and more efficient product and service delivery all have an impact on companies worldwide, innovation and its capacity to drive growth across all arenas is increasingly a fundamental issue. Firms seeking to exploit their potential are using innovation as a core element of their corporate strategy and embedding it into the very core of their organization. Innovation is the source of increasing value and differentiation in an ever more crowded and homogeneous marketplace. As such, how companies can build and develop their innovation capability is a critical concern. The following chapters detail how this has occurred.

References

Cortese, A. (2001). Masters of innovation. *Business Week*, **50**.

Economist Intelligence Unit (1998). Country Data (1990–1996).

EU Innovation Scoreboard (2001), www.cordis.lu/innovation-smes

HM Treasury (1998). *Innovating for the Future*. Department of Trade and Industry.

Interbrand (2001). www.interbrand.com

Jones, T. and Kirby, S. (2001). *Taking Ideas to Market*. John Wiley.

Nordstom, K. and Ridderstrale, J. (1999). *Funky Business*. Book-House Publishing.

Pavitt, K. (1991). Key characteristics of the large innovating firm. *Br. J. Management*, **2(1)**, 41–50.

Tidd, J., Bessant, J. and Pavitt, K. (1997). *Managing Innovation: Integrating Technological, Market and Organisational Change*. John Wiley.

Evolution of innovation capability

Introduction to Part 1

The last two decades have seen an increasingly faster development of the art and science of innovation than at any other period in history – faster even than the peak years of the Industrial Revolution. Companies across the world have embraced new technologies, created new processes, exploited new markets, formed new organizations and realized new strategies – all to enable improved development and delivery of new products, services and businesses. This has occurred not just in one specific lead sector but throughout industry, from computing and consumer products through to pharmaceuticals and retail.

As firms have sought to enhance their approaches to innovation in order to improve performance, they have evolved practice and, in doing so, created, built and integrated new innovation capabilities within the organization. Many have experimented with new ideas for stimulating, organizing, prioritizing, managing and enabling innovation to deliver increased benefits to the firm, its customers and its suppliers. Some of these ideas have failed or, although ideal in theory, have proven to be unsustainable in practice. Others, however, have worked well and achieved – and sometimes exceeded – the desired objectives. These have consistently delivered the improvements they were envisaged to, and as such have become a core part of the day-to-day practice within the originating organizations. Moreover, on the back of this, many of these improvements have subsequently been successfully migrated across sectors. They have proven themselves to deliver benefits in organizations large and small, and to enhance performance equally from one industry to another. For many firms these have, in effect, been translated into the mainstream of innovation practice and gradually become the standard *de facto* approach.

Reviewing the past twenty years, there have been three main waves of new approaches that have occurred across industry. These distinct waves have each had a different focus, followed different schedules and been comprised of differing techniques and approaches, and have all had a significant impact on corporate performance across the board. At the point of first development and introduction, these waves have all come to represent the leading edge of innovation practice for the time and, as each component approach has gradually been adopted across industry and become standard practice, have in turn stimulated the next wave of new ideas, and thereby the new edge, to take shape. As organizations have integrated the previous wave into the core of their operations to build their innovation capabilities, so new approaches that can be used on top of, in parallel with or sometimes even instead of existing methods have evolved innovation best practice. These three waves have, at heart, addressed several core common issues:

- 1980–1986: Putting the basics in place
- 1987–1993: Globalization and acceleration
- 1994–1999: Focus and integration.

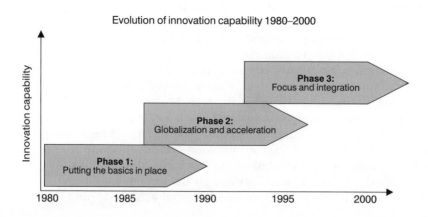

Evolution of innovation capability 1980–2000

The three waves of innovation capability evolution have had an impact on all aspects of a firm's operations, from strategy and process to organization. As you delve into the individual elements that comprise these waves of leading edge practice and examine where and when they were first introduced on a recognizable scale, the elements can be generically grouped into seven main areas:

1 *Strategic impetus* – the corporate theme that has driven innovation
2 *Market focus* – how innovations have been presented to customers
3 *Product attribute* – the differentiating feature for new products and services
4 *Activity effectiveness* – the key component for successful innovation delivery
5 *Development process* – how new products and services have been delivered
6 *Enabling organization* – the structure of the group delivering innovation
7 *External alliances* – how firms work with partners to realize innovation.

It is across all seven of these areas that individual improvements in innovation practice have occurred and continue to occur. As the edge of innovation practice has moved on, each time new approaches in these seven areas have emerged and been introduced.

Today, we are into a fourth wave of innovation capability development. Although many firms are still grappling with some of the issues presented in earlier phases of this capability evolution, there is, across different sectors, a whole new portfolio of approaches being tried out, proven to deliver improvement and thus being adopted by other firms seeking to emulate this. These are the new approaches to improving performance that will tomorrow become standard. We are now in the middle of this fourth wave of innovation capability evolution, and today this is the leading edge. Companies that are developing and refining the new techniques for innovation success are today at the forefront of innovation practice. They are 'innovating at the edge'.

This first section of the book focuses on the varied approaches that have, over the years, formed the first three waves of the leading edge of innovation. Through examining each of the seven component approaches that have been used and subsequently migrated into the mainstream, and highlighting leading adopters in each wave, it provides an overview of where we have come from and where some companies are now. In doing so, it not only gives a contextual framework for the development of an organization's innovation capability, but also identifies they key challenges for firms adopting these approaches both today and in the future.

3

Phase 1: Putting the basics in place

The first major period of recent advance in how organizations have taken their ideas to market occurred in the early to mid-1980s, when companies facing the challenges of increased competition and more rapid technological advancement sought to accommodate several new challenges. This was when firms as diverse as Sony, IBM and Dow all started to formulate product strategies as a distinctive element and dependency of their overall corporate strategy. How innovation could be used to create, develop and support an evolving portfolio of new products and services focused on future revenue and margin growth was being considered in a proactive manner for the first time. Product strategy emerged from under the wings of either overall business or marketing and sales strategies, and came into the limelight.

At the forefront of this was the increasing role of technology in creating and enabling the development and introduction of new products and services. From semiconductors to composite materials, database management software to the first call centres, the adoption of new technology became a core strategic focus for many companies, and as a means of effecting this the management of external alliances to facilitate the transfer of the appropriate technologies from lead innovators, universities and other research establishments became a key challenge. Understanding the technology, never mind selecting the most appropriate type for an application, was a major headache for many. Furthermore, ensuring that access, integration, upgrading and support were managed in a coherent and focused manner was, in many cases, frequently being seen less as a black art and more as a core corporate capability.

At the same time, although largely focused on their regional markets, companies were increasingly aware of issues such as quality and reliability. The advances being made by Toyota and other companies in the automotive industry were having widespread impact as more organizations adopted the total quality mantra in their bid to improve idea delivery and support. In addition, as growth generated from new products and services became ever more important, many organizations began to establish dedicated resources focused on idea creation, selection and delivery. To support this, they also began to introduce recently created improvements such as stage-gated development processes. Together this combination of focused resources and defined processes helped to deliver the first significant improvements in the efficiency of innovation activities across the board. This was thereby the first wave of improved innovation capability, where many organizations started to put the basic elements of a coherent approach to innovation in place.

3.1 Product strategy

During the post-war period, when attention was first being paid to product innovation activities and the supporting processes, there was constant growth in the number, range and type of new products being produced. As more disposable income became available for purchases and the real cost of production fell due to increased production efficiency, existing markets continued to grow and new markets, many outside the industrialized world, began to evolve rapidly. Simultaneously, new needs were becoming apparent and advances in new technologies were enabling fundamentally new consumer products such as colour TVs, transistor radios, dishwashers and instant cameras to be realized and launched. The corresponding, largely organic, growth of markets and opportunities led many manufacturers to produce more and more variants of products and broaden their product ranges, often diversifying into new areas to satisfy burgeoning needs.

However, while this resulted in a basically uncontrolled evolutionary development of company activities, technologies and resources as many manufacturers' new products were either led by the demands of the developing markets or pushed by newly invented technologies, this period was also the time when some companies began to think more strategically about what products to make and how to determine new product ranges (McGrath, 1995). During the early 1980s, manufacturers and service organizations started developing new product strategies (Cooper, 1984).

As leading companies Philips, IBM and American Express, to name but a few, were identified as using clearly planned product strategies and their respective methodologies explained, more and more paid attention to the area (Mintzberg, 1994). The significance of the different benefits to be gained from adopting alternative approaches, such as providing high volumes of product or service each with a low profit margin as opposed to low volumes of high-profit-margin products, was becoming more apparent. As many of the funding financial institutions also became interested in what new products firms were developing, details of which specific products would provide the best returns were first explored (Devinney and Stewart, 1988). Companies seeking to address the needs of developing markets began to reassess their new product lines, identify which were most appropriate to the market and their organization and focus attention on their development (Cooper and Kleinschmidt, 1987). As companies have since sought to access new markets and increase their revenues, the strategic perspective of which products to develop, where to produce them and how to deliver them has now developed into a sophisticated activity in its own right. As a key part of this, product design in terms of the visual and ergonomic dynamics was also first viewed as a key success factor. Product strategy became seen as a core activity within corporations – not just in large multinationals but also in many smaller companies, particularly those in areas dependent on high technology, where investment in innovation and product development is often high (Pavia, 1990). It was also during the early 1980s that companies first began to categorize the different approaches to product strategy that were available, the three key alternatives seen at the time being offensive, defensive and imitative strategies (Freeman, 1982).

- *Offensive* product strategies were characterized by significant R&D activity developing new technologies and processes to enable companies to be first to market with new products and services. As market and technology leaders, firms adopting this strategy were seen as being dependent on access to the latest information about emerging technologies, market trends, consumer behaviours and economic indicators. Although frequently considered to be high risk because of the uncertainty and the high levels of investment often required, this approach was also seen to be one where the returns were significant. Key exemplars at the time were Pilkington with its float glass products, chemical company DuPont and its Teflon coatings, and, in the financial services sector, Diners Club as the lead charge card product.

- *Defensive* product strategies were by contrast seen as being less dependent on creating the new market or technology, but more on developing it further. Using an organization's skills and capabilities in production, delivery, and sales and marketing, the main objective was to introduce competitively priced follow-on products and services in large volumes to gain a significant share of a growing market. Although evidently less risky than offensive product strategies, as it focuses on improving existing products, this approach relies on a very good understanding of markets and buyer preferences, coupled with an ability to identify and satisfy short-term expectations. Matsushita was the leader in this arena, being the most successful close follower of JVC in the VHS/Betamax war with Sony – largely achieved through efficiently introducing a continuous stream of market tracking incremental improvements to the core VCR products. Similarly, Microsoft's Word software was a successful follower of the preceding WordStar product, just as Nissan produced highly reliable but low-cost alternatives to Ford and GM vehicles.

- *Imitative* product strategies were in some ways similar to the defensive approach, as they focused on the provision of follow-on products and services, but rather than developing incrementally improved versions they relied more on taking advantage of localized markets and the ability to manufacture low-cost clones. Either through licensing patents or core technology acquisition, but without any significant R&D expenditure, many firms, often in developing countries, chose this approach to copy the market leaders, benefit from their earlier innovation and grow in domestic markets before competing on the world stage. Compaq's first PCs were IBM clones, using identical technology but at lower price; drinks companies Budweiser and Molson copied the 'dry' brewing process from the Japanese Asahi and Sapporo leaders; and in Korea Daewoo cloned GM and IBM products and Samsung started off by making low-cost versions of Sanyo TVs and Sharp microwaves. Compaq and Samsung particularly used low-cost, high-volume imitative strategies as the precursors to move on up the value-chain into the more profitable defensive and offensive approaches.

In parallel to these three strategies, outside the high technology areas several firms continued to pursue a niche traditional approach to product strategy. In established markets where there was little call for innovation at the time, firms such as Barbour, Aga, Le Creuset, Mont Blanc, Coutts, and Fortnum and Masons all continued to provide the same products year on year. By a dictate of fashion and clientele, a number of such areas where brand-linked established goods were able to create and satisfy demand, this approach continued to provide revenue, if not generate significant long-term profitability. This choice of product strategy was largely a result of consequence rather than intent. Organizations seeking to grow would rarely consider this as an entry strategy to the ever-increasingly competitive world of new product and service provision.

From around 1980, product strategy was thus first seen as a distinct but component element of overall corporate strategic intent. Raised from subordinate afterthought to an equal standing with marketing and production on the boardroom agenda, the determination of which products and services to provide, in which markets, using what delivery mechanisms and embracing what technologies to address which issues, were all, for the first time, being considered in a collective coherent manner. Although at the time emergent globally in organizations as varied as Braun, Unilever and IBM, one of the best examples of how a company moved from a pure technology-driven approach for development to a coherent offensive product strategy where technology adoption is coupled with leading edge design and clear market segmentation is Sony, the Japanese consumer electronics company.

Sony: technology meets design

Sony is the world's most successful consumer electronics company. By 2001 it had a turnover of $58.5 billion, employed over 180 000 people worldwide and was filing over 1350 patents per annum. As the company has grown and competed with keen rivals in its home base of Japan as well as internationally, over its fifty-year history it has consistently used the adoption and exploitation of breakthrough, and often disruptive, technologies to drive and underpin its product strategy. It has not all been plain sailing, but this is what the organization expects and is structured to accommodate. Being at the lead demands high levels of innovation, and there are therefore associated levels of risk. Mistakes will occur, particularly in such a highly competitive marketplace as consumer electronics, but, argues Sony, through leading and not following it will consistently outperform its competitors – the most significant and sustained of which has been fellow Japanese corporate Matsushita.

Sony's rise to pre-eminence in the consumer electronics market is almost entirely self-achieved. The company has outperformed not only its Japanese rivals but also many larger US firms such as RCA that have now all but abandoned the consumer electronics market. Sony's success was heavily influenced by the ability of its founders to anticipate the demands of consumers and develop products to meet those demands. Culturally Sony is a company that looks for employees with teamwork skills, but, unlike many Japanese companies, by motivating through salary rewards it also tries to create a competitive atmosphere within the organization.

A former naval lieutenant, Akio Morita, and a defence contractor named Masura Ibuka founded the company after the Second World War. In 1946 they established Tokyo Tsushin Kogyo (TTK) to develop their first product, a rice cooker. This product failed, but as the Japanese economy began to grow, TTK focused on developing electronic goods and developed a tape recorder based on, but offering improvements over, an existing US model. Seeing the potential in the recently invented transistor, Ibuka then acquired a licence from Western Electronic, and in 1954 TTK began mass production of a small tubeless radio that they named Sony after the Latin word for sound, Sonus. This product's success not only led to the company changing its name from TTK to Sony, but also kicked off a twenty-year period of continued technology-led innovation.

Between 1950 and 1979 Sony introduced nine significant disruptive technologies, including transistor pocket radios, colour televisions and consumer video cameras (Christiansen, 1997). However, since then the company has adopted a new strategy, different from the pure technology-driven approach of its first 30 years. Throughout the 1980s Sony established and followed a product strategy driven by the continued and sustained creation of technologically innovative products that were also class-leading in terms of industrial design and ergonomics. Sony's new big idea was miniature perfection (Jones, 2000). This two-pronged strategy enabled it largely to succeed in most of the arenas in which it competed, either through technology superiority in the case of the compact disc, or product design in the case of audio products, or even both in the case of the Playstation and its Vaio laptops. This change in strategy coincided with a shift from a single point of decision-making by CEO Akio Morita (until 1979) to a more Western-style multinational, where decisions are taken by cross-functional groups of experts drawing on inputs from market research, R&D, production and design.

The late 1970s had been a period of awakening for Sony. With a string of successes from the introduction of pure technology-led products, the launch of Betamax VCR in 1975 was the start of the company's first really major experience of product failure. Although initially brimming with confidence about the forthcoming video age and the ability of the Betamax to play the leading role in this, Sony was shocked by the way in which JVC and its arch competitor Matsushita stole the market with their alternative VHS format. Although the Betamax technology was superior, after a year of lobbying Matsushita chose to go with JVC and the VHS format. 'It pains me to reject Betamax, but the JVC product has fewer components. My company must choose the product that can be manufactured more cheaply . . . That is the only way to overcome the disadvantage of being a latecomer,' said a Matsushita executive at the time. This in itself is an insight into the attitude that would emerge within Matsushita during the following decade of following a defensive product strategy, mainly focused on regular updating of products to follow the market rather than lead with new breakthroughs. Despite extensive efforts in marketing and product development, and the support of fellow consumer electronics manufacturers Aiwa, Sanyo, Toshiba and NEC, Sony lost a vicious and costly battle between the rival formats and was eventually forced to withdraw the Betamax and switch to the now standard VHS format.

As well as a longer tape length, one of the key factors in the Betamax/VHS war had been access to software – through its part ownership of Universal, Matsushita had access to a major player in the film industry. Consequently, in 1979, when Sony initiated a joint development partnership with Philips for the compact disc, it also kicked off the acquisition of CBS records to ensure that, together with Phillip's ownership of Polygram, for this product the hardware technology leaders would also have access to the software required to ensure success. Product strategy in Sony was no longer just 'technology push', but a balance of new technology innovation supported by market access.

Walkman

According to corporate legend, Akio Morita commissioned the first Walkman so that his friend and co-founder Masura Ibuka could listen to classical music on long-haul flights. Much to the doubt of many in Sony, he then thought it would make a promising product for the mass market. The rest, as they say, is history. The Walkman defined key aspects of consumer behaviour throughout the 1980s and, in its continually evolving form, has been a mainstay of Sony's audio product range for over twenty years. Although the first model was by today's standards large, bulky and, in terms of sound quality and features, relatively basic, at the time it was a significant product advance that created and exploited a whole new market. For the first time it gave consumers a genuine portable music system that was also personal and, to some extent, private. However, since, technologically speaking, the initial Walkman contained nothing new (being effectively a design repackaging of existing components), unlike earlier Sony innovations it was difficult to protect. As competitors such as Aiwa, Panasonic (Matsushita) and Toshiba would all quickly produce their own imitations to capitalize on the growing market, from the start Sony had continually to develop and launch improved products focused on class-leading design and market positioning, wherever possible supported by new technology. Only by doing this could Sony maintain its lead and reap the financial and brand benefits.

Over the next decade there were many incremental improvements made to the Walkman product, most of which were quickly imitated. Some of these were introduced by competitors, but the majority by Sony itself as the company maintained predominance (Table 3.1; Sanderson and Uzumerii, 1990). Sony was the first to introduce an FM radio feature, in 1980; the first to reduce the product's size significantly, in 1982; the first to produce a waterproof 'sports' version, in 1983; the first to launch rechargeable models, in 1985; and, with the 'my first Sony' range in 1987, the first to introduce products focused on the child market. These developments, many orientated towards clearly identified target consumer groups, continually increased the number of models manufactured by Sony to a level well ahead of the competition. They enabled the company to nurture, protect and exploit the market, and to ensure that, twenty years after the introduction of the first Walkman, the product had become an icon of contemporary culture and synonymous with the whole personal stereo market.

Since the introduction of the Walkman, Sony has continued to innovate in technology, design and market positioning, developing and launching a number of key new product families including:

- The compact disc in 1982
- Digital audio tape in 1987
- The mini disc in 1992
- The DVD in 1995
- Vaio PCs and laptops in 1996
- The MPS memory stick in 1998.

Although now under ever-increasing pressure from traditional rivals such as Matsushita, Toshiba etc., as well as new competitors including Microsoft and the rapidly evolving Samsung, as the definitive consumer electronics company, Sony is still preeminent in its field and has become synonymous with successful product innovation. Moreover, as it has moved into music, film and game production, it has brought its focus on continual innovation to new markets and new competitors.

Table 3.1 Walkman innovation 1979–1988 (source: Sanderson and Uzumerii, 1990)

Feature	Company	Date	Imitated
Walkman	Sony	1979	Yes
Mini headphones	Sony	1979	Yes
AM/FM stereo radio	Sony	1980	Yes
Stereo recording	Sony/Aiwa	1980–1981	Yes
FM tuner cassette	Toshiba	1980–1981	No
Auto-reverse	KLH SOLO	1981–1982	Yes
FM headphone radio	Sony	1981–1982	Yes
Downsized unit	Sony	1982	Yes
Dolby noise reduction	Sony/Aiwa	1982	Yes
Direct drive	Sony	1982	No
Cassette-sized unit	Sony	1983	Yes
Short-wave tuner	Sony	1983	No
Remote control	Aiwa	1983	Yes
Detachable speakers	Aiwa	1983	Yes
Water resistance	Sony	1983–1984	No
Graphic equalizer	Sony	1985	Yes
Rechargeable	Sony	1985	Yes
Solar-powered	Sony	1986	No
Radio presets	Panasonic	1986	Yes
Dual cassettes	Sony	1986	No
TV audio band	Sony	1986–1987	No
Digital tuning	Panasonic	1986–1987	Yes
Child's model	Sony	1987	Yes
Enhanced bass	Sony	1987–1988	Yes
Voice-activated	Toshiba	1988	No

3.2 Regional products

As firms sought to develop appropriate product strategies and improve the effectiveness of their innovation activities, they also began to focus more on the needs of their markets. Determining product strategies that considered both the capabilities of the organization to develop and deliver new products and services, and the opportunities available in the marketplace, necessitated a good understanding of the market and its needs. Moreover, through the ability to evaluate prevailing trends, assessment of which particular new products and features were in demand was possible. To be able to offer products that could successfully compete in growing but ever more crowded sectors, companies therefore began to develop products that were as much 'market pull' as 'technology push'.

Largely due to the structure of distribution networks, organizational focus and location of existing facilities, during the late 1970s and early 1980s most companies first sought to develop products and services for their local markets (Day, 1994). These were the markets that were most accessible, incurred least distribution costs and, for many, were most familiar and hence best understood. Capturing user needs was at this time in its early stages of sophistication and had not evolved into the science it is today. As such it was quite natural for organizations to feel most comfortable developing and launching new products and services for the markets with which employees, their families and their friends were most familiar. In assessing issues such as the target market demographics, target customer profiles, current trends and social, political and environmental influences, as well as the more traditional potential market size, short-term market share and likely profitability, companies were focused on the opportunities and the potential return available for products on their home turf.

Even the majority of multinationals were, at the time, developing different product ranges for differing countries, seeking to focus on addressing specific local market needs with products and services configured to meet these needs (Bonnet, 1985). In the highly representative and arguably lead market of the automotive sector, international alliances, mergers and acquisitions had only marginal effects on products as companies such as General Motors maintained several different product lines in the US, including Buick, Oldsmobile, Cadillac and Chevrolet, as well as independent facilities in Australia producing Holden cars and both the Vauxhall and Opel brands in Europe. The US vehicles were typically large, smooth-riding cars ideal for long journeys on open roads, and with no particular concern for fuel efficiency. By contrast, the European products were more compact, had harder suspensions for good cornering round country lanes and narrow city streets and, due to the higher prices of oil, were more fuel-efficient than their American counterparts.

Companies focused first on their local domestic markets and secondly on export markets. As a consequence, the products that were developed at this time had strong cultural and national influences because they were designed primarily to address regional tastes. Products across the range from cars to domestic appliances could be clearly identified as being American, British, German or Scandinavian in origin, as much by their design as by their brand. Reflecting national identities to maintain appeal to their primary regional markets was, at this time, therefore a major issue for companies such as Braun, Laura Ashley, Fiat, and Bang & Olufsen (Bayley, 1979). If consumers identified with their home products and services, this was a major impetus towards the purchase decision. Although many were exporting some production outside their local region, by and large they were not designed for export and therefore made little attempt to address the frequently different needs. The exception to this was Japan, particularly in its automotive and consumer electronics sectors, where the export market was seen as key from early on. However, even here the export market was primarily considered to be the USA and hence, to all intents and purposes, this was the equivalent home market. Given the disproportionate spending power available in the USA, Toyota, Sony and their followers were designing products with the North American and not the European, never mind the African or even Sub-Asian, household in mind.

For many organizations, particularly those in the medical products, capital goods and transport sectors, this regional product focus was adequate. As long as competition remained largely local in both origin and focus, innovating and configuring products for home consumers was, although never simple, relatively predictable. If local needs were well understood and products suitably configured to deliver the required value proposition and provided at the right price point, then local innovation for local markets was for a time sustainable. However, for others (especially those such as GEC in the UK) involved in technology-dependent areas with high consumer demand, such as TV, radio and domestic appliance manufacturers, the emergence of low-cost products from Korea and Taiwan and ever-higher quality and technology-advancing competition from Japan was too great a challenge. For these companies there were only really two options in such markets – compete or get out. Often lacking the necessary consumer insights, technical innovation and production efficiency to compete without government subsidy, many chose simply to exit consumer sectors and concentrate on the less competitive and, at the time, more locally focused markets of defence, power and telecommunications. This was a strategy that paid suitable dividends for a while, but one that, for GEC/Marconi, was certainly not successful in the long term.

However, within the ever more competitive consumer electronics sector, one company that more successfully illustrated some of the issues in pursuing a focus on regionally driven and tailored products throughout the 1980s was Danish hi-fi company, Bang & Olufsen.

Bang & Olufsen – Danish design, Dutch technology

In a world of conformity and standardization, Bang & Olufsen has throughout its life fought to pursue a different path – one focused on high performance, simple operation and elegant design. Focusing first on the Danish and then the European high-end markets, this company grew to become a pinnacle of good design. However, although it overcame multiple challenges and continued to be a successful player through to the end of the 1980s, during the early 1990s its niche focus in a global marketplace brought it near to breaking point. Despite this, the company has drawn on many of its earliest values and ambitions to reinvent itself again as a clearly defined, if not major, player in the consumer electronics maelstrom.

Founded in 1925 by Peter Bang, a radio enthusiast recently returned from the USA, and Svend Olufsen, the dyslexic son of a West Jutland squire, Bang & Olufsen was established to develop and produce an innovative mains-powered radio, the B&O Eliminator. As one of twenty Danish radio manufacturers, B&O grew steadily within a crowded marketplace by focusing on developing new products at the highest end of the local market. Using the service mark 'The Danish Hallmark of Quality', over a thirty-year period the company introduced gramophones, loudspeakers, tape-recorders and an ever-evolving range of radio products. Although hit hard during the Second World War and following the Treaty of Rome in 1957 as Denmark considered joining the Common Market, B&O realized that without a protected local market, few if any of the existing small Danish radio companies would survive competition from larger German manufacturers such as AEG, Siemens and Grundig. B&O thus determined that, rather than trying to defend its local market, it had to establish itself within the larger European regional marketplace.

Introducing a series of innovative products ranging from its first stereo gramophone in 1960 to its first television in 1962 and, with the Beomaster 900, its first fully integrated music centre in 1964, B&O, although remaining a small Danish company, priced itself at the highest end of the market, positioning its products 'for those who discuss taste and quality before price'. Wishing to replicate the success of the Danish furniture industry at the leading edge of contemporary style and design, the company sought to set itself apart from other brands with 'sensitive, almost feminine' advertising to match its sleek and simple, yet technically advanced, product designs. Seeking particularly to distance itself from what it considered to be the 'aggressive, military look' of Japanese export products that started to enter the European market during the 1970s, the company built on the success of its Beomaster 900 by introducing the Beolab 5000, developed to 'create a European hi-fi format which communicates power, precision and identity'. Replacing competitors' rotary knobs with linear sliding controls, and framed gold panels with anodized aluminium extrusions, this flagship product not only defined the company's design strategy throughout the 1980s but also gave birth to the low sleek Beomaster 1900 product – which, due to its highly regarded design, was actually acquired by many museums across the world before it had reached full production.

With continued innovation in the hi-fi, TV and telephone markets throughout the 1980s, B&O consistently delivered high quality, simple, ergonomic, leading-edge design supported by the latest in applicable technologies. Its 1984 Beovox Red Line floor-standing loudspeakers, 1986 Beocenter 9500 music system, 1987 Penta tall-slim loudspeakers and its 1988 Beocom 2000 telephone all won design awards and maintained the company's position at the high end of the European market.

However, emerging from a marketing strategy that had seen sales outside Denmark as exports for many years, the company struggled to find the most appropriate distribution channels to move on from internally financed outlets that 'became small princedoms whose staff were more preoccupied with appearance than with their real job of selling products', where exclusive interiors were promoted at the cost of the products, towards more successful dedicated franchises. In addition, as the sound quality of Japan's increasingly global products improved in the late 1980s, in tandem with an ambitious global move from high quality British manufacturers such as Mission, ARCAM and Quad, B&O struggled to maintain its position in an ever-crowded marketplace. Having become cost-heavy and slow to react, and having, competitively speaking, inefficient production, margins on small niche sales were not sufficient to provide the necessary investment in innovation and product development. In 1988, losing technical leadership and being forced to concentrate more on the design side of its products, B&O had to form a strategic alliance with Dutch-based multinational Philips to provide cash and components. Although it had made it through the increasingly competitive 1970s and 1980s by focusing on providing niche products for its regional market, for the 1990s global reach and focus were clearly required, and these could only be achieved in partnership with a larger, more efficient multinational company – although at the time *Forbes*, the US business magazine, did not hold out much hope:

A beautiful face is not enough. Bang & Olufsen is the last of a dying breed. A two tiered share structure that keeps controls in the hands of the members of the founding families provides short-term guarantees for Bang & Olufsen's survival and for its stubborn insistence on uninspired policies. The cash infusion from Philips will cover the losses for a time, but the company's longer term prospects are darkening.

Since then the company has fought back. Formulating a new strategy in 1991, 'Break Point 1993', B&O reinvented itself largely from within. Accompanying previously unheard of significant redundancies, the company eliminated subsidiaries, reintroduced centralized management systems, and moved from mass production to become an order-producing organization. Several directors were replaced and, fully leveraging Philips ever-increasing technical input and component supply, the core internal design group started successfully to rejuvenate the company's product range. In the CD player market, the upright Beosystem 2500 with its CDs centrally located behind sliding glass doors and wall-hanging flat-panel loudspeakers was the first of several new globally focused products designed to compete with and distance the company from the stacks of black anonymous boxes that had become the industry standard. Since then, as it has continued to introduce an increasingly successful series of design-led products intended to appeal to the new high-end style-conscious market, B&O has arguably not only innovated new products but also innovated itself out of crisis to remain an independent company, linked to, but not controlled by, a multinational, and one that now uses global partnerships to survive.

3.3 Quality

The ever-increasing variety of new products available during the 1960s and 1970s led inevitably to greater and more defined requirements from consumers. One of the most significant of these was for higher product quality that was reflected in improved reliability, better construction, greater durability and increased value for money. Driven primarily by the success that Japanese manufacturers, particularly Toyota, had achieved in the US automotive market by focusing on quality, companies across a diverse range of product and service sectors all sought to emulate their market performance by adopting this as a key strategic issue (Hauser and Clausing, 1988).

Originally initiated by the US occupation forces bringing W. Edwards Demming to Japan to lecture on 'Statistical Process

Control' and the quality control methodology processes developed in Bell Laboratories, many Japanese companies embraced and adapted these approaches to support an underlying philosophy of improved product quality. From this, a number of enhanced processes were developed and implemented within Japanese industry. The first of these, Quality Function Deployment (QFD), was originally developed in Mitsubishi's Kobe shipyards in 1972, adopted by Toyota in 1978, and then by major US organizations such as Ford and Procter & Gamble in 1983 (Kogure and Akao, 1983). This was an industry-initiated process whose primary aim was to capture and convert the 'Voice of the Customer' into the product and process needs that profitably deliver what the customer needs and wants (Sullivan, 1986). It managed preferences across individual functional aspects of the development activity, providing mechanisms that wove the individual functional tasks into a coherent process. Although later found not to be as much of a short-term panacea as originally thought, QFD nevertheless provides companies with the potential to drive long-term improvements in the way that new products, particularly new variants of existing lines, are developed (Griffin, 1992). As such it is still widely used in the incremental innovation areas within the FMCG and automotive sectors. Following on from QFD, other management principles, including Quality Circles, continuous improvement and Total Quality Management (TQM), implemented the same philosophy of achieving greater product quality throughout industry. Concepts such as a 'House of Quality' became highly popular as a means of integrating the various techniques, and quality as a principle was applied not just to products but also within the context of overall processes and operations (Voss, 1994). Quality has now become a standard expectation for concerns as varied as manufacturing, finance and education, as organizations all seek to integrate it into their respective products and processes, aiming to set and achieve as high a set of targets as possible. Moreover, in the key areas of application, such as the automotive industry, aiming for zero defect production with no rework has now become a fundamental aspect of manufacture across the sector (Womack *et al.*, 1990).

However, from an innovation point of view, the big problem with the whole quality approach, and TQM in particular, is that it is focused on continuous improvement rather than major breakthroughs. It is ideal for followers, adopting defensive and imitative product strategies, where producing cheaper, more reliable clones are the core objectives. Although a key differentiator in the 1980s, taken by itself it now has very little to contribute to the innovation leaders who are focused on breaking the *status quo* and defining a new future. In many ways, if it is allowed too great an influence, in most organizations the whole quality approach can kill innovation and undermine creativity. It therefore has to be managed and utilized accordingly.

GE and Six Sigma

Fifteen years after it first adopted the quality approach through its Work-Out initiative, GE, the US-based multi-industry multi-national, has moved on to become a chief advocate for its latest incarnation, Six Sigma. Whereas GE used Work-Out to define how it behaved in the 1980s, it is now using Six Sigma to define how its people work and interact with the company's customers, with the aim of finding new ways to exceed expectations. Six Sigma is a process that seeks to focus the organization on delivering near-perfect products and services, and is based on the principle that if you can measure how many defects you have, you can system-atically figure out how to eliminate them and get as close to 'zero defect' as possible. There are three key elements – customers, process and employees:

- Customers are seen as the centre of activity, and therefore meeting their expectations is the core target of the organization
- Process wise, GE is examining the transaction cycle from the customer's perspective and using this to see where it can add value or improvement
- Lastly, through focusing on delivery through people, GE is seeking to involve all its employees in the approach, providing training and procedures to support practice.

Although GE believes that Six Sigma is the path to the future in terms of satisfying customers, many would say that this is really only an updated version of TQM by another name, seeking to reintroduce some of the practices that many US organizations tried to adopt in the 1980s but failed fully (and hence success-fully) to implement. In comparison to the Japanese companies who grew on the back of increased product quality, few Western firms ever took the principles down to the human level where, as a core element of people's attitude to work, results get delivered. No Western organization has benefited from quality to the same extent as the Japanese leaders, and particularly Toyota.

Toyota – quality-driven market entry

During the 1960s, Japanese steel companies began to export cheap steel targeted at the lowest tiers of the US steel market. As they captured these markets and drove prices down, Western producers exited these sectors and focused on the higher tiers where profits were greater. Throughout the 1970s the Japanese steel makers then improved the quality of their products and, to increase their margins, pursued the US companies into the highest tiers of the market. Today Nippon Steel and Kobe Steel are among the world's leading high quality steel producers, competing successfully with European manufacturers Corus and Usinor as well as US Steel. Toyota similarly used this strategy first to enter and then to lead the US automotive market.

The first car manufacturing companies to be established in Japan were Nissan Automobile in 1933 and Toyota in 1937. These were founded to prevent the American Big Three of Ford, GM and Chrysler from monopolizing the Japanese market. After the Second World War, Toyota was one of the first Japanese companies to establish what became the *Kanban* approach to mass manufacturing, which is focused on the production of only a limited number of parts for products. Learning from the US industrialists sent to help rebuild the Japanese economy, Toyota was a lead implementer of this approach. Later evolving to a non-stock philosophy or 'just-in-time' production, where small batches of supplies are delivered when they are needed, this, together with an increase in the quality approaches being developed in the steel and shipbuilding industries, laid the foundation of what rapidly became a highly efficient production capability.

In the 1960s, faced with limited growth at home, Toyota had entered the low end of the US market with its Corona model, a car so simple and reliable that it became the *de facto* second car across middle-income America. When the 1970s oil crisis caused many customers to look for smaller, more fuel-efficient alternatives to the large, gas-guzzling products from Ford, GM and Chrysler, Toyota was able to supply the right product, at the right place, at the right time and at the right price. However, faced with increasing competition in the low-cost area from other Japanese manufacturers such as Mazda, Honda and Nissan, from the late 1970s Toyota started to go upmarket, introducing models aimed at more sophisticated customers. Throughout the 1980s, Toyota launched the Corolla, Tercel, Camry, 4Runner and, later, the Lexus ranges into US and then global markets. In each and every sector that it entered, Toyota focused predominantly on producing products of higher quality than the competition. Fully leveraging its highly efficient just-in-time production processes, the company was able to outperform its US competitors in every area it chose to operate in, single-handedly forcing them into drastic improvement initiatives. For example, in reaction to Toyota, between 1979 and 1986 Ford cut $5 billion in costs and lowered its breakeven point by 40 per cent from 4.2 million to 2.4 million cars by introducing robotized assembly lines and laying off 40 000 people. Similarly, between 1979 and 1988 GM and Chrysler lowered their breakeven points from 5.5 million to 4.1 million cars and 2.4 million to 1.1 million cars respectively. These levels of reaction indicate just how dramatic the effect of Toyota and its fellow Japanese producers was on the key US marketplace.

Whereas Toyotas were once recognized as low-price, low-quality cars, the continued improvements that were made to Toyota products over twenty years meant that by the end of the 1980s they were the higher-price, higher-quality products against which US producers could not compete. Only the European BMW, Mercedes, Volvo and Saab brands prevented global domination. The continued introduction of highly reliable, good value-for-money products has enabled Toyota to today become the world's third largest automotive company and the maker of some of the highest quality products around.

3.4 Project selection

As companies defined new product strategies and implemented new development approaches, a key issue that correspondingly came to the fore was deciding which projects actually to pursue. From a resource perspective, a firm can rarely innovate in all the technology areas or markets that it would like to, so choosing which projects should be taken forward is a major decision. The ability to select winning new products therefore became one of the most sought-after core innovation capabilities across all sectors, and one where proficiency was often a compelling source of competitive advantage (Cooper, 1985). How this might best be achieved has been a core topic within innovation research for a number of years, and varied models and expert systems to aid in project selection have been proposed, developed and assessed (Souder and Mandakovic, 1986). These have ranged from the simple ranking of opportunities against revenue potential through more refined risk/reward matrices to complex algorithms considering market window, investment, technology availability, development time, competition, intellectual property protection, complexity and margin (Ram and Ram, 1989). Whichever method was adopted, it was during the mid-1980s that organizations first really recognized that deciding on which new products and services to develop was one of the most difficult management decisions within corporate innovation. In addition, it became evident that successful firms both use

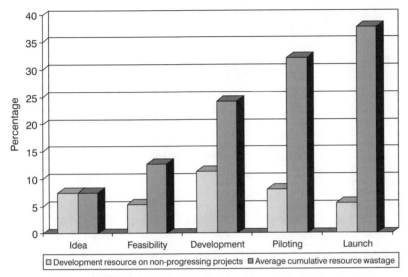

Figure 3.1 Development resource spent on non-progressing projects (source: Corus NPD Benchmarking Survey, 1999).

whatever tools and techniques fit best with their individual needs to mitigate the risk and also spend more time up front on this area. Two weeks extra spent deciding which project to pursue is a far better use of time and money than wasting six months on the wrong opportunity that will never realize value. Even today, over a third of product and service development spend is typically on projects that are not launched, with 66 per cent of resource wastage occurring after feasibility assessment (Figure 3.1).

Filtering the least attractive ideas prior to more detailed feasibility assessment has become a fundamental aspect of successful innovation in many firms, and better-performing companies typically use over 20 per cent of their development resource on the idea and feasibility phases. Given that on average only one in fifty ideas ever makes it through to successful launch, companies today typically aim to cull 75 per cent of their ideas up front with best-in-class performance currently running at 95 per cent. In the average company one in ten opportunities actually progress into full-scale development; in more efficient organizations this falls to one in forty (Figure 3.2).

So how do companies now select which new ideas to progress, and what methods do they adopt to cull the candidates down? The most widely adopted approach is to assess opportunities against defined criteria that are determined best to reflect both the opportunity and the ability of the company to deliver it

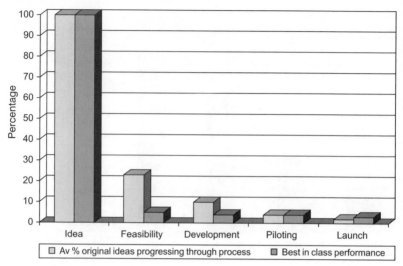

Figure 3.2 Progression of ideas through innovation process (source: Corus NPD Benchmarking Survey, 1999).

(de Bretani and Droge, 1988). Whilst varied factors addressing organizational, market and technology synergy are most frequently utilized for the latter, determining which measures to use to assess the opportunity from a financial perspective is often a less coherent issue. Traditional forecasting of likely annual revenue, profit margins and overall return on investment are still widely used. However, in some areas organizations have adopted alternative metrics. During the Internet boom, market share and number of customers was a key driver for companies seeking to emulate Amazon, whilst in the pharmaceutical world measures of value – either NPV or EVA – have become commonplace, and in telecommunications increasing ARPU or average revenue per user has become the dominant factor.

Although much of the analysis to aid project selection can be undertaken internally within an organization, during the 1990s the need to consider more comprehensively the needs of the potential users as well as the production and distribution processes began to play a more significant role in project selection. While the use of workshops, hall tests, consumer focus groups and user clinics was initiated largely in the FMCG and automotive sectors to evaluate existing products and new product concepts, together with traditional market research and largely more insightful cognitive research, these techniques have now migrated both across sectors and to a position earlier in the innovation process, where ideas and not concepts are being evaluated. Particularly in new service development in banking and retail environments, up front analysis of customer attitudes, preferences and behaviour now plays a major role alongside revenue projections in helping organizations determine which projects to pursue and which to terminate. However, although many of these project selection practices are now implicitly integrated into most innovation programmes and are thus seen as an essential part of the development process, with eight out of ten new products still seen as commercial failures, improving the effectiveness of project selection continues to be a major issue for many companies (Marcotti, 1998). Looking into the future and accurately choosing the winners from the losers is never going to be easy. However, through more appropriate, more effective and more efficient approaches to project selection, some organizations are finding that it is slowly moving from being a black art to a more predictive science.

Siemens Medical – quick filters

There is apparently an old saying in German business: 'If only Siemens knew what Siemens knows'. This sums up both the strengths and weaknesses of this major German electronics and electrical engineering company. It is a huge conglomerate with well-recognized technical brilliance but traditionally poor communication. Operating in 190 countries and employing 470 000 people, Siemens is a vast empire where knowledge and the opportunity for innovation are easily wasted. As a company it is currently embarked on a major change programme, and is spending one billion euros turning itself into an e-company with knowledge management, cross-business procurement, shared customer relationship management and re-engineering of the value chain all playing their part (*The Economist, 2001*). However, within this IT to light bulbs, automotive parts to semiconductor manufacturer, there is a five-billion-euro revenue business unit that has been pioneering its own approach to idea management. Siemens Medical Solutions business unit is one of many business units within the Siemens organization. Although one of the smaller parts of the company, it is nevertheless now one of the most profitable and one of the best at exploiting new ideas.

For many years the innovative medical products developed by this unit came from internally generated ideas and product concepts. The company has a long history of technology-led innovation introducing a series of successful products, including the first X-ray tube in 1886, the electric hearing aid in 1913, the first ultrasonic echography unit with real-time display in

1966, and the first magnetic resonance tomograph in 1982. Often working in collaboration with specific university research centres and a few choice customers, Siemens Medical had developed a regular flow of new products that gave it a steady, if not class-leading, position. However, by the late 1980s the company recognized that it needed to improve its innovation performance significantly and, in order to supplement the largely internal source of ideas and drive innovation within the company, it chose to increase its pipeline through growing its input of externally generated ideas. It opened its doors to a wider range of potential opportunities, and ideas and suggestions began to flow in to the organization at an increasingly high rate. Now faced with hundreds of potential projects instead of the traditional few, the company had to determine which were the likely winners and which should be left alone. With limited internal development resource, focus was paramount. However, with typical idea assessments taking between one and six months to complete, the available resource was quickly becoming snowed under with new opportunities to evaluate and little time left actually to develop and launch the new products.

The solution implemented within the company was to introduce a two-step approach to project selection, where first a 'quick filter' was used to reduce the candidates to a manageable flow and then a more intensive ' idea assessment' was conducted on those that made it through the filter (Redel *et al.*, 1998). This initial assessment had to be undertaken using incomplete and entirely qualitative information. In the first step each new idea was qualitatively assessed by means of a one-page questionnaire that included twenty key questions about possible customer benefits, business opportunities, possible implementation problems, and the company's strengths and weaknesses. This was the quick filter, and, using these answers, supporting software placed each idea as a point on an innovation opportunity chart. The ideas that were seen as being most promising were then ranked according to Siemens' latest corporate risk strategy.

With typical companies only launching one in fifty ideas, the key was to use the quick filter approach to get down to the one in ten as efficiently and as reliably as possible. However, the dichotomy here was that too harsh a filter would only let through a few, probably similar, opportunities, thus restricting innovation, whereas too loose a filter would most likely let through too many. The key was to choose the right twenty questions. It was crucial to differentiate clearly between the 'killer criteria' or the 'must haves' that had to be met and the secondary 'like to haves', and to concentrate on the former.

Step two was a more traditional in-depth quantitative assessment, where a cross functional team spent several weeks analysing the market, calculating the necessary investment and implementation costs, predicting possible revenues and profits, and evaluating the associated risks. From the most promising ideas, business plans were developed and submitted to an internal venture capital board that provided initial funding for their realization. Within the first year 450 ideas were evaluated, 70 per cent of which came from external customers and universities; eleven business plans were completed and three opportunities were implemented.

Five years on Siemens Medical was averaging more than one invention a day, and two-thirds of the products generating its $5 billion revenue were less than three years old. With major growth in the USA, the business unit now has 28 000 employees, is sourcing over 50 per cent of its new product ideas externally, and is promoting innovation management as being at the core of its organization. As a lead business unit, Siemens Medical is also seen as a centre of excellence within the overall organization, and as such is central to the company's recently initiated change programmes.

3.5 Stage gates

Throughout the evolution of innovation capability, the conceptual existence of an associated innovation process had gradually also developed. Driven by the underlying basic 'inception–creation–realization' inter-relationship of tasks for the exploitation of new ideas, as more and more people (and later companies) applied their knowledge and skills to the development of new technologies, products and services, so a more detailed understanding of the enabling process began to occur. However, despite a gradually increasing level of internal complexity, which was largely dictated by the mounting sophistication of the products and services being developed, it has also only been within relatively recent years that innovation has itself become widely recognized as a process as well as an activity. Whilst the large scale post-war growth of consumer-orientated, technology-exploiting, time-saving and value-adding products drew attention towards product development as an increasingly multifunctional activity, it is only during the last thirty years or so that serious attempts have also been made to model it as a process. While minor variations exist across different industrial and commercial sectors, innovation has largely been found to be a common process that applies equally inside and outside its traditional primary focus of manufacturing.

The same process is, at a generic level, common across the development of new products, services and businesses.

Although companies starting from Ford, Westinghouse, Hoover and AEG in the 1930s had all developed and introduced new products by following a series of discrete but interlinked activities, it was NASA who, throughout the 1960s and 1970s, first began to model the increasingly familiar process. In an attempt to coordinate, measure and manage the multiple technical developments required collectively to put man and machines on the moon, NASA described product development as simple linear sequential model. Using this as a guide, other organizations soon also began to adopt a structure to help them in turn to take control of their innovation and product realization processes.

However, it was in the early 1980s that a major step was taken in the modelling and management of the development process through the introduction of the 'stage-gate' approach (Cooper, 1990). Conceived by Robert Cooper of McMaster University in Canada, the stage-gate process became seen as the 'second generation' innovation process, as it not only broke the development of a new product or service into discrete phases but also introduced defined review points at the end of each phase (Figure 3.3). These reviews, or stage gates as they became commonly

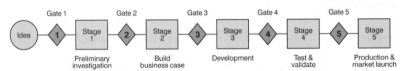

Figure 3.3 Stage-gate process (source: Cooper, 1990).

known, are clearly defined 'yes/no' progression points that provide organizations with the ability to measure and control the process and match subsequent funding to meet the requirements of each gate. The essence of the approach is that upon reaching each gate, a project has to meet certain predefined criteria and pass evaluation for progression. This ensures that no key tasks that should have been completed are missed out or are running late to the detriment of the overall project.

For example, for the feasibility assessment gate in its version of the development process, GPT, the British telecommunications company later to be renamed Marconi, required the following deliverables to all be in place (Jones, 1997):

- Marketing plan
- Market requirements specification

- Outline systems specification
- Business case
- Project management plan
- Outline manufacturing plan
- Outline customer services plan
- Outline test and verification plan
- Regulatory approval
- Risk analysis.

Over a twenty-year period, the stage-gate approach became the standard *de facto* process for all major organizations in their development and realization of new products and services. Companies as varied as Exxon, Hoechst, Visa, Microsoft and Guinness have all now adopted this as their core development approach, and have seen the associated benefits of clearer progression, easier replication across sectors and improved product quality all delivered into their activities.

The original standardized model assumed that the innovation process, initiated by the existence of some idea, comprised of five stages. However, this offers just one interpretation of a process that may or may not be familiar, for, over the years, there has been considerable debate over both the number of stages and their individual composition. For example, early work that had been undertaken in the late 1960s and later updated in the early 1980s by Booz Allen and Hamilton, a US-based consultancy with a more strategic point of view, recognized the process as being seven basic steps, expanding the first 'preliminary investigation' stage into three separate phases of 'new product strategy development', 'idea generation' and 'screening' (Booz Allen and Hamilton, 1982).

Innovation is by its very nature a multifunctional activity, where each of the various disciplines involved frequently takes differing leading, participative or consulting roles as a product, process or service is developed. So, unsurprisingly, their individual views of the process vary. Each functional area has developed and interpreted the process within these perspectives, imposing their own parameters onto the general structure. From a marketing perspective, innovation has, for instance, been seen as a nine-stage process (Kotler *et al.*, 1996). Additionally, incorporated between idea screening and business analysis are two more stages of 'concept development and testing' and 'marketing strategy development'. Both of these are clearly key areas of high marketing involvement and hence are seen as being of priority in a marketing-led interpretation of the process. By contrast, from a design perspective, innovation has been seen in a different light where the focus is very much on the core development activities.

One interpretation, now adopted as a British Standard for managing product development, portrays innovation as being a six-stage process (Pahl and Beitz, 1984):

1 Marketing
2 Specification
3 Concept design
4 Detail design
5 Manufacture
6 Sales.

Here the narrow focus of the design disciplines on the central development stages means that all the front-end activities are reduced to a single marketing stage followed by specification development. Although the core product development activity is represented in more detail, only the key areas of design interest are fundamentally addressed, with scant attention paid to other functions' areas of responsibility. Each of these individual interpretations of the stage-gate process has its own intrinsic value for the specific functions or disciplines concerned, but inherently biases the interpretation to the most influential function. As an alternative, a more holistic and pragmatic industrial view from Toyota saw the innovation process involving six core steps (Sasaki, 1991):

1 Specifying the product concept
2 Doing R&D that yields new processes and products that can be used in design
3 Analysing market and profit potential for each proposed new concept
4 Designing the product
5 Planning the production
6 Planning the marketing.

By focusing more on the integral activities themselves and what is actually undertaken within each stage, this provided a more task-orientated view. It shifted the perspective onto the actions required to deliver the defined outcomes and deliverables.

Across industry the adoption of the stage-gate approach, in whatever format it is configured by either the organization or the specific function leading innovation activities, has undoubtedly had a positive effect on new product and service development success. As it has introduced discipline and the opportunity for clearer and more controlled project management across innovations emanating from or driven by whatever discipline using whichever interpretation of the process, the stage-gate approach has brought about a step change in innovation efficiency. According to a 1997 best practices study, nearly 60 per cent of the firms studied used some sort of gated development process (Griffin, 1997). To highlight the benefits gained it is worth examining some aspects of the process of one of the earlier adopters of the approach, Dow Chemical, in a little more detail.

Dow Chemical – gatekeeper

The Dow Chemical Company is a leading provider of chemical, plastic and agricultural products to a wide range of consumer markets. With annual sales of $30 billion it addresses markets including food, transportation, health, personal care and building and construction in over 170 countries. Founded in 1897, it started life as a producer of bleach, and over the next fifty years developed new agricultural products as well as expanding into chlorine, bromine and plastics, including cellulose and polystyrene resins. It formed a joint venture, Dow Corning, with Corning Glass to produce silicones in 1943, and first expanded outside the USA ten years later; by 1960 overseas production accounted for 8 per cent of sales that were soon to exceed $1 billion per annum. With the introduction of a line of products for automotive applications in 1970 and the supply of 'Styrofoam' insulation for the Alaskan pipeline in 1975, Dow's annual sales soon exceeded $10 billion. By 1980 it was the world's largest producer of thermoplastics, and the range of products that were being created by the company had expanded significantly and the development process needed clear definition. The company thus looked towards the recently conceived stage-gate approach. As one of the lead implementers of this, Dow was also one of the first companies to use it to provide a common language across projects.

Labelled as the 'Development and Commercialization' process within the firm, the Dow interpretation had the usual five core stages:

1 Preliminary investigation
2 Build business case
3 Development
4 Test and validate
5 Full production and market launch.

Major impetuses for Dow's implementation of the stage-gate approach were the desire both to formalize and to control the development process and, at the same time, also enable a more customer-centric project structure. In a bid to accommodate increasingly high customer expectations, an additional activity early on during the development of the business case was to have lead customers participate directly in the creation of both the work plan and the schedule. Here they had direct input into determining the timing of reviews, as well as the ability to use individual gates as triggers for the contribution of their own resources.

As it implemented its five stage-gate process across multiple projects, Dow also used a 'red–green' chart to visualize and thereby report progress. For each project, the dates when it was scheduled to pass each monthly gate review were shown alongside the actual dates achieved. Projects that were on track or ahead of schedule were shown in green, whilst those missing the gate by more than a month were shown in red. This had the double benefit of not only highlighting the projects that were in trouble and needed attention or extra resources, but also indicating which gates (and hence which phases of the process) were most problematic for the organization to undertake efficiently.

In addition, to improve schedule reliability and resource planning, the team at Dow also broke down each of the main five stages into an extra level of detail (Near, 1998). For every elemental step of each stage of the process, a standard was created for how long it should take and the level of resources typically required. In order to account for the variation in project size and complexity, as the approach was implemented earlier projects were examined and, together with external benchmark information, a relationship between expected cycle time and complexity was also created. Based on this relationship the company was able to define guidelines that were relevant to individual projects. This helped the development organization to provide more realistic schedules and timings for the major phase reviews and also key launch dates, as well as the commitment to deliver to these.

Since its introduction, the stage-gate process has served Dow well and become an integral part of all its business unit's development activities. Over time it has inevitably evolved in the detail and composition of individual stage and gates, and also in how it is utilized across the company. To facilitate this and help each global business unit to understand where it stands with regard to the capability level of its individual process, and where to focus improvements, Dow developed a survey tool to evaluate relative performance. This was especially useful in encouraging the use of common practices and terminology across the company – a major benefit for such a large organization, where development opportunities increasingly crossed internal boundaries. By 1995, with annual sales first reaching $20 billion, Dow was facing this issue on a daily basis.

As the world's most productive chemical company, Dow has continued to introduce more and more product lines – now including everything from basic polystyrene, ethanol and vinyl chloride products through to high performance polyurethane and epoxy products. The most recent advance in the expansion of the development commercialization process for these and other new products has been the use of Web-based tools to enable improved interaction between all parties involved in the development and commercialization of new products. Effectively facilitating an automated stage gate and encouraging the re-use of existing information across projects, this has improved communication of deliverables and commitments. It is enabling better integration of individual projects into the overall product portfolio, improving documentation control, allowing the company to see projects and development progress by business unit, better prioritize risk, and balance resource supply and demand across programmes. Increasingly integrated with several e-commerce initiatives, the stage-gate process is continuing to underpin Dow's ability to innovate and deliver a continuous stream of new products into the market.

3.6 Product champions

The escalating growth of the marketplace, more exacting customer demands, increasing competition and the corresponding need to develop more new products that occurred during the 1970s and 1980s led many companies to identify new requirements for their organization. Unlike the ongoing manufacture of existing products, innovation was not a steady-state process. It could not be planned, controlled and managed in the same way, and for many organizations it could not be easily undertaken within the same environment. Product and service development was gradually recognized as being different. It required inputs from a range of differing functions at different times, and as such often placed extra demands on functions such as manufacturing and sales, whose day-to-day activities and focus were primarily on existing products (Jones, 1997). Innovation therefore had a different set of requirements, and it was the recognition of this that led many companies to establish dedicated resources for innovation and product development.

In the first instance, companies with active research and development activities sought to integrate marketing, design and manufacturing staff into development groups, and those without R&D facilities began to grow development capabilities through part-time or full-time secondment from within their production, sales and marketing departments. As organizations thus defined a responsibility for innovation, so they also began to provide dedicated facilities and, most significantly, identifiable funding. An increasing awareness of the importance of investing a share of revenue in innovation activities helped to encourage firms to assess their processes, identify areas for improvement, and implement appropriate procedures to control, manage and monitor both development programmes and the associated funding. This funding was vital, but it also had to be appropriate to the project. Large budgets themselves did not guarantee success, but rather, there was a need to recognize the individual requirements of the different stages of development programmes and then to arrange and allocate appropriate funding accordingly (Rosenthal, 1990).

As the importance of innovation as a corporate activity grew, its position within organizations became more prominent. As the source of the new products that could help a company capture greater market share and generate increased revenue, product and service development became more and more significant, in some companies gaining equal influence to the traditional power centres of marketing, sales and operations (Pulos, 1991). Increasingly organizations started to move towards empowering the development activity through both raising its profile and providing more dedicated resources.

With the growing recognition of the importance of innovation in enabling growth and an increasing awareness of the improvements available in the associated processes, during the 1980s many companies found their development activities becoming more and more complex. They were involving more specialist input, covering more dispersed locations, frequently requiring greater access to enabling technologies, demanding more resources and becoming ever more distinct from day-to-day operations. These developments collectively initiated a shift in the focus of development responsibility (Smith, and Reinertsen, 1991).

Whilst the initial recognition of a need for dedicated development resources had encouraged the provision of appropriate funding and facilities, the control of programmes had remained very much a role for senior management, many of whom often had additional responsibilities. As such, innovation programmes were often compromised as much by senior management inattention as by resource allocation (Pavitt, 1991). Companies such as HP, Procter & Gamble, and Citibank therefore began to also recognize the need for a new role in innovation; that of the product champion. Although there remained a requirement for senior management participation in phase reviews, the day-to-day project management responsibilities could largely be given to individuals who, as part of a core development team, had a full-time role to push projects forward (Mabert *et al.*, 1992). The focus therefore shifted to innovation being a recognized activity, supported by senior management but planned and managed from within.

Product champions were frequently drawn from one of the key functions such as R&D, design or marketing, and their role was often as much one of internal coach as external assessor (Griffin, 1992). They took responsibility not only for the control of a development programme and the delivery of outputs against set targets, but also for motivating the development team, insulating it from external influences and ensuring that the appropriate resources and facilities were provided as and when required. In essence, a major task for product champions was therefore to foresee problems, identify options and steer development programmes around obstacles. In some cases, and particularly when self-managed teams were later introduced, this resulted in far greater power residing within the development activity, as product champions added an internal negotiation role within the organization where, for example, they could discuss suggested changes in product specifications, determine what impact they would have upon the progression of a project, and then agree only to those that were most appropriate. This more devolved approach to project management was another major step towards further empowering the innovation activity within organizations.

Many of the early adopters of this approach were larger organizations, where the multiple demands on individuals' time and conflicting priorities between innovation and the steady-state production and sales activities were the most extreme. Of these, one of the most successful lead initiators was the Japanese manufacturer Honda.

Honda – developing a new Accord

The Honda Motor Company was established in 1948, and is now one of the world's leading manufacturers of automobiles and the largest producer of motorcycles. The company and its subsidiaries develop, manufacture, distribute and provide financing for the sale of its increasing range of cars, motorcycles and other power products, and have twenty-five separate manufacturing operations. Six of these are located in Japan, five in the USA, two each in Thailand and Brazil, and one each in Canada, the UK, France, Italy, Spain, India, Pakistan, the Philippines, Vietnam and Mexico. The automotive group accounted for 80 per cent of year

2000 sales of $6 billion, with over half of these being in the USA.

Although starting motorcycle production in 1949, it was not until 1963 that Honda launched its first car, the S500 sports car. Entering Formula 1 racing in 1964, the company secured its first victory the following year in Mexico. In 1966 it launched its N360 mini-compact car, and in 1972 the first Honda Civic debuted in Japan. In May 1976 the company first introduced the Accord, developed to 'redefine the concept of world's best family car'. Named car of the year in Japan, with low fuel consumption and anti-pollution measures as leading features, this was a major success for Honda, and production built up gradually, passing one million vehicles in January 1980. The second generation of the Accord was designed to further its predecessor's domestic success and initiate much sought-after initial export sales. With improved quality and a wider choice of engines, this model continued home sales and also established early US success, in many ways supported by the establishment of Honda's first overseas production plant in Ohio. This had been established in support of the company's philosophy of 'manufacturing where demand exists', thereby promoting localized production, and was the first Japanese car factory in the USA.

Both of these first two Accord models had been delivered using traditional functional approaches to new product development, taking advantage of collocation of input and ownership of resource, in combination with a strong idea of what the Japanese market in particular demanded and multiple research studies of what a potentially global car should be. For the next version of the Accord, scheduled for launch in 1985, Honda wanted to expand input, using a combination of Japanese and US facilities to ensure that the company created a stylish, competitive product that would be popular in both key markets. In particular, the company sought to integrate input to ensure that it exceeded current standards in five key areas:

1 Environmental impact
2 Driving pleasure
3 Safety
4 High efficiency
5 Value for money.

In a bid to overcome functional divisions, especially when research, development and design activities were to be increasingly geographically dispersed away from production and sales operations, the product champion concept was seen as a key element that would further enable more integrated design. Rather than using a sequential handover of responsibility, the company wanted to create a source of continuous dialogue throughout the design and development process (Lorenz, 1986).

To facilitate effective leadership of new product development programmes within Honda R&D Company, the firm's technology and new car development organization, Honda introduced the concept of product champions into the business and created what were termed Representatives of Automotive Development (RADs). These were Honda's highest-ranking product champions, and took on the role of super programme managers. Supervising the development programmes for a family of cars, RADs had to demonstrate a successful record of project management combined with engineering excellence. They would sit on the automobile planning board, Honda's highest-level car strategy council, along-side functional managers, and thereby bring a previously unknown level of influence on product strategy (Deschamps and Nayak, 1995).

For the first time in the company history, a new leadership of product development was thus created. Whereas in the past the functional hierarchy had defined product concept by consensus and individually driven the respective elements of the sub-sequent development within their individual arenas, with the introduction of RADs as product champions, ownership of the overall development programme resided with one individual able to call upon input and resources from any of the required functional groups – from marketing to design to production. Moreover, it was the responsibility of the RAD to justify the product concept to management, and coordinate input from market and technical research as well as feedback from produc-tion and sales areas of the company. In a business where the planning of a new product was far from linear, relying greatly on this frequently changing input from across the company, this central role was a new level of both authority and visibility of leadership. As well as being the leader of development and delivery of a new product, the RAD was also very much the overall product architect.

Each RAD managed a steering group to enable coordination of functional input. Termed the 'SED steering group' due to its main components of resource from sales, engineering and design, this provided the direct linkage between the overall product concept development and delivery and the business. By appointing RADs and empowering them with such authority to control the development, Honda changed two major perceptions across the company. In giving such responsibility to a group of managers representing the product side of the business, it gave leadership for projects to product-focused managers as opposed to the line hierarchy. In addition, it established an alternative career path that still led to senior positions within the organization.

Using this approach for the new Accord development, initiated in late 1982, involved coordinating input not just from Honda operations in Japan but also from two new facilities in the USA. The Ohio Centre of Honda R&D provided state-of-the-art product engineering, prototype development and testing facilities, whereas a Los Angeles Centre focused on product planning, market research and styling. Specifically established to help drive the expansion of the company in its main export market, these investments were seen as key to the success of the new product.

Throughout development, the change of focus to the product champion concept for programme management, enabling continuous interaction throughout development, had two key additional benefits (Bessant and Lamming, 1988):

1 Modification of the design during development ensured continuous improvement in efficiency in terms of reduced costs and improved quality
2 Rather than being on the receiving end of others' final decisions, production-initiated design improvements had a natural way of being communicated into the programme.

Developed in less than three years from concept to market – a class-leading achievement at the time, especially given the cross-country input and responsibility – the third-generation Honda Accord was launched simultaneously in Japan and the USA, rolling off respective production lines in June 1985. Over the next four years, this product quickly penetrated the US market whilst still performing well in Japan. Sales of 2.6 million in the USA and 0.7 million in Japan helped to push cumulative Accord production to over five million by July 1989. In 1988, US-built models were, for the first time, imported in to Japan.

Since then the Accord has continued to evolve. Using the same development philosophy led by RADs, the fourth generation, launched in September 1989, became the top-selling car in the US for the following three years, won its fifth consecutive first place in the JD Power Consumer Satisfaction index, and was named the best car in America in 1990 by *Car and Driver* magazine. In October 1992, production of fully assembled Accords started in the UK and a strategic relationship with Rover to co-develop new products was initiated the following year. By the launch of the sixth-generation global product in September 1993, cumulative production had passed eight million vehicles. In 1997, after seven generations, the Accord had become established as a major top ten product in over 140 countries, and over twelve million had been sold.

3.7 Technology transfer

As new technology became more and more influential in the development, production and operation of new products and services, a clear need arose for many companies to access the specific technologies that could offer them competitive advantage. Particularly at a time when many saw technology as the enabler of successful innovation and sustained corporate growth, bringing the latest developments into an organization for profitable exploitation was a key strategic target. In what became known as technology transfer, successfully facilitating this movement of new technology into a firm became a critical issue for many. Especially since most of the enabling technologies usually lay outside an organization's home territory, industry sector or market, this necessitated a higher level of external interaction than had been practice until this time (HM Treasury, 1998). Transferring any technology from an originating organization into a new host for exploitation was in many ways as complex as human organ transplants, and, without specific attention, rejection was similarly commonplace. Only by learning how to set the scene for the introduction of new technologies and put in place and affect the key conditions for a successful transfer did companies, both large and small, actually benefit.

First, the host firm had to identify and assess all the key external technological sources, including suppliers, research and technology organizations, and universities. This required knowledge of the appropriate sources and the ability to evaluate the technologies, in terms of both their innovativeness and their applicability (Roberts and Hauptman, 1986). By implication, this meant that companies that wished to use technology transfer as a key source of innovation, either instead of or to supplement internally developed capabilities, had to develop a good knowledge of what was happening where and clearly define the key criteria that would help determine which technologies could (and which could not) be successfully exploited by them. An organization had to develop the internal capacity, including the right mix of skills, to absorb the technology and adapt it to its own circumstances. At the time, the majority of firms accessed new technology through directly recruiting trained people from the originating organizations. Therefore, crucial to the technology transfer process were the people who understood and were comfortable with the relationship between the firm and the institutions that nurtured skilled personnel, new concepts and new technologies (Souder and Nasser, 1990).

Perhaps most importantly, a market or network had to exist that effectively brought together the users and sources of technology

(Hakansson and Laage-Hellman, 1984). Companies had to position themselves within a network of organizations that could collectively facilitate the transfer. Many of these grew up around key universities such as MIT, Stanford and Cambridge, but others were centred on the corporate research labs of companies including DuPont, AT&T and BT. These networks or alliances had to be managed in a manner appropriate to both the technology and the recipients (Nuerno and Oosterveld, 1988). Whilst some firms, particularly those operating in scientifically intensive areas, developed technology from close connections with organizations that populated the science and engineering base, others sought to join or establish alliances between organizations of differing technological understanding and capability. In these cases, it was the mix of organizations within the network that dictated the potential for successful technology transfer. Only through managing the structure and operation of the joint venture or network relationships could the needs of one partner be complemented by the knowledge and resources resident within another (Littler and Leverick, 1995).

One of the exemplars of technology transfer between organizations has been the British Technology Group (BTG). Originally established by the UK government to facilitate the transfer of new research and emerging technologies from British universities, BTG focused initially on a few key institutions and corporate hosts. However, as the organization developed both the capability and the reputation to act as the transfer intermediary, it widened its reach and acted as facilitator between corporate clients. Often taking a stake in a new technology, over the past twenty years BTG has become a listed entity at the forefront of the transfer of technology and management of associated intellectual property.

Internal transfer

In addition to this transfer of technology between organizations, transfer has also increasingly occurred internally. As technology utilized in one area has found applications in another, or developments from within corporate R&D laboratories have provided benefit in manufacturing sites, internal networks providing similar mechanisms to those that occur externally have also been established (Souder and Padmanabhan, 1989). To support such transfer, companies as diverse as 3M, IBM, DuPont, Shell, and France Telecom have all established either internal groups or procedures focused on technology transfer. Some of these have been integrated within existing corporate research groups and others have been separate entities with a stronger commercial focus. Some were shrouded in secrecy to protect corporate know-how; others became well known, and none more so than the future technology development and transfer group within Xerox.

Xerox PARC – technology transfer generator

Throughout the last thirty years of the twentieth century, one establishment in California was seen as the centre of innovation and technology transfer for the whole computer industry. Creating the core technologies that gave birth to most of the key elements of today's PCs, peripherals and the Internet, this establishment has been extensively criticized for being a financial drain on its parent, who arguably did not fully profit from its investment. This is a major misconception – just one technology developed here enabled the whole laser printing industry, and in doing so created billions of dollars in revenue for the parent company. Moreover, although not fully exploited internally, this establishment was the predominant source of technology transfer into partner and spin-off organizations that, amongst others, led to the creation of the first PC, the mouse, Ethernet connectivity and the Windows-style graphical user interfaces that underpinned the birth of Apple and 3com, and the sustained growth of Microsoft. Throughout this period, this was 'the centre of the computer revolution'. This establishment was Xerox Corporation's Palo Alto Research Centre or, as it is more commonly known, Xerox PARC, or simply PARC.

In 1970, in a desire to recreate the sort of technical hothouse that AT&T's Bell Laboratories had been in 1948 when it invented the transistor, Jack Goldman, the Xerox Chief Scientist, con-vinced his superiors in what was at the time a rather con-servative copying company to stake tens of millions of dollars and provide funding for what was seen as a renegade think tank in an abandoned building adjacent to Stanford University. Although Xerox management was more interested in marketable products than new technology and nearly killed it before it started, PARC became the place where the greatest gathering of computer talent ever was assembled. Its remit was to invent the future and create the technologies that would underpin the company a decade out. Led by Bob Taylor, a preacher's son from Texas with a background in psychology rather than engineering, and known largely for his ego, and Alan Kay, a visionary who dreamed of a machine small enough to tuck under the arm yet powerful enough to store books, symphonies, letters, poems and drawings, this establishment was conceived to position Xerox on the leading edge of technology.

It is important to recognize that at the time of its establishment, computers were viewed as large corporate machines for which users queued up to enter their punch cards for processing of calculations. PARC scientists, however, saw the computer as something that would 'serve rather than be served.' They envisaged that the computer should be easy and intuitive to operate, communicate on a human scale through a full-sized TV screen, and accurately display text and images as they were entered by keyboard or mouse. Most significantly, everyone could have one on the desk or, as Bob Taylor saw, under the arm. The computer should be a 'personal computer'. Over a twenty-year period, PARC created many of the technologies that enabled this.

Although Xerox itself had problems grasping some of the technologies that emerged, never mind exploiting them, the ideas and innovations that occurred went on to create some of the leading elements of the computer industry. A summary of just some of the developments that came out of PARC gives an indication of the effect that it has had on the computer industry, how we now work and how, in the twenty-first century, we do business.

First, from an internal technology transfer perspective within Xerox, the key achievements included:

- The Alto computer (1973–1980), which included the world's first Graphical User Interface (GUI), WYSIWYG (what you see is what you get) editing, bit mapped displays and overlapping windows, and the first commercial mouse
- Laser printers (1977), which provided a means of seamlessly transferring digital documents onto paper and became the basis for Xerox's multi-billion dollar printing business
- Ethernet (1980), which became the global standard for inter-connecting computers on local area networks, spawned a series of sophisticated network protocols, enabled distributed computing and led to new communication between Xerox copiers
- Multibeam lasers (1986), which emitted multiple beams rather than a single standard beam and thus increased the speed of printing (later, blue lasers have reduced wavelength and allowed higher resolution printing)
- Ubiquitous Computing (1988), which became the industry standard for connected computational tools and spawned several spin offs including MobileDocs and LiveWorks.

Although each is a significant and important success in its own right, these internal achievements are dwarfed by those that occurred through the technology transfer that took place via the migration of staff and their expertise outside the organization to other companies. Either through frustration at the poor take-up of their ideas within Xerox, or through disclosure to outsiders, there are four key (and now famous) examples of external exploitation of PARC know-how:

1. After creating Interpress, a programming system that reconciled the differences in image resolution of computer screens and printers, Chuck Geschenke and John Warnock left PARC to develop a new typesetting system that they named Postscript. To exploit this they founded a company called Adobe, a firm that would eventually become a $1 billion a year enterprise.
2. Alvy Ray Smith, co-creator within PARC of Superpaint, an image-manipulating tool, left to join George Lucas's Lucasfilm and later spun off Pixar, the leading digital studio that produced the computer generated movies *Toy Story* and *A Bug's Life*.
3. James Clark, one of the students on Stanford courses taught under PARC supervision, designed a graphical chip that he named 'the Geometry Engine'. This was the foundation of a whole new technology that could create, manipulate and move complex 3D images, a technology that he exploited through the creation of a start up – Silicon Graphics – the first of his three billion-dollar companies.
4. Most significantly, in the eyes of many industry commentators, is the migration of several PARC technologies into Apple. Through two 'show-and-tell' demonstrations of Smalltalk, an object-orientated graphical interface, to Steve Jobs and his team of engineers, Xerox revealed key elements of the 'look and feel' of what first became the Lisa interface and, in 1984, the Macintosh, the product that turned the company from a respected niche player into a major computer manufacturer.

Taken together with the internal achievements, these four examples highlight the impact that PARC technologies and their associated transfer into commercial applications had on the whole computer industry during the 1980s. As a single source of some of the major disruptive technologies in computing, Xerox PARC was clearly pre-eminent.

Gradually fuelled by the recognition of just what they had created, Xerox has since improved its own exploitation of the technologies that have been invented. As well as supporting a continuous stream of innovative products within the copier market, PARC has also spun out over thirty new companies, including Optidem (which became Cipher Data Products), Synoptics Communications (later Bay Networks then Nortel), ParcPlace Systems (which became ObjectShare), Semaphore

Communications, dpiX, and Uppercase. Xerox PARC now has a budget of $65 million, employs 250 researchers and, together with its sister research centres in Webster (New York), Ontario (Canada), Cambridge (England) and Grenoble (France), is the centre of innovation and technology development for the Xerox Corporation – an organization that, on the back of many of the technologies to come out of PARC, has itself grown to be a $18.7 billion turnover multinational employing 92 500 people globally.

References

Bayley, S. (1979). *In Good Shape: Style in Industrial Products.* Design Council.

Bessant, J. and Lamming, R. (1988). Design for efficient manufacturing. In: *International Handbook of Operations Management* (R. Wild, ed.), Cassell.

Bonnet, D. C. L. (1985). Integrating marketing variables in the early stages of the new product process to support the design and development of technologically advanced new industrial products. *Q. Rev. Marketing*, **Autumn,** 7–11.

Booz Allen and Hamilton (1982). *New Product Development Management for the 1980s.* Booz Allen and Hamilton.

Christiansen, C. M. (1997). *The Innovator's Dilemma.* Harvard Business School Press.

Cooper, R. G. (1984). New products strategies: what distinguishes the top performers. *J. Product Innov. Management*, **1,** 151.

Cooper, R. G. (1985). Selecting winning new product projects. *J. Product Innov. Management*, **2,** 34.

Cooper, R. G. (1990). Stage-gate system: a new tool for managing new products. *Bus. Horizons*, **May–Jun,** 44–54.

Cooper, R. G. and Kleinschmidt, E. J. (1987). Defining the new product strategy. *IEEE Trans. Eng. Management*, **Aug,** 184–93.

Day, G. S. (1994). The capabilities of market-driven organizations. *J. Marketing*, **Oct,** 37–52.

de Bretani, U. and Droge, C. (1988). Determinants of the new product screening decision: a structural model analysis. *Int. J. Research Marketing*, **2,** 91–106.

Deschamps, J. P. and Nayak, P. R. (1995). *Product Juggernauts: How Companies Mobilize to Generate a Stream of Market Winners.* Harvard Business School Press.

Devinney, T. and Stewart, D. W. (1988). Rethinking the product portfolio: a generalised investment model. *Management Sci.*, **Sep,** 1080–95.

Freeman, C. (1982). *The Economics of Industrial Innovation.* Francis Pinter.

Griffin, A. (1992). Evaluating QFD's use in US firms as a process for developing products, *J. Product Innov. Management*, **9,** 171–87.

Griffin, A. (1997). PDMA research on new product development practices: updating trends and benchmarking best practices. *J. Product Innov. Management*, 429–58.

Hakansson, H. and Laage-Hellman, J. (1984). Developing a network R&D strategy. *J. Product Innov. Management*, **1,** 224.

Hauser, J. R. and Clausing, D. (1988). The House of Quality. *Harvard Bus. Rev.*, **May–Jun,** 63–73.

HM Treasury (1998). *Innovating for the Future.* DTI.

Jones, R. (2000). *The Big Idea.* Harper Collins.

Jones, T. (1997). *New Product Development: An Introduction to a Multifunctional Process.* Butterworth-Heinemann.

Kogure, M. and Akao, Y. (1983). Quality Function Deployment and CWQC. *Quality Prog.*, **16(10),** 25–9.

Kotler, P., Armstrong, G., Saunders, J. and Wong, V. (1996). *Principles of Markets – The European Edition.* Prentice Hall.

Littler, D. and Leverick, F. (1995). Joint ventures for product development: learning from experience. *Long Range Planning*, **Jun,** 58–67.

Lorenz, C. (1986). *The Design Dimension.* Basil Blackwell.

Mabert, V. A., Muth, J. F. and Schmenner, R. W. (1992). Collapsing new product development times: six case studies. *J. Product Innov. Management*, **9,** 200–212.

Marcotti, G. (1998). Stay tuned to consumer taste. *Financial Times*, **31 Mar,** 21.

McGrath, M. E. (1995). *Product Strategy for High Technology Companies.* Irwin.

Mintzberg, H. (1994). *The Rise and Fall of Strategic Planning.* New York.

Near, D. (1998). New product metrics: measuring and motivating product and portfolio performance. PDMA Conference, October.

Nuemo, P. and Oosterveld, J. (1988). Managing technology alliances. *Long Range Planning*, **March,** 11–18.

Pahl, G. and Beitz, W. (1984). *Engineering Design.* Design Council.

Pavia, T. M. (1990). Product growth strategies in young high-technology firms. *J. Product Innov. Management*, **7,** 297.

Pavitt, K. (1991). Key characteristics of the large innovating firm. *Br. J. Management*, **2(1),** 41–50.

Pulos, A. J. (1991). Is there such a thing as design management? *Design Rev.*, **Spring,** 64–70.

Ram, S. and Ram, S. (1989). Expert systems: an emerging technology for selecting new product winners. *J. Product Innov. Management*, **6,** 89.

Redel, T., Stroetmann, B., Beier, M. and Kirchner, H. (1998). Innovation management in the medical industry, technology strategy and strategic alliances. R&D Management Conference, Madrid.

Roberts, E. B. and Hauptman, O. (1986). The process of technology transfer to the new biomedical and pharmaceutical firm. *Research Policy*, **Jun,** 107–20.

Rosenthal, S. (1990). Building a workplace culture to support new product innovation. Boston University Round Table.

Sanderson, S. M. and Uzumerii, V. (1990). *Strategies for New Product Development and Renewal: Design-Based Incrementalism*. Arthur D. Little.

Sasaki, T. (1991). How the Japanese accelerated new car development. *Long Range Planning*, **Jan,** 15–25.

Smith, P. G. and Reinertsen, D. G. (1991). *Developing Products in Half the Time*. Van Nostrand Reinhold.

Souder, W. E. and Mandakovic, T. (1986). R&D product selection models. *Research Management*, **Jul–Aug,** 36–42.

Souder, W. E. and Nasser, S. (1990). Managing R&D consortia for success. *Research Technol. Management*, **Sep–Oct,** 44–50.

Souder, W. E. and Padmanabhan, V. (1989). Transferring new technologies from R&D to manufacturing. *Research Technol. Management*, **Sep–Oct,** 38–43.

Sullivan, L. P. (1986). Quality Function Deployment. *Quality Prog.*, **19(6),** 39–50.

The Economist (2001). Electronic glue. *The Economist*, **Jun 2**.

Voss, B. (1994). Quality's second coming. *J. Bus. Strategy*, **Mar–Apr,** 42–6.

Womack, J. P., Jones, D. T. and Roos, D. (1990). *The Machine that Changed the World*. HarperCollins.

Further reading

Cooper, R. G. (1997). *Product Leadership: Creating and Launching Superior New Products*. Perseus.

Edgett, W., Kleinschmidt, E. and Cooper, R. (1998). *Portfolio Management for New Products*. Perseus.

Hiltzik, M. (2000). *Dealers of Lightning: Xerox PARC and the Dawn of the Computer Age*. Orion.

Lewis, M. (1999). *The New New Thing: A Silicon Valley Story*. Hodder and Stoughton.

Pande, P. S., Neumand, R. P. and Cavanagh R. R. (2000). *The Six Sigma Way*. McGraw Hill.

Robson, M. (1988). *Quality Circles: A Practical Guide*. Gower Publishing.

Sata, M., Brannen, N. S., Katsuhisa, Y. and Naritoshi K. (2002). *Honda*. Oxford University Press.

4

Phase 2: Globalization and acceleration

With the fundamental elements of defined product strategies, access to technology and dedicated resources in place and all focused on creating and delivering ideas into the local market-places, the next step forward for many leading organizations occurred between 1986 and 1994. This was the second wave of improvements to corporate innovation capability, and the associated approaches were, for nearly a decade, seen as leading edge practice. As globalization simultaneously opened new markets and increased the sources of competition, several key advances in approach were implemented. From a market perspective, the ability and the need to embrace a worldwide marketplace meant that the focus for idea delivery had to change. Rather than address just their local needs, organizations had to accommodate a wider diversity of end product and service requirements that differed from area to area. At the same time they had to ensure that sufficient commonality was present in the delivery and support of their products and services to benefit economically from scale. Examples of how companies tackled this dichotomy include the use of common automotive platforms across multiple markets but with local customization to regional needs, and a similar effect in the consumer electronics industry with shared components for multiple products.

Allied to this commonality was the increasingly important role of the brand in communicating and supporting new ideas. Whether this was in the form of multiple brands applied to common products or, as in the case of Nike, the extension of a single brand across multiple global product ranges or, as with Coke and Procter & Gamble, how to use a common brand across multiple products, each of which were customized to local tastes and consumer behaviours, or, as with Intel and Nutrasweet, the introduction of ingredient branding, the increasing significance of the brand in the delivery of new ideas became core practice for many firms. In parallel with this, in order to create and deliver the best new products and services it became doubly necessary to focus both on doing the right things and on doing them quickly. This led to organizations trying to focus more on their core competencies and at the same time accelerate their idea delivery. This correspondingly facilitated the introduction of fuzzy-gate development processes to speed up decision-making, multi-disciplinary teams to engage all functions simultaneously, matrix organizational structures to accommodate team/functional align-ments and allegiances, and increased involvement of suppliers to reduce cost and complexity. All of these were elements of a more complex corporate innovation capability that was quickly becom-ing a key differentiator in the marketplace between winners and losers. Throughout this period, these and similar issues were therefore all shown to deliver benefit across companies large and small, and became seen as the new standards.

4.1 Core competencies

Whereas the development and implementation of a product strategy had focused companies' attention on the products that they could develop for their markets within individual business units, in the early 1990s an alternative perspective of focusing on the organization's core competencies as the basis for new business creation was promoted and, particularly in sectors where com-panies had diversified operations, widely embraced. Largely led by Hamel and Prahalads' work, which formed the basis of their article 'The core competence of the corporation' (Prahalad and Hamel, 1990) and the subsequent business bestseller *Competing for the Future* (Hamel and Prahalad, 1994), identifying and exploiting core competencies became a key strategic focus for many firms. As organizations found competition increasingly severe, many began to assess which core products, technologies and markets were closest to the heart of their current or planned capabilities and which could drive growth, and, in an increasing range of instances, used this as the basis for reshaping their strategy, organization, products and, in some cases, industry (Irwin and Michaels, 1989).

Core competencies were seen as a platform for competitive advantage both in existing operations and as the basis for the development of new business (Baker *et al.*, 1994):

- NEC, for example, conceived, developed and leveraged its core competence in semiconductors to become a world leader and a first-tier player in telecommunications and computing products. NEC determined that semiconductors would be the company's core product and, rather than undertaking extensive expensive R&D, entered into a wide range of alliances to build the necessary capabilities quickly and cheaply. The company moved from manufacturing switching and transmission equipment into mobile phones, fax machines and laptops, as it used its ability in designing and manufacturing semiconductors as the key building block upon which all its successful products were based.
- Sony's core competence in miniaturization was key in enabling it to deliver a continuous stream of class-leading products throughout the 1990s.
- Philips' leading capability in optical media was at the time seen to underpin not only the compact disc in 1982, but also the myriad of related by-products such as CD-R, CR-RW and DVD that has been the mainstay of much of the company subsequently.
- 3M's core competencies in adhesives, substrates, coatings and advanced materials have spawned over 60 000 new products, most of which are different combinations of these four areas.

Core competencies were seen as the collective learning in an organization, and to have three key attributes:

1 The potential to access a wide variety of markets
2 The ability to contribute significantly to the perceived customer benefits of an end product
3 They are difficult for competitors to imitate.

In terms of composition, an organization's core competencies are based on its capabilities, which can in turn be seen to be combinations of skills, facilities and structure. Some of these capabilities are viewed as being the competitive capabilities that have a positive impact on competitive advantage, but not all. Rather, a competence is a unique network of both competitive and non-competitive capabilities, linked together by business process (Gallon *et al.*, 1995). It is the ability of an organization to consolidate corporate-wide competencies that is seen as the real source of competitive advantage. An organization's core competencies are thus the competencies that underpin its long-term competitiveness by providing customer value, competitor differentiation and extendibility. A core competence is thus truly core when it forms the basis for entry into new markets (Prahalad and Hamel, 1990). Typically, a world-leading organization has only four or five core competencies. If a company lists more than this, then several are likely to be component capabilities.

Moreover, companies also began to recognize that just as competencies were built up of individual capabilities, then end products or services were similarly dependent on core component products, each of which is the physical embodiment of one or more core competencies. One of the most widely quoted examples of this has been Honda, whose core products are the engines that leverage the company's core competencies in transmissions, power-trains and precision engineering. These core products are then components of the end products of cars, motorbikes, chainsaws, tractors, lawnmowers, snowmobiles and even Formula 1 racing cars. In order to develop new products with a high level of corporate synergy, determining which relate to and rely on core competencies as opposed to non-core competencies or capabilities thus became a key determinant for project selection and an essential aspect of innovation strategy. No longer was the desire to deliver this product into that market using a chosen technology the essence of product strategy; this had to be underpinned and focused around core competencies and hence core products.

As companies have since sought to follow the credo of core competence-led strategy, some have succeeded in refocusing their businesses but others have failed. Not recognizing that building core competencies can take decades and is not simply the divestment of a few none-core business units has been perhaps the most common misconception. However, equally, firms have not fully understood that successful product strategy has become focused not just on building the core competencies but also on exploiting them, and exploiting them in the most advantageous manner. The translation of core products into end products requires the skills to translate them into products and services that customers want to buy, and this does not follow naturally. As Philips found, defining the core competencies to exploit did not imply that consumers would purchase the company's products when competitors' products more successfully understood and addressed user needs, leveraging both technological capability and marketing nuance. However, one company that was identified as a leader in core competence thinking at the time and has also successfully translated its core competencies and products into a continued series of competitive market leading end products is another Japanese manufacturer, Canon.

Canon – Optics R Us

Canon started out as the Precision Optical Instruments Laboratory, which was founded in Tokyo in 1933 to design and manufacture cameras that could compete with the dominant German models of the time. Re-branded as Canon in 1935, the company developed its capabilities in photographic equipment production over the next thirty years to become one of the new leaders in the 35-mm camera market. Seeking to exploit its technical prowess in additional areas, in 1962 the company developed a plan to enter the business machine market and over the next decade launched new calculators, copiers, typewriters and billing machines, opening manufacturing and marketing subsidiaries worldwide. In 1975 Canon developed an early laser-beam printer, and the following year entered the fax machine market. During the 1980s the company introduced the first bubble-jet printer, the first copier with replaceable cartridges and the first plain paper fax, together with colour copiers, laser printers and digital copiers, and a constant stream of class-leading compact, SLR, video and digital cameras. By 1990, Canon employed 62 000 people and had annual sales in excess of 1.8 trillion yen, 78 per cent of which came from its business machines products.

Over this time Canon had identified and built up core competencies that both underpinned its products and enabled it to move into new markets. Its four core competencies in precision mechanics, fine optics, microelectronics and electronic imaging formed the key building blocks upon which all its successful products, from cameras and imaging systems to printers, faxes and copiers, were based (Table 4.1). As such, they provided the company with evident competitive advantages in all these areas and enabled it to compete with such a diverse range of rival organizations as Pentax and Kodak in the camera market and the industry giants of Hewlett-Packard and Xerox in the business machines arena.

Canon achieved this not only by developing the core technological capabilities but also by identifying and defining industry leading core products that other manufacturers would source as components for their own end products. Unlike Xerox, who focused on internal exploitation of its laser printer technology capability, Canon developed its core product of the laser printer engine to a point where it was a key component of the end products of a wide range of companies including Apple, HP and Samsung. By 1995 Canon had 84 per cent of the world manufacture of desktop laser printer engines, even though the company's share in the laser printer business was less that 20 per cent.

Table 4.1 Deployment of Canon's core competencies – 1992 (source: Hamel and Prahalad, 1994)

Product	Precision mechanics	Fine optics	Micro-electronics	Electronic imaging
Basic camera	X	X		
Compact camera	X	X		
Electronic camera	X	X		
EOS SLR camera	X	X	X	
Video still camera	X	X	X	X
Laser-beam printer	X		X	X
Colour video printer	X		X	X
Bubble-jet printer	X		X	X
Basic fax	X		X	X
Laser fax	X		X	X
Calculator			X	
Plain paper copier	X	X	X	X
Battery-powered PPC	X	X	X	X
Colour copier	X	X	X	X
Laser copier	X	X	X	X
Colour laser copier	X	X	X	X
Still video system	X	X	X	X
Laser imager	X	X	X	X
Cell analyser	X	X	X	X
Mask aligners	X		X	X
Stepper aligners	X		X	X
Excimer laser aligners	X	X	X	X

In addition, in order to ensure cross-business transfer and utilization of the developed capabilities, Canon also encouraged its staff to share new technologies and insights. Critical people were regularly rotated around the camera, copier and professional optical products businesses, and when one business unit was investigating new product opportunities, its first point of contact was the experts in other areas. When the reprographics group initiated development of microprocessor-controlled copiers, it turned to the photoproducts group that had developed the world's first microprocessor controlled camera for guidance.

Throughout the 1990s Canon exploited its four core competencies, developing and launching a whole series of new products ranging from the world's first integrated laptop, bubble-jet printer and A2 digital colour copier to the award-winning IXUS APS compact cameras, and along the way producing over eighty million bubble-jet and laser printers. Today Canon is the world's leading manufacturer of both business machine products and cameras. In 2000 the company had over 85 000 employees working in over forty countries, and total sales of $24.2 billion. It continues to invest in new technology, spending $1.8 billion a year on R&D, and for five years has been in the top three corporations receiving US patents, generating $137 million in revenue from patent royalties alone. How Canon maintains this position will be a product of both how it continues to develop and exploit its four core competencies and how it keeps innovating in technology, product design and marketing.

4.2 Global products

An emerging focus on increasing export opportunities in international markets developed throughout the 1980s, causing more and more companies to seek to capitalize on the available benefits and, as a key element of this, to unify their product ranges across countries and cultures. Led mostly by the Japanese high-technology consumer electronics market, organizations began to develop global products – products that would appeal to local and export markets alike, were thus the same the world over and could therefore be sold worldwide without modification. By creating products that satisfied common needs, organizations could increase sales and reduce costs. By embracing the opportunities available, from adopting standard designs and acquiring the associated ability to reduce the number of product lines being supported, companies were able to focus more on core means of improving global product quality and profitability across their product range (Quelch and Kenny, 1994). They sought to improve product integrity (Clark and Fujimoto, 1990).

In order to facilitate this globalization, organizations identified common needs that could be addressed by their increasingly standardized products. More than ever before this defined a focus for market research activities – and specifically, those centred on gaining an understanding of the customer. Since the same products were now being sold in Japan, Europe and the USA, companies had to be certain of their target markets and, in particular, to ensure that they fully understood the requirements of the target customers in all markets. Only by producing accurate profiles of designated worldwide users of new products could companies isolate the commonalities and integrate the key associated features within their products. Thus firms had to develop the capabilities and build the resources to stay tuned to the needs of the global customer (Caulkin, 1997).

The consequences of this move towards common global products influenced not only the products and services themselves, but also initiated a number of changes in the way in which products are developed. Although initially many companies maintained their existing innovation capabilities either within or close to their home manufacturing facilities, as more sought to better understand global customer preferences, some (like Honda) established development centres in their larger export markets. As well as setting up new overseas manufacturing sites to produce their new global products, Japanese car manufacturers, American IT suppliers and Korean electronics firms alike also founded a number of research laboratories and design centres across Europe and the USA (Clark and Fujimoto, 1992). By locating some of their key development capabilities and resources in these markets, they were able to get closer to their customers, better understand their preferences, and subsequently develop such successful global products as the Mazda MX-5, the Logitech MouseMan, and Samsung's range of fax machines and microwaves.

Wherever possible, companies sought to exploit the opportunities for the same product to be provided in all markets. For some, such as those mentioned above, this was possible. Either through function or desire, PCs, calculators, sports cars and jeans could and did all find, or create, similar demand in the USA, Europe and Asia. However, in many areas a fully global product was not possible. Sometimes for regulatory or legislative reasons, but more often due to subtle differences in local needs or tastes, many companies wishing to introduce global products found themselves introducing a standardized offering with varied components. Unilever, for example, tried to create a global product offering in the personal care sector. Using its *Lynx* brand in the UK, labelled as *Axe* elsewhere, even this major global FMCG encountered numerous problems. Not only did Latin America, North America, Europe and Asia all require alternative odours, but gel consistency was also different, as was (due to poor cross-regional coordination) bottle shape, cap fitting and label colour. Yes, the company did have a global product from a product portfolio perspective, but not one that was actually the same worldwide in terms of physical reality or associated economies of scale. Although Prozac is the same product worldwide, the labelling and secondary packaging varies from one region to another to comply with local legislation. Similarly, Diet Coke is different across the world – from a branding perspective it is called Coke Light in Europe, the sweetener used is different in the USA and Europe, the can shape varies from country to country, and because only the concentrate is produced centrally, the taste varies globally in line with the local water supply to canning and bottling plants.

Recognizing that globalization of product portfolios was not as easy to achieve in all areas as had been originally thought, many companies started to go global on an underpinning component and platform basis but not in every element. Similar levels of cost reduction could be achieved by sharing key parts but allowing for localized cultural or stylistic tweaking; commonalities could be addressed without imposition of a bland global common denominator. This approach was practised across sectors from consumer electronics and pharmaceuticals to foods and financial services. However, by far the most successful and widely recognized mass product globalization through common platform exploitation was in the automotive sector, this time the world's largest car manufacturer, Ford.

Ford – same car, different face

The Ford Motor Company will forever be associated with its founder, Henry Ford, and its first mass-produced car, the Model T. From 1908 to 1927 this was the product that brought motoring to the people, and as a consequence was in its own way a global product. Over the next fifty years Ford expanded operations both under its own name in the USA, Europe and Australia, and, through M&A activity, under the additional brands of Mazda in Japan, and Mercury and Lincoln in the USA. More recently, with the creation of its Premier Automotive Group (including Jaguar, Volvo, Aston Martin and Land Rover), the company has also grown its brand portfolio in Europe.

Although largely successful in their own right, each of the Ford divisions had been under growing competitive pressure throughout the late 1970s and early 1980s. Toyota, Honda and, increasingly, Nissan were hitting the US market hard with high quality products, and in Europe GM, VW, Peugeot Citroen and even Fiat were all gradually taking market share in one segment or another. As global supply outstripped demand and overcapacity became the key threat across the whole industry, the provision of new products that met and hopefully exceeded consumer expectations in each market was key and achieving this in the most economical but value-adding manner was clearly the preferred route. In 1980 Ford determined that, wherever possible, it would share product platforms across regions to allow multiple vehicles to be provided into the global marketplace using the same core elements. Moreover, across all products additional components, from exhausts and windscreens to door handles and seats, would be shared to minimize variety, reduce stock and hence maximize economies of scale.

The first product to emerge following this philosophy was the 1982 Sierra in the UK, or Taurus in Europe and Australia. Although initially not launched in the USA, this vehicle was by and large identical in all three markets, save for the name badge. Identical chassis, identical body and common parts were all exploited to the full. This was followed by a relaunched Escort/ Focus compact car. However, although they were an initial success the bland design of these products, conceived to appeal to all, did not achieve the sales they could have. Under increasing pressure from GM's Vauxhall Astra/Opel Kadett and Vauxhall Cavalier/Opel Vectra lines, as well as better value and arguably more sophisticated products such as the Peugeot 205, VW Golf, Audi 100 and Fiat Uno, as the decade progressed Ford was forced to reappraise its global product strategy. In essence, the company had to both improve the common global products that it was providing under its own name and better integrate and exploit the opportunities available from its newly acquired additional brands. What resulted was a two-pronged approach.

Under the Ford brand, the company relaunched its core mid-sized vehicle as a global product. Labelled the Mondeo in Europe and the Taurus in the USA, this was designed to reclaim the core 2.2-children family car market. Although it sported different body panels on either side of the Atlantic, over 90 per cent of the vehicle was the same, with shared high-volume common parts, and could thus be priced very competitively in all markets. In addition, at the bottom of the range a new edge style was introduced in the small simple Ka product, which was again available worldwide, and in the intermediary segment the Escort was eventually replaced by a global Focus product. In parallel with this, and also under the Ford brand, product variants were created to appeal to niche sports markets. In the USA the Probe was introduced, based on the Mondeo/Taurus platform, and in Europe the Puma utilized common platform and production with the Focus. Despite a major failure of product positioning with the Scorpio executive replacement for the longstanding Granada line, with the subsequent extension of the edge style introduced on the Ka product across the core car product range, Ford gradually repositioned itself as one of the lead innovators in the automotive sector.

Outside the main Ford brand, the company determined similarly to share product platforms wherever possible. Starting with the Mercury Sable, the company first re-branded tweaked versions of the core Mondeo/Taurus platform before moving on to its newer acquisitions. After buying Jaguar in 1990 for £1.6 billion, Ford invested a further £1 billion over the next few years to rebuild the company, improve product quality and create the basis for new global products. Although it continued development of the class-leading XJ saloon and XK8 sports car, which share few components with other Ford products, Ford did use the Lincoln LS as the basis for the Jaguar S-type and the Volvo S80, and the Mondeo for the smaller Jaguar X-type as well as the newer Volvo S40. Although sharing platforms and many components as well as common production facilities, Ford was smart in allowing Jaguar to design its own engines in order to maintain prestige impact. As a result, Jaguar production expanded from 50 000 to 200 000 in less than four years. Similarly, with the later acquisition of Land Rover from BMW as part of the Rover fallout in 1999, Ford took advantage of the opportunities for global products in the Sports Utility Vehicle (SUV) segment. Having earlier re-badged the Nissan Terrano as the Ford Maverick, Ford moved on to multi-label the Ford Explorer/Lincoln Aviator/Mercury Mountaineer in the USA and then, after acquisition, re-badge the Land Rover Freelander as both the Ford Escape and the Mazda Tribute. Collectively, these product extensions across multiple brands further reinforced Ford's position in the marketplace. By leveraging such high quality, well designed, leading global products into multiple markets using its multiple brands, Ford has regained the top slot in the industry as well as critical acclaim. By 2000 the Ford Motor Company had increased its turnover to $141 billion, employed 345 000 and, despite emerging problems due to declining demand in its key US market, was again seen as a global leader.

4.3 Brand significance

The 1980s was the era when brands generally moved from being simply a means of identifying goods to being a representation of core product values, and rose to prominence as the names and logos of organizations such as Coca Cola, Sony, BMW and McDonalds gained truly global recognition. However, it was in the early 1990s that building the significance of the brand became a core focus within innovation (King, 1991). Whereas up until this time brands had been largely collective and developed to support and promote an organization's specific products, such as Rowntree's Kit-Kat chocolate bars and P&G's Ariel soap powder, during the 1990s companies like Nike, Virgin, Starbucks and, more latterly, FCUK and Amazon all started to create new products and deliver new services that supported and extended the reach and scope of the corporate brand. This resulted in a mutual and increased interdependency of product and brand, and hence greater brand significance.

Customers now not only purchased a product or service, but also received a brand experience designed to increase brand awareness and loyalty. What Nike achieved with sports clothes, Virgin did with music retailing, airlines, holidays, financial services and then on-line car, energy and wine purchasing. Diners at T.G.I. Fridays do not go there to get a burger and fries; they go to gain an experience. Likewise, Starbucks believes that 'customers see themselves inside our company, inside our brand – because they are part of the Starbuck's experience'. Companies as diverse as the UK bank First Direct, the GM offshoot Saturn and clothes retailer Gap all created experiences for their customers that reinforced the brand with the product and raise its significance in the mind of the consumer (The Forum Corporation, 2001).

The role of a brand in conveying a specific set of values to consumers had previously been seen as delivering up to four levels of meaning, as it communicated product attributes, promoted benefits, inferred impressions of the buyer's values, and projected a personality (Kapferer, 1992). However, as marketers developed the influence and impact of brands, the role grew most in the last two fields of value and personality. As companies such as Gillette and BMW built product portfolios and enhanced awareness, developing brand loyalty and increased brand recognition, in many cases the value of the brand equity became one of the organization's most significant assets. Much of the nearly 100-fold gap between Microsoft's 1996 market value of $85 billion and its fixed asset value of only $1 billion was associated with the value of the brand and intellectual property (Caulkin, 1987); likewise the five-fold differences between market and book values of food companies such as Nabisco, Kraft and Nestlé.

Brand value became a strategic issue for many leading organizations as they sought to enable both corporate and shareholder growth. With its first survey of the world's most valuable brands in 1991, the consultancy Interbrand brought the issue to the fore. Ten years on, the company's annual table of the top 100 brands has gained sufficient foothold in the corporate psyche to have a dedicated issue of *Business Week*. By 2001, the Interbrand survey (Table 4.2) showed that, despite the recent economic downturn, the Coca Cola, Microsoft and IBM brands were all worth over $50 billion, and twenty-seven organizations had brands valued at over $10 billion. Moreover, of the top 100, twenty-three were brands that were implicitly linked with identifiable new products and services such as Nokia, Amazon, Dell, SAP, Yahoo and Duracell.

Table 4.2 The twenty-five most valuable brands 2001 (source: Interbrand, 2001)

2001 rank	2000 rank	Brand	Country of origin	2001 brand value ($bn)	2000 brand value ($bn)	% change
1	1	Coca Cola	US	68.9	72.5	−5
2	2	Microsoft	US	65.1	70.2	−7
3	3	IBM	US	52.8	53.2	−1
4	6	GE	US	42.4	38.1	11
5	5	Nokia	Finland	35.0	38.6	−9
6	4	Intel	US	34.7	39.0	−11
7	8	Disney	US	32.6	33.6	−3
8	7	Ford	US	30.1	36.4	−17
9	9	McDonald's	US	25.3	27.9	−9
10	10	AT&T	US	22.8	25.6	−11
11	11	Marlboro	US	22.1	22.1	0
12	12	Mercedes	Germany	21.7	21.1	3
13	16	Citibank	US	19.0	18.8	1
14	15	Toyota	Japan	18.6	18.8	−1
15	13	Hewlett-Packard	US	18.0	20.6	−13
16	14	Cisco Systems	US	17.2	20.1	−14
17	19	American Express	US	16.9	16.1	5
18	17	Gillette	US	15.3	17.4	−12
19	−	Merrill Lynch	US	15.0	−	−
20	18	Sony	Japan	15.0	16.4	−9
21	20	Honda	Japan	14.6	15.2	−4
22	23	BMW	Germany	13.9	13.0	7
23	22	Nescafé	Switzerland	13.3	13.7	−3
24	21	Compaq	US	12.4	14.6	−15
25	−	Oracle	US	12.2	−	−

Within the evolving innovation of new products and services, this growing importance of the brand had a number of major implications. Not only did new products have to reflect the values and personalities associated with their respective brand, but also, as a key means of developing the brand, it was through the introduction of new products that these values were modified. Whether developing new core products such as the Ka, or extending the product range with variant products such as the Probe and the Puma, organizations such as Ford sought to maintain a symbiotic relationship between its brand and its products as their mutual dependency increased. Particularly in the automotive, communications, electronics and food sectors, where the increasing similarity of products in looks, functionality and performance had diminished relative product differential, it was the impact of the brand, and the values associated with it, that became more and more significant (Sharp, 1993). As this impact continued to increase, organizations innovating new products and services sought to maintain and protect their brands through addressing the incorporation of proprietary technology in products (such as canned 'draught beer') to enhance the brand image and differentiate from own-label products, promoting component suppliers like Nutrasweet and Dolby through ingredient branding to increase customer confidence, and embedding covert anti-counterfeiting mechanisms in clothes, videos and drinks to prevent brand erosion though piracy (Lorenz, 1994). Although Nike, Volkswagen and AOL all successfully leveraged their brands to mutually support their new products and services, with a 2001 brand value of $35 billion, by far the most successful exploiter of brand significance during the 1990s was micro-processor manufacturer Intel.

Intel – it's what's inside that counts

Not many years ago, if you mentioned the word 'microprocessor' you would be likely to get mystified stares from most consumers. Few knew anything about the microprocessor, even though it was the 'brain' that powered the computer. However, today many personal computer users can recite the specification and speed of the processor, just as car owners can tell you if they have a 1.6-, 1.8- or 2.0-litre engine. The awareness of Intel has grown along with the awareness of the chip. This can be credited to the Intel Inside Program, which was launched in 1991. The promotional campaign represented the first time a PC component manu-facturer successfully communicated directly to computer buyers. Today, the Intel Inside Program is one of the world's largest cooperative marketing programmes, supported by some thousand PC makers who are licensed to use the Intel Inside logos. Since the programme's inception in 1991, over $7 billion has been invested in advertising by Intel and the computer manufacturers that have carried the Intel Inside logos. This has created an estimated 500 billion impressions, while building Intel's worldwide name.

In 1968, two scientists left Fairchild Semiconductor in Cal-ifornia to establish their own company. Robert Noyce and Gordon Moore, later famous for Moore's Law, the most quoted law of the IT world, founded Intel to develop and manufacture high performance silicon chips for the fast-growing computer industry, introducing the world's first microprocessor in 1971. For more than three decades, Intel Corporation has developed technology enabling the computer and Internet revolution that has changed the world. Today, Intel supplies chips, boards, systems, software, networking and communications equipment, and services that comprise the 'ingredients' of computer architecture and the Internet.

From the dawn of the personal computer in the late 1970s, marketing was mainly driven by computer vendors and software publishers. Although its processors were helping to drive the rapid increase in performance, which in turn helped systems to run more smoothly, quickly and reliably, Intel relied on its PC vendor customers to convey this message. Intel had little brand identification among users, who knew no more about the processor than they did about the company that built the transistors in their radios. In fact, computer users were generally unaware of what advanced processors were available.

By 1977 Intel had grown to 10 000 employees and continued to expand its own production capabilities, which, largely through the launch of an IBM PC based on the Intel microprocessor in 1981, were generating an annual turnover of over $1 billion by 1984. As revenue increased to $8 billion Intel grew to hold over 80 per cent of the PC chip market, but despite this, was little known outside Silicon Valley and a few computer enthusiasts. Intel believed people needed to know more about the processor and the company behind it, and so in 1989 an Intel marketing manager, Dennis Carter, formed a small group and for the first time launched a programme aimed at marketing a microprocessor, the 386SX, to the Information Technology managers who purchased PCs for business. This effort was highly successful – IT personnel learned about the new 386SX and converted to it rapidly. However, several challenges quickly emerged – specifically, the issue of trademark protection. In the late 1980s Intel assumed that its 386 and 486 processors were protected trademarks, thus preventing other companies from using them, but the courts ruled that this was not the case and the door was opened for rivals to use them at will.

In order to communicate the benefits of new processors to PC buyers it was important that Intel transfer any brand equity from the ambiguous and unprotected processor numbers to the company itself, while simultaneously raising awareness of its name. Intel invested billions of dollars in developing cutting-edge technology, and billions more in assuring performance and reliability. A stronger brand was needed to communicate this to consumers, separating Intel from the pack. Clearly, marketing directly to the end user was a novel idea for a semiconductor company. Although the company was widely recognized among computer manufacturers, the brand had little name recognition amongst end users. The media raised questions as to whether a pure technology company could play in the same league as Proctor & Gamble, General Motors and McDonalds. Even to many within the company, the campaign seemed a stretch.

In addition, although the processor was a key component of personal computers, it was after all only a component. To market this component to the PC buyer effectively, it was important to work with the manufacturer of computers. The processor was buried deep inside the computer and, despite its significance, it was hard to tell which processor any PC contained before it was purchased. Intel studied successful consumer marketing techniques and examined tactics used by well-known companies supplying a component or ingredient of a finished product such as NutraSweet, Teflon and Dolby. They also began a variety of marketing experiments and envisaged how a branded ingredient programme would play out in the computer industry. Key to this strategy was gaining consumers' confidence in Intel as a brand and demonstrating the value of buying a microprocessor from the industry's leading company. At the suggestion of its advertising agency, Intel adopted a new tagline for their advertising: 'Intel. The computer inside.' Using this to position the important role of the processor and at the same time associating Intel with 'safety,' 'leading technology' and 'reliability,' consumer recognition and confidence would hopefully soar. That would create a new pull for Intel-based PCs. Later, this tagline was shortened to 'Intel Inside'.

The important role of the microprocessor was being communicated, but to be truly effective the ingredient status of the microprocessor needed to be dealt with. In 1991 the company therefore developed the Intel Inside cooperative marketing programme. The heart of this programme was incentive-based cooperative advertising. Intel would create a co-op fund where it would take 5 per cent of the purchase price of processors and put it in a pool for advertising. Available to all OEM (Original Equipment Manufacturer) computer makers, it offered cooperatively to share advertising costs for PC print ads that included the Intel logo. The benefits were clear. Adding the Intel logo not only made the OEM's advertising dollar stretch further, but it also conveyed an assurance that their systems were powered by the latest technology. The campaign was launched in July 1991, and by the end of that year 300 PC OEMs had signed on to support the programme.

Once the OEM programme was underway, Intel started print advertising around the world to explain the logo to consumers.

Television was especially effective in communicating the Intel Inside message to the consumer. In early 1992 Intel debuted its first TV advertising, stressing speed, power and affordability, made by *Star Wars* director George Lucas' Industrial Light and Magic Company. It used state-of-the-art special effects to take viewers on a sweeping trip through the innards of the personal computer before hovering over the campaign's core focus – the then new Intel i486 processor. Along with such TV advertisements, Intel added a distinctive and memorable three-second animated jingle displaying the logo and playing a five-tone melody. Starting in 1995, the now-familiar tone helped to 'cement a positive Intel image in the minds of millions of consumers'.

The marketing investments quickly paid off in terms of consumer mind-share, aided by the high-profile launches of the Pentium and Pentium Pro microprocessors. The advertising results were stunning. From a standing start Intel became one of the most valuable brands around, ranking third in the 1993 Interbrand survey with a value of $17.8 billion, only lagging behind longstanding leaders Marlboro and Coca Cola. In 1991, Intel research indicated that only 24 per cent of European PC buyers were familiar with the Intel Inside logos. One year later that figure had grown to nearly 80 per cent, and by 1995 it had soared to 94 per cent. By the late 1990s the campaign was widely regarded as a success. Intel's innovative marketing helped broaden awareness of the PC, fuelling consumer demand while prices continued to plunge. Intel became a lightning rod for the computer revolution. When Intel's 'Bunny People' characters danced their way across the TV screen, during a break of the 1997 SuperBowl, 'they became nothing less than the whimsical icons of a go-go PC industry', according to *Advertising Age*. Intel had arrived in the public consciousness as a world-class player. Its brand was known worldwide, its name synonymous with the computer industry.

This campaign for the first time really brought attention to components rather than just end products, and ensured a unique linkage between brand and product, where brand significance became as important as technical performance in the purchase decision. As such, it prompted increased promotion of components in other areas ranging from Shimano gears and brakes on mountain bikes and GoreTex breathable fabrics in outdoor clothing through to DuPont polymers in kitchen worktops. It has increased global awareness of both Intel and microprocessors and, despite increasing competition from rivals such as AMD, Intel remains one of the premium world brands. By 2000 Intel had a turnover of $33.7 billion and continued to invest over 10 per cent of revenue in R&D, and, although dropping two places to number six in the Interbrand rankings in 2001 with a value of $34.7 billion, the Intel brand is unique in being so well known. Alongside Cisco, Intel is the only component brand in the top 100, a position underlying the company's achievement in raising both its brand significance and value.

4.4 Speed to market

Throughout the 1990s, the issue that perhaps received more attention in the field of new product and service development than any other was accelerating the process – reducing time to market, or achieving rapid product development. However it was phrased, as the advantages of developing more and more products more and more quickly to improve market share, generate additional revenue streams, maximize profitability and support profit growth were all recognized, this single issue of increasing speed to market came to the forefront of many organizations' thinking (Reinertsen and Smith, 1991). Customers expected a continuous pipeline of the very latest products and technologies to be available to them as quickly as possible, and so manufacturers had to react:

- Honda took less than four years to move from drawing board to showroom (Kiley, 1989)
- Honeywell required only 12 months to develop thermostats, which had previously taken four years (Bussey and Seaese, 1988)
- Xerox cut its copier development times down from six years to three (Reiner, 1988)
- AT&T took less than a year to design a new phone – down from its previous two years
- HP took only 22 months to develop its Desk Jet Printer – down from 54 months (Dumaine, 1989)
- Merck reduced some of its new drug development from ten years to four.

To achieve this a wide range of different techniques were implemented across organizations, from front-end research and core development activities through to delivery and customer support operations (Gold, 1987). Several organizations also began to examine how they could accelerate the up-front technical and market research activities. Market research was more efficiently integrated into both ongoing customer sales support and emerging technical evaluations, as detailed later; companies such as Nike began to incorporate consumer evaluation of prototypes into their overall innovation programmes to capture and accommodate user preferences and attitudes; manufacturers such as Raytheon pursued multiple evaluations in parallel to increase the choice of technologies available for implementation; R&D personnel spent more time with customers to gain better understanding of end-user applications of their technical developments; and, as mentioned earlier, organizations such as Siemens introduced two-step idea evaluation approaches to filter out the least attractive opportunities and so enable better resource utilization and faster migration into development.

Significant efforts were being employed and deployed to reduce development time by tweaking the core enabling process. Each stage of the development process was streamlined through simplification of operations. New technologies such as 3D CAD were used to enable early visualization and rapid prototyping; customers were involved early on to provide guiding input into product and service configurations in development; wherever possible appropriate activities such as detail design and tooling preparation were conducted in parallel; market testing of concepts and the organization of product launches were eliminated; and external suppliers and vendors were better integrated within the project teams and hence the process (Milson *et* al., 1992; Towner, 1994). By adopting such techniques, numerous organizations began to gain from the acceleration of many of their core development programmes.

In the operational arenas, firms also implemented an increasing variety of techniques and approaches to improve the speed at which products and services could be delivered to customers and thereafter maintained. Dell put in place the necessary infrastructure to ensure next day delivery of its computer products, UPS promised next day parcel delivery, and Amazon guaranteed delivery of books within three days. First Direct provided twenty-four-hour customer service for its banking services, and Shell ensured that 80 per cent of calls to its business-to-business product units would be dealt with by the first point of contact. Pioneered by low cost rivals Easyjet and Ryanair, airlines embraced Internet technologies to drive down costs and decrease transaction time to a point where 80 per cent of bookings were taking place on-line. Cable and Wireless promised fault resolution for its telecommunications services within eight hours of notification, and UK car rescue organizations such as the AA, RAC and Green Flag established procedures to ensure that engineers were with customers within the hour.

Collectively, such enhancements to the ways in which companies conceived, developed and delivered their products and services ensured that throughout the 1990s speed of delivery increased significantly across multiple arenas. However, within one sector, the fashion industry, there was one company that used speed to market as both a differentiator and the key enabler for improved service that resulted in sector leading growth. That company was the Spanish clothing company, Zara.

Hot couture at the House of Zara

What began as a small lingerie manufacturing company in Northern Spain with a mere starting capital of $25 in 1963 is today one of the world's fastest growing fashion businesses. Not only is Zara rapidly increasing its share of the market, but it is also changing the way high-street fashion retailers go about doing their business. Zara has shelved traditional fashion logic and approach – there are no four seasons at Zara to adhere to, only continuous changes, with stores receiving new stock every two weeks.

Zara was founded by Amancio Ortega initially to sell lingerie and pyjamas, but the entrepreneur expanded into high-street fashion and the first Zara store was opened in 1975. Today the company has some 450 stores worldwide, and is looking at expanding with *circa* 150 stores a year. Inditext, of which Zara is subsidiary, floated on the Madrid Stock Exchange in May 2001, making Ortega Spain's richest man. The company's stock was oversubscribed twenty-seven times, and raised some $1.8 billion for the initial share sale of a 23 per cent stake of the company. This was at a time when retail fashion shares were doing less well in a market where the economic slowdown was hitting spending and European retailers were laying off employees to deter the failing profits.

The company has to maintain its competitive edge to continue to succeed in a market where customers are fickle and margins are easily squashed by mistakes in the design-to-stock process. Although Inditex is more profitable than its competitors, earning 99 cents on every 10 euros in sales compared to Hennes & Mauritz's 84 and Gap's 64, it has to attract more shoppers to keep the sales growing in its expanded network of stores. The Zara brand is aimed at fashion-conscious young individuals who see clothing as perishables – what is fashionable today will inevitably be out-of-date tomorrow; designs are worn just as long as they are credible amongst peers. This emphasizes the need for Zara to keep in touch with the customer. If it fails at this and at delivering what the customers want fast, the people who keep Zara's revenue growing will move to the next store along the high street.

Zara's headquarters in La Coruna is the home for the company's design team, the 200 designers who are responsible for selecting the right colours, materials and shapes for the clothes to be supplied to the stores. What differentiates Zara from its main rivals and peers, the Swedish Hennes & Mauritz, US-based Gap and their like, is the incredible speed at which designs are taken from concept to final product in store. This can take up to ten months at H&M, whereas Zara manages the same within one month – sometimes as little as two weeks.

Zara also maintains an image of always being on the pulse of the latest fads and fashion must-haves by providing its customers with an ever-changing selection of clothes. Zara's production is in-house, and this enables the company effectively to test how designs are doing in the stores. If a certain design is not selling, it can easily be changed to accommodate customer demand. Often stores are only supplied with a small number of a certain design, and if it sells well the production of this item is accelerated and the stores supplied with more merchandise. This effectively means that Zara tests its products in stores rather than at a pre-launch stage, using real customers as lead users. As the company can change designs based on the reaction gained in the stores, mistakes have less of an impact on the final bottom line. As the designs and what is supplied in the stores are so dependent on customer say, the number of designs that are not welcomed by customers and consequently have to be sold at discount are also fewer than industry average. Any items that fail to attract the customers can be changed within Zara, and later supplied back to the stores with an enhanced design.

The company's designers also follow the marketplace by meticulously studying both the fashion shows and the high street; Zara knows that its customers are influenced by the expensive *prêt-a-porter* lines of the fashion houses in Milan, Paris and London, but they also interpret designs to accommodate their lifestyles and thus become a fashion force of their own. These are Zara's influences – the top-down supply of fashions and the customer view of these. The company simply provides its customers with new designs more often than its rivals – and at that speed, it still manages to provide what customers want.

Zara has succeeded in taking the customer to the centre of its design process and thereafter vertically integrating the entire production process to ensure that the right designs are reaching the right stores at the right time. Mistakes are, of course, made, but these are rectified quickly. Based on feedback from the network of stores, Zara's production facilities can change the colour or add new details to a design and thus ensure that it will sell. All its stores are linked to the headquarters with a computerized communication system that allows personnel to share ideas and input customer feedback and reactions. This information is then shared with the headquarters, thereby allowing the adjustment of volume and style of orders to accommodate shifts in customer demand. Zara aims at keeping the company's image an up-to-date and fresh one through being close to the customers; this also limits the mistakes in the designs and, through having more than one delivery per month, the company quickly sees what is selling and can pull any designs that do not sell quickly enough. Zara minimizes inventory, and thus keeps operating costs down. The company integrates all stages of value creation in the design and processing of fabrics, manufacturing of garments, and the sale process itself. Approximately half the clothes are manufactured in plants owned by Inditex. Some 80 per cent of garments are manufactured in Europe – mainly in Spain and Portugal.

From the beginning, Zara has kept logistics as a core capability essential to being able to supply the merchandise at the right time. This is one of the reasons that Zara maintains its production centres mainly in Europe; this cuts the delivery time and cost to minimum, albeit possibly not allowing for the cheapest production of the merchandise. With logistics that deliver fast, the overall strategy of 'fashion now' is strengthened. Zara's main distribution centre is located in La Coruna in northwest Spain, from where new lines are shipped to all the stores several times a week. In Europe, fleets of trucks deliver the merchandise, covering a distance of more than seven million kilometres a year. Shipments to more distant stores are made by airfreight, thereby cutting the time between the placement of the order and the reception of the merchandise (Inditex Annual Report, 2000).

Zara provides fashion considerably quicker than any of its rivals, and this is what the company's success is based on. A sketch of a design can be in the stores as quickly as within a few weeks. Aiming to produce fashion designs that are regarded in the same manner as perishable items such as foodstuffs, Zara has succeeded in creating a company that exists to supply for the fashion conscious who may or may not use a design more than once. The company has managed to expand and gain market share in a highly competitive industry in uncertain times through disregarding traditional fashion logic. The company updates its designs at a continuous pace, rather than focusing on seasons as traditional fashion retailers have done. Zara is putting its customers at the centre of the design and production process through the computer network that connects all stores and by which customers' feedback and response to designs are fed to both the manufacturing and the business sides of Zara, allowing volumes and designs to be altered. The speed at which Zara brings designs to market – whether imitations of the catwalks or in-house creations inspired by current trends on the streets and clubs of Europe – is what at the moment allows Zara to expand at its ambitious space. And as Inditex's CEO José María Castellano highlights: 'This business is all about reducing response time' (CNET Investor, 2001).

4.5 Fuzzy gates

The introduction of stage-gated development processes benefited organizations' ability to manage innovation programmes through tracking progress and undertaking regular reviews, often linked to capital and resource commitment. However, for many firms, this was not the answer to all their needs.

Whilst enabling a higher degree of control and understanding of progression of a project through the process, such gates originally required tasks to be checked off against predetermined lists and thus often made the overall ideas-to-market process slow. With the introduction of improved versions of the approach to include cross-functional gates that were more holistic to capture the whole process, there was less rework, earlier detection of failure, better launch and shorter elapsed times (Devinney, 1995). However, projects were still forced to wait at each gate until all tasks were completed and, so as not to stray from a process through which all projects had to progress, any significant overlapping of activities was largely impossible.

As smoother progression through a development process became an increasingly common issue, several companies began to look across their innovation activities for opportunities for improvement. Areas examined included enhancing cross-functional interaction at the start of projects, particularly between the traditionally divergent disciplines of R&D and marketing, greater and earlier involvement of both suppliers and customers to ensure that new products and services were being configured in the most economical and desirable manner, and, throughout the process, means of focusing the organization on the right measures to drive the changes in behaviour that would deliver improved performance. One example of how an organization addressed this last issue is Hewlett-Packard, which, in 1987, introduced a 'return map' to focus the whole development organization on key metrics (Figure 4.1). Rather than measuring and hence motivating teams around the completion of individual phases within the development process or meeting the defined criteria associated with individual gates, the company went for more holistic higher-level measures that unified differing groups around common time and financial targets.

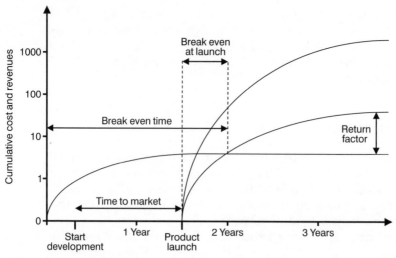

Figure 4.1 HP return map.

From a time perspective, a dual focus on both 'time to market' and 'break-even time' (or time to profit) had two benefits. Shifting individual aims towards a more collective 'ready for launch date', when all the varied elements required to deliver a new product or service into the desired markets were in place, was designed to help teams to work together so that the overall project succeeded rather than just the ingredient elements. Moreover, the focus on break-even time helped to balance any sense of unnecessary haste from rushing to meet an early launch date with the benefits to be gained from getting the product right. Since a quick market entry of a product that did not fully meet customer needs or compete successfully with rival offerings would result in a lengthy break-even time, considering the two metrics together helped teams to balance speed with both quality and value.

In parallel with these two time-based measures, financial targets of 'break even at launch' and 'return factor' helped to integrate the post-development, marketing, sales, distribution, and support activities into the overall picture. Break even at launch, although a time-based measure, was driven by product profitability and so encouraged the organization to maximize value through achieving the most appropriate combination of sales and margin required to cover the investment. Rushing to achieve high sales volumes to capture initial market share at the expense of profit due to heavy discounting, for example, was therefore implicitly discouraged. Similarly, measuring and rewarding all those involved on the basis of the return on investment (or return factor) achieved at a defined point in time after launch helped to ensure both that development costs were kept as low as possible and that profitability was maximized. Together these two implied a greater focus on efficiently creating and delivering competitive new products and services.

In terms of the core development process itself, such targets implied and demanded an evolutionary development over the existing stage-gate approach. Driven by the increasingly important need for speed, in order to overcome unnecessary delay and enable smoother progression, third-generation processes therefore sought to accommodate the need for certain tasks to overlap during a development programme (Cooper, 1994). Through modifying the individual gates to become more 'fuzzy' and allow 'conditional go' decisions, a degree of fluidity could be introduced into the process that allowed phases to overlap. This enabled some activities to continue apace even though some parallel elements may not yet have been fully completed. Requiring teams frequently to work with partial data, such advances required greater fluidity in overall programme management and a more holistic view of overall project progression. In addition, by being more outcome rather than task focused, these processes permitted organizations to build prioritization models and, through a shift in authority away from phase reviewers towards programme managers, enabled projects to move through the process with more flexibility than was possible using more rigid stage gates.

As innovation became generally viewed as a multifactor process that required a high degree of integration at both intra- and inter-firm levels, which was increasingly being facilitated by IT-based systems, as an evolving process itself it became more and more complex (Rothwell, 1992). However, despite this evolution and the introduction and modification of gated control mechanisms, it still followed the same basic framework that it had done from the start. Although many different models of the innovation process were developed, discussed, adopted and subsequently improved upon, and many used different metaphors or focused on different aspects of innovation activities, most organizations agreed that there was still a common sequence (Tidd *et al.*, 1997). Fuzzy gates changed the management but not the structure of the innovation process.

However, while many companies benefited from the identified advantages of fuzzy gates, others suffered from some of the limitations. These included the higher stress associated with pressurized teamwork, straining of resources due to complex and increased demands, mistakes being made due to steps being skipped, and other unexpected inefficiencies arising from some stages of the process being more open to time reduction than others (Crawford, 1992). Thus, when determining how to organize and run innovation programmes, all of these benefits and impacts had to be taken into consideration and a balanced value judgment made (Sasaki, 1991). Only by determining which techniques and practices were most appropriate to individual organizations' resources, capabilities and products could those that provide greatest benefit be implemented.

Amongst the many firms who embraced fuzzy-gate development processes as a key component to improving their ability to deliver timely innovation during the early 1990s was US-based photographic equipment manufacturer Polaroid.

Polaroid – instant cameras

While more recently suffering from its inability to compete successfully with long-term rivals Kodak and the more adept new kids on the block, Fujitsu, in the early 1990s Polaroid was a major player in the photographic equipment sector. Based in Boston, the company's main product lines were primarily film and instant cameras that, in 1992, were generating an annual turnover of over $2 billion. The existing range of cameras had been on the market for over ten years and, with an end to some initial patent protection on the horizon, Polaroid was anticipating rival products to appear, particularly from Fujitsu. The company was therefore keen to reinforce its position as market leader. As sales of existing products began to drop off at the beginning of 1993, it was clear to the firm that a new design had to be launched as quickly as possible in order to extend product profitability. Significantly the company chose not to develop this product in the USA but instead managed the project from the UK manufacturing facility in Scotland – the first time that a Polaroid product had been developed outside the USA.

Although using the same optics from existing designs and only upgrading a few elements of the electronics, as a key means of differentiating the new product from the 1980s range Polaroid wanted to significantly enhance the visual and ergonomic details of the camera. Using UK-based design consultants in conjunction with a selection of leading toolmakers and moulders, together with production expertise from within Polaroid, a team was put together in December 1993 and formal project kick off followed in January 1994. Under the overall control of a new product manager within Polaroid, the joint team was working to a tight schedule. Launch was scheduled for October, in time for the critically important Christmas market.

In order to minimize time to market, the team made extensive use of the latest CAD/CAM systems and solid modelling software to create three-dimensional representations of the product. These were based on the designers' concept drawings, and provided the key mechanism through which interaction across the team could take place. Although using a phased development programme, there was no time for anyone to hang around, so the reviews had to be fuzzy to accommodate the inevitable variability in progress in each area. Specifically, the interaction between the designers, production engineers and toolmakers for the creation of the moulds for the main product case structure was a key area requiring flexibility. Traditionally tool-making would commence only when a design had been finalized and, at that time, typically took up to six months to complete. This was the major bottleneck and so, in order to reduce its impact, initial tool making was actually initiated far earlier than normal, when the design was still being developed.

At the first review point at the end of February 1994, the conceptual design was finalized and initial vendors to provide key components had been identified. Toolmakers had been selected and briefed with data transfer mechanisms and file formats all agreed. In addition, detailed design of the overall body had been started, with initial CAD models being created to provide a common reference framework for all plastic moulding definition. In order to enable parallel development of as many aspects of the product as possible, key interface points between parts were agreed and their dimensions fixed. This gave every designer and engineer a number of common reference points that could not be changed.

Following acceptance of the concept by the full team, engineering layouts were prepared and initial three-dimensional computer models were released to the toolmakers, who were then able to start tool design and prepare the metal bolsters from which the final mouldings would be made. As complex surface models were subsequently created to assess form and ergonomics, block models were produced via CNC machines running directly from the designers' software. Using stereo-lithography technology, which had recently emerged as a key rapid prototyping tool, the first components were modelled, and by April the first fully working prototype had been produced. This was used to not only assess the visual and ergonomic features of the new camera but also to evaluate the full engineering design of every component and their respective fit to the key interface points agreed previously. Several prototypes were provided to Polaroid's marketing department for evaluation, and by the time of the design review in May, feedback had been duly received and a number of slight modifications already incorporated into the three-dimensional computer models. Tooling had by then progressed to a point where the toolmakers had created the majority of their patterns ready for final processing once the final design was fully approved. In addition, moulders had already been involved and were ready to create first samples as soon as the tools were complete.

Unlike traditional programmes, where the design review would initiate many of these activities, everything that could conceivably be done up front had been. Using partial data, but continually discussing what the final data would most likely be, the majority of the suppliers and subcontractors had already done over 50 per cent of the work that would have normally only just be being initiated at this stage. Consequently the design review itself was less of a 'yes/no' decision and more of a final check prior to a formal release of all the three-dimensional data to the toolmakers and vendors. This release occurred two weeks later after final completion and sign off of the full engineering and design definition.

As toolmakers finished their work, the designers produced twelve fully working prototypes using a combination of stereolithographic and vacuum casting techniques. These were sent out as advance products for dealer liaison and for internal briefings across Polaroid, as well as for use in advanced photo shoots that would enable the fast production of promotion and packaging material. During the last week in July, first production samples were received from the toolmakers to check consistency against original design intent and data. These were provided to the manufacturing facility where, together with additional samples from other vendors, they were then used as part of initial engineering pilot builds where complete cameras were first assembled on the production lines that had also been prepared in parallel over the preceding couple of months.

The final review in mid-September was where mass production would usually be approved. However, since production start up had already been initiated two weeks before and all packaging was now in stock, this formal review was again more of a final check to plan that inventory build-up to meet anticipated market demand could occur. Following the successful meeting of all key criteria, production was subsequently ramped up during the last two weeks of September, ready for worldwide launch in mid-October. Polaroid then went to market with a new product in the shortest time the company had ever achieved – six months from blank sheet of paper to fully working prototype, and nine months to full production. The Spectra model gave new lifeblood to the Polaroid range and lifted sales back up to 1992 levels for the next three years.

Epilogue

Although this product successfully maintained Polaroid's sales for a while, in the longer term the company was unable to sustain the competition from rivals' digital products. Whilst working on new technologies such as 'Opal' ink-jet photo-quality printing and the 'Onyx' digital printing from wireless devices process, and continuing to refine its ability to rapidly develop and launch new products, under new CEO Gary DiCamillo the firm focused more and more on short-term fashion-led innovation. As Polaroid first produced the Spice-cam and then the Barbie camera versions of its core product, and next introduced the temporarily successful low-priced i-Zone camera, the new core teenager market soon tired of the fad and moved on to Fuji, Kodak, Canon and Sony digital products. Running out of cash reserves for new products in October 2001, Polaroid filed for Chapter 11 bankruptcy protection.

4.6 Matrix organizations

As the cross-functional demands of innovation and product development grew in line with more complex products and markets, so the impact on the enabling organization also increased. Whereas the early 1980s had been characterized by the establishment of dedicated development resource and the emergence of the role of product champions within companies to drive project progression through the organization, the late 1980s and early 1990s were when truly multidisciplinary teams operating within matrix-based organizational structures finally came to the fore.

Innovation is, by consequence of its cross-functional nature, an activity dependent on collaboration. Whether inter-business or intra-company, this collaboration is what drives people to create, develop and exploit new ideas in the most effective manner. Consequently, issues such as information sharing, trust and understanding are all key drivers of collaborative success (Anderson and Nauras, 1991). From the inter-business perspective, where organizations seek to gain mutually from sharing costs, sharing risks, gaining market or technology knowledge, collaboration typically occurs through both application- and technology-based networks (Meyer, 1997). Key to this is the ability for companies to see collaboration as a route of success where contribution, trust and equal benefit are core. Similarly, within organizations these same issues drive effective intra-company collaboration. Whereas the alternative silo attitude restricts sharing of information, minimizes knowledge transfer and increases development risk, collaboration between some, or all, of the key functional disciplines involved in innovation could significantly improve project success:

- Through encouraging collaboration between R&D and marketing, projects could typically be better focused, more achievable goals could be agreed, there would be less misinterpretation of group perceptions, and new products and services could be planned that have greater synergy with both the organization's technological capabilities and the needs of its core markets (Griffin and Hauser, 1996).
- By integrating design and manufacturing through such initiatives as design for manufacture and assembly, better products could be launched earlier, the number of components could be optimized, assembly time could be minimized, and overall development times could be reduced (Pugh, 1991).

Intra-company collaboration was thus seen to have a clear and measurable impact, not just on the development process, but also on the products themselves and how well they function, look, feel and ultimately perform in the marketplace. Within the organization the most appropriate mechanism for achieving this level of collaboration was seen to be through the use of teams. By establishing an environment where the key development functions could work together throughout the process, progression of a project through that process was made smoother (Ulrich and Eppinger, 1995). Multifunctional teams were seen as the ideal *modus operandi* for development activities, and became commonplace in the majority of successful manufacturing companies and service provision firms alike (Arthur D Little, 1991). As they used teams as a core means of improving interdepartmental integration, firms realized benefits from the hierarchical structures being overcome by the team's ability to cut across traditional vertical lines of authority and decision-making (Larson and Gobeli, 1988).

However, key to such team-based intra-company collaboration was an appropriate task-based culture and enabling organizational structure. Whereas traditional role-based cultures common in government, banking and other bureaucratic, hierarchical organizations place most importance on activity segregation, with the role taking precedent over the individual, task-based cultures are more project orientated. Whilst functionally aligned organizations provide a significant barrier to the establishment of successful teams, as the predetermination of individual roles fights against the adaptability required to achieve shared goals, task cultures place the emphasis on getting the job done. The structure most commonly adopted in such cultures has been a net, or matrix, where power and influence resides at the interstices of the net (Mintzberg, 1988). Such structures attempted to make the best use of an organization's resources and to preserve a balance between workflow requirements and functional management. Although belonging to 'vertical' parent functional, geographic or even business unit groupings from a resource ownership perspective, matrix organizations enabled individuals to be simultaneously focused on developing and launching new products and services as part of 'horizontal' cross-functional or cross-business project teams. The associated culture was one where individuals balance their own roles both as part of a project team and home discipline. With decision-making residing primarily with the team, it provided organizations with a highly flexible approach, as project teams could be formed, abandoned and reformed quickly, enabling the company to react quickly – a key attribute when needing to accommodate high levels of market sensitivity.

That said, matrix organizations were later found not to be the global panacea that were initially considered. Control is still largely retained by top management through allocation of projects, people and resources, but little day-to-day control can be exerted over working methods or procedures. The associated culture requires a favourable climate where the product is always the centre of attention. Moreover, because of the opportunity for confusion from working for two masters, companies often had to bias the matrix to provide priority, either by splitting long-term and short-term objectives for the individual between the functional and project managers, or by introducing independent resource coordination. Although opening up communication, conflicts do occur within matrix organizations typified by reduced functional manager control, poor resource allocation and diminished individual identity. In particular, matrix organizations perform best when the company is experiencing growth. When resources become scarce, the associated competition that develops between groups frequently necessitates rules and procedures that can be counter-cultural. In times of hardship, task-based matrix organizations are consequently often forced to change to role-based or even centralized power cultures to provide control and direction.

However, throughout the late 1980s and early 1990s many firms did adopt a matrix structure as the key organizational shift to drive improved innovation and project performance. Companies as diverse as BP, HP and Procter & Gamble adopted matrix organizations to enable improved cross-functional interaction on projects. However, in terms of direct impact on performance, by far the most effective cross-business adoption and subsequent adaptation of this approach was achieved by the Swedish/Swiss engineering conglomerate ABB.

Asea Brown Boveri (ABB) – global matrix management

When Percy Barnevik became CEO of ABB in 1983, he inherited a major challenge. The Swedish/Swiss engineering company had an export-orientated, technocratic culture that many regarded as over-centralized and bureaucratic. The company's 1300 business units operated as national fiefdoms with high local autonomy but little global coordination. The company faced excess capacity, weakened demand, and increased competition from global competitors.

To combat these threats, Barnevik introduced a two-stage strategy focused on first restructuring and then global growth. Restructuring was initially drastic. Barnevik retained only 10 per cent of corporate HQ staff; the remainder went to operating companies, projects or redundancy. In addition, a new global matrix structure was introduced to give managers responsibility for both local markets and global products. The decentralized business unit structure demanded strong horizontal integration processes to ensure that the entire organization leveraged and benefited from the specialized expertise and knowledge in its units. The role of country managers was to articulate customer-focused, local market strategies, whilst the global product managers' tasks were to develop and champion worldwide strategies to capitalize on economies of scale and coordinate and approve R&D and product development around the world.

Part of the glue that held this matrix together was ABACUS; ABB's sophisticated and fully-automated management information system. This tracked thirty-two performance measures across 5000 profit centres, and compared the variance between budget forecasts and actuals. Most importantly, it allowed data to be broken down both by global product line or business segment, and by country or company. It provided accurate and timely information to the filed operations and ensured that managers around the company received the same information at the same time, regardless of their hierarchical level. For the first time this allowed the company to coordinate and control operations and projects, keeping all managers equally well informed.

Barnevik's personal schedule was gruelling as he travelled the world to communicate the changes – he estimates that he spent 80 per cent of his time travelling and presented 5000 PowerPoint slides during a single year. This was also accompanied by a new corporate identity and a policy that made English the official corporate language. As a result of all the changes implemented, between 1988 and 1992 revenues grew from $17 billion to $30 billion, with return on assets simultaneously improving from less than 10 per cent to almost 19 per cent. ABB was voted 'Europe's most respected company', and was described as the 'post-multinational company of the future'.

During the mid-1990s, ABB moved its matrix towards a regional focus on three trading blocks – Europe, the Americas and Asia. In part this was a response to the growing importance of large projects within ABB that were neither country- nor product-specific. Nonetheless, by the late 1990s further issues became apparent. ABB's customers were predominantly global corporations, and so regional boundaries were diluting. The industry as a whole continued to be highly competitive, and the 'multi-domestic' focus made it more difficult for ABB to capture scale economies than it was for competitors with focused product development and manufacture in single locations. The matrix structure also led to exhaustion and conflict between staff. ABB responded by splitting itself into smaller segments and abandoning its regional structures (Barlett and Ghoshal, 1993). Segments and business areas now took global responsibility with country managers reporting directly into the group. Additionally, ABB was moving away from its engineering heritage towards a more knowledge- and service-orientated culture. This, in turn, placed a much greater emphasis on developing technology and managing global leadership, challenges that later proved significant.

4.7 Supplier partnerships

Whilst technology transfer alliances enabled organizations to source, acquire and integrate new enabling technologies to allow new product platforms to be developed, other external relationship developments within the innovation community have focused on improving alliances with vendors and customers. Through encouraging the integration of suppliers within the development process, primarily by establishing appropriate partnerships, a wide range of benefits have been achieved to both the process and the developed products. Although supply chain management is a universal business practice, comparatively few organizations have achieved effective supplier involvement in product development. Companies that excel in this area have entered into partnerships with their suppliers and worked together to realize mutual gains and achieve strategic goals. GlaxoWellcome's Zebulon development team shared strategic goals, including improving customer responsiveness, in an era of rapidly increasing complexity to help meet demands of reduced costs, increased flexibility, and ever-faster speed to market. Such alliances occurred between suppliers and customers throughout the innovation process, in the early concept development and product planning stages, the core detail design and prototyping activities, and right through to product launch (Magrath and Hardy, 1994).

Pioneered initially by some of the Japanese car manufacturers, such as Toyota, both at home and subsequently abroad in their transplant facilities, supplier partnerships have now become commonplace across industries (Cusumano and Takeishi, 1992). Today they exist not just throughout their parent automotive sector, but also occur widely in the electronics, IT, consumer and pharmaceuticals fields. In addition, the principles of partnerships have more recently migrated into such varied areas of application as the healthcare, aerospace and construction industries, where non-adversarial relationships have gained ground as standard practice on large-scale projects. During the early 1990s, world-class organizations first selected suppliers according to various criteria that went beyond traditional cost-per-unit considerations. Companies that worked in close partnership with a few select key vendors were able to take advantage of their suppliers' special competencies, leveraging them to achieve both significant operational, economic and productivity benefits and also increased input to new product development activities. The increased intimacy achieved through partnerships allowed some firms significantly to reduce their supplier base, often by over 90 per cent, enabling companies to forge closer relationships with their remaining suppliers and leading to lower total costs, lower inventories, improved working capital and better products. Narrowing the supplier base also benefited the remaining vendors, who usually increased business volumes in exchange for lower unit pricing. By working together, companies were thus able to pool talents and resources, yielding substantial gains in product cost, quality, flexibility, system responsiveness and overall performance:

- Motorola used pareto analyses to focus its attention on the top 3 per cent of its thousands of suppliers. Since supplies typically make up 60–80 per cent of a product's costs, this allowed the company to achieve the most of its cost-cutting efforts.
- Exxon worked to reduce its supplier base by 25 per cent each year. One plant had two suppliers generating over 80 per cent of purchase volume.
- AT&T used quality initiatives in its relations with supplier partners, helping it to improve the quality of its integrated circuits twenty-fold.

From a product and service perspective, the associated direct benefits from these partnerships included less product variation and lower costs through standardization of components. In addition, target price agreements derived from the advanced negotiation of agreed profit margins were also established (Anderson and Nauras, 1991). In particular, partners were able to identify which organization in the supply chain could perform a specific task at the highest quality and lowest cost. The pharmaceutical company Novartis worked closely with suppliers to provide an expanding array of packaging designs and materials in the consumer market. Partners assisted them in balancing the needs of shelf life, manufacturing, distribution, marketing and profitability.

In terms of the innovation process, core advantages occurred mainly through the reduction of development costs and faster time to market. By involving suppliers such as component manufacturers, IT vendors, toolmakers and moulders throughout the process – but particularly early on – and also by forming long-term contractual relationships with them, organizations were able to achieve high levels of consistency between design and supplier processes. To encourage a continual flow of ideas and improvements, some companies began to reward and recognize partners with additional benefits, such as preferential bidding for new work, cash back for achieving performance-based objectives, and sharing of savings identified in cost-reduction efforts.

Technology also greatly enhanced cooperative development. Communication tools such as extranets, electronic data interchange, common CAD/CAM platforms and management software gave partners instantaneous access to shared information. In some cases the partners' operations became integrated as one through technology. Sportswear manufacturer Reebok was able to reduce its new product lead times with distributors from six weeks to 24 hours via electronic linkage. Through increased availability of and associated common access to detailed and, most significantly, shared process data, the overall process was thus accelerated, often providing benefits such as early availability of prototypes.

In addition, rather than choosing one or two ways of working with their vendors, several companies employed a plethora of communication tools. Organizations were increasingly using cross-functional, cross-corporate teams to promote the exchange of objectives and ideas and encouraged interaction with key suppliers at all levels of the organization, particularly upper management. While telephone and video conferencing were most common forms of interaction, more effective communication of ideas often hinged on personal interaction. Consequently, advisory councils, conferences, and problem-solving teams with suppliers were frequently put in place to support ongoing communication. Furthermore, top companies co-located personnel, rotating employees at partner sites for months at a time. Chrysler had 400 partner engineers co-located at its facilities, enabling constant sharing of ideas and a greater mutual understanding of strategies, goals and capabilities, saving over $1.2 billion – a benefit that was shared with the suppliers.

Moreover, by having repeated close working relationships, particularly through partnerships during the core design stages of the development process, problems that arose were identified earlier and, as a consequence, fewer changes necessitated (Bonaccorci and Lippami, 1994). Purchasers, designers, engineers and managers all gained a deepened appreciation of the capabilities, needs and objectives of their partners, and took this knowledge back to enhance further the process improvement efforts of each organization. Dell worked with its suppliers to reduce the number of human interactions in its supply chain, helping them decrease the reject rate of new products by 40 per cent while decreasing the overall failure rate by 20 per cent.

As a core means of improving existing structures, leveraging supplier partnerships has now become a major issue in innovation and new product development across all industries. Although suffering a downfall in sales in the first couple of years of the twenty-first century, one organization that refined its approach for supplier integration to a leading position throughout much of the twentieth century was UK-based retailer Marks & Spencer.

Marks & Spencer – long-term partnership

Marks & Spencer is one of the UK's leading retailers. Serving 10 million customers a week in over 300 UK stores, by 1997 the company also traded in thirty-eight countries worldwide – including the USA, where it owned Brookes Brothers. Approximately half the group's overseas stores are franchised to local partners. The group sells clothing, footwear, gifts, home furnishings and foods under the St Michael trademark, whilst the smaller financial services group comprises operations of the group's companies providing account cards, personal loans, unit trust management, life assurance and pensions, and accounts for 4 per cent of revenues. Marks & Spencer uses agreements instead of contracts with suppliers, solidifying relationships that remain strong for years. Some of its suppliers have provided goods and services for over 100 years. While many other UK high-street retailers gradually shifted to source the majority of their clothes from overseas throughout the 1980s and 1990s, up until 2000 Marks & Spencer still bought the majority of its products from British-based suppliers. The company is often credited with single-handedly ensuring the survival of at least part of the British clothing industry.

Founded in Leeds, England, in 1893 by Michael Marks, a Russian-born Polish refugee, and developing into a partnership the following year with Tom Spencer, a former cashier from a wholesale company, Marks & Spencer evolved from a single market stall to having shops in every British high street. Growing steadily, during the 1920s, Marks & Spencer broke with British retailing tradition by eliminating wholesalers and buying clothes direct from manufacturers. Marks & Spencer became a byword for reliability and high quality, giving the firm a unique reputation within the UK marketplace.

Key to this had been a combination of ensuring high standards throughout its production and new product development activities together with an increasingly close relationship with a few select suppliers, some of which, such as Coats Viyella, Courtaulds, William Baird and Dewhirst, had been with the company virtually from the start. By the late 1980s Marks & Spencer had brought into place its Global Sourcing Principles, which established a minimum acceptable entry standard for each supplier and an expectation that each supplier would steadily raise its standards. Essentially, suppliers competed for the lucrative contracts based on a combination of quality, value and innovation. As explained by a director of the company:

A key factor in business success is forming strategic partnerships. Marks & Spencer have established strategic relationships with a select number of suppliers. The value in these relationships is that we work closely together, more than you would expect to see with any other commercial arrangement. For example, we are prepared to share with those partners our strategic company plans and they reciprocate by sharing their development programmes with us. A strategic business partnership is about sharing a vision of the future. It's about understanding how we can combine our products and services to add value to the business operation and ultimately to bring the benefits created by that added value to the customer.

Dewhirst was, and still is, a typical supplier to Marks & Spencer. As a long-term partner, the company was fully integrated with both production and development activities, working together to develop new product lines. By the early 1990s, Dewhirst was selling 88 per cent of its goods to Marks & Spencer. Although, like its competitors, it was expanding operations outside the UK to include Malaysia, Morocco and Indonesia, and aiming to increase offshore production to 70 per cent by 2002, both companies continued to share ideas and explore new fabrics, new processes and new styles. Again as explained by M&S executives:

> *Quality suppliers who embrace partnering benefit from these reduction efforts as well, obtaining increased volume that easily compensates for any reduction in unit pricing. Likewise, process and product enhancements that increase a company's market share also increase the volume for the company's suppliers.*

Developing long-term general agreements with key suppliers is seen by the company to strengthen these relationships. Such agreements exhibit a high level of trust and interdependency, avoiding the adversarial roles typically assumed in contract negotiation and execution. Whereas world-class supplier agreements are seen to often last the life of a product, or for at least five years, for Marks & Spencer exclusive supplier relationships such as the one with Dewhirst can be considered to have lasted over 100 years.

By the mid 1990s, Marks & Spencer dominated clothes retailing in Britain (Table 4.3). In 1997 it sold £4.3 billion of clothing, footwear and gifts, giving it a 15 per cent share of the UK market and about 35 per cent of the UK underwear market. Having also built a reputation for high quality food as well as providing its own branded range of financial services, the company overall had a turnover of £8.2 billion, profits of over £1 billion, and a market capitalization of nearly £17 billion.

Table 4.3 United Kingdom clothing retailers market share 1997 (source: Competitive Intelligence/Company Reports)

Position	Retailer	% share of UK market (1997)	Annual turnover £m (1997)
1	Marks and Spencer	15.0	8243
2	Arcadia Group	7.2	1399
3	Storehouse	6.5	1250
4	C&A	4.7	844
5	Next	3.5	639
6	Sears	2.9	524
7	River Island	1.6	285

Since then, although Marks & Spencer has continued to leverage its supplier relationship across its businesses, things have unfortunately not gone so well. Competitors such as Next, Gap and new arrival Zara have innovated better and more quickly, providing more attractive products offering greater value for money; public and institutional confidence have both declined; stores in Europe have been closed; and by 2001, with revenue stagnated at £8 billion, profits had tumbled by over 80 per cent to £146 million and market capitalization had been more than halved to £7.6 billion. In a bid to regain its mantle in its core UK marketplace, during 2001–2002 Marks & Spencer introduced new designer lines of products as well as, for the first time, a separate brand – 'Per Una' – created by George Davies, founder of long-term rival Next. Together with the use of celebrity advertising and revitalized food products and continued innovation in its use of supplier partnerships, performance has since showed signs of recovery. However, it remains to be seen whether Marks & Spencer will prosper for another 100 years.

References

Anderson, J. C. and Nauras, J. A. (1991). Partnering as focused market strategy. *Calif. Management Rev.*, **Spring,** 95–112.

Arthur D Little (1991). *The Arthur D Little Survey on the Product Innovation Process.* Arthur D Little.

Baker, H., Jones, W. and Nicholas, M. (1994). Using core competencies to develop new business. *Long Range Planning*, **Dec,** 13–27.

Barlett, C. and Ghoshal, S. (1993). Beyond the M-form: toward a managerial theory of the firm. *Strategic Management J.*, **Winter,** 23–46.

Bonaccorci, A. and Lipparni, A. (1994), Strategic partnerships in NPD: an Italian case study. *J. Product Innov. Management*, **11,** 134–45

Bussey, J. and Seaese, D. R. (1988). Speeding up. *Wall Street Journal*, February 23.

Caulkin, S. (1997). The knowledge within. *Management Today*, **Aug,** 33–7.

Clark, K. B. and Fujimoto, T. (1990). The power of product integrity. *Harvard Bus. Rev.*, **Nov–Dec,** 107–18.

Clark, K. B. and Fujimoto, T. (1992). *Product Development Performance: Strategy, Organization and Management in the World Auto Industry.* Harvard Business School Press.

CNET Investor, May 23, 2001.

Cooper, R. G. (1994). Third generation new product processes. *J. Product Innov. Management*, **11**, 3–14.

Crawford, C. M. (1992). The hidden costs of accelerated product development. *J. Product Innov. Management*, **9**, 188–99.

Cusumano, M. A. and Takeishi, A. (1992). Supplier relationships and management: a survey of Japanese, Japanese transplant and US autoplants. *Strategic Management J.*, **12(8)**, 563–87.

Devinney, T. M. (1995). Significant issues for the future of product innovation. *J. Product Innov. Management*, **12**, 70–75.

Dumaine, B. (1989). How managers can succeed through speed. *Fortune*, February 13, 53–9.

Gallon, M. R., Stillman, H. M. and Coates, D. (1995). Putting core competency thinking into practice. *Res. Technol. Management*, **38(3)**, 20–28.

Gold, B. (1987). Approaches to accelerating product and process development. *J. Product Innov. Management*, **4**, 81.

Griffin, A. and Hauser, J. R. (1996). Integrating R&D and marketing: a review and analysis of the literature. *J. Product Innov. Management*, **13**, 191–215.

Hamel, G. and Prahalad, C. K. (1994). *Competing for the Future*. Harvard Business School Press.

Inditex Annual Report 2000.

Interbrand (2001). www.interbrand.com

Irwin, R. A. and Michaels, E. G. (1989). Core skills: doing the right things right. *McKinsey Q.*, **Summer,** 4–19.

Kapferer, J. N. (1992). *Strategic Brand Management: New Approaches to Creating and Evaluating Brand Equity*. Kogan-Page.

Kiley, D. (1989). Can VW survive? *Marketing Week*, **May,** 18–22.

King, S. (1991). Brand building in the 1990s. *J. Consumer Marketing*, **Fall,** 43–52.

Larson, E. W. and Gobeli, D. H. (1988) Organizing for product development projects. *J. Product Innov. Management*, **5**, 180–90.

Lorenz, A. (1994). Brands fight back. *Sunday Times*, April 3.

Magrath, J. and Hardy, K. G. (1994). Building customer partnerships. *Business Horizons*, **Jan–Feb,** 24–8.

Meyer, M. H. (1997). Revitalise your product lines through continuous platform renewal. *Res. Technol. Management*, **32(3), May–Jun,** 9–11.

Milson, M. R., Raj, S. P. and Wilemon, D. (1992). A survey of major approaches to accelerating product development. *J. Product Innov. Management*, **9**, 53–69.

Mintzberg, H. (1988). *Mintzberg on Management*. The Free Press.

Prahalad, C. K. and Hamel, G. (1990). The core competence of the corporation. *Harvard Bus. Rev.*, **68(3)**, 79–91.

Pugh, S. (1991). *Total Design: Integrated Methods for Successful Product Engineering.* Addison-Wesley.

Quelch, J. A. and Kenny, D. (1994). Extend profits, not product lines. *Harvard Bus. Rev.,* **Sep–Oct,** 153–60.

Reiner, G. (1988). Cutting your competitor to the quick. *Wall Street Journal,* November 21.

Reinertsen, D. G. and Smith, P. G. (1991). The strategist's role in shortening product development. *IEEE Trans. Eng. Management,* **Jul/Aug,** 18–22.

Rothwell, R. (1992). Successful industrial innovation: critical success factors for the 1990s. R&*D Management,* **22(3),** 221–39.

Sasaki, T. (1991). How the Japanese accelerated new car development. *Long Range Planning,* **Jan,** 15–25.

Sharp, B. M. (1993). Managing brand extension. *J. Consumer Marketing,* **27(3),** 11–17.

The Forum Corporation (2001). *Experiencing the Brand – Branding the Experience.* www.forum.com

Tidd, J., Bessant, J. and Pavitt, K. (1997). *Managing Innovation: Integrating Technological, Market and Organizational Change.* John Wiley & Sons.

Towner, S. J. (1994). Four ways to accelerate new product development. *Long Range Planning,* **Apr,** 57–65.

Ulrich, K. T. and Eppinger, S. D. (1995). *Product Design and Development.* McGraw-Hill.

Further reading

Barham, K. and Heimer, C. (1999). *ABB: The Dancing Giant: Creating the Globally Connected Corporation.* Pitman Publishing.

Bevan, J. (2001). *The Rise and Fall of Marks & Spencer.* Profile Books.

Handy, C. (1993). *Understanding Organizations,* 4th edn. Penguin.

Jones, T. (1997). *New Product Development: An Introduction to a Multifunctional Process.* Butterworth-Heinemann.

Reinertsen, D. G. and Smith, P. G. (1991). *Developing Products in Half the Time.* Van Nostrand Reinhold.

Womack, J. P., Jones, D. T. and Roos, D. (1990). *The Machine that Changed the World.* HarperCollins.

Website

www.intel.com

5

Phase 3: Focus and integration

The third major phase in the evolution of organizations' capability to deliver competitive, value adding and sustainable new ideas came into place in the final few years of the twentieth century. As the ability to use flexible supply chains, global branding and cross-cultural teams became the norm for many organizations, the two key differentiators that came into play in this were focus and integration – focus in terms of the customer and how to deliver an idea; integration, in terms of sharing information, skills, technologies and effort.

Differentiation for the end user became a key issue because global products and services were now commonplace: BodyShop, Gap and H&M were on every major high street and in every mall; Hyatts and Sheratons provided the same menu to identical rooms worldwide, all with the same soaps and bed linen; and MTV, CNN, Discovery channel and HBO were available from every cable operator. Ensuring that customers perceive a tailored service or individualized product has driven the concept of mass customization of niche products using common platforms and modular components across sectors, from Dell to Mercedes to Amanpuri resorts and Banyan Tree boutique hotels. The economies of scale are still there, but to consumers there is an impression of individuality and focus on satisfying their specific requirements.

Launch management as a discrete activity emerged in both the pharmaceutical and consumer products sectors at around the same time. For reasons of both complexity and speed, companies in both sectors first saw the opportunities and realized the benefits to be gained for coherent multi-country launches on schedule and into the right market sectors. Enabling such new products and services to be delivered on a global scale and still produce profit had demanded a previously unimaginable level of cooperation and integration between organizations. Not only did companies now start choosing to work more closely with all stakeholders, from suppliers, distributors and retailers to customers, investors and analysts, but they also began working in partnership with their competitors. Companies recognized that, in many areas, only by working together to establish new global standards could they individually create the environment in which their new ideas could be successful. As a consequence, there has been increased integration of R&D activities internally, and more firms became part of cross-industry networks.

Supporting all these advances was an increasingly major role for the management of knowledge across innovation programmes. From conception to delivery, the need to deal with more complex products and services being developed by a range of different stakeholders implied the necessity for improved information flow both within organizations and across partner groups. This, the most recently completed phase of innovation capability evolution, thus became the stage where the last full wave of improved approaches to innovation were proven and subsequently moved across sectors into the mainstream operations of an increasing number of adopting organizations.

Integrated R&D

As organizations refined their product strategies and focused on their identified core competencies in order to manage their access to new enabling technologies, they also established, developed and enhanced supporting technology strategies (Ford, 1988). These were often targeted on supporting innovation in one or two key areas with any individual business unit. During the mid- to late 1990s, many organizations began to face the major challenge of successfully integrating the associated R&D strategies within their overall business strategy. Whilst new technologies had enabled companies to develop innovative, high quality products within discrete markets, how these activities and the overall approach to their management better fitted with the everyday cross-business operations of production, distribution and sales was being increasingly recognized as an issue (Kodama, 1992). This had an impact on three levels:

1 How the R&D activities within an individual business unit could be better integrated with other activities within that business unit

2 How R&D activities within one business unit could be better shared across the technology development areas in other business units

3 How new product and service applications across a firm's customer base and product portfolio could be better supported and exploited with existing technologies.

This integration started to happen at all stages within the innovation process. From the establishment of interdisciplinary business and R&D groups to manage and review new programmes, to the utilization of different skills within projects themselves, the overall level of cross-functional cooperation began to increase significantly. For instance, during concept stages technical and market assessments were more commonly being carried out together, whilst during development R&D personnel are increasingly becoming involved in the planning of marketing activities and remaining part of the team right through to launch (Anderson and Tushman, 1991). By 1998, researchers at IBM typically spent 25 per cent of their time with customers, focused on creating new products and services for them. This compared to less than 5 per cent in the early 1990s. People involved in undertaking and managing research activities had to become more flexible, more adaptable and more willing to change (*New York Times*, 1998).

Ensuring that all elements of the organization, and particularly traditional centres of innovation such as R&D, became closer to the market was viewed as an imperative for improved customer understanding and more effective leverage of new technologies. Sometimes through partnering with lead customers but mostly by improving cross-business unit interaction, creating new linkages became seen as core mechanisms for driving fuller exploitation of technological capabilities. From the increasing understanding of customer needs and core business activities gained by R&D personnel, and the greater awareness of R&D programmes from people across the business, particularly when there was a high level of innovation present, individual R&D and business strategies gradually became more aligned, interdependent and hence mutually supportive.

However, in encouraging this integration firms found that it could be over-managed, as some of the most effective interactions still occurred on an informal basis. As many companies, such as Mazda, Lucent and Unilever, all sought to achieve globalization of R&D and establish strategically located facilities across the world, the greatest difficulties were largely organizational as firms tried to balance decentralization and serving local markets with centralization and the economies of scale thereby achieved. The key to achieving truly effective global product development and marketing activities was seen to be access to information, and it was the sharing of communal and frequently technical data that enabled efficient innovation programmes to function (Devinney, 1995).

Creating and maintaining accessible data warehouses became a major challenge for many. As companies first implemented web-based interfaces to improve access to information, so the need to ensure that common standards were adopted across business units and partners subsequently grew. These required greater visibility and awareness of insights without compromising speed and relevance.

Across all levels of innovation operations, facilitating success-ful integration between R&D and other business activities demanded more frequent and open communication where all available information was shared across the scope of projects' operations (Kodoma, 1992).

Lastly, companies such as GE and DuPont also began to pay attention to some of the 'softer' people issues. In order to encourage researchers to become more versatile, to look proac-tively for new opportunities for their technologies and to be more open to external interaction, rewards and incentives were duly modified. Aligning core motivational drivers such as peer group recognition, time and, occasionally, monetary awards to corporate ambitions for greater sharing of technology and information was a major first step (Miller, 1997). In addition, providing R&D leaders with a better grounding in business management, improving team-building skills and encouraging them to take greater respon-sibility for cross-business unit technology strategies was also new. In effect the role of R&D leaders evolved into one of integrating technology across the enterprise (Larson, 1998). Together these changes brought about what has come to be seen as a revolution in the role and positioning of R&D within the organization.

One organization that placed particular emphasis on integration of R&D activities to drive improved cross-business exploitation of technologies during this time was US-based multinational 3M.

3M: innovation exploitation

3M's distinguishing strength is its entrepreneurial drive to transform three dozen technology platforms into a constant and consistent new product flow, providing new solutions for new customers in new markets.

3M's growth has come through a desire to participate in many markets where the company can make a significant contribution from core technologies, rather than be dominant in just a few markets.

(3M Annual Report, 2000)

The US-based multinational 3M has for the past 100 years been seen as a leading organization that is consistently creating new ideas. As it has invented and reinvented numerous ideas, focused on its core capabilities and expanded across multiple sectors and created new technology platforms, and developed innovative products for both new and existing markets, 3M has gained a reputation as a global leader in taking new technology innovations to market. There have been some bad patches, just like with any organization, but by and large the reputation that has been built and promoted around 3M is well deserved. Through the various different approaches adopted, the organization has developed an environment that encourages innovation and the mechanisms to exploit it. As it has evolved, it has taken a lead in providing the necessary support culture, processes and opportunities to drive innovation and the creation of new ideas into the heart of the company. Recently the company has had to improve the cross-business exploitation of its technologies as a key enabler for higher innovation performance.

3M: a brief history

The Minnesota Mining and Manufacturing Company, 3M,was founded in 1902 in Two Harbors, Minnesota, on the shore of Lake Superior, when five businessmen agreed to mine a mineral deposit for grinding-wheel abrasives. However, the deposits proved to be of little value, and the company quickly moved to nearby Duluth to focus on sandpaper products. Although there were several years of struggle, when the company gradually mastered quality production and built up a supporting supply chain, new investors were attracted to 3M, and early technical and marketing innovations began to produce successes. The world's first waterproof sandpaper, designed to ease the health problem of sanding dust, was developed in the early 1920s, and a major milestone occurred in 1925 with the invention of masking tape – an innovative step toward diversification, and the first of many Scotch-brand pressure-sensitive tapes.

In the next decade, technical progress resulted in Scotch Cellophane Tape for box sealing, for which customers began to find many additional uses, including multiple consumer applications. Drawing on expertise in bonding mineral grit to sandpaper, 3M also brought out new adhesives to replace tacks in bonding upholstery, and sound-deadening materials for the auto industry's new metal-framed cars.

A roofing granule business was also developed in response to the need to make asphalt shingles last longer. In the early 1940s 3M was diverted into defence materials for the Second World War, and this was followed by new ventures such as Scotchlite Reflective Sheeting for highway markings, magnetic sound recording tape, filament adhesive tape, and the start of 3M's involvement in the graphic arts with offset printing plates.

In the 1950s, 3M introduced the Thermo-Fax copying process, Scotchgard Fabric Protector, videotape, Scotch-Brite Cleaning Pads and several new electromechanical products. In the 1960s, dry-silver microfilm was introduced alongside photographic products, carbonless papers, overhead projection systems and a rapidly growing healthcare business of medical and dental products. Markets further expanded in the 1970s and 1980s into pharmaceuticals, radiology, energy control and the office market, and globally to almost every country in the world. During the 1990s the company set new sales records of over $15 billion annually.

In 2000, 3M achieved record sales of $16.7 billion and experienced one of the highest levels of innovation in its history, generating $5.6 billion – nearly 35 per cent of sales – from products introduced in the previous four years, with over $1.5 billion of sales coming from products introduced in 2000 alone. To continue to drive this further, in the same year 500 patents covering new innovations that will form the basis of future products for the company were filed by 3M in the USA alone.

Context: building a tradition of innovation

Creating an organization where such levels of innovation performance have become both expected and achieved has required clear focus on facilitating effective and continuous idea creation. Key to this has been the building of a supportive and motivating environment, something that 3M sees as its 'tradition of innovation' (Coyne, 1996). The six core elements of 3M's corporate culture that have been seen to contribute to this tradition of innovation are:

1 Vision
2 Foresight
3 Stretch goals
4 Empowerment
5 Communication
6 Recognition.

Since the early days of the company these six elements have been the drivers of continuous innovation and growth for the organization, and today, as 3M seeks to push itself to even higher levels of performance for its second century, they are still the fundamental backbone to the way in which the company has defined and evolved the corporate culture to support successful innovation.

Vision

The first element in creating the 3M tradition of innovation is to declare the importance of innovation and make it part of the company's self-image – hence the 3M vision to be 'the world's most innovative enterprise and preferred supplier'. Employees across the company are continuously reminded of this, and that their focus should be on achieving it. In addition, to consistently check that what the organization thinks it is doing is aligned to this vision, its customers are regularly consulted on their opinions about 3M and whether its claim to be the world's most innovative enterprise is true.

Foresight

Understanding customer needs, the trends in their industries and the changes that are heading their way, is also seen as core in 3M. However, this is far from easy, for reliably getting customers to indicate what their needs are, what problems they encounter and what solutions they might be looking for can be very difficult. The issue is that there are two levels of needs; the articulated kind, where a customer recognizes it and can voice it openly, and the unarticulated kind – problems that people do not know that they have. This second type is clearly far more difficult to find, and, for 3M, this requires far greater insight into the customer's environment. However, although this is often much more difficult to capture, the rewards that stand to be gained from finding the unarticulated need and then addressing it can be very substantial.

Stretch goals

The third element in the building of 3M's innovation culture has been the adoption of a number of stretch goals designed continuously to push the organization further. There are two key goals that have been in place in the company for years, one focused on the medium term and the other more immediate:

1 The company had the aim of deriving 30 per cent of all sales from products introduced in the previous four years in place throughout the second half of the twentieth century. This set the medium-term focus for the organization as it sought to achieve this target, and when in the late 1990s meeting it

became a regular occurrence, it was changed to an increased stretch goal of 35 per cent – a target that a performance in 2000 of 33.5 per cent came very near to achieving.

2 To help achieve the improvement in this medium-term goal, there is also a more immediate target designed to create a sense of urgency across the company. For many years this was to have 10 per cent of sales from products introduced in only the last year, and again, as performance increased, so this goal was increased in the late 1990s to 15 per cent – a target which, by comparison, the 2000 performance of 8.9 per cent is someway off meeting. This goal is designed to ensure that the organization is more selective about what new ideas it pursues as it seeks to focus its resources on those that will provide the greatest return.

Empowerment

A fundamental component of the 3M philosophy has always been to give people responsibility and trust. William McKnight, who joined 3M in 1907, became president in 1929 and then chairman of the board in 1949, and is credited with first creating an environment within which innovation could occur, laid out two basic principles for empowerment of employees way back in 1948:

> *As our business grows, it becomes increasingly necessary to delegate responsibility and to encourage men and women to exercise their initiative. This requires considerable tolerance. Those men and women to whom we delegate authority and responsibility, if they are good people, are going to want to do their jobs in their own way.*

As a guideline for this, all technical staff in 3M have, for the past fifty years, been encouraged to spend 15 per cent of their time on projects of their own invention, giving them the time and space to experiment, make mistakes and learn but, most importantly, feel in control of what they are doing and how important the organization believes this to be. The message is clear – if you have a good idea and the commitment to work on it, then go for it, even if it is at odds with 3M management. In essence the company has in some ways encouraged a healthy disrespect for management, specifically allowing people to pursue their own thing, rock the boat, but also potentially come up with something totally new for the company.

> *Mistakes will be made. But if a person is essentially right, the mistakes he or she makes are not as serious in the long run as the mistakes management will make if it undertakes to tell those in*

authority exactly how they must do their jobs. Management that is destructively critical when mistakes are made kills initiative, and it's essential that we have many people with initiative if we are to continue to grow.

Real empowerment also means toleration of mistakes, as people have to know that if they try something and it fails, they will not be punished. The alternative serves only to reduce risk taking, encouraging taking the easy option and never really putting people in the position to come up with anything radically new. This is true not only in the R&D world of 3M, where failures can sometimes be hidden, but also in the more visible areas of the company, such as marketing. For every 1000 ideas only 100 are ever developed enough to be considered as projects, and only a few of these actually make it to launch. Even then, over 50 per cent of new products launched onto the market are failures. This ratio is expected, and hence the environment is designed to accommodate it, and to allow people to learn from their mistakes in the hope that the next time round the insights gained will help to improve the chances of success.

Communication

Open and extensive communication is also seen as a core issue at 3M. This is three way – management needs to communicate broad direction and vision to the labs; the labs need to be able to communicate new opportunities to management; and marketing and innovators across the organization have to be able to communicate with one another. Indeed, a recent study of communication patterns within 3M showed that, unlike many organizations where the strongest communication typically occurs between operations, management and sales as they seek to maximize revenue from existing product and service lines, in 3M the dominant communication flows are between R&D, marketing and senior management as they drive forward new ideas as the future of the company (Jones, 1998).

Recognition

The final element in 3M's innovation culture is their system of reward and recognition. Foremost, the company does not believe in financial rewards. No huge bonuses are given to the best researchers, as high performance innovation is expected from them. What the organization does do is recognize innovation in a very public manner, and it has several award programmes covering all areas of the business from R&D to marketing to manufacturing and administration. For R&D there are a series of awards, partly determined by peer nomination. The ultimate is election to the Carlton Society, essentially the 3M hall of fame. Promotions are also different in 3M. The company has adopted a dual ladder career system, where technical people have a choice. To progress, they can move into management as is common in many organizations, or they can be promoted into more advanced technical positions. However, whichever option they choose, the salary, benefits and other privileges are the same. Promotion does not require people to move from the areas of the company where they flourish into management – it is their choice.

Cross-business exploitation

With these six elements firmly in place, 3M thus created a corporate environment where idea creation is the norm, where innovation is expected, and where people both desire and feel able to take their ideas forward. How transferable this is to other organizations with an existing culture in place and how well the 3M approaches specifically apply to smaller companies are both common questions asked by commentators. However, 3M recognizes that corporations must adapt and evolve if they expect to survive. Competitors will always bring products or technologies into the market that will change the basis of competition. To succeed, 3M sees that it has to be the company that innovates and the company that is at the forefront of idea creation.

Of particular significance to the company is communication across sectors, and especially across technology platforms. One of the areas of greatest concern for the company in the 1990s was an apparent stagnation as the varied divisions across the company, from healthcare to industrial tapes, and from data storage to office products, began to operate in silos as independent business units each pursuing their individual aims. Although still successful, it was recognized that the opportunities for cross-business exploitation of new technologies were not being fully realized. Therefore, major efforts were made to improve cross-business communication of new technology platforms. Micro-replication technology, creating precise three-dimensional patterns on a variety of surfaces, began when 3M researchers were looking for improvements that could be made to a plastic lens in overhead projectors. The adoption of this technology allowed the subsequent plastic lens to perform better than the much heavier conventional glass lens. Since then, micro-replication has spread, first into other optical applications such as more reflective material for traffic signs, and later into non-optical areas such as fasteners, connectors and data storage disks.

To encourage initial cross-sharing of technologies, the company defined three basic ground rules:

1 Products belong to divisions but technologies belong to the company – they should and must be shared
2 Multiple methods must be used for sharing information, from intranet to technology forums and audits
3 Networking is the responsibility of everyone; if someone calls you, you are expected to spend your time helping him or her out.

However, even with this in place performance was not considered to be good enough for 3M, and after major restructuring in the mid-1990s and the spin-off of its data storage and imaging businesses, in order to progress further the organization started driving several key initiatives across the entire company. These were all focused on improving performance. Three particular initiatives were introduced in 1999 to put together and enable the components for even better cross-business R&D exploitation and integration:

1 *3M Acceleration (strategy).* To drive the capability to generate greater returns on the $1 billion annual R&D investment, the 3M Acceleration initiative focuses on both shortening development cycles and sharpening focus. By identifying opportunities to reduce the laboratory to marketplace journey, the company is implicitly looking for more exploitation opportunities for emerging and existing technologies. Identifying these across the business is seen as a key mechanism for achieving the desired improvement in time to market performance. In addition, the specific sharpening of focus on growth areas with the best returns is stimulating the individual business units both to identify and to share their insights on the most attractive product and market combinations for innovation. As these needs are communicated across the company, they are prompting managers to search for existing solutions that already meet the requirements.
2 *Six Sigma (process).* As in GE, the adoption of the increasingly standardized Six Sigma process across the whole company is, in its broadest context, aimed at the key areas of lowering costs, increasing sales, satisfying customers, developing managers, increasing cash flow and making the whole organization faster. Whilst this is having an impact on all areas, with new technology and product development it is being particularly used to improve customer understanding, not just in terms of existing markets but also for potential

cross-selling opportunities. From a market pull perspective this is modifying the technology exploitation process to increase the number and variety of end product applications across the business and its customer base.

3 *Global products/local execution (organization).* The company has traditionally operated with a global market – a single source paradigm. Individual centres of excellence exist within 3M and provide new technologies. Individual business units focused on the associated exploitation are therefore largely geographically located in either the most appropriate market or the skill supply country. As such, although there is good sharing of ideas and technology, employees were largely experienced in only one culture. This was seen as a key barrier to global product delivery. Although 3M is a global company, many of its staff are local in outlook. This was especially true for the majority of its US-based workforce. To improve global thinking and execution, the company consequently introduced its global products/local execution initiative to encourage people to work outside their home environments. Taking on board practices within some pharmaceutical and automotive companies, 3M is using the increased movement of people across its business to improve awareness of different cultures, different customers, and hence new opportunities. In its bid to deliver new technology faster and more pervasively, this human initiative is complementing the other two strategic- and process-based changes.

Mass customization

The globalization of markets had a profound impact on the nature of social, political and economic interaction. Business was now being conducted differently, management precepts were being overturned, exports and imports had lost their meaning, and organizations were no longer being thought of as hierarchies but more as networks and organisms. However, despite these changes and the growth in the number and range of global products, little initially changed in the more subtle focus of many of the outputs of product and service development. Despite decentralized marketing and sales activities, many development capabilities remained centralized and focused on delivering global products and services for one or two prime markets, one of which was often the home market. The products that were developed through global programmes focused on the gross commonalities in the marketplace and not on the more niche requirements of many consumers. However, what in the mid-1990s began to drive globalization of innovation was not so much an improved means of operating development activities, but rather a better way satisfying the particular demands of local standards and regulations and, more significantly, the variations in consumer tastes and styles (Devinney, 1995). This gave rise to the need for mass customization – the provision of highly individual products and services on a mass scale. As companies sought more fully to address the needs of the consumer, as opposed to the customer, many of the principles for targeting profitable niche markets that had first been developed and refined in the food and drinks industries found influence in wider product fields (Foxall and Haskins, 1986). As organizations operating globally used common component suppliers and modularity to achieve worldwide commonality, many began to address the challenge of using the same capabilities to enable economic mass customization of their products (Pine, 1993).

By identifying the key issues that engender products with specific cultural or niche appeal, companies started to modify elements of their products better to address these markets. Whilst commonplace for several years in, for example, watches (Swatch), the practice of mass tailoring product configurations to specific users also became increasingly adopted in more general fields, including industrial goods, medical equipment (Toshiba) and paints (ICI), as well as in other consumer-orientated product areas such as:

- Spectacles: Vision Express – tailored lenses within an hour rather than a week
- Photographic processing: Fuji – multiple formats available within thirty minutes instead of five days
- Domestic appliances: Maytag – next day delivery of preferred model and features.

In the automotive sector, following the adoption of common platforms across different brands to enable globalization, mass customization first manifested itself in the use of the same elements in such varied embodiments as MPVs, coupés and sports car formats, as well as the more traditional saloons, hatchbacks and estates. By the late 1990s this had become a key element of product strategy within most car manufacturers as they all sought to extend the concept in their desire to offer customers greater choice but without a negative impact on their production effectiveness. A recent study by McKinsey, the consultancy, estimated that eliminating the losses associated with producing cars to meet a demand that never materializes could be worth up to $80 billion a year to the automotive industry (McKinsey, 2001). Building to order is the Utopia, but is unfortunately not a reality in an industry where typical order-to-delivery time is 42 days. Customers have to wait that long despite their initial expectations usually being of delivery within two weeks at most. However, while the aim of achieving the three-day car continues to be a target for the industry today, towards the end of the twentieth century some motor manufacturers started making significant progress, particularly through leveraging and refining their approaches to mass customization.

As a result of its partnership with Honda, in 1993 the British car manufacturer Rover launched the 600 series with a significantly reduced variety of available options. The Rover 600 had only thirty possible combinations: six models available in only five colour/fabric combinations, using only three different engines, with options such as air bags, CD players, air conditioning and ABS fitted as standard on some models and unavailable on others. This compared with the twenty different models, eleven different colours, eight engines and twelve optional extras (or in other words 1500 possible combinations) that had been available on the preceding 800 series, and was typical of the European build philosophy at the time. This rationalization was both a reflection of the company's inability to cope with providing the customer choice expected and its desire to be more package-focused in its product offerings. The Rover/Honda approach to meeting customer expectations was, as with several other manufacturers such as Peugeot, Fiat and Renault, focused on segregating their target market into distinct group profiles and then configuring individual product options and combinations around them. Thus if customers wanted a CD player fitted as standard they would also get air conditioning, whereas if they preferred a sunroof they would also get a radio cassette. The segregation and segmentation was typical, logical and, within the markets served, largely successful, but it clearly did not allow for the more individualized customization of the product expected higher up the market. Although the 600 series was, in the end, one of the most successful products that Rover had produced for years, successfully repositioning the brand and leading to the company's subsequent takeover by BMW, the practices adopted were certainly less able to accommodate the level of customer choice offered by the new parent, an exponent of greater flexible manufacturing prowess focused on economically delivering mass customized products.

During the 1990s there was a major change in the way that many European car manufacturers, and particularly the German firms of BMW, Mercedes and VW, evolved their ability to handle individual customer orders. By 2000, around 19 per cent of cars ordered in Europe were custom made compared with less than 7 per cent in the USA (*The Economist*, 2001). In Germany, the proportion of cars built in response to customer orders placed directly or indirectly with the factory was running at 60 per cent. This has been achieved through the ever-increasing sharing of platforms and components introduced to achieve economic globalization in the late 1980s, in conjunction with greater integration of design and production processes and cutting down on non-core procedures. Typically, production of a volume vehicle takes only two days, but also involves forty days of handling paperwork, accessing parts and scheduling a slot in the manufacturing process. A key delay here occurs in the paint shop, where changing from one colour to another takes several hours at a minimum. The solution adopted by Mercedes for its Smart car is to have interchangeable body panels that are hung onto the core metal chassis, thus allowing for almost real-time colour selection. The colour of any vehicle is thus fully flexible within the palette of options provided, and can be changed with no negative impact on production time. This approach of limited stock holding of key time-consuming elements is also used by VW for its most recent ranges of Audi products, all of which are now designed around a standard aluminium sub-frame. A further advance initiated to enable mass customization in the late 1990s was the incentivization of fleet buyers to place their orders in the troughs of a highly cyclic average purchase cycle, thus reducing bottlenecks and increasing the overall ability of manufacturers to assemble products to customer requirements as quickly as possible. Furthermore, another innovation introduced into this sector during this time was the creation of regional distribution centres to act as buffer stocks between the factory and dealer, and the use of the Internet to search across these centres for existing vehicles that match an individual customer's requirements. The result – an increase in the proportion of car buyers who get the exact specifications they request, up from 25 per cent to 76 per cent over the decade.

Today, mass customization is largely seen an extension of the built-to-order philosophy most extensively used by companies to shorten delivery times, trim work in progress and provide the customer with a bespoke product. The approaches developed in the automotive sector have migrated into others, and the 'any colour as long as it is black' philosophy is now history in most areas. However, throughout the 1990s, one organization outside the automobile sector has been seen to be the leader in the adoption, adaptation and creation of new advances in the mass customization of products. The company that leveraged this to greatest effect was Dell, the world's number one PC manufacturer.

Dell – as you like it

Most people are well aware of how Dell usurped Compaq as the PC industry leader in the late 1990s through leveraging direct sales over the phone and Internet. Many are experienced in ordering laptops and desktops from the company with the ability to not only specify model, processor speed, display, memory and modem but also operating systems, installed software, support service provision, Internet connectivity and, in some cases, colour. These are all standardized options that can be configured best to meet the customer needs. Customers can choose exactly the specification of product that they want, with no trade-off in price or in delivery time. In addition, the multiple alternatives of purchase, lease or loan also provide the purchaser with a degree of financial customization.

The key enabler of this level of flexibility is the way in which the products are themselves designed. Dell restricts the options available for customer selection to a number of predefined key modules, each of which is universally inter-compatible. Through maintaining sufficient stocks of each module, the company is able to offer its customers an apparently wide choice whilst at the same time ensuring that product assembly always occurs in less than four minutes (or six if you include software installation). No matter what options the customer selects, Dell can rely on its ability consistently to assemble, ship and deliver the desired product to the designated address within 24 hours of order placement. Although this necessitates holding higher stocks than advocated by some proponents of lean production, it undeniably allows Dell reliably and continually to mass customize the vast majority of its products. Essentially a highly-tuned flexible manufacturing system coupled with direct multichannel customer interaction, Dell, as the new leader in the PC industry, continues to grow at a rate of twice the sector average, largely by offering its customers a class-leading combination of quality, price and perceived personal service.

Innovation integration

Whilst the significance of innovation and creativity as major factors within product development success has been known for some time, the late 1990s was when it hit the mainstream in product marketing (Johne and Snelson, 1990). Through the mid- to late 1990s, companies began to promote innovation as the core of their product message. Building upon but not replicating existing brand values, an increasing number of manufacturers and service providers began to emphasize technical, product and market innovation as a key element of their propositions. Lexus adverts identified the 327 new innovations included in their latest car, Saab similarly highlighted the 1265 changes in the new version of its 9–5 model, Dyson identified over 100 patents protecting its latest vacuum cleaner as the key message in its promotional campaign, and NEC claimed over 15 000 patent applications as an organizational achievement. More recently this innovation performance has been turned around to provide an underlying opportunity for customers to themselves become more creative. 'Canon patents five ideas a day to enable you to have hundreds' and similar advertising campaigns have moved internal innovation performance to the forefront. By 1998 no corporate AGM was complete without the mention of innovation; many organizations appointed directors of innovation, and even companies as diverse as British Airways and American Express all had to have an innovation strategy.

Government agencies and consultants worldwide stopped talking about good design and quality as the drivers of product success as they had done throughout the 1980s. Instead innovation was the answer to everyone's problems. Innovation was suddenly a global panacea for corporate competitiveness, and organizations including the Design Council, the Department of Trade and Industry and the CBI in the UK alone all put up the innovation flag as the mantle of future prosperity. Even the big five management consultancies established innovation service offerings as they sought to jump onto the bandwagon, extend their service portfolios and not lose clients to the more established, and in many cases more experienced, innovation specialists.

However, despite all the sudden interest and hype, just as with e-commerce, not all organizations benefited from innovation. Many tried but, through lack of understanding, vision, commitment, integration or implementation, some failed. Those that succeeded used innovation as part of an overall corporate ambition, and as such leveraged the opportunities to their best effect. Of the firms who prospered, many (such as ARM, Genentech and Amazon) used technology as the key enabler, whilst others (such as First Direct, Sony and Thomson) used innovation as a cross-company issue to bring together opportunities for collective exploitation. However, of all the possible examples, one firm highlights the benefits that could be gained through using and promoting innovation to move forward and up the value chain. That company is South Korea's Samsung Electronics.

Samsung Electronics – incessant innovator

Samsung Electronics is one of several companies that exist within the Samsung Corporation, the largest of Korea's five major *chaebol*. With sales in 1999 of over $87 billion, it has overcome the financial crisis of 1997 and emerged as a global powerhouse in its chosen arenas of operation. Moreover, in comparison to its *chaebol* counterparts Hyundai, Daewoo, Lucky-Goldstar and SK, Samsung has also made a significant and world-leading shift from follower to leader in its introduction of innovative new products.

Founded in 1938, Samsung started out as an exporter of dried fish, vegetables and fruits produced around Korea to Manchuria and Beijing. This was followed by sales activities focused around flourmills and confectionery machines. After Korea's Independence from Japan in 1945, the economy became unstable and the Korean War decimated the economy. In January 1951 Samsung began the first step of its grand idea to rebuild Korea's economy by entering the manufacturing industry. It started by substituting imported goods with domestically produced products. Following the 1960 revolution and the subsequent military coup, as one of the emerging *chaebol*, Samsung gradually expanded its operations and decided to move into five core strategic key areas for the future – electronics, chemicals, heavy industries, shipbuilding and aerospace. Over the next decade it duly founded and developed five associated companies:

- Samsung Electronics Co. Ltd (1969)
- Samsung Fine Chemicals Co. (1973)
- Samsung Shipbuilding Co. (1974)
- Samsung Heavy Industries Company, Ltd (1974)
- Samsung Aerospace Industries, Ltd (1977).

Although all five of these have since grown both organically and through acquisition activity to become major organizations in their own right, it is Samsung Electronics that has made the greatest progress through moving up the value chain. In 1969 Samsung Electronics was established to 'help develop Korea's electronics industry into a worldwide competitor.' The founding Chairman, Byung-Chull Lee, believed that 'electronics is a value-added industry that requires technology and skilled labour and has great growth potentials both at home and abroad'. He felt that electronics was exactly the type of industry Korea needed at that stage of the country's economic development, and one in which most significantly sustainable long-term competitiveness was possible.

From the start the objective was to enter into large-scale production of key products, and the initial route was through the manufacture of imitation products, many based on those of Japanese competitors. Kicking off with joint production of its first black and white TV in 1970, with Japanese manufacturer Sanyo, the following year Samsung produced its own model for the local market and started to export in 1972. A move into home appliances created the company's first refrigerators and washing machines in 1974 and, with the introduction of its first colour TV, by 1978 Samsung had exports over $100 million and had become the world's largest producer of black and white TVs. A partnership with another Japanese manufacturer, Sharp, in 1979 saw the company's move into microwave ovens, an area that it would quickly come to dominate. With subsequent moves into air-conditioning units in 1980, personal computers in 1983 and video recorders in 1985, using technology as the key driver for internationalization, by 1986 Samsung was exporting products back to Japan as well as to Europe and the USA. The company had R&D centres in Santa Clara and Tokyo, manufacturing sites in Portugal, the UK and the USA, had delivered over 10 million colour TVs, and was the world's largest producer of microwave ovens. By 1990 the company had produced 20 million colour TVs and, with its development of 16M DRAM chips, was the world's thirteenth largest semiconductor manufacturer.

Samsung next set itself the target of becoming one of the world's top five electronics companies through building a reputation for innovation, world-leading technology and high quality, not low-cost, production. In 1993, having recently entered the mobile phone market and also achieved $40 billion in annual sales, after years of imitation Samsung determined that the only way forward was to move from follower into leader and to do this by innovating in every arena that it could. The company recognized that 'cheap and fast' production was a thing of the past and that, to succeed in the long term, it had to equip itself with capabilities in brand power, logistics and intellectual property management to complement its existing strengths in semiconductor technology, mechatronics, fine processing and mass production. As the core of this, it had to 'make innovations in its work processes and its way of thinking'. Samsung had to 'become customer and market orientated and develop and accumulate new technologies'. Moreover, the company went as far as to proclaim that it could become number one in the world if it strove for 'innovation in everything' and became known as 'the leader of change and innovation'.

Accompanied by a new logo, Samsung's 1993 'New Management' policy signalled a complete overhaul of the organization and a turnaround in how it approached its business globally. The company started to pursue a full-scale quality drive and world-best strategy. 'New Management' implementation began by encouraging individual employees first to make 'changes within themselves, striving to care more for others and to behave ethically'. Today, performance at Samsung is measured in qualitative instead of quantitative terms. Moreover, international competitiveness is an overriding objective, achieved through multi-faceted integration of facilities as well as the development of global information systems. Samsung's ultimate goal was to achieve improvements worldwide by succeeding as a top-tier enterprise in the early years of the twenty-first century.

Samsung recognized that total, unrelenting customer service is not just desirable but is also the only way for a company in the consumer electronics sector to survive. To that end, the company implemented a 'Line Stop' system, which allows any worker to shut down production if a defect is found. Moreover, like GE and 3M, Samsung adopted the Six Sigma programme and other advanced quality control methods. Employees in the field who are closest to the customer were also empowered with much greater decision-making authority. Rapid 'one-stop' services were offered, and Samsung promulgated a 'Customers' Bill of Rights' as part of its ongoing efforts to improve both product and service quality.

Determined to eliminate outmoded practices, employees were encouraged to 'change everything except their spouses and children'. As such, the company's reform efforts were systemic, penetrating every aspect of the organization. For example, Samsung adopted new work hours so that employees arrive earlier and leave earlier, giving them more quality time with their families. Senior managers are required to leave their offices and visit the field regularly to ensure the best understanding of company operations. Samsung then put all business processes, procurement, production, sales and logistics on-line. In concert with this rapid on-line management and response, the company has also implemented restructuring to ensure the most focused commitment to customer service from the perspective of building a truly global enterprise, in tune with emerging business trends worldwide.

Over the following seven years, Samsung duly moved from good quality emulator into technology-rich leader. All of its subsequent products were, in one way or another, innovative and class leading. From the world's first 256M DRAM chip in 1994 to the world's lightest CDMA phone, the fastest CPU and the first 30-inch LCD in 1997, the company constantly innovated, with the first mass-produced digital TV in 1998 and the fasted 1G CPU in 1999. Despite a major restructuring in 1997 due to Korea's economic problems, resulting in the sale of ten of its business units, by 2000 Samsung was still Korea's leading *chaebol* and Samsung Electronics was not only the world's leading manufacturer of microwaves, but also had the largest market share of eleven other product areas (including LCDs and digital TVs) and was winning design awards across Europe, Japan and the USA for its mobile phones, notebooks and monitors. In particular, with its 'Samsung Digitall – everyone's invited' slogan, the company has committed to digital technology as the core competency needed to expand the number of its world-leading product lines. With a 2001 product range extended to include integrated TVs, MP3 players and mobile phones with integral TV and MP3, Samsung continues to use and extensively promote innovation as the key enabler of corporate growth and driver on continual evolution.

Launch management

As organizations became more experienced and more efficient at creating and developing new products and services, attention was increasingly focused on achieving successful market exploitation of innovations. As improved interaction between functions such as R&D, design and production had brought about smoother, quicker and more focused progression of new ideas from concept to launch, the challenge that many companies began to face in the late 1990s was in improving the introduction to the marketplace. Given that the often extensive investments made in development had to be recouped as quickly as possible, achieving as fast a market penetration as possible, building up market share and gaining as large a margin as possible all contributed to a shorter break-even time and a higher return on investment. As quicker technology introduction reduced market windows, and greater and faster innovation imitation limited first mover advantage, more and more similar products were being launched into an ever more discerning marketplace. As a consequence, getting the preparation for, undertaking of and follow-up on new product launch became increasingly significant as an overall driver of success. Key to this was the interaction between the product creators, the product suppliers and the product promoters during the initial launch into the market. In other words, launch management as a recognized capability within firms began to move to the fore across multiple sectors.

One of the arenas within which effective launch management was first highlighted as a core competence was the pharmaceutical sector. For a blockbuster drug that typically cost $500 million and up to ten years to develop, early recuperation of investment was paramount. With potential sales of $500 million to $1 billion within the first three to four years an industry norm, getting the launch right was critical. During the late 1990s leading companies were often spending between $100 million and $500 million on a broad range of marketing activities, approximately 20 per cent of which occurred pre-launch, with the remaining 80 per cent for launch and post launch media advertising and medical promotional campaigns (Best Practices LLC, 2000). What made this such a challenge in this sector was that these launches were often both global and multicultural, and therefore required not only coordination of production, distribution and sales activities as with any product, but also, by the nature of the high levels of legislation and regulation present within the industry, such issues as local packaging, trials, certification and government approvals had to be addressed. As firms such as GlaxoWellcome, Pfizer and Merck all endeavoured to coordinate these complex activities they implemented new levels of organizational alignment, with marketers especially playing an increasing role in shaping and planning product strategy. Often creating a dedicated cross-functional launch team for each new product, some members of these teams would get involved in the development process at an early stage – sometimes up to six years before launch. Requiring input from all key areas of the organization, from research and clinical trials to production and sales, in some cases launch teams became seen as stewards of the products through the journey from molecule to established drug. As such, issues including supply chain management, brand management and global product positioning all came under the influence of the launch team. Creating an integrated approach where individual team members' areas of responsibility would change in both scope and prominence throughout the launch process became, in its own way, a mirror of the multifunctional team approaches being used within the development process.

The key attributes of a successful product launch within the pharmaceutical sector that emerged during this time were seen to include:

- Building and sustaining sales force enthusiasm using a combination of information provision through early products awareness, regular communication and continued training, with incentivization via such elements as uncapped bonuses and well-defined compensation systems.
- Using innovative market research to enhance product positioning and brand development through ensuring that clinical developments activities are focused on real and not perceived needs, and providing accurate and insightful data to facilitate dialogue between the scientific and marketing communities within a firm.

- Leveraging co-promotion partnerships by forming strategic alliances with other pharmaceutical companies with no directly competitive product, and where a marketing and sales alliance could double the size of the sales force in areas where quick market entry and maximum impact was seen as key.
- Using thought leaders such as academics and key consultants to both identify key health guidelines and market windows of opportunity up front in the overall market positioning process, and become advocates of new products, either through speaking with physicians directly or via conferences and journal articles.
- Building early awareness within the medical community through education of consultants and physicians around health guidelines, by a combination of publication in research journals and sales representatives supplying product samples to test and thereby hopefully facilitating large-scale switching from existing products.

In this highly defined sector, such elements of a coordinated and coherent product launch could be leveraged to great effect. However in other faster moving, less predictable and in many ways more competitive sectors, additional organizational capabilities were also being introduced to affect an efficient product launch. Logitech highlighted some of these, with the successful introduction of its Mouseman 2 product in the computer peripherals sector of the consumer electronics industry.

Logitech – mice and men

Logitech designs, manufactures and markets human interface devices that connect people and computers. Retail and OEM (Original Equipment Manufacturer) offerings include pointing devices such as mice and trackballs, as well as game controllers, keyboards, PC video cameras and multimedia speakers. Now the world's largest manufacturer of mice, employing 4000 people worldwide, in 2001 it produced its 200 millionth mouse. Headquartered in Fremont, California, in 1995 it was however still seeking to reinforce its position with the global launch of its new MouseMan 2 product.

Founded in Switzerland in 1982 to produce interface equipment for the fast-developing computer industry, over the next decade Logitech grew significantly. The early move of its operational headquarters to the USA coincided with the company becoming the major supplier of mice to most of the leading PC manufacturers, including IBM, Compaq and HP. In addition, in the mid-1980s

Logitech also started to market products directly to retail under its own name. It was soon a global operation, with manufacturing facilities in Taiwan, China and Ireland, design occurring in the USA, Ireland and Taiwan, and marketing activities being run regionally: Europe from Switzerland, Asia from Taiwan and the USA from California. By 1994 Logitech was investing 7 per cent of turnover directly into new product development, launching an average of twenty-five new products per annum.

By 1990 Microsoft had moved into the interface device sector and released a number of mice to compete with Logitech, particularly in the high end of the retail space where, at the time, Logitech had 40 per cent market share and products typically sold for around $50. Although Logitech had launched its successful MouseMan product in 1991 and updated it in 1993, with improved comfort and weight, Microsoft were known to be preparing another new model, the J-mouse, for launch the following year. To compete, Logitech therefore had to introduce another innovative product to maintain its lead position. In October 1994 Logitech successfully launched two versions of MouseMan 2, a new mouse developed by an international team of engineers, consultants and marketing personnel from the USA, Italy and Ireland and taking less than a year from concept to full-scale production. By the end of the year, Logitech's Ireland facility was manufacturing 140 000 units of the MouseMan 2 each month to satisfy the growing market demand. Key to this success had been the way in which the launch had been managed.

The development of the MouseMan 2 product focused on introducing a number of innovations into the marketplace. It was to be available in two forms, Classic and Sensa. The Classic model was pitched at the middle of the market and incorporated advances in ergonomics to provide a snug fit with the hand, improved responsiveness, smoother action and fewer compo-nents. It was largely an evolutionary step on what had gone before, and the market was therefore well known to the company. By comparison, the market for the Sensa model was more uncertain. Positioned at a premium for the high end of the market, this product would share the same elements and provide identical performance and functionality to the Classic model. The differ-ence was in its appearance, for this was the first time a new process called 'cubic printing' was to be used on a mass-produced item to provide a number of different colour, texture and pattern combinations for the product's external surface. Seeking to emulate the high-end Mont Blanc and Lamy pen market in quality and variety of finish, this was a major step for a market within which all existing products were previously only available in the uniform industry standard grey.

Like other leading companies, Logitech had been using a multifunctional team-based approach for product development, led by a senior manager who had undertaken the role in addition to his other responsibilities. Moreover, individual team members had also been available for work on multiple projects at a time. Whilst this approach had delivered good products, there had traditionally been problems with both resource availability and, as a consequence, hitting deadlines. Projects had also been driven by marketing, which had, understandably, always wanted as early a launch date as possible. Consequently, what was required and when would be stipulated by marketing, and all other activities were reverse scheduled backwards from this date. Since there was extensive consultation across the company before the launch date was set, projects would often progress as planned – but not always. Although team members would try their best to achieve individual targets, more often than not a series of minor delays would build up during a development programme, resulting in a late launch. As deadlines were all very tight to hit as earlier launch date as possible, any unforeseen problem or minor iteration would have an impact on the overall schedule, which was managed by programme managers who, due to their position in the hierarchy, had little authority. In addition, they had little knowledge of the product itself and so found it difficult to see opportunities, in say tooling lead times, to reduce the time to launch.

For the Mouseman 2 project, a number of changes were introduced to overcome such problems and reduce the possibility of any unforeseen delay. Central to these was the establishment of a new approach for launch management. Across the company, the concept of a 'product availability date' was implemented. This was not the launch date, but the point at which half the first month's worldwide requirement for a new product had been manufactured and was in stock ready for global supply to retailers. The computer industry as a whole had developed a reputation for late launches, and this was an attempt to rectify this. Once all parties involved in development and introduction had agreed to the product availability date, it could not be changed. Everyone had the opportunity to be involved in the determination of the date, but thereafter the onus was on each individual to meet his or her commitment and deliver. Late launch was not an option. As a consequence, project schedules were not based on idealistic minimums but on what the team members guaranteed they could deliver. Although the overall project was therefore scheduled to last slightly longer than with the traditional approach, since no delay was acceptable and none would occur in any component task or activity, it would in theory actually turn out to be quicker.

The second major change for the project was the selection and role of the core team leader. Rather than having a senior manager as a part-time leader, a full-time position was given to a programme coordinator who had extensive experience of product development and had recently been part of a similar, but not identical, project for the company. He acted as the product champion. The mould was also broken in that, for the first time, the leader was not an engineer, and he was given more responsibility than had been available on any previous projects. Whereas the individual team members committed to their elements of the product availability date, as the one ultimately in charge, the team leader had overall accountability and was in turn given greater authority. Rather than having to ask senior managers for resources, he was able to object to insufficient funding or insist on extra support for any inexperienced members of the team when required. As product champion he was undoubtedly in charge, and as well as being able to delegate roles to the team he could also protect them from any unwanted external distraction from elsewhere in the company.

The third major change introduced for this project was in the team itself. Whereas previously individual members had multiple commitments, for the MouseMan 2 project all members of the core team were full time and all their previous responsibilities were assigned to others for the duration of the project. Together these were a major shift for Logitech, but one that it was felt would improve the ability to hit launch with a competitive and innovative new product in two forms simultaneously. Starting in January 1994 with a strategy review in the USA, the core team was therefore formed. Comprising eight personnel, including the team leader, design engineer, manufacturing engineer and quality engineer in Ireland, a marketing manager and a consultant industrial designer in California, a colour consultant in Milan and an electronic engineer in Switzerland, this was a truly multi-national core team. Drawing on an extended team of twenty-five additional resources, ranging from marketing strategists and CAD operators in the USA to production engineers in Taiwan and a prototyping facility in Scotland, this was a high-profile project for the company.

There were inevitably a few ups and downs during development, but with key operational mechanisms such as sharing of common databases and weekly cross-team update sessions, underpinned by frequent additional intra-team communication and two weeks of co-located working at key points, the overall project progressed exactly to schedule. In the first week of August, 1000 units were produced on a new assembly line in Ireland. These were used for evaluation to assess pre-launch readiness, and after passing this test, full-scale production was initiated for the core product and the supporting packaging and software, all fully configured to local language and retail requirements. In July 1994 Microsoft released its product late but to market acclaim, and gradually took number one slot in the retail market. The Logitech MouseMan 2 product was launched worldwide in October 1994, on time and in perfect position for the Christmas market. Within three months the Mouseman 2 was the market leader, production was running at full capacity, and Logitech had regained leadership from Microsoft. Coupled with two differentiated versions of an improved product, its combined enhancements of increasing team leader authority, making the core team all full time and, most significantly, introducing the product availability date concept to guarantee launch, had paid dividends.

Continuous development

In line with increasing market requirements for more frequent new launches and product updates, the demand for a continuous series of new product introductions also grew. Ever-shorter product lifecycles demanded constant innovation. With the expected product life for laptops dropping below eighteen months and financial services companies refreshing their product offerings on a bi-annual basis, an overall expectation of a continuous release of new products and services from innovation leaders subsequently arose. With the ability to track changing customer and business trends and react sufficiently quickly to pump out a constant stream of new services to match the associated needs, in the late 1990s companies were able to move closer and closer to real-time research, development and launch.

With the advent of the Internet as a primary delivery channel for many businesses and an alternative sales channel for others, a core mechanism for developing, testing and launching a constant series of updated offerings to an increasingly fragmented customer base finally became realizable across all sectors. No longer did firms have to keep a product on the market for a year before considering an updated version; the constant introduction of a stream of incrementally enhanced versions was now possible. As firms became ever more familiar with the principles of a disciplined development process with regular and then more fluid decision-making, so the ability quickly to adapt new procedures and accommodate increasingly variable input and expectations grew. As the end of one project and the start of another became less distinct, component phases of development overlapped completely and the lines between different product releases became blurred, the core innovation process itself became more and more continuous. Ideas went in and products came out. It became increasingly difficult to determine where and when one version of a product or service was replaced by another, as the transition itself became continuous. Innovation could no longer just be seen as a jump from one state to another, but itself became the series of minor incremental changes that were being continually introduced. Over a period of time there was a distinct change, but to the customer this was gradual. From being an activity separated from the day-to-day steady-state operations and sales environments by its very need for a different culture, innovation itself gradually became a steady-state component of the business structure.

In the case of on-line products and services in particular there was a fundamental change in the development process, where gates as distinctive review points between concept and launch disappeared. In an arena where the delivery mechanism of the Internet is itself ever moving and ever evolving, how new products and services have been developed has similarly experienced constant change. Whereas traditionally a concept had to be frozen before progressing into detailed design and development, this was no longer the case. Although certain parameters had to be defined, the flexibility of web-based development meant that several key design decisions could be left until a later stage – after, say, some initial concept testing with prospective customers had been conducted. The development of on-line services became more and more of an iterative process, where the original vision, the design, the execution and the customer all involved and fostered interaction. Whilst conventional development processes required a final design to be approved prior to production or service provision, again this was not so rigidly enforced. In a bid to test out multiple final options and combinations and so choose only the ones that fitted best with user testing, many aspects of the look and feel as well as the detailed content of on-line services could be left loose until later. Different options could now be trialled with users in controlled environments, where their individual preferences for alternative formats, layouts, navigation and even the basic colours, images and fonts could be investigated and evaluated both openly and covertly. Moreover, as there were often multiple new features, enhancements, products or even services being continually introduced, there was no final review point for launch as the concept of a discrete launch date itself was slowly disappearing to be replaced with a whole series of mini-launches.

Alternative Internet products

In essence, continuous development processes were increasingly being used to evolve three different types of web site, each with their own characteristics and thus each requiring a slightly different approach. These three can be seen as channel, software and product sites.

Channel sites

As an additional (or even the only) marketing and sales channel for an organization, web sites are in a state of continuous development. In creating a façade where customers can access information about a new product and service, configure, order or purchase goods or services, firms have had to ensure that their sites are being continuously updated either with new content or new features. Companies quickly learned that their existing and potential customers alike expect the very latest offerings and therefore also expect to be able to find out and acquire them. Rather than an annual rejuvenation of catalogues, brochures and order forms, firms can renew these virtually instantaneously at minimal expense. Moreover, core business processes such as order handling, transactions and additional service incorporation can be facilitated in a smooth and non-interrupting manner.

Where the web site acts as a channel for marketing and sales, product innovation and service improvement is often focused on making the use of the site more efficient to the user – the better the user experience, the more likely the user is to return, complete an order or increase their basket size. Tesco, the UK retailer, aims at increasing average customer spend on-line, which can be done through more effectively allowing customers to fill their basket, register and check out. These processes can be continuously improved based on customer feedback, and will not disrupt the shopping experience for existing customers. For companies like BP, Sony and Cartier, for whom web sites are primarily marketing channels, the rate at which new offerings can be included is dictated by the conventional means in which they are being developed. A new oil, Walkman or watch has to be created before it can be specifically marketed. However, the updates to the web sites can then be instantaneous.

Software sites

In a similar vein, but with different application, software sites have also been relentlessly updated through continuous development. When the product being delivered is no longer physical but can be downloaded directly onto the user's desktop, the sites that enable this delivery have embraced an even higher level of development. Particularly for companies like Adobe and Macro-Media, which provide products such as Photoshop, Acrobat and Dreamweaver – all now part of many a customer's application package – the opportunities that have been presented and taken for perpetual innovation have been significant. As customers have been able to register on-line, the software providers have been able regularly to prompt for updates to be downloaded. Often at no cost, this has presented near instantaneous delivery of incremental improvements to the applications themselves. From new features down to the fixing of bugs in earlier versions, as soon as the improvements have been completed by Adobe or Macro-Media they have been able to offer them directly to their customer base. No longer restricted to annual release cycles, this has driven both continuous development of the software applications them-selves as well as the associated delivery.

Product sites

Organizations that have web sites that are themselves the product, such as eBay and Hotmail, have faced equally demand-ing challenges for continuous development of both content and format. These on-line services exist only in the virtual world, and as such have been the focus for all development activities within the respective organizations. Here there have rarely been such things as new launches for additions to functionality, as these have been constantly drip fed onto the site. New features have been developed, tested and added continuously. Once an opportunity is identified, either by the organization or, increas-ingly, by its customers, means by which these can be accommo-dated are investigated and prototyped almost at will and then subsequently introduced onto the sites. Frequently focusing on the reaction of customers to such additions, the trialling of improvements has been conducted live as the main web site itself has become a beta test environment. If the enhancements work and meet with customer approval, they have been retained and further developed. If not, then they have simply been dropped. In this way, such sites have almost taken on a life of their own as they have grown in reach, scope and functionality in an almost organic manner. The instant nature of these changes means that services can be updated to respond to market changes, as well as to customer feedback. The innovation has been occurring proactively and reactively in a constant arena of ongoing development. Two lead examples of this are eBay and MSN.

eBay – customer-driven development

The massively successful Internet trading site is a lead user of direct customer involvement in its everyday innovation processes (Hof, 2001). eBay has become a master of harnessing the communications power of the Internet, not just to let its customers give direct feedback to the company leadership, but also to track their every movement so that new products and services are tailored to just what they want. As the company seeks to try out new ideas, such as the 'Buy it now' feature, it watches customer reaction and waits for immediate feedback. eBay is run like a democracy, with customers playing a major role. Its customers, the 38 million buyers and sellers who trade on its site, have the kind of influence over the on-line auction site that most consumers and businesses could never dream of exerting on conventional companies. They are, in many ways, eBay's *de facto* product development team, sales and marketing force, merchandising department, and security detail all rolled into one. It is not just that they have catapulted eBay from a little on-line garage sale into a global marketplace; they also crowd eBay's on-line discussion boards, posting 100 000 messages a week to share tips, point out glitches and lobby for changes. By using the Internet to tap into the talent and imagination of its customers, eBay has multiplied its innovation team by millions. If a retailer tried to do this, it would have to interview every single person leaving every store, post a list of what each thought of the shopping experience, then ask each of them to write up a merchandising plan and call suppliers to arrange deliveries. That's what eBay's customers voluntarily do each day, and thus the innovation and change on the site becomes an everyday activity through which the service evolves better to meet customer needs.

MSN – Microsoft's development lab

MSN, Microsoft's Internet portal, was first set up in 1995. As Microsoft Network, its original focus was as a 'media play' providing content including news, sport and e-commerce. However, through MSN, Microsoft found that it had a direct relationship with consumers different to anything it had previously experienced. Whereas Windows and Office software purchases and upgrades had driven traditional Microsoft customer relationships, prospective new customers were visiting MSN as a portal or entry point to other sites. As the default homepage on Internet Explorer, Microsoft was able to make MSN the first point of contact for its customers each and every time they went on-line. In addition, when in 1997 the company bought Hotmail, the free e-mail service, Microsoft was able to direct the millions of users to MSN every time they sent an e-mail. Furthermore, through amending the Explorer browser software it was also able to send users to the MSN site whenever they mis-spelt a web address. Over a period of three years MSN changed from being a media service to become one of the top three portals on the Internet, alongside AOL and Yahoo. With 110 million active users of Hotmail and 42 million users of Internet Messenger, Microsoft's on-line chat service, by 2001 MSN was achieving 270 million visitors a month.

MSN has lost money throughout its life and many consider that it will, in itself, never be profitable. However, this does not matter to Microsoft, as the real point has never been to generate revenue (Harvey, 2001). Instead MSN serves a mix of purposes, including research and development, testing software, advertising and product distribution. The instant interactive relationship with customers that MSN provides for Microsoft has become an ideal testing ground for new products. Its customers have increasingly been asked to download and try out beta software that is still in development and provide comments and feedback, giving Micro-soft its own continuous user acceptance development and testing lab. Software updates and even major upgrades are developed in collaboration with active users in a two-way process. Not only do MSN users act as testers for Microsoft ideas; they also suggest new ideas and thereby themselves initiate new developments. This creates a constant cycle of continuous development as hundreds of new features and products are simultaneously defined, created, tested and introduced. One example of how this has been used is in the development of a service called Passport, which helps users to create a digital on-line identity to store personal information that the user wishes to disclose. Hotmail users first tested this as a beta version as a quick way for them to leave the site and ensure that their mail was all closed. Feedback and suggestions gained from this drove both Passport's initial release and subsequent evolution. It has since been developed to include credit card information, medical data and even diary information, to enable improved on-line bill payment, ticket purchasing and holiday booking. Now renamed Sign In.Net, it is being continually refined and updated in collaboration with MSN and Hotmail users as the advance application for Microsoft's .Net platform strategy that the company sees as a major element of its future.

Further applications

The continuous development of new services, especially for web-based delivery, has clearly become a capability that several leading organizations have embraced. However, as technology has evolved apace and new enabling software has come into being, firms operating off-line have also been presented with the opportunity to enhance their innovation processes further. With the ever-increasingly modularity of products being facilitated by mass customization, particularly where information technology is a major player, fast and frequent updates have also become a reality for companies as diverse as Dell, Schlumberger and Datamonitor. Although not immediately applicable to large-scale automotive and aerospace product development, especially in the information-dependent service sectors, continuous incremental innovation and hence continuous development processes are becoming more and more commonplace.

Knowledge management

In the post-industrial era, a firm's success has come to lie more in its intellectual assets than in its physical assets or natural resources. High skill requirements, new information technologies and the accelerating pace of change have initiated a shift in the way many companies compete. Firms have therefore begun to recognize the need to organize and coordinate their intellectual and knowledge sources to allow them to become more responsive (Ruggles, 1998). With the growth in both the level and quality of data required to develop new products and services, many organizations started to focus on how best to acquire, control, manage and retain this information. As more and more companies first reached similar levels of proficiency in many of the organizational and operational activities associated with innovation, it was the ability of a firm to learn more quickly than its competition that was seen as a sustainable source of competitive advantage. Companies began to compete on their ability to improve their performance faster and more efficiently than their rivals, and so they required new ways to recognize, encourage, enhance and build upon people's capacity for learning (Maira and Scott-Morgan, 1995). Whilst an organization's knowledge of technology, products and markets has always been critical to its competitive success, and had been identified as such, up until around 1996 it was not so much seen as being in need of explicit management (Caulkin, 1987). However, as the leverage of knowledge to support new development became more significant, companies began to try to manage it actively and to adopt the art and practice of organizational learning (Senge, 1990). Furthermore, in parallel with the recognition of the need to develop their knowledge bases, companies also began to acknowledge the value of their 'intellectual capital', and searched for new ways of exploiting it and locking it into their businesses (Stewart, 1997).

In the late 1990s, knowledge management became a desired (if somewhat over-played) solution to improving an organization's ability to innovate. Quite correctly, it was seen as being the combined mechanism and philosophy that could make any learning or insight that exists within an organization available to any project or team whenever and wherever it is needed. For some, this pointed towards extensive yet accessible increasingly web-based information management systems that could operate across and within a company's infrastructure. For others, it was more linked to a greater openness and exchange of information as it ensured that employees within an organization all recognized that allowing sharing of their individual insights did not give away power but rather enabled the company as a whole to gain. This was underpinned by the dual recognition that if you share information you do not lose it, and that there is a hierarchy of knowledge, starting at the bottom with data and moving up through information and insight into knowledge at the highest level.

Particularly in high-technology areas, where new ideas are the currency of innovation, the value of corporate knowledge can be highly significant (Bukowitz and Petrash, 1997). As the importance of intellectual capital as a corporate asset, especially in new product development, gained acceptance, increased attention was focused on the area of organizational learning as a solution to the problems of how to promote it and, of greater significance as more and more individuals moved between companies, how to retain it. Knowledge management was therefore recognized as a process that amplifies the knowledge created by individuals and crystallizes it as part of the knowledge network of the operation (Nonaka, 1991). To enable this to occur, knowledge management focused on connecting people with other knowledgeable people and with information, enabling the conversion of information to knowledge, encapsulating knowledge to make it easier to transfer, and disseminating knowledge around the company. Only by achieving this could companies develop their intellectual capital, improve their learning and, as a consequence, continually develop competitive products (McKee, 1992). One of the early leaders in this was the Swedish insurance company Skandia.

Skandia – knowing and doing

Skandia is one of the most innovative companies in financial services today. Established in 1855, it was Sweden's first stock insurance firm. It has been an international company since it began, with offices around the world, and has been active in the USA since 1900, in Latin America for more than forty years, and in Japan for about thirty years. Today the group holds euro 120 billion in assets under management, employs 5600 staff and is active in 20 countries worldwide. Skandia has undergone a profound transformation in recent years, from an insurance company with a main emphasis on property and casualty insurance to what it is today: a focused, global savings company. This savings business has expanded rapidly, entirely through organic growth driven by the creation and delivery of new services. Over the last decade, Skandia has consistently out-innovated most of its competitors in developing new and better investment and insurance products. The key elements in this have been a focused strategy and a deep commitment to people, underpinned by the use of knowledge. Most companies would claim to have these things, but Skandia's difference amounts to much more than a corporate catchphrase (Jones and Kirby, 2001).

In the early 1980s, much of the asset management industry was highly vertically integrated. Companies performed fund management, product development, packaging, administration and distribution in house, and this model worked – proprietary funds represented 80 per cent of sales in the USA in 1980. However, by 2000, proprietary funds accounted for just 30 per cent of sales. Skandia's strategic revolution was to turn its attention purely to product development, packaging and administration. It was the first financial services company to reject the industry wisdom of vertical integration. At the back end it bought investment performance from a host of other fund managers, and at the front end it left distribution to banks and financial advisors. As a strategy, the group's focus on product development, packaging and administration allowed it to stay focused on areas of greatest return and opportunity for innovation. However, it takes genuine bravery and belief to run in the opposite direction to the rest of the industry. The Skandia vision states, 'Faster, smarter, better at helping our distributors serve their clients.' This has been continually refreshed and renewed by a consistent ability to set unreasonable goals as a way of driving perpetual corporate renewal. However focused, strategy and unreasonable targets are only a part of what allows the group to make consistently high quality and innovative products.

The other component of Skandia's success is down to its people policies. Jan Carendi, Skandia's chairman, is the man who was primary architect of the strategy, but most of what Jan talks about is people and in particular values, education and renewal. 'If you treat your people with warmth, charm, intimacy and caring, they will ruthlessly destroy your competitors.' A key belief in Skandia is that a truly innovative and entrepreneurial culture is a vital competitive asset. This is accomplished in a number of ways, described below.

Skandia's balanced scorecard, introduced in its earliest form in 1993, includes a focus on human factors that is almost exclusively concerned with the extent to which employees feel that managers and peers contribute to the innovative culture. This survey is backed up with a strong commitment to the accountability of line managers for the culture that is to be found within their work units. Over-performance can be used as a way to identify and share knowledge, whilst identified under-performance is used as a catalyst for development and feedback. Since the introduction of this, the company has also created a number of tools to visualize and report its intellectual capital:

- The Skandia value scheme shows the building blocks that make up its intellectual capital
- The Skandia Navigator is a future-oriented business-planning model that forms the basis of Dolphin, its PC-based business control software package.

Both are used in combination to measure knowledge use as accurately as possible. However, despite the precision of Skandia's values-based scorecarding, a key assumption for the company is that building control systems is just as expensive as investing in building employees' understanding. As Carendi says, 'If you think competence costs a lot – try incompetence'. Learning at Skandia is therefore both a strategic priority and a managed process, and it is combined with the recognition that quality learning does not come cheaply. Skandia's scorecard, for example, captures the per capita cost of training and development for each individual. Much of Skandia's management effort is focused on the development of a culture élan that supports the company's ability to build and maintain profitable relationships with intermediaries and to be consistently innovative. Values and culture are much more than a slogan at Skandia. Senior managers are genuinely committed and HR systems are highly focused. A similar rigour is brought to the learning process. Education is thus also part of what enables the process of continuing renewal. Carendi talks about the challenge of 'turning around a successful company'. Many companies lose out when success breeds complacency and boom turns to bust. To achieve repeated and extraordinary success requires a fusion of collective wisdom into the culture, structure and systems of the organization – 'no-one is more clever than everyone'. In practice, this means a continual critical re-examination of past assumptions to avoid becoming blinded by success.

Today's businesses operate in an environment where knowledge is the primary wealth-creating resource. This has led Skandia to develop new work methods, competencies and processes based on the knowledge that exists within it. The company carries out this kind of development on a daily basis. Through these processes emerges the accelerated growth that represents Skandia's intellectual capital, which it sees as its combination of 'customer capital', 'human capital' and 'organizational capital'. Many of these are invisible to traditional accounting methods and systems, but the company believes that they are the innovative source of the company's future value. Whereas traditional accounting focused only on a company's financial capital, as it began to understand the challenges of the new economy, intellectual capital and the supporting knowledge management processes were seen more accurately to represent the major share of the Skandia's total value. That is why the company had actually been developing its intellectual capital management practices since the early 1990s.

Skandia's success rests on innovation, strategic discipline and culture. Whilst it stands as an example of strategic focus as a way of building success, its real point of differentiation is its powerful centre of attention on values-based management and education to create a culture that is a genuine source of competitive advantage through the successful and continual leverage of knowledge.

Competitor collaboration

The establishment of research networks to nurture new technologies and their derivative products, the use of technology transfer programmes to enable new techniques and processes to be adopted, and the creation of corporate joint ventures to resource development programmes and exploit the opportunities available, had all laid the foundation for increased corporate interaction for innovation. The growing level of cooperation throughout projects between organizations, their customers and their suppliers that developed during the late 1980s cemented many of the interactions in longer-term relationships, and a decade later, in several lead fields, a move towards competitor collaboration, later to be termed as 'co-opetition' by some, began to emerge. This was not immediately as much of a cross-industry advance as supplier partnerships had been but, with early success in a few high-profile arenas, was soon quickly developing as a major opportunity across sectors as diverse as financial services and chemicals.

Within the automotive sector, discrete actions including common platform sharing enabled new alliances to be forged for appropriate projects. Not focused on a full-scale integration of product lines, this specifically targeted move resulted in, for example, a number of joint MPV development programmes between companies such as Ford and VW and Peugeot–Citroen and Fiat, who, in other areas of the market, were in direct competition with each other. Having recognized and started to exploit the advantages to be gained from platform sharing across some of their individual business units, these firms did not initially have existing platforms that could be immediately adapted for this growing but still niche market. Therefore, more as a reactive tactic, with volumes not yet justifying individual investments for single brand competitors, and in their desire to compete with Renault's Espace product in particular, they grouped together to share new product development.

These competitor alliances differed from earlier joint ventures such as the Honda/Rover and VW/Seat relationships, where there was coordination and sharing of development resources, components and production facilities across complete product ranges. Whereas these types of joint venture were long term and integrated throughout the R&D, design, manufacturing and business strategies, the new collaborations between competitors were more short-term partnerships, formed to enable the parties involved collectively to overcome common challenges and help address the specific needs of the market or industry at one moment in time (Anderson and Nauras, 1991). They could form the basis of long-term relationships, but, given the pre-existing competitive positions, more often they have been temporary marriages of convenience. As such, the way in which they were both operated and managed differed both from one collaboration to another and, more significantly, from other more long-term strategic alliances. However whilst the attraction of such alliances could be significant, there are several limitations, in particular relating to corporate know-how. As competitors work together on new developments a level of sharing of information and, often, strategic intent is essential, but at the same time issues such as ownership of intellectual property as well as customer and market information can be very sensitive. In addition, the common understanding of working practices required for successful collaboration could potentially lead to depletion of individual core competences and consequential erosion of competitive advantages. Most firms choosing to follow this approach have as a result been careful to define clearly the scope of their cooperation, as well as any agreed limitations.

Although always wary of antitrust proceedings and accusations of forming anti-competitive cartels, similar partnerships also began to exist in other sectors such as aerospace and computing, where competitive collaboration even occurred between Airbus and Boeing for shared avionics technologies, and between IBM, Motorola and Apple on early elements of RISC-based computing.

WAP – Nordics together

In the alphabet soup that is the telecommunications industry, there have been many and varied initiatives over the years. From NMT and CEPT to UMTS and CDMA, acronyms have consequently increasingly propagated the language. However, within this melee several developments have successfully entered the mainstream of popular culture. GSM and 3G are the primary elements that have now become part of our everyday vocabulary. Whilst many of the initiatives have sprung from individual companies as well as cross-industry forums, some have been self-initiated by companies coming together to tackle an issue collectively. This is especially true in the case of Wireless Application Protocol, or WAP. In the face of ever-spiralling technological alternatives, shifting alliances and increasingly diverse competition, during the mid- to late 1990s a number of telecommunication equipment manufacturers found that pragmatic partnerships with the competition was an effective way to create and exploit new business opportunities.

Nokia, the Finnish mobile phone giant, had humble beginnings. From its start as a wood pulp mill in 1865, the company evolved first into a paper and chemicals conglomerate, adding rubber at the end of the nineteenth century. As a producer of footwear and tyres, the Nokia brand developed through the 1920s, and the company later expanded into cable manufacture to satisfy the local need for power transmission and telephone networks. By 1967 the electronics part of the business generated 3 per cent of the overall net sales. During the 1970s and 1980s Nokia invested heavily in building its technology businesses, developing new network platforms, computers and early mobile handsets. Driven by new legislation, the company joined several Swedish companies, including Ericsson, in the development of a car-phone based mobile network that was launched as Nordic Mobile Telephony (NMT), the world's first multinational cellular network in 1981. By 1988, Nokia had become the largest information technology company in the Nordic Countries and Europe's number three producer of televisions. However, during the recession of the early 1990s the company chose to focus exclusively on telecommunications and divest itself of all non-core operations.

Working together with Ericsson on the development of the Nordic Mobile Telecommunications system had been a first experience of joint working between the two companies, and this took another step forward with the creation of a new global system, GSM, led by France Telecom. Faced with multiple local mobile solutions being developed across Europe, from TACS in the UK and C-Netz in Germany to RTMS in Italy, in 1982 the Conference des Administrations Européenes des Postes and Telecommunications (CEPT), which comprised the telecommunications administrations of twenty-six European countries, decided to establish a new specification for pan-European mobile communications. Named Groupe Speciale Mobile (GSM), this was quickly established as a means of enabling roamed mobile services across the Europe and its dependencies. With NMT already in existence as a multinational network in Scandinavia, it was not surprising that Nokia and Ericsson subsequently played a major role in the development and deployment of the new GSM system. Nokia made the first GSM call in Finland in 1991. Within a year there were thirteen networks operating in seven countries – a figure tripled twelve months later when the first ever text message was sent in Finland, again by Nokia. By December 1996 there were 120 GSM networks operating across the world in over 80 different countries, many of which ran on Nokia equipment. All this put Nokia in a leading position for the future development of mobile communications in both voice and data services.

Just as the browser war between Netscape's Navigator and Microsoft's Explorer was reaching its peak, it was apparent that, for the forthcoming mobile Internet, a common micro-browser approach across manufacturers would be better. It would clearly be ineffective for Nokia to have one system, Ericsson to have another, and other manufacturers either to have to create their own versions or to side with one of two camps. Nokia in particular was keen to introduce some element of predictability into the future evolution of the mobile Internet, and was therefore open to defining the first major stage of the data journey in conjunction with a few select leading partners (Brown, 2000). From Ericsson's perspective, the attraction of working with Nokia to form a *de facto* standard as soon as possible was a key issue, as it would quickly define the cross-industry route. With a multitude of concepts there was a substantial risk that the market could become fragmented – a development that neither of the involved companies would benefit from.

Whereas the move to create NMT had been mainly legislative, and GSM had been largely an overall network operator desire to enable roaming from one country to another, this partnership was more in the hands of the manufacturers themselves. Nokia and Ericsson had to work together proactively with whichever other companies needed to be involved to create the next step change in mobile data services. Microsoft was keen to promote the concept of the mobile Internet as being a stripped-down version of the existing PC-based Internet, but the two mobile phone manufacturers wanted a simpler solution. The cost of incorporating the necessarily complex filtering would have been prohibitive, and hence, despite the pressure, an alternative route was required. The preference was therefore for a dedicated micro-browser specifically designed and dedicated for use with mobile phones. Small file sizes could accommodate the low memory constraints of handheld devices and the low bandwidth limitations of the GSM network. By implication, although the solution would have to support conventional web HTML and XML languages, a new version would have to be specifically designed for small screens and one-handed navigation without a keyboard.

The key third partner for Nokia and Ericsson was therefore Unwired Planet, later renamed phone.com and subsequently Openwave. Based in Redwood City, California, this company was a leader in Internet software and was to become the world's largest mobile Internet software developer. The proposal was to create a combined protocol for mobile devices that contained key elements of the three companies' respective technologies:

- Phone.com's HDML (Handheld Device Markup Language) and HDTP (Handheld Device Transport Protocol), used for describing content and user interface
- Ericsson's ITTP (Intelligent Terminal Transfer Protocol), which handles communication between server and mobile device
- Nokia's TTML (Tagged Text Markup Language), which enables its Smart Messaging concept Internet access technology.

After a period of intense negotiation during 1995–1996, the cooperative initiative between the three culminated in the creation of WAP, the Wireless Application Protocol, which provides a method of communicating across wireless networks quickly, securely and efficiently. With the ability to integrate databases, dynamic content and messaging, this ran on all networks equally, including ever-multiplying IP-based networks.

With the development of WAP, the delicacy of the venture was apparent to all parties. Being open and giving away information was more difficult than originally envisaged. Although patents were less of an issue here than in other areas of future cooperation, such as Bluetooth, ensuring that the value created by the group was shared appropriately with no single firm dominating was key. This was greatly facilitated by the fact that all three companies were looking to follow similar business models for the generation of revenues for the technology, rather than having competing requirements and influences.

To encourage and facilitate cross-industry adoption of this application protocol, the three partners also formed the WAP forum. This brought together over twenty-five wireless operators, nineteen device manufacturers, fifteen infrastructure companies and twenty software developers, and resulted in the release of WAP 1.0 in April 1998. Quickly becoming an open world standard, established by industry rather than regulators, WAP has since been used for application development across many devices and technologies, from handsets to PDAs.

Despite its sometimes over-hyped qualities and capabilities at the time of launch, it is undoubtedly the cooperation between the three key players that was one of the major propellants of widespread acceptance of WAP, allowing the standard to be quickly developed and integrated into a wide range of products across the mobile arena. Although not initially as successful as predicted, largely due to misrepresentation and positioning in the market by several lead network operators, WAP did gradually gain a strong foothold in the mainstay of mobile communications. With the launch of WAP 2.0 in August 2001, the protocol further embedded its role as a lead standard for a new generation of more advanced GSM-based mobile devices. Incorporating improved security and more varied style sheets, as well as better and faster text transfer, this paved the way for the services that would soon be available on the subsequent GPRS and 3G networks.

Although some organizations are reluctant to adopt such partnerships within their development programmes, usually for the lack of incentive to do so, as much as for the fear of disclosure of sensitive information, many have been increasingly experimenting with competitor collaborations and gaining shared benefits. This has now occurred not only in the identified high-technology areas, but also in sectors as diverse as food, chemicals and pharmaceuticals. As an effective means of initiating and operating innovation programmes, when appropriate, this type of relationship continues to grow significantly in its application.

References

Anderson, J. C. and Nauras, J. A. (1991). Partnering as focused market strategy. *Calif. Management Rev.*, **Spring,** 95–112.

Anderson, P. and Tushman, M. L. (1991). Managing through cycles of technological change. *Res. Technol. Management*, **May–Jun,** 26–31.

Best Practices LLC (2000). *Best Practice in Global Pharmaceutical Launches.* Best Practices LLC.

Brown, A. (2000). On Coopetition, The New World of Communication, **December,** 37–41.

Bukowitz, W. R. and Petrash, G. P. (1997). Visualising, measuring and managing knowledge. *Res. Technol. Management*, **Jul–Aug,** 24–31.

Caulkin, S. (1997). The knowledge within. *Management Today*, **Aug,** 33–7.

Coyne, W. (1996). *Research and Development at 3M. Annual Innovation Lecture.* DTI.

Devinney, T. M. (1995). Significant issues for the future of product innovation. *J. Product Innov. Management*, **12,** 70–75.

Ford, D. (1988). Develop your technology strategy. *Long Range Planning*, **Oct,** 85–95.

Foxall, G. and Haskins, C. G. (1986). Cognitive style and consumer innovativeness: an empirical test of Kirton's Adaption–Innovation Theory in the context of food purchasing. *Eur. J. Marketing*, **3/4,** 63–80.

Harvey, F. (2001). Microsoft's direct connection to the customer. *Financial Times*, December 31, p. 7.

Hof, R. D. (2001). The people's company. *Business Week*, December 3.

Johne, F. A. and Snelson, P. A. (1990). Successful product innovation in UK and US firms. *Eur. J. Marketing*, **24,** 7–21.

Jones, T. (1998). Functional Interaction: Diagnosing Interface Relationships in New Product Development. PhD thesis, Salford University.

Jones, T. and Kirby, S. (2001). *Taking Ideas to Market.* John Wiley.

Kodama, F. (1992). Technology fusion and the new R&D. *Harvard Bus. Rev.*, **Jul–Aug,** 70–78.

Larson, C. F. (1998). *Industrial R&D in 2008.* Industrial Research Institute.

Maira, A. N. and Scott-Morgan, P. B. (1995). Learning to change and changing to learn – managing for the 21st century. *Prism*, **Third Quarter,** 5–13.

McKee, D. (1992). An organizational learning approach to product innovation. *J. Product Innov. Management*, **9,** 232.

McKinsey (2001). The false promise of mass customisation. *McKinsey Q.*, **3.**

Miller, J. A. (1997). Discovery research re-emerges at Dupont. *Res. Technol. Management*, **Jan–Feb,** 24–28.

New York Times (1998). IBM opens the doors of its research labs to surprising results. *New York Times*, July 13.

Nonaka, I. (1991). The knowledge creating company. *Harvard Bus. Rev.*, **Nov–Dec,** 96–104.

Pine, B. J. (1993). Making mass customisation happen: strategies for the new competitive realities. *Planning Rev.*, **Sep–Oct,** 23–4.

Ruggles, R. (1998). Why knowledge? Why now? *J. Centre Business Innov.*, **1.** Ernst & Young.

Senge, P. (1990). *The Fifth Discipline: The Art and Practice of the Learning Organization.* Currency Doubleday.

Stewart, T. A. (1997). *Intellectual Capital: The New Wealth of Organizations.* Nicholas Brearley.

The Economist (2001). July 12.

Further reading

Dell, M. (2000). *Direct from Dell.* Harper Collins.

Gundling, E. (2000). *The 3M Way to Innovation: Balancing People and Profit.* Kodansha.

Jones, T. (1997). *New Product Development: An Introduction to a Multifunctional Process.* Butterworth-Heinemann.

Stewart, T. A. (1997). *Intellectual Capital: The New Wealth of Organizations.* Nicholas Brearley.

Summary to Part 1

Together, the varied enhancements to organizations' ability to innovate that have been introduced over the past years have evidently moved thinking and practice forward. From first putting the basics of an effective innovation capability in place, to then tuning it to deal with the challenges of addressing globalization of both products and markets and the need to accelerate innovation delivery and, lastly, on to improving focus on customers' needs and increasing the level of integration both within and across businesses, there has been a clear evolution. There has been a massive shift in how firms across all industries now develop and exploit their ideas, and this has primarily been driven by the way in which they have adopted and adapted the respective improvements.

As the three waves of new approaches to innovation that have been introduced found success in one sector and then been successfully migrated across industry to become the new industry best practice, so have elements of their embodiments been adapted. What was first introduced as the new approach in the consumer electronics sector has, as it has transferred across, been modified to suit the particular needs of the chemical and financial services industries. Product strategy, mass customization and innovation integration are all finding their new homes in the likes of BASF, Exxon, Citibank and CSFB. Similarly, many of the new ideas such as quality, product champions and global products that were first generated and initially introduced in the automotive sector have found applications in arenas as diverse as cosmetics, education, energy and transportation. The essence of the overall philosophy remains the same, as do the fundamental tools and techniques, but, usually through initial experimentation and adaptation, the details gradually change either in scope or focus to fit the specific requirements present.

Across all seven core areas of focus, the gradual evolution of organizations' innovation capability has facilitated continuous improvements in the way in which firms have tackled the increasingly complex challenges that they have faced in creating and delivering successful new products and services.

Strategic thinking has moved on from first considering the need for a distinctive product strategy as a key component of overall corporate ambition to a focus on identifying and developing organizational core competencies, and then to improving cross-business integration as new applications of capabilities and technologies are exploited.

Firms have changed their market focus from providing regional products and services primarily addressing local requirements to identifying and satisfying the common needs of global customer bases, and then on to using mass customization as a core enabler for meeting more specific niche user attitudes and desires whilst still maintaining economies of scale.

As quality, consistent product performance and reliability have become prerequisites across all areas, organizations have embraced the increasing significance of the brand in under-pinning and communicating product attributes, and, more recently, have rushed to increase the perceived and actual levels of innovation integration across their product ranges.

From improving the prioritization, evaluation and selection of which new ideas can offer the greatest benefits, companies have invested in enhancing cross-business interaction first to deliver increasingly quicker speed to market, and have then sought to introduce more effective launch management activities to enable faster and deeper market penetration.

The underpinning core development process used to drive, manage and enable successful innovation delivery has also evolved from the initial stage-gate phased approach to one with flexible fuzzy gates that permit more accelerated development, and, particularly in the new economy, to a more continuous approach where the resulting products are themselves in a constant state of gradual evolution.

The enabling organization used for innovation has similarly transformed from first being a dedicated resource within com-panies, and the introduction of product champions to manage and motivate development to matrix structures, allowing multi-disciplinary teams to operate, on to an increasing leverage and management of organizational knowledge to facilitate even higher levels of sharing of information and insights.

Lastly, the relationships with organizations external to the firm have progressed from the initial customer–provider interaction of technology transfer to closer supplier relationships throughout the development process, and, in latter years, to increasing levels of collaboration between competitors on areas of common strategic interest.

As the earlier elements have become standard practice and very much the hygiene issues that all effective companies consider and accommodate, the later approaches have been adopted to enhance capability. Although not all of the most recent improvements are yet fully transferred across all sectors, many are on the way. Whereas issues such as supplier partnerships, core competencies and brand significance are now evident in all areas, those such as launch management and competitor collaboration are still only in their initial stages of cross-industry migration. However, as serendipity is achieved, it is only a matter of time before these too become common parlance in all sectors.

The leading edge of innovation practice has evidently both moved and evolved. Some firms who were innovating at the edge in the 1980s have continued to do so again in the 1990s, either by changing their own perspectives and building new capabilities or being early adopters of the new ideas that have been developed and proven by others. Some have made an advance and, for a time, stuck with it, incrementally refining their approach to deliver ever-increasing levels of efficiency and effectiveness, and leaving other organizations to take the lead in the introduction of the next step change. Those that have been at the forefront in the past may well be again in the future, but in these early years of the twenty-first century there are now a host of new companies who are innovating at the edge.

Part 2

Innovating at the edge

6

The edge today

Today, as the innovation leaders strive to take the next step in the evolution of this increasingly fast, diverse and complex arena, there are a whole new set of issues coming onto the horizon for many firms. Like mass customization, ingredient branding and total quality management, some of these are being developed first in one sector and will then transfer across to others in the next few years, whilst others are more generic in application from the start. In an increasingly competitive marketplace, leadership in the ability to conceive and deliver groundbreaking innovation is becoming ever more of a core competitive advantage. This latest phase of the evolution of organizations' innovation capability is pushing new boundaries and challenging firms' preconceptions across the spectrum, forcing them to re-evaluate some of their core activities and processes and, if need be, reinvent themselves.

- Leading the charge are a number of organizations who are very much breaking existing preconceptions and reinventing their respective marketplaces. Following its early success with vacuum cleaners, Dyson is once again redefining the domestic appliance market with its new washing machines and, in an equally mature and saturated marketplace, Smint are shaking up the confectionary food sector. Likewise, eBay and Egg are both leveraging the opportunities from the connected economy to change customer expectations and cause fundamental change in the trading and financial service industries.
- With the advance of the Internet as a sales and distribution channel, mass customization of products is evolving into true personalization and delivery of tailored services unique to the

individual. In parallel with mySAP, myCNN and FT.com all becoming established for Internet-based personal content and service delivery, Nokia are moving the concept of post-acquisition product personalization forward with the increasingly wide range of physical and software options available for its phones, and, with the arrival of digital TV, fully personalized programming and advertising is now a reality.

- An increasing focus on the underpinning needs of customers is similarly driving increased interest in discovering and capturing the values by which purchase decisions are being fundamentally influenced. Led by companies such as Nike, greater psychological and behavioural science input to the innovation process is prompting more and more companies to search for the unarticulated needs that have to be satisfied at the start of projects and to use these as reference points throughout delivery.

- The increasing convergence of new technologies, especially mobile communications and PCs is driving companies such as IBM, Dell, Motorola, Microsoft and Nokia to share development and also the supporting intellectual property rights. In contrast to the great video debacle between Betamax and VHS, DVD products are now being developed through cooperation between Sony, Toshiba, Matsushita, Philips, Panasonic *et al.*, while Ericsson, Motorola, Nokia and partners are leading Bluetooth, the new wireless applications standard, which has over 200 companies involved in its development and exploitation.

- Driven by the fallout of the dot.com bubble, an increasingly diverse range of organizations are re-evaluating their core and non-core businesses and looking to a combination of internal and external investment to support new innovation programmes. From early stage venture capital firms to multinationals, the way in which the availability of finance can be used to increase the chances of ultimate success for new technologies, new products and even new businesses is being redefined. From Nestlé and Unilever to Scipher and BTG, companies are using such investment to increasingly beneficial effect.

- Enabled by fully integrated networks and processes, firms across several lead industries are collaborating virtually. Collaborative product and service development is increasing cross-industry involvement and further reducing development timescales. Led by Covisint in the automotive sector and c-Medica in the medical device industry, new means of organizing for innovation are becoming a day-to-day reality.

- Lastly, organizations are using ever more inventive strategic partnerships to exploit the value and reach of their brands.

Virgin is the most visible originator of this approach, with its multiple business operations across the travel, retail, financial services and entertainment sectors, but others such as Centrica and Manchester United are moving practice another step forward. In alliance with an ever-expanding range of leading partners, from Nike and Vodafone to MBNA and BskyB, this football club in particular is adopting increasingly inventive value- and margin-sharing propositions to extend its core brand's reach and increase associated revenues.

Together, these issues are ensuring that the way in which individuals, companies and even governments innovate and deliver new ideas to the market continues to evolve at an ever more rapid pace. Fuelled by shorter product lifecycles, more fragmented markets, fewer barriers to competition and, in many cases, reduced resource availability, these approaches are very much defining the next wave of new innovation capability. As more and more organizations emulate the leaders in their desire to improve performance, this is the new leading edge of innovation practice.

7

Market breakers

Until now, companies have embraced a series of evolving and in many ways incremental new approaches to improving their strategic intent for innovation. From the first emergence of product strategy as distinct from (but implicitly linked to) corporate strategy, to a focus on core competencies and the underpinning capabilities that can differentiate a company from its peers, then to an increasing cross business use and reuse of developed technologies, platforms, processes and approaches, over the past twenty years firms have clearly shifted and built upon the core strategies that they pursue. While for many organizations that may still be making this journey there are now clearly mapped out next steps to follow in the evolution and development towards a more sophisticated strategic approach, for others who have already moved along with or just behind the leading edge of innovation practice there is the problem of determining what else they can do.

With the successful implementation of the varied organizational and process improvements that have emerged in parallel with the strategic evolution, companies have improved their individual and collective capabilities to bring innovations to market more quickly, exploit more recognized customer requirements, and share knowledge and insight. As a result, for the leaders there is now arguably little to differentiate between the strategies that they use for creating and delivering new products and services. Merck, AstraZeneca and GSK all adopt similar strategic approaches, and the only difference can be considered to be how effectively the different companies implement and execute them. Likewise, although some are still marginally ahead, Sony, Matsushita, Samsung and Philips all share similar strategies, processes, investment profiles and even organizational structures. In the eyes of several firms we have reached a plateau where the leading innovators are now all pretty well aligned in their perspectives of how to create and deliver new products to their customer bases, and the differences are only in the detail.

The Internet

For some, particularly those with an interest in promoting and supplying the services and infrastructure that support the Internet, e-business and m-commerce are still seen as the new battlefield. Despite a short-term downturn, investment in faster networks, larger servers and more consultancy support will, according to many of the respective providers and stakeholders, still be the route for guaranteed success. However, as the dot.com–dot.bomb cycle has demonstrated, there is a significant difference between the hype and reality. The Internet is an effective new tool, a cheap sales channel, a flexible customer relationship mechanism and an efficient means for improved working. It is not in itself a strategic shift for innovation; a bad idea is still a bad idea whether or not it is delivered through the Internet. Poor decision-making, ineffective management, misaligned organizations, inefficient processes and resource wastage are barriers to successful innovation in both the real and virtual worlds. Internet successes, including Amazon and Yahoo, are good ideas that through leveraging the operational and tactical opportunities provided by the Internet have delivered the results. They have done this by learning from earlier developments in the real world. Ideas have been selected against key criteria so that those that are implemented address identified needs, deliver value, are scaleable, can be continuously updated, exploit external supplier and partner relationships, leverage the technology and, perhaps most significantly, provide something new. Boo.com, letsbuyit, exite@home, clickmango, Chemdex and an increasing list of failed or failing Internet business have delivered services that in one or more of these aspects have not come up to the necessary standard to compete. Hindsight is clearly a wonderful and somewhat artificial perspective, but it is probably fair to say that sustainable success on the Internet has so far been shown to rely on building and exploiting some of the innovation capabilities that have been developed and proved in other arenas in the past.

Market breakers

So, given this apparent levelling of the real and virtual playing fields of innovation as companies that have been open to learning and change have individually evolved their capabilities to broadly similar levels, where, it may be asked, is the key strategic move that will redefine the competitive landscape emerging today? It is coming from high-level redefinition of business focus. Whereas in the past we have experienced a largely evolutionary development of strategy, we are now seeing the emergence of revolutionary thinking. Incrementalism is no longer sufficient, for the leaders today – the companies that are successfully innovating at the edge of practice – are 'market breakers'. Faced with markets within which the existence of too many products offering broadly similar features and supported by nearly identical customer propositions have become the norm, firms wishing to make a significant impact are looking for opportunities for major change. Companies as varied as SouthWest Airlines, its European counterparts EasyJet and Ryanair, and New World wine producers such as Penfolds, Rosemount and Montana are all trying to identify means by which they can break the rules and redefine the whole marketplace, not just a niche served by a few products and services. To do this they are deploying a range of approaches for using new technologies, new customer–supplier relationships and, especially, new ways of successfully creating and sharing value. A few clearly identifiable organizations operating across the industrial spectrum are using innovation to change fundamentally the dynamics of the markets within which they operate or enter. Through the combined development of significantly improved value propositions and deployment using the most effective delivery mechanisms, companies such as Dyson, SMINT, eBay, Egg and Google are all causing massive change in their respective sectors as they introduce new products and services that recalibrate what their customers, and hence the wider market, see as the new norm. These are not the only examples, but they are some of the most prominent.

Dyson – cleaning up the market

With the launch of its Contrarotator washing machine in November 2000, Dyson, the UK-based domestic appliance manufacturer, was once again setting out to take on the sector incumbents and use innovation to redefine the marketplace. Seven years after the launch of the company's first Dual Cyclone vacuum cleaner it was again making waves across the industry. The product of four years of R&D, over £25 million – an industry-leading investment in innovation of 16 per cent of turnover – and, as expected, packed full of new innovations, the Dyson Contrarotator is based around the principle that with two drums rotating in opposite directions the quality, speed and efficiency of the wash cycle is much better than the conventional single-drum design used by all other manufacturers. Positioned at around twice the price of competitive products, as with the company's earlier vacuum cleaners, Dyson is seeking fundamentally to recalibrate the value proposition delivered to customers.

Now well-known internationally through the extensive promotion of the company's products and James Dyson's positioning as a leading entrepreneur by the media, the story of how a lone inventor overcame rejection to set up and head the most successful domestic appliance company of the modern age is probably familiar to many. However, for those unaware of this, in summary the key points behind the Dyson cleaner story are:

- After early success as the inventor of a number of products including, in 1974, the ball-barrow, a wheelbarrow with a ball instead of a wheel to improve traction and with no chance of sinking as it is pushed across soil and lawns, in 1978 James Dyson began to investigate why conventional vacuum cleaner bags clogged so easily. His avenue of invention went towards high-speed cyclones, where centrifugal forces could be used to cause any particle contained within an airflow to be thrown out to the edge of a container. Four years, several patents and over 5000 prototypes later he produced the world's first bag-less vacuum cleaner, a product that, unlike its competitors, could not only accommodate waste materials from dust to glass and liquids, but also, due to the cyclone technology, did not suffer any degradation of suction as it filled up.
- Rejected by all the existing manufacturers, including Hoover, Electrolux and Panasonic, allegedly to protect the highly profitable bag replacement market worth over £100 million in the UK alone, in 1991 the product was entered for and won the International Design Fair prize in Japan. It subsequently went into limited licensed production as the G-Force, addressing the Japanese premium market at a retail price of $2000 a piece. Quickly imitated as a lower-cost product and distributed by US network marketing company Amway, a lengthy legal battle over patent rights followed. This, when it was won, together with the licence income from Japan, provided Dyson with the capital required to set up a small research centre and factory in Wiltshire, England. The resulting product, the DC01, launched in 1993, was the first in a range of models that quickly

dominated the sector. Offering new levels of performance into a largely stagnant marketplace, it was a huge success across the world. By 1995 the DC01 was the UK's best-selling vacuum cleaner, within eight months of launch it became the best seller in New Zealand, and Dyson had also won the largest ever export order for electrical goods to Japan.

- By 2000, with an increasing range of product variants available, sales of Dyson Dual Cyclone vacuum cleaners had grown towards market domination. In the UK Dyson was selling 100 000 units per month, had 53 per cent of the floor-care market, was outselling its nearest competitors nine to one, and occupied nine of the top ten best selling slots. Moreover, with over 20 per cent of the market, the company was also brand leader across Europe. Faced with falling market shares, reduced revenues and potentially massive losses in their floor-care business units, Electrolux, Hoover and Panasonic all started to produce their own bag-less cleaners, which bore a strong resemblance to the Dyson products. So strong was this resemblance that one by one they have all been successfully prosecuted for patent infringement. In a high-profile defeat in 2001, the courts ruled that Hoover had infringed a 1980 patent and copied Dyson's designs in the manufacture of its Vortex bag-less cleaner range. As its market share continued to fall from a high of 25 per cent in 1990 to less than 10 per cent in 2000, Hoover was forced to suspend sales of the Vortex and go back to the drawing board.

A key aspect to all this has been the redefinition of the value proposition offered to customers. Although clearly offering improved performance, with its '100 per cent suction 100 per cent of the time' promise duly delivered, coupled with award winning product design, when it was first introduced into a mature, saturated and low-margin UK marketplace the Dyson product was priced at £300, twice the price of the existing best-selling products from Electrolux and Panasonic. Conventional business school wisdom for a mass market product would have pointed to either price-based competition, where similar performance is offered for less money than existing products, or performance-based competition, where improved quality, reliability or speed are offered at the same price point. Both of these were rejected. Primarily because in 1993 the company was small, had few economies of scale and had a limited advertising budget, Dyson believed that in order to generate sufficient profit and, in comparison to existing products, to reflect the value of the innovation that the firm was providing, it had to price high. Electrolux, Hoover and Panasonic dominated the market and controlled many retailer and distribution channels. Accustomed to their existing perception of the value proposition they did little initially to compete, believing that the oddity that was the DC01 was no threat to their substantial and apparently solid revenue streams. Unfortunately for them, they were wrong. To the surprise of many, not only were customers prepared to pay twice the price for the new Dyson products when replacing old cleaners; as the reputation for quality and performance grew, households across Europe also threw out their recent Electrolux, Hoover and Panasonic purchases and upgraded to a Dyson. Even in a rather dull sector, Dyson showed that if offered a new product that exceeds existing market expectations and provides superior design and performance, even at a price premium, consumers will embrace it.

Fuelled with success, with the Contrarotator washing machine Dyson is now learning from its earlier experiences as it yet again seeks to redefine another market sector. Competing with some but not all of the same established players as before, this time the market knows what is coming, and companies including Maytag, Miele, Whirlpool and Zanussi believe that they are ready to defend existing turf and market share. However, they are in for a tough time, for the Dyson product is already scoring high on performance and design. Protected by over fifty patents, the fundamental element is the dual tub, which, the company claims, enables the product to wash twice as clean in half the time. Rather than the 'drop and flop' action of a single drum, clothes are moved far more during the wash by the double drum's increased flexion and agitation of the load, and hence there is greater exposure to the detergent. By simulating and potentially improving on the more thorough washing that is surprisingly achieved through hand washing, in comparison to a conventional machine the Contrarotator cuts a typical weekly wash of 14 kg down from 5 hours 54 minutes to 2 hours 18 minutes, halving power costs. In addition, as claimed by Dyson, the product can get clothes cleaner in 15 minutes than a conventional machine can in an hour. However, it is not just in fields of technology and design that the company is seeking to compete with its second range of products. Supported this time by enthusiastic rather than sceptical retailers, all now eager to be first to sell the products, together with a growing on-line sales channel, Dyson is going for scale from the start. Two products were introduced into the market in 2000–2001, the first of which won several design awards. Six months after launch both were in the top ten UK sellers, with the £1000 CR01 competing for top slot with Zanussi and Bosch products priced between £400 and £450. On this basis it looks as though superior performance, design and exceeding expectations, and not price or features, are again key to a successful value proposition. Profits for the growing Dyson Technology Company for 2000 were £35 million, up £9 million on 1999, on a similarly increased turnover of £226 million.

Smint mints – power in a packet

Even by comparison with the domestic appliance market, many would consider that the mint sub-sector of the confectionary market was not a prime candidate for a revolution. Although the food and drinks industry as a whole is an ever-evolving test-bed for new ideas, from microwaveable ready meals and dual-pot yoghurts to self-chilling drinks cans, the confectionary business is itself rather sedate. Even industry leaders such as Nestlé and Cadbury are relatively cautious and slow to introduce innovations, and when they do, they are largely incremental rather than revolutionary. New flavours or new sizes of product are more likely to be launched to extend an existing product portfolio slowly, rather than introducing a totally new product. In fact, the average time between totally new product introductions in this highly conservative sector is round about ten years! Within the mints sub-sector, innovation has traditionally been even more lethargic. In the USA, Altoids have been the stalwart for years; in the UK, Extra Strong mints were introduced in the late 1970s. Globally, Tic-Tac, Mentos and Polo had become increasingly established as the leaders throughout the 1980s, with each taking a good share of the market. The *status quo* has, however, been fundamentally disrupted by a new arrival on the scene, and one that is typically priced at three times the competition. This mint is Smint.

Originally launched in its home Spanish market in the mid 1990s, with its distinctive dispenser and powerful taste, Smint was a hit from the start. It quickly became a domestic best seller for its parent Chuba Chups, an organization that made its name in the conventional lollipops sector and has since become the world's largest manufacturer and the market leader in eighty different markets. The product of a $3 million R&D investment, Smint was specifically targeted at broadening the company's market from the child and youth and into the adult markets. With the uniquely designed 'one-at-a-time' dispenser for added convenience and hygiene, Smint provides consumers with a perfectly packaged hit of flavour that is also sugar free, made with a plaque-fighting sugar substitute, and has now been tested and approved by dental associations worldwide. Taste and health simultaneously!

Following export success in the UK in the late 1990s, using Chuba Chups' extensive network, global distribution followed in

2000. With an international presence from San Francisco airports and Stockholm nightclubs to Tokyo restaurants, London sandwich bars, Bangkok street sellers and Milanese food-stores, often displayed prominently at the point of purchase, Smint is a huge success. The biggest thing to hit the emerging market of 'power' mini-mints for adults, it quickly gained ground and in 2001 pushed long-term global leader Tic-Tac into the number two position in 90 per cent of the markets in which it was available. Furthermore, it has even taken a significant share of the high-value breath-freshener market.

By 2001 the Smint range of flavours had expanded from the original mint to include peppermint, lemon, peach, liquorice and wild berry. Provocative media campaigns included eccentric TV adverts in Korea, Smint cocktail receptions in London nightclubs, sponsorships of Snowboarding competitions in France, a plan to convert the Millennium Dome in Greenwich into the world's largest advert, and a highly innovative web site, www.smint.com, all of which helped to promote Smint as a different product in an overcrowded market. Again, as with Dyson, to the amazement of existing players, people were prepared to pay a heavy premium – sometimes up to 400 per cent the price of its competitors. Although the proposition is different, it is sufficiently compelling to overcome the price barrier and thereby deliver a significant benefit to its manufacturer. This is both high volume and high margin. It is a proposition that with innovative and coordinated promotion has totally redefined the rather dormant global mint market.

eBay – the go-between

'Disappears faster than a dot.com company', proclaimed a recent advert for Hyundai cars. Unlike many of its fellow dot.coms, eBay will not be disappearing any time soon. Even according to the ever-insightful Red Herring, eBay is 'the definitive online market-place'. The story goes that Pierre Omidyar founded eBay as an online auction site when his girlfriend was collecting Pez sweet bottles. How did eBay grow from swapping children's sweet containers into a company with ten times the market value of Sotheby's in five years?

The Eureka moment was when Omidyar noticed that his girlfriend suffered from a lack of 'market liquidity' in the pursuit of her hobby. Collectibles – the kind of stuff that is traded in car boot sales and market squares all over the world – are bought and sold avidly, but the trick to buying is to be in the right place at the right time. This of course is easier said than done – to succeed, you need to know what seller, in what market, in what town, in what country, on what day will have the right object at the right price. All over the world, second-hand dealers make money by exploiting this problem. By knowing their markets better than anyone else they profit from customers' imperfect knowledge and the high cost to consumers of searching for products.

Omidyar saw how Internet technology could cut through these market imperfections by creating what amounts to a 24-hour, global car boot sale. He aimed to create a Nasdaq-like market for a wide range of goods, but with a twist: 'I wanted to give the power of the market back to individuals, not just large corporations,' said Omidyar. Sellers initiate an auction by posting a description of the product on the eBay website. Buyers use the company's software to make bids, and to complete a transaction the seller and winning bidder simply negotiate payment and shipping details between themselves. eBay provides copious advice on how to do this, but does not act as an intermediary. eBay's users transacted $2.25 billion of gross merchandise sales in the first half of 2001, and eBay itself made $148 million gross profit on net revenues of just $170 million – a gross profit margin in excess of 80 per cent!! Even taking into account costs like marketing and IT, net profit margins are 20 per cent compared to an average of 15 per cent for the largely mature businesses of the S&P 500. It is one of the few dot.com companies that have been robustly profitable, almost from the start. What explains eBay's success? The answer includes equal measures of luck and judgment. Omidyar's understanding of the Internet's potential was truly ahead of its time, and was rooted not in technology *per se*, but in an observation of a genuine, unmet consumer need.

When eBay was founded, Internet commerce had only just been permitted by the Internet standards governing body, the browser had been invented one year previously, and public debate was about whether the Internet would ever be used by anyone except technology geeks. At such an early stage it requires a genuine leap of imagination and a willingness to take risk to create a new business, and eBay was able to translate this early insight into genuine first-mover advantage. First-mover advantage has been one of the shibboleths of the dot.com era – usually meaning little in practice other than an ability to burn cash quickly on expensive marketing and non-proprietary technology. eBay gained a genuine advantage by being the first on-line market place to gain scale. If I want to sell goods, I much prefer taking them to a market with 100 buyers instead of just one. Similarly, if I'm buying, I prefer a market where there are lots of people selling. This simple truth creates a virtuous circle for eBay – the more people who use it, the more valuable it becomes to each of its users and the harder it becomes for a competitor to challenge it. eBay reinforces this virtuous circle by allowing buyers to review sellers to provide the element of trust that can be missing when sales are not conducted face-to-face.

As it has grown exponentially, first in the USA and then globally through a combination of both organic expansion and acquisition, eBay has successfully profited from redefining several key markets. Classified ads in newspapers, car boot sales, the antique business and even the leading auction houses have all been affected. The combined elements of the size of addressable market, transparency of costs, scalability of the technology and attractiveness of the on-line community have together positioned eBay in a largely unassailable position. In many ways eBay has capitalized on the logic of low-cost transactions to build an ideal business model. With very low working capital, zero distribution (as buyers and sellers arrange this themselves), zero product liability and very small marginal cost to grow the business as each new customer requires a small amount of server space and customer service, it is in many eyes the perfect e-commerce business. With a market capitalization even in late 2001 of $15.3 billion and a P/E ratio of 175, it is a very healthy business.

Going forward, eBay has to sustain its growth to maintain its share price, as the true test of a company's innovative capacity is whether it can keep inventing beyond its first idea. For eBay, there are three strands to that strategy; expanding into new territories, new markets and new products. Fortune has smiled upon eBay in the pursuit of its first goal. The dot.com crash has enabled it to move quickly into new countries by buying up local companies that had copied its business model but were subsequently forced to sell at fire-sale prices. The company is also seeking to move away from its original consumer-to-consumer model by leveraging its technology to provide virtual storefronts for SMEs. In addition, its purchase of Half.com also added fixed-price trading to the offering. Perhaps most difficult of all, the company has now also entered the second-hand car market through its partnership with Auto Trader, a used car dealership. In 2001 this alone generated sales of over $1 billion. Time will tell how successful these business extensions will be, but eBay stands as a great example of a company that was the first to understand how new technology could meet an old but unidentified human need to redefine a market.

Egg – beating the competition

Egg is one of several UK-based Internet banks, but it is different to the rest. It has led the pack both in terms of the products and services that it has offered its customers and in the way that it has uniquely used these customers to enable it to create and provide value, thereby changing the market. What started out as a foray into retail banking for a large insurance group was, from its launch, intended to upturn the whole investment market, break down industry barriers and provide greater transparency for customers. As it moved towards break-even on schedule in late 2001, despite the Internet downturn, Egg had successfully navigated the consumer, technology and investor journeys to a point where, with imitators in its wake, it could realize its intent.

When it was launched in 1998 by the Prudential, a global life and health insurance company, the only competition to Egg came from the existing high street banks. By and large the big four banks' lack of innovation had been responsible for the low interest shown by UK consumers in the financial services sector. With the exception of First Direct, a 24-hour telephone bank within the larger HSBC organization, which had pioneered improved customer service and lower banking fees over a number of years, none of Barclays, NatWest and Lloyds were setting the world on fire – why should they? After all, they were banks. With its strange name and unique claim to tailor its range of products to suit the specific needs of each individual customer, Egg was a new venture over which many had doubts. The Internet frenzy was clearly an opportunity but, with leaders such as Amazon still making ever-greater losses, the conservative financial community was dubious of the new arrival's long-term prospects.

Attitudes quickly changed, though. The plan from the start had been to use high-interest savings and then low-interest credit cards to build up a significant customer base that Egg and the Prudential could then leverage within and across the financial services sector. The initial aim was therefore to use a simple telephone and Internet savings account offering top rate of interest to ideally build up about 500 000 customers over its first twelve months, and then to introduce an Internet-only credit card. However, without even using the advertising it had scheduled, Egg took off like a rocket. With one month it had its 500 000 customers, and moreover, the deposits were enormous. The average amount on deposit in savings accounts across the UK in 1998 was £3000. Egg's customers invested an average of £15 000! Ten weeks after launch Egg had £1bn on deposit, and within seven months the company found itself hitting its five-year target of over £5 billion in cash reserves. This was unprecedented in the history of UK financial services. Although there were obvious operational problems associated with training call centre staff and accelerating the roll out of technology to cope with the potentially overwhelming demand, it was clear that Egg had started some-thing. As a consequence, other Internet banks were set up, all with similarly unusual names. The Cooperative Bank launched smile.co.uk, the Abbey National started Cahoot, and the Halifax joined in with IF. Moreover, the main banks, especially Barclays, LloydsTSB and, via FirstDirect, HSBC, all accelerated their move on-line. Attracted by the prospect of the lower costs of Internet banking, Barclays and NatWest also set off down a retail branch closure programme that, after protest from its more traditional customer base, later had to be reversed.

With an innovative TV advertising programme including a subverted use of celebrity endorsement to establish the brand and subsequent commercials that were built around the company not recognizing stereotypes, all backed up by a strong offer, Egg quickly established the idea that its products could be configured to meet each individual's needs. The launch of the Egg Card in October 1999 as the first true credit card designed for the Internet provided market-leading rates, 0 per cent six-month balance transfers and cash-back on purchases, something that established players such as Barclaycard could not compete with. Within twelve months Egg had over a million credit card customers with an average balance of £1750 – twice the national average! In addition, as it introduced loans where the rate and duration were flexible to meet individual circumstances and mortgages that offered a variety of rates as well as flexible payment options, Egg soon became a major player in the UK. It next added insurance to its portfolio, and created Egg Shop to increase website traffic and enable customers to transact with a number of on-line retailers, where purchases were guaranteed through the Egg Card. More-over, with an innovative link up with Boots, the retail chemists, the company provided a joint credit card/loyalty card branded as a Boots product but 'powered by Egg' and targeted at Boots 12 million existing loyalty-card holding customers. Within two years of its launch, the company had 27 per cent of on-line credit card accounts and 88 per cent brand awareness, and egg.com was the third most visited e-commerce site in Europe. A partial flotation as Egg plc in June 2000 was heavily oversubscribed, raising an extra £150 million, but with the Prudential still holding 79 per cent of the equity.

With a competitive portfolio of products and a large and surprisingly loyal customer base, even when rates were dropped Egg was in a strong market position – although owing to the competitiveness of its products it was losing money. However, this was expected and all part of the strategy. The next move would begin to reverse losses but at the same time continue to deliver value to its customers. Whereas savings accounts, credit cards, loans and even insurance were conventional and easily understood, the increasingly sophisticated area of investments was considered to be more complex for the consumer and had therefore commanded high margins for providers and brokers alike. With transparency and mutual benefit as two of its core brand values, Egg wanted to break this mystique and change the market. Using its customer base of 1 million largely high-income, and hence very attractive, individuals as a collective prospective investor, Egg negotiated a wide range of extremely competitive rates with investment fund providers. Whereas traditional fees for individuals seeking to make stock market or unit trust investments had been around 5 per cent, Egg was able to reduce these to as low as 1 per cent. Passing on a sufficient share of the savings to its customers to make investment through Egg more competitive and easier than any alternative route, but at the same time retaining a percentage of commission, the company was able to use this as a means of generating much-desired revenue for its shareholders.

The March 2000 launch of the Egg Investment Fund Supermarket, where customers could choose and easily manage a wide range of unit trusts and ISAs from a growing number of fund managers, was a major breakthrough. Representing over 30 per cent of the UK's collective investment market, the twelve lead fund managers signed up to Egg together managed over £55 billion. The Egg Investment Fund Supermarket fundamentally changed a whole sector of the financial services industry, as the transparency and lower costs became apparent to all. Individual investors no longer needed to pay high commissions, and other intermediaries such as AMP's rival ample.com offering were quickly established. Although Egg's success has initiated imitation, with its first-mover advantage, high brand awareness and continuous stream of innovation, it is unlikely to be overtaken by any emulator. By the end of 2001, with 25 million people on-line within the UK, Egg had established itself as both a market leader and a market breaker. With 1.8 million customers it had, against some analysts' expectations, broken even and, with an expansion into the German, French and Italian markets in partnership with Microsoft, was well on the way to being a dominant player across Europe.

Google – search me

A final example of successful market-breaking innovation is the search engine Google. Launched in 1998 by Sergey Brin and Larry Page, two Stanford students, Google quickly developed a cult reputation as the fastest and most accurate search engine in cyberspace. Although there were hundreds of existing search engines already in operation, Google was able to use its reliability and accuracy to devastating effect on its rivals. By April 2001 it had pushed aside earlier and more heavily marketed competitors such as Ask Jeeves, Alta Vista and Infoseek to become the most popular search engine in the USA, with an index of 1.3 billion entries compiled by the company's 10 000 computers picking 1000 pages a second. Named after the googol, the mathematical term for the number one followed by 100 zeros, and including 50 PhDs in its 220 staff, whereas other search engines use the principle that relevance is based on repetition, Google measures a page's pertinence according to whether other sites, especially popular ones like Amazon, have already linked to it. Also, unlike the early entrants into this arena, Google has not relied solely on revenue from advertising but has also licensed its proprietary know-how to other websites, portals and WAP providers, including Netscape, Yahoo in the USA, and Vodafone and Virgin in the UK. Typically charging $1 million licence fees per company, revenues reached $50 million in 2002, giving the company a potential value at IPO of up to $250 million in the height of a recession.

Summary

Dyson, Smint, eBay, Egg and Google are all market breakers, using innovation to refine fundamentally the sectors within which they provide their products and services, and changing customer attitudes and expectations as they do so. They are not unique, but they are all highly visible. Other, often smaller, companies are attempting to achieve equally dramatic effects across industry, some in similar mature markets and some in faster, more dynamic and continually developing sectors. No matter where, as a clear strategy for creating and exploiting value, breaking an existing marketplace through redefinition of the current proposition is evidently bearing fruit, and is even providing similar benefits to those traditionally gained from the creation of totally new markets.

8

Product personalization

As mass customization enabled the first provisioning of individual products and services on a large scale, more recent advances of product configuration have been driven by allowing even greater tailoring to user needs. Moving on from mass customization, several organizations are now taking advantage of the ability to offer large-scale post-purchase personalization of products and services. Whereas the type of mass customization exemplified by Dell during the 1990s enabled customers to specify the product or service that they would receive from the factory, shop or garage, the most recent advances in allowing individual tailoring of products have been focused on post-acquisition – after the purchase has been completed and the product delivered or service activated. No longer is customization restricted to what happens before the product reaches the customer or a service is activated. Today the prospect of unique products and services configurable by, and centred on, the user is finally becoming a reality.

Levis has taken mass customization of jeans forward with its 'Original Spin' products providing the ability to have 'made to measure' products cut to your body-scanned size in store, sewn and shipped direct to the home within two weeks. Similarly, Nike has gone a further step forward with its customized clothing and accessories under the 'choose it: build it: buy it' proposition. Using its e-commerce sales channel, Nike.com, you can now not only select colour, size and fit, but also have your name sewn in or printed onto trainers, shirts and eyewear. These both take the approaches of Dell etc. into the clothes industry, thus recreating a level of bespoke tailoring on a mass scale. Volvo also launched its latest model in the USA exclusively on the Internet, offering customers up to 1 million variations according to their colour choices, interior preferences, engine and extra feature requirements. In addition, as with Egg's loans and mortgages, from a service perspective companies are using customization to offer clients apparently individual products. Just as car insurance is influenced by personal details and track record, BUPA, a UK medical insurance group, is providing similarly 'tailored' health insurance and, somewhat more controversially, a number of other health companies are already using genetic information to group customers into different risk categories and hence offer individualized differential rates. As more and more applications are similarly exploited, mass customization of products and services pre-delivery continues to develop and evolve. However, none of these advances help post-delivery.

Personalization of a product or service is now coming to the fore in a number of sectors, and is allowing the user to determine the configuration, appearance, functionality and performance of the products themselves. Driven first in the software arena, personalization of interfaces has become commonplace. Barclays, a leading UK bank, allows its on-line customers to personalize their experience, from naming accounts through to determining which transactions appear on the screen and in what order, and detailing what particular aspects of the available data they wish to be presented with. As well as customized news feeds, the *Financial Times* and *Wall Street Journal* both allow users of their on-line versions to configure their own pages of stock portfolios in a similar way to those provided by Self-trade, Schwab, Sharepeople and Ameritrade. MySAP, myCNN and myMSN likewise allow companies and individuals to customize their favourite web pages to provide exactly the information they want in the format, layout and detail they each prefer. Equally Amazon, eBay, Starwood and many other organizations make extensive use of cookies to enable returning customers to be presented with personalized pages full of recommendations, profiles, order histories and the like.

While these software-enabled and mostly Internet-based solutions are providing customers with ever-increasing personalization in the virtual world, in the real world true personalization is only now just entering the mainstream in a couple of key lead arenas. Without doubt one of the greatest drivers on product and service provision in the first decade of the twenty-first century, product personalization is first being seen and experienced in the more real world areas of mobile phones and digital television.

Nokia phones – any colour, even black

Nokia, the Finnish company that exploited the opportunities presented by the advent of mobile telecommunications to turn itself from a tyre manufacturer to the world's leading mobile phone producer, has been the figurehead of product personalization in the first years of the twenty-first century. One of the pioneers of the GSM technology that came to dominate first- and second-generation mobile networks in all but the USA, Nokia has continuously led the way in innovating in both technology and design. Unlike its great rival and sometimes partner, Ericsson, which in 2000 was forced to recognize its inferior capabilities for phone product design and production and form a joint venture with Sony, the more consumer-centric Japanese electronics company, Nokia has managed to retain prime position in the handset market despite continued and aggressive competition from the likes of Motorola, Philips, Panasonic, Samsung and Siemens. Although starting with no track record in consumer products, Nokia has successfully complemented the introduction of smaller handsets, longer battery life, larger phonebooks, infrared communication and clearer reception with an ever-evolving redefinition of mobile device design. Although occasionally temporarily leapfrogged by NEC, Siemens, Motorola and even Ericsson, as Sony did over a decade before with the Walkman, Nokia has continuously maintained the leading position in ergonomics, styling and user-interface design. Alongside the introduction of the leading 9000 and 9110 communicators providing combined PDA and phone functionality for mobile Internet access, Nokia launched the widely praised chrome 8810 in 1998, which was exhibited in the Museum of Modern Art in New York, and, in December 1999, the 7110 WAP phone. These raised Nokia to design icon status in some arenas. It is, however, with its core 3000 and 6000 series phones that the company has brought product personalization into the mainstream.

For so long considered to be a technology-led product purchase, mobile phones had during the 1990s significantly reduced in product size, increased in performance and improved in ergonomics and industrial design. However, throughout that period customers got what they bought – the product came in a standard form with the only personalization options being the selection of one of six preloaded ring-tones. The Nokia phones introduced in late 2000 and 2001 have, by contrast, driven product personalization into the mass market – even entry-level handsets such as the 3310, 6250 and the 2002 released 8310 now allow owners to reconfigure multiple aspects of the product to suit their individual preferences:

- Over 15 000 different Nokia ring-tones, from Beethoven to Britney Spears, can be downloaded through multiple providers and intermediaries; alternatively you can compose your own
- Over 20 000 different colour snap-on covers are available in multiple outlets from newsagents to nightclubs across the world; if none of these suits your taste, then other firms, such as Photofone, will create one-off fascias from photographs or any graphical design you like
- Over 10 000 different graphical display images are available for downloading onto the phone; again, if none are satisfactory, users can also create their own individual images
- In addition, such features as voice dialling are allowing even the core call connection itself to become personalized to the user's own voice and word preferences.

Coupled with 500-space phonebooks, the ability to link specific ring tones to separate callers, predictive text input and the ability to participate in multiplayer networked games, even in advance of the more advanced GPRS and 3G networks, Nokia handsets operating on GSM and CDMA networks have enabled millions of their users to take a standardized product and configure its visual, audio and aural interfaces to their own individual requirements – a level of personalization that raises expectations not only in the mobile device sector but also across the whole consumer goods arena. As such, in this area alone product personalization is clearly already a key focus.

Interactive digital television – suits you

Although the identified Internet sites have already allowed a good level of personalization of content selection and presentation, and, with their handsets, Nokia has clearly made significant headway in the physical as well as the software domains, at the time of writing, the arena within which product personalization is making most progress and providing the highest level of individual dedicated tailoring is that of interactive digital television. Originally launched in the UK in 1998, digital television is being rolled out across Europe and is rapidly becoming a mass-market medium. Already reaching over a third of the UK population by the end of 2001, overall penetration across Europe as a whole is predicted to move from 18 per cent in 2002 to 51 per cent by 2005 (Figure 8.1). In addition, the planned switch-off of analogue television services between 2010 and 2015 will eventually convert all of Europe to digital television. The same is set to happen across the Americas, the Middle East and large parts of

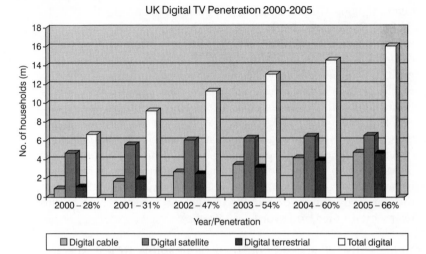

Figure 8.1 UK digital TV penetration 2000–2005 (source: Datamonitor/Mason Communications).

Asia, albeit on different, mostly slower, timescales. Digital television ownership is forecast to match Internet-PC ownership by 2005 and, with the analogue switch-off, looks set to overtake it thereafter.

Digital television is more than merely a channel for broadcasting pictures and sounds. It is a unique product and services delivery channel that offers operators the ability simultaneously to send and receive multiple signals to and from individual customers, and also enables these customers to select and individually configure a huge range of TV, audio, shopping, banking, gaming, communication and information services. For the consumer, digital TV offers more than a combination of the Internet and TV; through the use of a number of key technologies, viewers (or more correctly users) can not only access all the traditional TV programming but also determine their own personal schedule, pulling programming from over 100 different channels. They can also time-shift any programme, use e-mail, send images, use instant messaging and group chat, as well as browse the web, pay bills, shop, gamble and even run applications such as word processors and financial spreadsheets.

Digital broadcasting

With traditional analogue TV, material was captured, stored on tape cassettes and, when scheduled to be aired, distributed over satellite, cable or terrestrial networks to the consumer, who received and simultaneously viewed it, usually via the same unit – a television. Although digital broadcasting has the same core stages, there are three key benefits gained from the fact that the material is in a digital format. These are:

1 Compression – the ability to send more information through the same distribution channel
2 Manipulation – the ability to change, edit, recreate and modify the information
3 Quality improvement – there is no erosion of performance, so the thousandth copy is just as good as the first.

Together these represent a significant improvement over the analogue system. However, by itself, digital broadcasting is not a fundamental shift in the paradigm. That shift is provided by the exploitation of digital broadcasting through interactive digital television.

Digital television

Whereas digital broadcasting is the digital transfer and manipulation of sounds and pictures, digital television is all about using key technologies to engage the audience interactively as individuals, in a manner that, according to providers, 'enriches the user experience'. The days of passive audiences being fed fixed diets of sound-and-picture programming are over as digital television evolves from the total passivity of traditional television to absolute interaction. To achieve this, it relies on three key elements:

1 An *applications programming interface* that allows the creation and presentation of content apart from traditional pictures and sound
2 A *conditional access system* that allows limitations to be placed on the content – for example, who can access it or when it can be accessed
3 A *set-top box,* an electronic terminal that receives and decodes the digital signals, then presents the information on a TV screen.

The applications programming interface is multimedia in the fullest sense. It caters for the delivery of pictures, sound, text and graphics. Not only this; it also allows for each of those elements to be controlled by a computer programme or application. This controllability is significant, and opens up immense possibilities regarding what can be done. The simplest change is the inclusion of extra material or information that can be optionally viewed. This includes still pictures, short film clips, pages of textual information, animations, charts, and audio clips. At the press of a button, during or after a programme, viewers can select and view the extra content at their leisure. This can be extra reference material for educational programmes, or humorous out-takes from an entertainment show. The BBC's award winning *Walking with Beasts* digital broadcasts in 2001 allowed viewers to access an additional six hours of footage. More advanced uses include interaction where viewers can, for example, take part in a quiz show, selecting answers with the remote control, or vote to influence the story line of a drama or provide immediate feedback on a current affairs programme. Channel 4's *Big Brother* had over 4 million people interactively voting for house evictions, and over 700 000 UK residents voted for their favourite act during the 2001 MTV awards.

The conditional access system is a tool-kit for securing content. It allows broadcasters to set limits on accessing the content, including who can access it, when, where, for how long, and how often. It can control access to content based on several criteria, including channel, individual programme, geographical region and subscriber profile. More significantly for the user, it can also put other limits on the content, such as the right to view, the right to skip adverts, the right to record, and how long after transmission a recording can be used.

Set-top boxes are not new to television, for they were required for analogue television delivered via cable and satellite. Neither has their fundamental purpose changed. However, in digital television they have also taken on a new role of running applications, or computer programmes, either individually or in parallel. Manufacturers have developed decoder chips that can handle three channels simultaneously to allow, for example, the user to view one programme while recording two others at the same time. When combined with a programming interface, a TV and a remote control or keyboard, set-top boxes, with their versatility as computing devices, thus provide all the components of a fully interactive multimedia terminal in the home. Set-top boxes are evolving from devices that decode television signals to complete multimedia terminals. One of the most fundamental developments here has been the addition of a hard drive that has two immediate effects – the persistent local storage of information, and a several-thousand-fold increase in storage capacity. This has enabled them to become personal video recorders. Competing with the Gemstar TV guide, from the same company that invented Videoplus VCR technology, products such as TiVo and ReplayTV are all revolutionizing viewing habits, mainly due to their sophisticated automatic programme selection and record-ing capabilities. Launching their first product in 1999, TiVo, based in San José, California, has been the primary mover in this space. Using strategic alliances with Sony, Philips, DirecTV and AOL, TiVo digital video recorders are providing early, dedicated content to users, enabling them to watch 'what they want, when they want'.

Electronic programme guide

Whilst these three elements are the key enablers for digital television, the killer application is the electronic programme guide, or EPG. Digital television signals include information about both content that is being broadcast and content that will be broadcast in the future. This information is used to fill the EPG, which offers an on-screen listing of all the programmes available across all the available channels for a week ahead. It contains the standard programme titles, start and finish times, and also information about each programme such as the type, key actors, directors, a synopsis, and other related information. Unlike Teletext listings, the EPG is not limited to a single presentation of the information. It can be used to show content by genre or by time of broadcast, irrespective of channel. Thus, for instance, it allows a user to select only sports programming, or to pick out all *Star Trek*, *ER* and *Friends* episodes across all channels. It is like having the world's most reliable flatmate – you can stagger home and find the pick of a night's primetime viewing waiting for you (Vine, 2001). It is and will continue to be the most used application on the set-top box, and, as such, offers rich commer-cial opportunities for advertising and other promotions. Because the programme listings are not restricted by channel or time, it is having a fundamental effect on the idea of channels, channel branding and channel loyalty. It is also challenging operators and content generators to come up with new ways of engaging and retaining audiences.

TV access

Equipped with all this technology, digital TV is providing a whole range of services that can be extensively personalized. The access to hundreds of channels of DVD-quality TV programmes is the major pull, but the ability to store large amounts of data locally has considerable implications for the delivery and utilization of content. Time-shifting and recording material for viewing at a later time have been the most immediate uses, but when combined with the electronic programme guide, as mentioned earlier, products such as TiVo can also record material automatically, without intervention from the viewer. If allowed by the operator, adverts can be skipped or concentrated into longer segments, thus permitting users to configure movie watching into the form they prefer. The consumer becomes the TV scheduler. Peak-time programming becomes an outdated concept as people choose what they want to see, when they want to see it and in what order. Moreover, coupled with the ability to access the full range of content that is being transmitted there is also the opportunity to retrieve information and movies on demand. Operators can download several movies overnight and offer them on an on-demand basis. Alternatively, a viewer can order a specific movie for watching a few days in advance. Such schemes are allowing operators from BSkyB down to offer specific, popular movies on demand, and a large library of movies on 'near-demand'.

Furthermore, as interactive services and content can be individualized to the viewer, operators are also configuring dedicated programming schedules for their customers. Digital television allows for significant, detailed profiling of viewer habits and behaviours – so much so that a highly sophisticated model can be built up of what appeals to individual viewers and what doesn't. TiVo already learns what you like to watch. Clearly valuable to advertisers, this also allows any provider to track one individual's viewing and create a unique TV channel comprising of only the specific programming that the profile suggests. As an alternative to creating their own schedule using the EPG, the capability is also there for thousands of people to automatically have their own individually tailored and fully personalized TV channel populated with only the content they desire, or their profile determines.

Small computer programs, or applets, are also being transmitted to the viewers' homes and run on the set-top box much as any computer program would. While identical applets can be delivered to multiple set-top boxes, the data they use can also be individualized to each home. It is this use of a common applet with individual data that makes interactive TV so efficient for the operator, yet also so appealing to the end user. For example, in a quiz game, where the user attempts to answer questions on a variety of topics, it is relatively easy for the operator to download thousands of questions from a huge range of topics in a very short time. Users can select which topics they would like to attempt, thus giving the impression of interactivity, while not requiring any information to be sent back to the broadcaster. This is in operation with *Mastermind* on the Discovery channel, and *Who wants to be a Millionaire?* on ITV2 in the UK, both of which allow interactive users to 'compete with contestants'.

Perhaps the simplest innovation in digital TV is, however, the use of meta-data, the extra text-based information transmitted alongside programmes, and similar to Teletext. This information can be presented on screen, in a variety of font styles, colours, positions and effects. Users can, for example, select the language for subtitled films, or, during a premier league match, request statistics on teams or individual players, such as the number of goals scored this season in comparison to the last. This is what enables the BBC to supply the wealth of accompanying information for its *Walking with Beasts* programmes as well as the option for alternative narrators. Digital TV is providing consumers with unique viewing, unprecedented in its flexibility and personalization. Both theoretically and practically, each viewer has a different experience in terms of schedule and content – a truly individualized service.

Internet access

Over and above TV programmes, the increasingly common additional service that is being provided to customers via digital TV is access to the Internet. However, while the interactive experience with digital television is in many ways similar to that of PC-based interaction, it is not the same. A television can display just over half the detail that a monitor can, so Internet content that has not been designed to take account of a television's limitations has to be reformatted. In addition, the means, speed and limitations of navigation vary and, more significantly, the environment within which it is used differs: PC-based Internet browsing is based on close proximity, proactive, largely mouse-driven interaction, whereas, given the traditionally more passive, distant entertainment role of the TV, digital TV Internet services have to fulfil different requirements. Moreover, due to the technical implications of offering full Internet access to all sites, operators are presently focused more on providing a 'walled-garden' selection of predetermined but still user configured and selected sites. This all means that digital TV Internet services operate at a reduced level compared to traditional PC versions. Although penetration will ultimately be higher, for a good while, functionality and choice will be lower than available through PC access. Providers are therefore also looking for other ways to entice customers.

Personal communications

Digital TV brings together two new concepts for television – two-way communications and point-to-point communications – major changes for what was once considered the ultimate one-way broadcast medium. E-mail and messaging were both key services contributing to the success of the Internet and, in a world where content is considered king, some commentators consider them as key enablers for digital television. However, whilst e-mail is already available and has significant potential, it is messaging that many feel will be the SMS of the digital TV world.

Whereas e-mail, in the form of text-based messages, has been available via TV for a couple of years, the ability to use it to send attachments from simple text files and spreadsheet documents through to pictures and sounds, computer programs and movies, is only just emerging. Although a huge opportunity in terms of customer engagement, this does, however, present a number of significant technical and commercial challenges for operators, and hence they are backing the growth of messaging services similar to those that originated in computer systems of the 1960s. Messaging, or 'chat' as it is sometimes known, is where people congregate in a virtual world, and type messages to each other – AOL Instant Messenger and MSN Messenger are the two main leaders for PC-based access. The communication is entirely text-based, and there are two main types of chat; group chat and person-to-person chat. Messaging distinguishes itself from e-mail by its immediacy and content type. It is conducted much like a lively conversation, with short statements or comments from one party followed by a reply from the other party. Messaging is now directly changing television-viewing behaviour, as friends can chat to each other while watching *Will and Grace*, *Sex in the City* or *The West Wing*, or, by using a chat room, members can discuss a current programme or related issue. Because of its simplicity, immediacy, ease of access and lack of requirement for significant data storage, messaging is therefore the primary means of personalized communication via digital TV.

Personalized advertising

The other major arena for personalization is that of advertising. Whereas analogue television advertising is focused on getting a message across and building brand awareness, new capabilities are available on digital television, including measuring advertising effectiveness, viewer profiling, giving extra information on request to viewers, arranging for the viewer to be contacted about the product, allowing the viewer to purchase the product, and even creating personalized adverts. These together arguably create a win–win–win situation – for the consumer, for the advertising agency and for the advertiser. The advertising agency wins by being able to target the campaign more specifically; the advertiser wins by being able to identify who was interested in or purchased their products, and in what circumstances; and the consumer wins by only receiving adverts that are of specific interest.

One of the most basic measures that digital TV can provide is whether or not an advert was watched. Instead of having to rely on questionnaires with statistical samplings of the population, advertisers can identify exactly how many household TVs displayed a particular advert. Digital TV viewing habits can be combined with other measures, including age and sex profiles, lifestyles, and number of dependents, geographic location and profession. The success of an advertisement can therefore also be considered in context of the content, and viewing habits can be monitored and recorded, including the way users switch channels during the adverts.

Digital television also enables the purchase itself, something that is both arguably compelling for the viewer, and beneficial for the advertiser. What makes it even more convenient is that there is no need in most cases to enter credit card details, billing addresses or delivery addresses, as the operator has all of this information already. For consumers without credit cards, the alternative is to have the goods added to the television subscription.

What a viewer watches not only depends on which channel is on, but can also be influenced on individual profile, or indeed a range of other considerations. This applies equally to advertising and to regular content. There is therefore the capability for full individualized tailoring of advertising configured to suit buying behaviour or even personal preferences. One option is to offer different advertisements for the same product. This choice of advert is based on the viewer's profile and allows much more finely focused advertising, with a commensurate rise in effectiveness. Advertisers offer adverts for entirely different products simultaneously. This is especially useful for companies such as Unilever and Proctor & Gamble, which have a variety of products aimed at different markets. The advert shown in each home is for a product that matches the profile for that individual household. For example, the drinks company Diageo can simultaneously promote a Smirnoff Ice to a flat of young adults, and Guinness to a more mature household.

Together with the additional increase in TV-based banking, commerce, learning and on-line and off-line gaming, these provide a truly groundbreaking prospect for service personalization. Each can be considered by itself to be a major advance, but collectively the ability to configure the core TV content and scheduling as well as to individualize advertising, commerce, gaming and learning are all significant evolutionary developments in innovative product development.

Where next?

Many organizations across the spectrum of products and services are already working on ever more imaginative ways of delivering the option for post-delivery personalization. These range from conformable mice and pens that mould themselves to the user's hand like clay, and self-regulating car dashboard lights that respond to the driver's retinas, through to more IT-enabled home and financial services that learn user preferences and adapt configuration and performance to suit. Wherever they may exist, such opportunities for product personalization are being seen as differentiators for users in their purchasing decisions, and, through experience and interconnectivity, they are providing ever more options for the provision of additional products and services based on emerging user preferences and attitudes.

Further reading

Reuters (2001). *Interactive Television in Europe: Beyond Digital Broadcasting*. Reuters.

9

Values recognition

As companies are becoming ever more capable of providing exactly the right new product or service for their customers' expressed desires, the big question is, how can you find out what is it that they actually want? It is clearly apparent that, through the use of the sophisticated technologies now available, we can today really at last begin to configure products that specifically match user requirements, but how can we accurately identify these? With the wealth of product choice now available to consumers, whether retail or business based, with the vast array of over-lapping brand propositions being offered and with the exponentially increasing variety of enabling technologies accessible by all, how can firms find out what it is that will prompt a shopper to become a customer? How can companies identify the unique user needs so that they can then create or configure the product to meet them? The answer is that several leading firms are now moving beyond traditional techniques to address attitudes and not demographics. User-centred design has prompted the development of user-preference based research and, through the use of new approaches from the worlds of psychology and behavioural science, targeting customers' underlying attitudes, values and even beliefs is now being recognized as a key focus for increased innovation.

Customer segmentation

In several sectors, many companies are still using very traditional means of identifying and classifying user needs. Perhaps the most recognized approach has been the use of market segmentation to group actual or potential customers into defined categories. Some of the traditional banks are probably some of the least developed here, as many still use gross income as a delineation of service provision. Customers earning under £30 000 will get a standard offering whilst those above this threshold will be offered something extra – maybe a personal banker, more colourful cheques or even lower interest loans. Equally, credit card providers such as MBNA and American Express will use the pure financial measures of salary and spending to differentiate between who should and who should not be offered gold, platinum or even black status, credit limits, rates and perks.

Similarly, many telecommunications companies are focused only on knowing how much time customers spend on the phone and when during a 24-hour cycle this occurs. The key metric of average revenue per user that is used by analysts in the industry to rate different providers' financial performance is also used by operators to evaluate and categorize customers. In a world where revenue has been linked to peak and off-peak minutes, this type of classification of user needs has been sufficient; however, as offerings become more complex, it becomes redundant. As mobile companies such as Vodafone and Sprint have been increasingly providing monthly packages including 'free minutes' within service provision, they are seeing customers as one of up to four different types of user and, as fixed network providers are becoming more data- than voice-focused and wish to charge accordingly, they too are having to segment their customer base in a more sophisticated manner.

In retail sectors, market segmentation of customers, and hence their likely purchases centred on stereotypical needs, can run to over ten different groupings including both age- and wealth-based classifications. Students are differentiated in their buying habits, and hence requirements, from school leavers who are living with parents, and flat-renting working couples are classified differently from first-time buyers or new parents. Socio-economic as well as demographic postcode-based profiling are used to support and define the segments for sectors ranging from car dealerships through to restaurant chains, in determining both sites and menus. For the big supermarkets, where store location, catchment areas, checkout throughput and revenue per square foot are all key drivers of performance and margins, customer segmentation is taken to a higher level, with up to forty different types of classification. Tesco, the UK-based supermarket, uses its loyalty card to identify and record the exact customer purchases and patterns, and hence opportunities for additional cross-selling either through discount promotions or direct mail campaigns. In many ways this takes the approach to its extreme and enables mass segmentation of the company's customer base down to the segment of one.

Airlines are similarly becoming ever more sophisticated in the way in which they use customer information, and with frequent flyer cards. The blue, silver and gold levels of membership used by British Airways are linked to both the frequency and the type of travel that customers undertake. Long distance is clearly more rewarding than short haul, but only if you have the right type of ticket. Unlike other airlines, such as Virgin Atlantic and United Airlines, for whom distance and class are the only parameters for reward, BA is more subtle: A BA economy class trip from London to Paris can earn customers more points than an economy trip to New York. The difference is in the price paid. This therefore applies a certain pressure, particularly on corporate travellers, in the choice of rates. In addition, since all flights are tracked, destinations are likewise recorded, and through even basic use of data-mining techniques, patterns can be identified. These enable 'two for the price of one', 'full fare upgrade' and 'inclusive hotel stay' offers to be specifically targeted to individual customers for the appropriate type of, as well as actual, destination at the right time of year. By tracking the past behaviour of each customer BA, Tesco and their imitators are able to segment needs at an individual level, configure incentives, mass-customize offerings and simultaneously extract the highest value from them.

Customer involvement

Such IT-enabled sophistication has been shown to be all well and good for service-based firms, where repeat business from customers is the ideal, but it is less applicable to new product innovation or the creation of new services of which customers have no previous experience. Whereas basic socio-economic and demographic profiling can provide a stereotype to be used for the development of new products and services, companies now have to get far closer to the customer. With no previous customer history on which to base decisions, more detailed information on the individual is required. At one level this can be provided by market research firms, who can build detailed profiles through the use of more and more sophisticated data-mining of multiple information sources ranging from electoral roles and driving licence records to customer profiles from energy suppliers, and membership lists from organizations as varied as the AA, American Express, Lands End and *The Economist*. While such approaches can and do provide many firms with detailed breakdown of age, income, buying patterns and user preferences, they do not reveal too much about the underpinning values that drive personal attitudes – which in turn influence purchase decisions.

One way of getting closer to understanding the customer that has been in use for some time is the involvement of lead customers or a selection of target users in the development programmes themselves. As part of wider 'voice of the customer' initiatives, organizations as diverse as Ford, Proctor & Gamble, Shell, Citibank and Coca Cola have been using a wealth of techniques to bring customers into their varied development programmes in order originally to express preferences between alternative product concepts prior to production, and more recently to help define key future product requirements. Hall tests, focus groups, workshops, interviews and even observational analysis have all been used across multiple sectors in a bid to try to either identify key needs that can be met or, more commonly, to determine which products or features (such as colour, size, form and texture) are most liked by potential buyers. Especially towards the end of a project, as final decisions are being made, companies are commonly using beta-test environments to soft-launch their new ideas, try out different configurations with customers, and determine which work best:

- Egg's investment supermarket concept brought together forty-plus providers to enable their customers to pick and choose where to invest their money within an overall portfolio. The new innovation was a combination of individual management and reduced fees from collective purchasing. Faced with a major launch of a new product into a highly competitive environment, the company chose first to run a controlled pilot with 100 sample customers for a month, fully simulating investment and access to funds. Trying out alternative user interfaces, sales support and IT systems together with lead consumer validation, this exercise provided the organization with the opportunity to select the most appealing interface combinations as well as providing a test environment within which they could validate operating processes, debug their software and check customer care procedures so that the subsequent hard launch to an eager yet critical customer base was an unqualified success.
- Similarly, Virgin Atlantic was faced with a key decision for its new Upper Class seating. Having gradually acquired many new customers from British Airways, United and American Airlines due to superior service and more competitive pricing, the company planned to introduce a major innovation into their

fleet but wanted to check the impact before launch. Virgin had a highly innovative radical design of seat that was scheduled for integration across its fleet, but, before going ahead with roll out, it first conducted a month of controlled tests in a simulator. Carefully selected customers spent a night 'flying to New York' in the new seat or an alternative, less radical design, and provided comments throughout the 'flight'. The results of this piloting gave Virgin valuable feedback on customer likes and dislikes, the ability to modify the design where necessary, and the confidence to go for a full launch across the fleet. Virgin launched the radical design, winning industry praise, design awards and even more customer recognition for innovation.

Such customer involvement is now being taken an extra step forward through direct involvement in ongoing live development activities from the beginning. In the business-to-business environment, lead customers are increasingly being used as the basis for new products and services. From telecommunications to chemicals, firms are creating specific new offerings around the needs of a single user to define a new product it can then sell on to similar customers. By building a bespoke product around the dedicated needs of a Dell, GM or Merck lead customer, firms such as AT&T, Qwest, DuPont and Bayer can create a sector-based innovation that can then be resold onto HP, IBM, Ford, Honda, Pfizer or GSK. In the consumer domain where one individual's needs are potentially too narrow for such dedicated product configuration, firms are now involving customers more widely in the definition of all aspects of the product and service that they provide. As highlighted earlier, eBay and MSN are both highly active in this.

Customer behaviour

What these ways of working are beginning to achieve is a better understanding of the unarticulated need. Whereas, if asked directly as part of a research study or even on the street, what they would like a new solution that is being developed to be like, potential customers, both business and retail, will undoubtedly give such answers as:

- Low cost
- Easy to use
- Reliable
- High performance
- Competitive.

These are all valid, but are also all equally meaningless. They could be applied to anything from a car or a DVD player through to a photocopier or a bank account. As with the use of approaches such as QFD a decade ago, they tell you the obvious or the incremental. People will want something that is slightly better than what they are used to, but rarely can they articulate a significant innovation. Quite naturally, people are relative in their expressed opinions and therefore will inevitably provide relative comments. For real innovation to be possible, firms want a far greater insight into customer preferences. They want to be able to get under the skin and dig down deep into what it is that drives the individual, so that this can then be understood and used as the basis for a new product. Companies want people to express such requirements as:

- Trust
- Freedom
- Flexibility
- Lifetime value
- Advice.

These, and other equally emotive rather than purely rational wishes, are key to enabling clearer definition of customer needs, and hence of new product specification. There is a fundamental difference between articulated requirements and unarticulated needs. It is accessing this type of input from customers that is now helping leading innovators define, create and then deliver the next big thing as far as users are concerned. The problem is that these are generally hidden and hence difficult to identify. Beneath individuals' concrete actions, attitudes and behaviours lie their personal beliefs and core values. It is these beliefs and core values that influence the attitudes and behaviours that then have an impact on their personal preferences, and it is therefore understanding these core values that is key. This is now the focus of several companies' early stage research activities for many of their innovation programmes. Accessing these is the key to understanding what it is that people want, what they need and, ultimately, what they will buy.

Nike

One of the best users of what are increasingly behavioural research techniques within the innovation arena has been the US-based sportswear leader Nike. The company established a cognitive research group specifically to look at human factors, psychology and consumer-based product evaluation questions in a desire to 'place the consumer at the centre of the development process'. By immersing themselves in the daily lives of target customers, they focus more deeply on the experiences of the consumer. By going to the customer rather than bringing the customer to them, the Nike team watches and talks with consumers wherever they happen to be, whether at home, in the office or in the gym. They try to understand the motivations and attitudes that underpin behaviour, and develop insights about the core needs and expectations that influence consumer decision-making. Using a selection of audio and video techniques as well as observational analysis, interviews, shadowing, traditional focus groups and usability testing, they seek to address such issues as preconceptions, first impressions and functionality, as well as evaluating competitor product performance, acceptance and brand perceptions (www.cognito-inc.com). As a result they are able to identify the specific buttons that need to be pressed by the company's products that will ensure that a teenager attending school, a young mother staying at home or a girl at the gym will want to buy the specific cross-trainer, vest or eyewear product that Nike has developed around her defined needs.

Customers and brand values

Equipped with such insights regarding consumer behaviours, attitudes and underlying values, companies are also increasingly using them in their configuration and development of the brands used to promote their products. Nike is clearly a master at this. Brand values as a set of issues or messages that represent a product or an organization are nothing new, but the way in which they are being used to link more directly with the values of the individuals that are seen as the target customers is changing. Egg is built around the ethos that its products and services are tailored to individuals. As such, its brand values are 'simple', 'transparent', 'mutually beneficial', 'empathetic', 'modern', 'fresh' and 'liberating' (Curtis and Simms, 2001). These are all used to communicate directly with the customer base with which the company believes it has shared points of view and even beliefs. Brand values are increasingly standing for something, and as such are being used by people for conscious and subconscious points of reference as they search out the products or services that match their needs (Jones, 2000). There is therefore a potential linkage between the brand values and the hidden customer values that companies are seeking to address and promote as they change the relationship that they have with their customers. Brands make the promises that the products are meant to deliver. The strongest brands have extraordinary power, as they attract, sustain, nurture and, in theory at least, develop such elements of the relationship as customer loyalty and common ownership.

Clarks – breaking new ground

A good example of how all these elements have been successfully brought to bear in a new product development is Clarks, a 175-year-old footwear company renowned for comfort and quality, especially in children's shoes. With a turnover of over £800 million, selling 38 million pairs of shoes per annum, it is one of the UK's most significant privately owned companies. It has been in a process of transition, evolving from its UK, Quaker roots to become an international shoe brand, and as part of this initiative in 2001 it worked with London-based design group PDD to research and define a design brief for a new generation of active footwear that would appeal to a new customer group.

Latest lifestyle developments indicated a significant growth in demand for active leisure clothing and footwear, a fast-growing market for companies from Nike and Timberland in the USA to Karrimor and Berghaus in the UK, but not one traditionally serviced by the Clarks brand and its high street retail outlets. The company was seeking not only to develop a new product but also to extend the brand into a new market sector meeting the needs of active walkers. Knowing that the sector offered potential of itself was no help to those tasked with developing the 'winning' design solutions. What the designers, engineers and marketers needed was a much closer appreciation of what walkers valued most, and for what reasons. From this the team could create the Clarks blueprint for 'delighting its customers'.

Some fundamental questions needed early definition – especially, what type of footwear would appeal to the needs of the market. Recent trends had seen diverse product innovation from professional '*boots*', hybrid-hiking '*trainers*' through to robust walking '*shoes*'. In addition, the Clarks brand needed to discover the optimal balance between heritage, comfort, value and fashion. In the words of Chris Towns, the company's new products manager:

> I needed to understand the buying habits, end use and expectations of our new consumer. Understanding walker motivations can only be guessed at from within the confines of your own office.

Using its ethnographic research team, PDD's approach was to involve consumers and retailers directly as 'co-developers' together with the core team. Key to this was the immersion process through which the team achieved an intimate understanding of needs in the real life context of use. In-home video interviews were conducted, with a wide range of leisure and walking enthusiasts exploring how people's footwear wardrobe reflected individual lifestyles. The cross-functional teams also personally participated and shadowed walkers across different activities in the mountains and fells of the UK's national parks. This helped identify the real-life experiences in differing terrain and climatic conditions, and gave meaning to generic customer wishes such as 'comfort', 'fit' and 'safety'. In addition, the team observed the retail shopping experience in both high street and specialist outdoor shops to provide point of purchase insights and aid the development of new retail brand marketing proposals.

The customer behaviour research helped the team to interpret the clues and quickly to identify the insights and opportunities leading to the definition of a compelling design specification. The approach helped to bridge the divide that often occurs between identifying market potential and realizing innovative solutions. The co-development approach continued throughout the in-house design, development and testing phases. Prototype field trials were used to prove out both the physical and emotional delivery of the new feature benefits and overall brand experience. The ethnography techniques also gave a number of soft benefits beyond the definition of the physical boot. The cross-functional knowledge-sharing helped team focus, improved decision-making cycles and gave confidence regarding how best to direct R&D investment. As a result the new product, the Clarks Active Mover range, was developed and launched in under a year – setting new standards for walker comfort and versatility both on and off the mountain.

As such methods are becoming better known across industry, recognition of the underpinning values of users and customers is gaining wider audience. Coupled with higher levels of sophistication in delivering innovation, the associated up-front identification of what is, and what is not, a real need is also migrating from one sector to another.

References

Curtis, J. and Simms, J. (2001). *EBrand Leaders: An Insight into 50 of Britain's Strongest Brands*. Superbrands.

Jones, R. (2000). *The Big Idea*. Harper Collins.

10

Patent pooling

Over recent years, as knowledge and know-how have become ever-greater sources of competitive advantage, so the role of the associated intellectual property has increased. Fuelled initially by technology transfer, and more latterly by increased cooperation between companies, intellectual property (IP) has moved from a defensive problem concerned with revenue protection to one more focused on value generation. As this change has occurred, so the varied mechanisms being used to affect it have also evolved. Today, in an ever more IP-aware marketplace, several major organizations are increasingly using IP as a key part of their innovation strategic approach. As more firms begin proactively to share their IP to generate value, patent pooling has now become the latest activity for focus in several market-leading arenas.

Intellectual property

Intellectual property has mixed origins. Patents can be traced back to the fifteenth century, copyright to 1662, design right to the end of the eighteenth century; and trademarks to 1875. However, these are all dates when these varied forms of IP first existed in a legal and hence executable sense. It was the scholars of ancient Greece who were the first to be concerned about who should be recognized as authors of work, although at the time this was purely from the perspective of intellectual ownership and acknowledgement of creativity rather than concern about any economic rights.

In terms of protection of invention and the ability to secure revenue from the ownership of intellectual property, it was developments in a number of fields that brought IP into being as a legal entity. For patents it was the move by the English Crown to provide specific grants of privilege to favoured manufacturers and traders that kicked off activity, whereas for copyright it was the advent of printing that eventually promoted formalization of intellectual property for the evolving industry. For design right it was the growth of textile production that prompted associated protection, and for trademarks it was the idea of differentiation between distinctive providers of a trade or service, and the associated goodwill that existed that first gave birth to the concept of protection in this field. Over the five centuries since patents started the IP bandwagon rolling, to today, where protection of business methods, software, genes and internet images is driving IP to the forefront of many organizations' thinking and growth strategies, there has been a massive change in the perception and context of what IP is – let alone how to manage it.

IP protection

Within the field of corporate innovation, patents were increasingly seen as the key mechanism for protecting organizational know-how throughout the twentieth century. Although some post-war use of this approach was initially seen as being anti-competitive and preventing corporate creativity, as new technological breakthroughs delivered whole new fields of IP, by the 1980s patents were seen as an essential part of a firm's competitive advantage. This was particularly emphasized by the definitive legal case that brought the scope of patents and the value placed on them to the fore.

Kodak vs. Polaroid: an insurmountable wall

In the late 1960s the instant photography market began to boom, with sales of cameras accounting for 15 per cent of the market. One company, Polaroid, whose total annual sales were still only one-tenth of those of its arch rival Kodak Eastman, dominated it. Whilst developing its core technology, Polaroid had been careful to protect it with a wall of patents that prevented its competitors from copying it. However, as Polaroid flourished the market became so attractive that in 1969 Kodak's R&D division decided to begin 'Project 130' to develop its own instant camera and film.

In its path were two obstacles; first, the patents held by Polaroid, and second, the fact that Kodak had earlier worked with Polaroid in a joint development project, during which Polaroid had revealed some of its future products to Kodak's engineers under a non-disclosure agreement. Mindful of any potential infringement that might occur, Kodak even took the step of hiring an attorney to advise them during their R&D programme. As Polaroid was already selling a product, customers had come to recognize its camera as the instant camera in much the same way that early Hoovers became synonymous with the vacuum cleaner. If Kodak were to compete, then it would inevitably have to develop something similar, but the patents and confidentiality agreement prevented this. Faced with a potential deadlock, Kodak pursued a strategy of allowing its staff to develop designs that might infringe the patents and even issued a memorandum to its staff saying that they 'should not be constrained by what an individual feels is potential patent infringement'. At the same time, the firm worked to rule that any potential infringement would be invalid, as the Polaroid patents were not likely to be strong enough to be upheld legally.

On 20 April 1976, Kodak finally launched its own new instant camera to much fanfare. Seven days later Polaroid responded with a lawsuit claiming infringement of twelve of its core patents. The ensuing trial took nine years to complete, and in the end decided that Kodak had indeed infringed seven of these patents. It was then a further five years before the scale of the damages could be determined. By the time this was finished in 1990, the instant camera market, which had peaked in 1978, had largely been superseded by 35-mm compacts and the advent of digital photography, but the judgment was clear and its impact significant.

What was the total cost? The best estimate is a total of $3 billion. Of this, $925 million was in damages, $1.5 billion was the money lost in the closure of Kodak's instant camera manufacturing plant (where 700 workers had to be laid off), $500 million was spent buying back and destroying all the 16 million cameras that had already been sold, legal fees amounted to $100 million, and the remainder was the written off cost of R&D. In addition to the trial, Kodak then faced a class action lawsuit from people who had bought their cameras. To settle this, it established a $150 million fund to compensate the owners with payments of between $50 and $70 each.

Polaroid's patent wall destroyed Kodak's instant camera business and played a major role in bringing the issue of IP to the notice of a wider audience. Since the initial Polaroid lawsuit raised awareness of the power of IP in 1976, companies globally have improved the way in which they both use and also try to circumvent patent protection. Patent walls or patent thickets have subsequently become commonplace as a means of keeping competitors out.

A longstanding user of patents since its first was granted in 1901, Gillette developed its Sensor shaver with IP concerns at the forefront of the product strategy. Although there were seven designs that could have been used, the company selected the one that could be protected with the most patents. The razor has over twenty patents covering the functionality of the razor right through to the click of the box when opening it. For its subsequent 1998 Mach 3 shaving system, Gillette spent $750 million on research and used thirty-five core patents to protect key technologies, product features and manufacturing methods.

Managing IP

Alongside this use of IP for protection, during the mid 1990s there was also a parallel focus on IP exploitation and the more effective management of the corporate portfolio. Managing your IP is all about exploiting the knowledge that you own. This may be knowledge that has been converted into tangible assets such as patents; it may be knowledge that you are aware of; it may be knowledge that is hidden; it may be intangible assets such as your brand, or even know-how that exists within your organization. Whichever, these varied types of knowledge can all be seen as intellectual property, and as such are something that can be used to create or destroy value. For firms that have evolved to generate value from their IP, managing it has three core components:

1 Recording the IP the company owns
2 Analysing the value of this IP
3 Exploiting the IP to maximize revenue.

Managing IP is increasingly seen to be part of a company's strategy, part of its organizational structure, and even a core capability – not a task delegated to patent agents and attorneys. Management has become distinct from maintenance: managing IP is now a responsibility of the company; maintaining it, whether in terms of drafting, filing or updating applications, is the responsibility of patent agents and attorneys, who are most commonly external to the organization. In this new approach, managing IP has been elevated to a key commercial concern for many firms (Fitzsimmons and Jones, 2001).

Several technology companies, including Dow and DuPont, have created IP management departments, and even divisions, to manage their portfolios and extract the maximum value from them. However, in the eyes of the *Wall Street Journal*, the company that has made the most noise from its considerable achievements in this area has been IBM. Within a two-year timeframe, $10 billion of value was created from the company's IP portfolio.

IBM: mining patents for gold

In 1998, Lou Gerstner, head of IBM, was concerned at the low return that was being gained on IBM's $5 billion R&D budget. He therefore challenged three of his executives to find a way to generate a greater return from the money the company was investing. The solution the three proposed was for IBM to become a component supplier and integrator for a range of OEM (Original Equipment Manufacturer) customers. The board agreed their strategy, grandly titled 'IBM's OEM strategy for the Twenty-first Century', in late August 1998, and soon the IBM Technology Group or ITG was born. This new group combined the mass storage division, which had previously been IBM's component supply operation, with its microelectronics, printing and network hardware divisions.

At the time the IBM database held over 12 000 patents, with another 2500 being added each year. For eight years in the 1990s, IBM filed more patents at the US PTO office than any other company. Its patent portfolio covers the fundamentals of computing, cryptography, software, storage networking, PC and server architectures, and semiconductor design and manufacturing. It is said that anyone working in the computer industry has at some time infringed an IBM patent! The subtle sub-strategy of the technology group was to use IBM's massive array of patents to challenge hardware manufacturers for potential infringements, and encourage them to settle through cross-licensing agreements. Some of these would be in the form of IBM supplying the company with its components in lieu of royalties.

The greatest change in IBM's thinking was that instead of using its patents as a defensive mechanism to protect its research work, it began to use them as an aggressive commercial weapon to generate sales. In the words of Tony Baker, Head of Business Development at ITG, 'Getting a return on that Intellectual Property is a very active program at IBM'. In some instances ITG even understood what technology they wanted from their competitors, and used a potential patent infringement case to get it! The list of licensees during 1999 alone includes the cream of the computing world:

- The storage company EMC agreed to purchase $3 billion in IBM disk drives in a cross-licensing deal to resolve a potential dispute when their previous licensing agreement with IBM expired.
- Cisco signed a cross-licensing deal, which led to a $2 billion deal, whereby IBM exited the network hardware market by selling its routing and switching patents to Cisco, in return for Cisco agreeing to purchase IBM storage devices and PCs.
- Acer required access to IBM's patents for the next generation of its PCs and computing devices. In a deal valued at $8 billion, Acer bought LCDs, storage devices, networking and processors from IBM, whilst IBM purchased $1 billion of Acer LCDs, which it then resold.
- 3Com was eager to access IBM's patent portfolio to speed up development, and so signed a $2 billion cross-licensing deal in which each was given access to the other's patents.
- Dell agreed a $16 billion component deal to supersede a previous licensing agreement. This effectively saved Dell tens of millions of dollars, as, rather than having to pay IBM licence fees and buy its components, the company agreed to buy components from IBM in lieu of licensing fees. This was expenditure it would have had to incur anyway.

In a later case, IBM wished to use Dell's ordering system, one of its greatest competitive advantages and something Dell had itself protected with two business model patents. In a second deal, initiated by IBM, Dell cross-licensed these patents in return for formalizing a licensing agreement on another set of patents it had been found to be infringing. In IBM's words, 'This removed an inhibitor to a potential relationship'. The success of ITG has been phenomenal. In the first six months of 1999 it generated roughly $8 billion in revenues in a mix of pure licensing revenues and component sales. The goal for 2002 is $20 billion!!

Aware of IBM's success, Xerox similarly formed Xerox New Enterprises to develop and market its 8000 patents, a move analysts believe will create over $24 billion in new wealth for the company's shareholders if it generates only half the revenue per patent that IBM now earns. Moreover, this revenue is almost all translated into pure profit, as the costs associated with the creation of the IP in the first place have already been absorbed.

New companies

While these firms are all long-established technology-rich product manufacturers that have generated their extensive patent portfolios as a consequence of long-term innovation focused R&D

activities, other newer companies have recently been taking a different approach. Foremost are the chip designers ARM and Qualcomm. As the global chip manufacturing industry contracted significantly in 2001, sales growth for these two firms grew by over 30 per cent (Wendlandt, 2001).

ARM: chips in everything

In just over 10 years, ARM has grown into one of the world's leading technology companies. First founded in 1985, and incorporated in 1990, this small Cambridge-based FTSE 100 and NASDAQ listed firm started off designing and manufacturing the first RISC processors for use in the products of two companies – Acorn in the UK and Apple in the USA. However, as originator of a new type of chip, the company had ambitions not to become a manufacturing competitor to larger established firms such as Intel, but instead to put ARM designs into as wide a marketplace as possible. This was to be achieved through licensing. With the first licences granted to GEC and Sharp in 1992 and, more significantly, Texas Instruments in 1993, an ever-increasing list of companies have since become ARM IP customers. Digital, NEC, Samsung, Yamaha, Philips, Lucent and Hyundai, as well as Sony, HP, IBM, Matsushita, Seiko, Qualcomm, Toshiba, Fujitsu, 3Com, Motorola and Mitsubishi are just some of the firms who took out licences to ARM technology during the 1990s. Revenues in 2000 were over £100 million and, with profits before tax of over £35 million, were up 97 per cent on 1999, ARM has become a favourite technology stock with many investors. Employing just over 500 personnel worldwide by the end of 2001, ARM's market capitalization was over £4 billion as its shares led the UK performance rankings (*The Observer*, 2001). The company has become a role model for IP exploitation. With a revenue stream based wholly on royalties, by 2001 its designs for 32-bit RISC chips were commonplace in handheld games, PDAs, in-car entertainment, data storage systems and imaging equipment, taking over 70 percent of the market share. In addition, ARM IP is fundamental to a stream of GPRS and 3G mobile phones.

Qualcomm: gaining predominance in 3G mobile through IP exploitation

Qualcomm is one of the world's fastest-growing companies, and regularly tops *Business Week* ratings for strategic and operational excellence. The company has shipped over 200 million chipsets and provides software to enable advanced communication, particularly through mobile devices. Like ARM, Qualcomm saw its future in revenue generated from licensing leading-edge technology, and over the past few years has positioned itself accordingly.

The company started life in San Diego in 1985 as a provider of contract R&D services to the Californian aerospace and defence industries. Over the next 10 years Qualcomm became the largest fabless semiconductor producer in the world, but chose to put future focus on commercializing its wireless CDMA (Code Division Multiple Access) expertise that now generates substantial revenues from licensing. By 2001 it had over 1000 engineers dedicated to CDMA technology development, and over 1300 patents granted or pending in the USA alone.

The US government originally developed the CDMA technology introduced commercially into the market by Qualcomm in 1995. CDMA codes separate transmissions so multiple data streams can share the same radio channel. It enables very high-speed transmission of up to 2 megabits per second compared to 9.6 kilobits with the existing GSM technology. CDMA2000, the latest digital version of the CDMA technology, is specifically designed for 3G mobile communications, and its growth is accelerating rapidly as licences are issued and CDMA-based 3G mobile products are launched.

Qualcomm's main competitors in the mobile technology arena are Ericsson and Nokia, whose 2G GSM technology dominated the European and many Asian markets. Within the USA, three different and non-interoperable technologies, one of which was Qualcomm's IS-95, competed for 2G mobile, but none ever achieved dominance. However, in a bid to create a global standard for 3G mobile, in 1999 Ericsson and Qualcomm signed an agreement to make CDMA2000 the world standard, with both companies supporting the technology through patent cross-licences. Nokia and Qualcomm were discussing a similar agreement in July 2001.

In 1999, Qualcomm spun off its consumer products division to Kyocera and increased gross margin from 32 per cent to 62 per cent. In July 2000, the company announced that it was also spinning off its integrated circuit and system software businesses so that it could concentrate more on the CDMA2000 technology and its future evolution. Although this was scrapped a year later due to the downturn in the technology sector, this highlighted Qualcomm's aim to have its main revenue streams as licences from its patents for CDMA and other wireless technologies rather than from manufacturing.

Qualcomm is actively licensing its CDMA technology to the likes of Microsoft and Motorola in the USA, to Matsushita and Mitsubishi in Japan, and to LG Telecom and Intercube in Korea. By the middle of 2001, over 100 communications equipment manufacturers had taken out licences. All licensees pay the same flat rate royalty per chipset, thus guaranteeing Qualcomm a predictable and steady revenue growth. The revenue for 2000 was over $3 billion, leading some analysts to predict that, owing to its pre-eminent position in CDMA technology, Qualcomm will dominate this industry by 2005.

Generating such value from IP is, however, not restricted to high-technology firms and the field of patents. Similarly large sums are also becoming commonplace in non-technology areas, and especially in the media. From the reality TV of *Big Brother* and *Survivor* to game shows such as *The Weakest Link* and *Who wants to be a Millionaire?*, licensing revenues for their parent organizations (including the BBC, Endemol and Celador) have been substantial. However, despite their prominence, these are all secondary when compared to a TV show for children: *Teletubbies* is in a league of its own.

Teletubbies: child's play?

The Teletubbies are Tinky Winky, Dipsy, Laa Laa and Po; large, baby-like characters, each in a different, bright colour, who speak in a simple language using words such as 'Eh-oh'. Ragdoll Productions created the Teletubbies in response to a request by the BBC for a programme aimed at two-year-olds, a slot they believed was not being addressed by their current range of children's productions. Since their first screening on the BBC in 1997, it is estimated that by 2001 over a billion children in 120 countries around the world had seen them.

Most of the income from a programme such as *Teletubbies* does not come from the sales to the TV stations, but from the merchandising rights. These are licensed to third parties, allowing them to produce items such as videos, T-shirts, souvenirs and other items with a likeness of the original characters. Copyright and a trademark on the name protect the likeness. Given the huge profits that can be generated from a successful series, these rights are extremely valuable, and one of the key issues in managing them has been licensing them.

The creators, Ragdoll Productions, licensed the rights to BBC Worldwide for the corporation to sub-license onto merchandisers in specific territories. In the USA, the rights holder was itsy bitsy Entertainment. For receiving a share of the income, both organizations are responsible for policing and co-prosecuting any potential infringements. BBC Worldwide has been very active in defending the rights to protect its value. It has requested the removal of images of the Teletubbies from numerous websites; in March 1999 the BBC sued Wal-Mart for selling dolls called Bubbly

Chuppies, which in the BBC's view were too similar to the Teletubbies; and it also considered taking action against an individual who had registered the domain names teletubbies.com and teletubbies.co.uk.

The success of the management of the Teletubbies IP was highlighted by Kenn Viselman, the CEO of itsy bitsy Entertainment, who, when the Teletubbies were introduced into the USA on the PBS channel, stated that 'You're looking at a major multimillion-dollar property'. He was right – in October 2000, it was reported that in the three years since 1997 the Teletubbies had already generated over £1 billion in merchandising, of which the BBC alone has received £90 million. Today the Teletubbies are licensed in ninety countries and translated into thirty-five languages, the most recent being Russian – where they are shown on state television under the name 'TelePuzikis'.

New developments

Across all types of IP there is an accelerating pace of change in both scope and application. The ability to patent gene sequences and computer software is, together with the global implications of the recent TRIPS agreement, having a profound effect on what organizations are, by and large, successfully seeking to protect and exploit. Copyright of software, books and particularly music in the Internet age has come under the spotlight, especially through the cases of MP3 and Napster. In addition, the increasingly aggressive stance of many corporations such as McDonalds and Nike in implementing the rights associated with the respective trademarks and design marks is also bringing these latter two into focus. Today, managing the IP portfolio has become an organizational capability requiring understanding of all the latest developments and issues across the whole IP arena and, by implication, a capability that itself will continue to evolve apace.

In such a rapidly evolving arena, the state of the art in managing intellectual property is developing and gaining interest across industries. For many organizations for whom managing IP is a new issue, state of the art is being seen in the perspective of best practice, and the putting in place of the internal capability to define an IP exploitation strategy, implement it, and thus create value. By contrast, for companies who are experienced in managing IP at a basic level, state of the art is more to do with knowing which emerging practices are defining the leading edge. For those seeking to evolve rather than establish their IP management capability, it is the implications of the new types of patents that are being granted and the new strategies that are being adopted by leading players to create value that are of interest. These new strategies include patenting business models, patent exchanges, securitizing IP revenue, and the rebirth of patent pooling.

Algorithms and business methods

No area has generated more heated debate in the IP arena than the patenting of business processes and software, in which the USA leads the charge. Consider 2001 statistics from the European Patent Office, where US nationals filed 52 per cent of all patents for business methods although they only filed 28 per cent of patents overall. Similarly, at the UK Patent Office, 31 per cent of all business method patents were filed by US nationals, compared to 10 per cent of patents overall. These are all focused on protecting means of delivering services rather than the enabling technologies or products themselves. Examples of well-known patents for business methods include Priceline's claim to a computer-based buyer-driven reverse-auction procedure, which it is using to sue Microsoft Expedia for selling airline tickets by the same method, and Amazon's 1-Click shopping method, which it has used to sue Barnes & Noble.

Patent exchanges

As companies realize that they have non-core patents that they would like to license or sell, the challenge becomes how to reach out to a large enough audience. One way is to use a new breed of web site that classifies and describes the patents, taking a commission on those sold through the site. An example is www.yet2.com, which is supported by a host of large companies such as Pitney Bowes, Motorola and Siemens. Another more specialized example is the Virtual Component Exchange at www.vcx.org, which offers to license IP cores for semiconductor chips. Manufacturers can license a number of cores and build them into an integrated circuit. Examples of companies offering their IP include ARM with their non-leading RISC processor cores, Arc Cores, and Imagination Technology Group. The VCX site also helps companies negotiate licences through their TransactionWare software. At the other end of the spectrum are sites such the Walmart Innovation Center, which invites anyone to send in details of their invention. The centre then assesses whether any part of it can be patented, and offers to help in this in return for a commission.

Securitizing IP

Some IP has such strong and reliable income streams that companies can now securitize them to receive the income today instead of in the future. Called Asset Backed Securitization (ABS), this is a growing phenomenon, particularly in the music industry. The first to offer these types of bond was the singer David Bowie, when Prudential Securities issued $55 million worth of 15-year bonds backed by the royalties from the publishing and recording rights to 300 of his songs. Other artists said to be considering ABS include Crosby, Stills & Nash, The Rolling Stones, Prince, Neil Diamond, and Luciano Pavarotti. The concept is just as applicable to any entertainers, whether pop stars, classical musicians, opera singers, conductors, authors, movie producers or TV personalities.

Patent pooling

One of the biggest concerns raised about the human genome project has been about the potential lack of reasonable access to the technology for future research and development activities. In the mid-1980s, some elements of the scientific and patent communities argued that the research should be openly available, whilst others, many of whom owned key patents, preferred to enforce these as protection against external exploitation. When scientists completed a draft sequence of the human genome in 2000, the desire to profit from their investments drove private companies and public universities alike individually to claim as much intellectual territory as possible. Aware of the value, they have sought to control both the commercial and public use of key technology and know-how. As the debate over whether or not such core information should be made publicly available for research continues, one of the major drives has been to create a dedicated patent pool.

Patent pooling is where a company assigns its patented technology to a 'pool' of patents that must all be licensed if a company is to build a certain product. It is a way of creating a *de facto* standard. This is where the action is today. As more and more companies seek to be part of the IP exploitation opportunity and use IP to help define the operational and commercial parameters within which new technology can exist, sharing IP through patent pooling is an approach that is gaining interest across the innovation realization world.

A patent pool is a collective intellectual property rights organization. It is an arrangement amongst multiple patent holders to aggregate their patents so that they share from the whole portfolio. It is an agreement between two or more patent owners to license one or more of their patents to one another or third parties. A typical patent pool makes all pooled patents available to each member of the pool and usually offers standard licensing terms to licensees who are not members of the pool. In addition, a portion of licensing fees is normally allocated to each member according to a predetermined formula.

Key benefits from patent pooling include:

- Facilitating rapid development of a new technology by quickly formalizing a new common standard
- Reducing effort and resources used in setting up and reviewing individual cross-licensing arrangements
- Creating an efficient mechanism for obtaining rights to a patent technology dependent on input from multiple companies
- Distributing risks from additional research and development amongst members of a pool to provide an additional incentive for more innovation
- Providing an institutional exchange of technical information not covered by patents but supporting the development and introduction of new technologies.

Rather than having to negotiate directly with each company, licensees prefer to license from the pool, which acts as a one-stop shop. It also helps them by quickly identifying all the patents they need to license. None of the companies contributing to the pool can withhold the licensing of their patents to a company unless the pool acts in an unreasonable manner. Moreover, they rely on the pool to enforce the patents. Critics point out that patent pools have several anti-competitive effects; they can inflate the cost of patented goods, they provide shields for invalid patents, and they can eliminate competition by encouraging collusion and price fixing.

Patent pools are, however, not new in concept. What is new is how they are now being used. In the past, mega-pools have been created to enable an industry to become properly established when different firms have held patents on the basic building blocks. Examples of this include the sewing machine, aircraft and automotive industries, which each collectively pooled patents in the early years of the twentieth century in order to enable common products to be created. In these cases representatives of the various members of each pool participated in the valuation of patented technology, resulting in every licensee being charged a royalty agreed by a pool committee. Although appearing to be rather bureaucratic, these mega-pools established the common cross-sharing of the diversity of technologies that underpinned the three industries. The automotive pool had 79 members and 350 patents when formed in 1917, and over 200 members and 1000 patents by 1932. As industry norms were created these mega-pools became a part of patent history, and as companies renewed their interest in patents as a defensive tool throughout the 1960s and 1970s, the opportunity for pools declined (R.P. Merges, 1999).

As industries have converged and the establishment of common platforms has become more and more significant to common success, patent pools have recently been reborn as a key mechanism for enabling reasoned cooperation. Fuelled by the success of bipartisan technology developments, such as the compact disc developed by Philips and Sony, as much as the desire to avoid reruns of the costly VHS/Betamax war of the late 1970s, especially in areas such as consumer electronics, sharing intellectual property between and across companies has once again gained prominence. Indeed there have been three areas where patent pooling is now having a particularly strong influence in the successful creation and exploitation of new technologies.

MPEG-2

The MPEG-2 pool began as an agreement between nine patent holders to combine twenty-seven patents that are needed collectively to define and enable an international standard known as MPEG-2 video compression technology. Initially established in late 1995, this pool was an outcome of the definition of this standard, and forms the basis for storing, transmitting and displaying digital video. Under the pooling agreement, the patent holders all license their MPEG-2 patents to a central administrative entity known as MPEG LA. Based in Denver, this is essentially a licensing agent that administers the group's intellectual property on behalf of the members. Grown to include fourteen patent holders and fifty-six essential patents by 2001, the MPEG LA licensed the group's patent portfolio to third parties who could then manufacture products that meet the standard.

In many ways the MPEG LA has become an institution rather than a one-time transfer of rights. It has a governance structure, a set of internal rules and a permanent procedure for evaluating new technologies as new patents are granted all over the world. There is also a mechanism for redefining royalty split amongst members when a new patent is added to the pool. Licensing to over 200 companies as diverse as Hitachi and Motorola, the MPEG-2 pool was the first in recent years to demonstrate tangible success.

DVD – two pools

Another recent example is with DVDs, where there are two competing pools. The successor to CD technology, the DVD (digital versatile disc) is a high-volume digital storage medium that can be used for data, image, video and audio applications. In 2001, the DVD market was worth over $30 billion. As with MPEG-2, in late 1995 a multi-firm standards group declared a standard for DVD technology when four core members (Philips, Sony, Matsushita and Toshiba) of a ten-member consortium entered into a patent pooling agreement to administer the licensing of DVD patents.

Unfortunately, full agreement over exploitation and royalties between all ten members was not forthcoming and, irritated by increasing delays to definition of the common standard for products that they wanted to launch, the original inventors of the CD, Sony and Philips, formed their own pool. They were quickly joined by Pioneer to form the three-firm '3C pool'. In 1997, Toshiba, Matsushita, JVC, Mitsubishi, Hitachi and Time Warner duly formed their own '6C pool'. Analysts warned that in the absence of a single unified pool, the price of DVD technology would increase, as the lack of a common approach would raise licensing costs. For the 3C pool the portfolio royalty is set at 3.5 per cent of net selling price for each DVD player sold and $0.05 for each disc. For the 6C pool, the respective rates are 4.0 per cent and $0.075.

With over 16 million DVD players shipped in 2000 alone, the two pools are nevertheless proving their individual worth as enablers of wider IP exploitation and faster revenue generation. However, to try and improve this further, the DVD Forum is trying to bring both pools together to form one global standard.

Bluetooth: sharing IP to maximize technology application

Finally, Bluetooth, the technology underpinning new wireless applications that was initiated by Ericsson, the Swedish telecommunications company, now also exists as a patent pool owned by a special interest group led by Ericsson, IBM, Nokia and Toshiba. This enables both shared development and wider and faster market penetration.

With the experience of jointly defining the NMT and GSM standards for mobile communications with Nokia, when Ericsson was deciding how best to exploit its emerging Bluetooth wireless technology, partnership was a clear favourite. Essentially a low-cost, low-power, short-range, yet fast and reliable radio interface that can act, for example, between mobile phones, their accessories and other data products, Bluetooth was first envisaged in 1994. Ericsson realized that, as it had nearly done with GSM and was also doing with WAP, the secret to ensuring worldwide take-up of the technology would be to establish a truly global standard quickly, and to do this with other lead companies.

In 1997, the company therefore approached several other manufacturers of portable electronic devices to develop the wireless technology. The following year, Ericsson, IBM, Intel, Nokia and Toshiba duly formed a patent pool, the Bluetooth Special Interest Group, leading to the release of version 1.0 of the technology in late 1998. This technology comprises both hardware and software, and, by creating the core pool from companies that have stakes in the underlying IP, they can share development effort both in terms of cost and resource while at the same time addressing a far wider market than could have been achieved individually.

With high levels of interest fuelled by the rapidly converging mobile and computing sectors, Bluetooth has quickly gained a strong foothold. Although there are potential competitors such as 802.11b-based Wi-Fi high-speed wireless LAN, other companies such as 3COM, Lucent Technologies, Microsoft and Motorola all joined in as promoters of Bluetooth in 2000 as the first products using the technology began to appear on the market. From Motorola's perspective, 'it was essential that they became part of the group as the combined product set across all companies will set the standard'. In addition, only by being at the heart of the development activities could it too share learning and experience as part of 'an organization whose whole is greater than the sum of its parts'.

With the partnership firmly in place to drive and promote development, Ericsson created Ericsson Technology Licensing specifically to license the Bluetooth technology and help companies such as South Korea's Samsung build Bluetooth technology into their PDA, printer and network products. One year later, membership of the Bluetooth adopter Special Interest Group passed 2000 – virtually every major communications and electronics company in the world – and Bluetooth is the fastest ever growing *de facto* global standard. Forecasts by Cahners-Instat anticipates that, by 2005, 700 million Bluetooth devices will be shipped annually – all using the same core technology underpinned by the shared IP made available through a single patent pool.

Together with other pools, such as those for digital video broadcasting, flat panel speakers, new synthetic fibres, and the 1394 external bus trademarked Firewire by Apple and iLink by other partners including Compaq, Matsushita, Sony and Philips, these approaches are all redefining IP exploitation across multiple industries.

References

Fitzsimmons, C. and Jones, T. (2001). *Managing Intellectual Property.* Wiley.

R. P. Merges (1999). *Institutions for Intellectual Property: The Case for Patent Pools.* University of California at Berkeley.

The Observer (2001). Key Data. *The Observer*, Business Section, 18 November.

Wendlandt, A. (2001). A chip of light emerges in the gloom. *Financial Times*, 20 October.

11

Investment integration

The Internet fallout

The fallout from the Internet and technology boom of the late 1990s brought several different elements of the investment in innovation into sharper focus. As the collapse of boo.com, clickmango, excite, chemdex and the like showed all too well, just as with the hype generated around some of the railway pioneers a century earlier, this was no guaranteed bet. As even the share prices of those companies that survived took a massive hit, with firms like Lastminute.com suffering 90 per cent falls from £3.50 to 35 p over an 18-month period, it was clear that the investment gravy train was no longer in the station. The early successes like Amazon, eBay, Netscape had fuelled an explosion of venture capital input into Internet and technology opportunities, with annual investment rising from $10 billion in 1996 to over $50 billion in 1999 in the USA alone. This in turn had generated an investment rush into the associated shares as investors bought into stocks with the single intent of selling them on at a higher price to maximize their profits. As momentum investing took off and the bubble grew and grew, the underlying fundamentals of company performance, its products, its market and its management capability were forgotten. It was only when these underlying fundamentals in many of the new firms were shown to be so poor that they began to affect the perceived value of the stock that the bubble burst. With the fear of being the one left holding shares in a worthless company, investors reacted. Their expectations of continuous growth of new companies at crazy rates were hit by less than incredible results and so confidence was shattered.

Without the experience to put all this into context, panic set in, the frenzy became a rout, and buy became sell.

It was clear that investment in innovation, no matter whether new technology, new products or new businesses, was still bound by the same parameters as had been in effect for the previous twenty years. No matter how much money is poured into an opportunity, if the original concept is flawed, then so will be the outcome. Likewise, if the firm or group of companies responsible for delivering the new proposition do not have the necessary experience, capability and management skills, then odds on it will result in failure. All the traditional critical success factors of having a unique product, a clearly defined market, a differentiated strategy, a structured process and the most appropriate enabling organization were all again shown to be true and to hold equally in the virtual world as they had been proven to do in the real world. Nothing had really changed. For a couple of years, inexperienced people had ended up running companies with too much cash and no feel for effective management. When things had got tight, the lack of any tools, processes or even business structures had meant that even when more experienced managers were brought in, there was little that could be used to save the companies.

Role of venture capitalists

Within all this, one area that was pushed to the forefront of media and hence public attention had been the role of the venture capitalist (VC). Although in existence within the world of corporate finance since the end of the nineteenth century, it was the technology boom that brought VC input as backers of new opportunities in technology and business development into the mainstream. Since the equity funds provided by venture capitalists, unlike bank loans, do not have to be repaid by the entrepreneur, they were seen as risk-free and valuable inputs to developing and exploiting a new idea. Moreover, with in excess of a thousand VC firms active globally, the sources of such capital investment were multiple. Either operating through the traditional approach of providing firms in which they invest with a non-executive director to act as a steward on the journey to IPO, or, as the bubble took shape, in a more hands-off, money-only manner, venture capital input to the technology boom was considerable.

Led by successful US-based firms such as Matrix Partners, who backed Sycamore Networks, and Kleiner, Perkins, Caufield and Byers, who were originally behind Netscape, venture capitalists grew apace (Lewis, 1999). However, in the explosion of invest-ment the traditional role of the venture capitalist as the board level steward, able to get things addressed as and when needed, was in many cases usurped by new blood investing in whatever seemed attractive. This recruitment of inexperienced people into VC firms meant that, when the time came, there was a dearth of talent capable of saving companies that were not meeting their much-hyped forecasts. As sure bets turned to evens and then fell further, the standard success rates for venture capital investment across the industry fell to around 20 per cent. Only one in five investments would deliver a return. Compare that with the typical success rates for new product development of around 50 per cent! Although the rewards and hence the risks could arguably be considered to be higher than those in 'traditional industries', this difference was not sustainable in the long term and hence was a key influence in the withdrawal of venture capital investment during 2001.

Role of incubators

In parallel with this rise in venture capital investment there was also a similar growth in the use of incubators. Again, although in existence for a number of years – first within university science parks in the 1960s, in government-sponsored research establish-ments in the 1970s and then in regional development agencies in the 1980s – it was during the late 1990s that incubator growth took off. Growing from 700 worldwide in 1990, there were over 3400 incubators of one form or another in operation by 2000 (Barrow, 2001). As physical sites for new start-up companies, attached to universities or for-profit science parks, or virtual homes for new ideas within corporate environments, incubators were increas-ingly seen as an ideal approach for nurturing and funding new opportunities. Cambridge Science Park hosted a wealth of companies, including Cambridge Drug Discovery, Tadpole Tech-nology and Zeus, whilst MIT and its graduates were credited with creating an average of 150 new firms per year. Amongst a growing list of corporate backers, IBM established the IBM–Conxion Dotcom Incubator Programme, Lycos created LycosLabs, Apple took a $15 million stake in Akamai, EDS invested $1.5 billion in new venture incubation, and News International set up Oxygen, led by Elizabeth Murdoch. In addition, stimulated by the success of idealab and John Kao's Idea Factory, even the major consultants got in on the game. Andersen Consulting invested over $1 billion, McKinsey established Accelerators in 1999 to 'turbo-charge' the launch and growth of new e-businesses, Bain created bainlab linked to the firms existing venture capital arm Bain Capital, and even PWC and Ernst and Young formed their own incubators. Attracted by the opportunity to create high-value companies and the need to stop the haemorrhaging of talent to new start ups, several companies across the industrial landscape all used the idea of incubators to address the challenges they were facing. However, in the fallout as Oyxgen shares fell 98 per cent and companies like Webvan (an early Andersen Consulting off-shoot) lost $5 billion worth of market capitalization as its shares fell from $34 at IPO down to 10 cents in April 2001, corporate enthusiasm declined and the remaining incubators became more focused.

Investment integration

In the wake of this rise and fall in enthusiasm for investment in new ideas, there has now been a more recent reappraisal of how new technologies and businesses are best supported and how investment is duly made available. The Internet frenzy had shown to many the risks that go with innovation, but at the same time it had also increased awareness of the benefits to be gained from successful, efficiently managed and appropriately leveraged investment integration within the innovation process. Learning from the experiences of the late 1990s, companies large and small are now revising their approaches to funding new ideas, and for some, both the technology rich and conversely the slow movers, now is the time that new levels of investment are being made available.

Whilst a few select companies such as 3M and Siemens have had long-established internal funding mechanisms to support internal innovation, for others the idea of having an investment approach to new product and technology development is a relatively new concept:

- Whereas Hewlett Packard was a natural investor in the Internet, creating its $1 billion Garage Programme for new start-up companies, it has learnt from others' mistakes and stays out of the early stages, preferring to work with a range of partners who oversee the selection process before up to $2 million of additional HP finance is provided to newly backed firms to purchase (mostly HP) equipment and services. In addition, through a support network it also positions access to leading hosting, communications and service providers such as Cononus, Qwest, Inktomi and EMC.
- At the other end of the corporate scale, Nestlé created a $120 million science and technology venture fund in October 2001.

Following success with developing its £7 billion Alcon pharmaceutical business, this new fund is focusing on supporting opportunities in areas such as genomics and other life sciences, as well as packaging, with the aim of providing an alternative path to innovation delivery to that of going through one of the traditional business units.

- Similarly, having failed to get anything going during the boom, Unilever has followed Nestlé by establishing a stand-alone venture capital fund to develop promising ideas that do not fit into its core food and personal care businesses (Jones, 2001). Having tried to incubate several potential spin-offs, including myhome (a home-cleaning service) and Lynx-branded barber shops, with limited success, Unilever has now joined together with private equity houses to create a fund to nurture innovations using a mix of company and venture capital funding.

These and similar initiatives within the corporate space are reigniting investment in innovation across the arena. Companies are learning from the mistakes of the recent past and looking for new ways to integrate internal and external investment in new opportunities, but this time with the appropriate levels of experienced management input to support companies. More and more often using venture capitalists as part of a network of specialist input that can be appropriately deployed, led by firms such as Bessamer Ventures and Witness Hermann Hauser, these are being adopted to address the challenges of exploiting new opportunities in all three main arenas – universities, corporations and start-ups.

University innovation exploitation

Universities are increasingly a key source of new innovations and, in order to bring them to fruition, a major user of external investment support. They provide an ideal environment within which fundamental research and early stage development can both take place and, as commercial imperatives dictate, are increasingly being encouraged to exploit emerging technologies by governments and other funding institutions alike. However, although keen to enable such exploitation to occur, by their very nature they are often difficult organizations for the exploiting organizations to work with. Some institutions, particularly Cambridge and MIT, but also more recently UMIST and Imperial College in the UK and CalTech and Washington State in the USA, have been at the forefront of commercializing their research through the creation of spin-offs, joint ventures and licensing collaborations, but for most universities this is not an easy journey.

The biggest challenge within the academic environment is typically that politics, consensus-driven decision-making and multiple committees frequently have an impact on the ability to build successful commercially minded exploitation teams around the scientists who are creating the new technologies. Although such scientists may well want to be part of a spin-off company, the universities usually prefer to keep them as part of the academic community. More than just for educational purposes of delivering lectures, this is primarily because of the need to fulfil the requirements for funding. Since universities are largely judged on the strength of their academic research bases and the associated ratings that these merit, as organizations they are loath potentially to lose some of their best people to a spin-out firm. As such, the theoretically simpler but often logistically and commercially more complex route of licensing technology has been the traditional approach.

In addition, although there is a desire to benefit from the exploitation, there is often a reluctance to commit the necessary additional resource. Frequently viewing the prior research and development activities undertaken to move new technology to the 'proof of concept' state as investment by the institution, universities are typically unwilling to provide additional time to take it further. As many universities (particularly those for which innovation exploitation is a totally new activity) do not recognize the level of legal and financial work involved in identifying and matching up potential partners, sharing the effort and hence the future, often overpriced, value accordingly can also be a major issue. Business plans can take far longer than necessary to develop, negotiation between academic and corporate organizations can be lengthy, and the inevitable physical move out of the university environment at some stage of the exploitation can be complex.

Lastly, the human dimension of the people who have created the new technology themselves is sometimes a blockage to exploitation. After years of academic life, individuals can be reluctant to leave the security of university tenure for the cut-throat reality of the commercial world. Furthermore, when they do, problems can occur due to both tension created between those who move out and those who are left behind, and the universities continuing to believe that they are still in charge of what have actually become ex-employees. Nevertheless, when all these varied issues are successfully accommodated, usually through the establishment and implementation of a sound and disciplined investment integration process, as shown by Cambridge and MIT with their establishment of world leading spin-offs, the benefits can be significant.

Corporate innovation exploitation

As highlighted by the recent moves of Nestlé and Unilever, even for the more traditional and conservative companies there is an increasing incentive to reap the rewards from new ideas irrespective of whether they are inside or outside the core business. However, as HP shows, for the more technology-based firms, enabling spin-out companies to emerge and grow can also have a direct impact on the core business as they open up new products and services for existing customers. In addition, from the spin-out companies' perspective, having access to the parents' customer base from the start sometimes provides them with established market channels and the guarantee of early sales. Brightstar, a technology spin-out from BT, is another example of this, where the BT equity stake in Brightstar rises in value as the mother ship offers its existing customers the associated new technology.

In addition, the chances of success are further increased by the fact that the technologies that are usually the core of the new innovation have normally been pre-screened internally within the parent company and found to have a better chance of exploitation outside. This key decision is something that alternative innovation exploitation paths, whether via universities, consultancies or small start-ups, cannot provide. For these there is no choice but to create a new venture, whereas for the multinational the internal route for exploitation through an existing business unit is always the first choice. Additional benefits also include the ability to leverage the parent company's existing capabilities in market research, intellectual property protection and financial and legal matters, as well as to gain direct access to people with the experience and skills that are most suited to the new venture. Moreover, most companies can use their financial and market positioning to protect their fledglings in the all-important first few months of going it alone.

Although, as corporate entities, commercial focus is clearly far greater from the start than in most universities, within large multinationals there can also be some similar barriers to be overcome. These are especially focused on how the people directly involved react to the changes that they are inevitably forced to experience. Whilst for some the opportunity to lead a spin-out or spin-off business to exploit a new technology may be the ideal career move both in theory and in practice, for others it can be fraught with issues. Especially for individuals who may feel stuck in a large, slow company, the idea of being part of a fast-pace, sexy spin-out can be very attractive. However, when the reality of having to leave the company pension scheme, operate with no secretarial support and have no company car hits home, the choice can quickly become less attractive. The dilemma for the company is that it is the experienced people who are most needed to make a spin-out a success who, for personal reasons, may be the least willing to move over, whereas new and relatively inexperienced recruits with little to lose will be lining up to join in. However, if only the younger volunteers join in, you are back in the no-experience-but-lots-of-cash Internet dot.bomb spiral. If older, more experienced managers are given safeguards about pensions and guaranteed something to fall back on if the venture fails, then the necessary motivation, enthusiasm and energy to make a spin-out a success can be lacking. Balancing these human, and often highly emotional, considerations is one of the critical decisions for corporate innovation exploitation.

Start-up innovation exploitation

By contrast with the other two, the small start-up route for innovation exploitation is the one with the greatest risk and hence, without expert support and suitable investment, the least chance of isolated success. Besides the lack of a parent organization to provide subsidized facilities, ready made access to customers, additional resource and credit facilities, the key challenges faced in this context are often the lack of an established network to tap into for advice, fewer contacts, less experience, and potentially unproven technology. Whereas corporate spin-out companies have often benefited from an initial incubation period within the parent prior to creation, for start-up companies they are themselves the early stage of the development and exploitation process. At the beginning there is no one to help to create a sufficiently professional business plan to gain funding, no one other than the few entrepreneurs involved and their friends have a vested interest in success, and it is also more difficult to get investors' attention. However, largely because of these barriers, small start-ups cannot afford to hang around and are therefore typically faster moving and focused on gaining revenue, whether from investment funding or actual sales, as quickly as possible. Consequently, although a high risk in terms of the lack of natural support, such companies are often more dynamic, more eager to succeed, and more pushy in the marketplace. With no safety net to fall back on, start-up firms have to succeed or fail – there is no middle ground.

Investment process

Irrespective of context, the overall investment process is largely generic. As with the innovation process that it seeks to support, when working with external investment there are key decision points and associated criteria that drive the release of resource and progress. Often happening at a rate implied by the nature of the innovation being exploited and the type of enabling organization being used, how investment is managed appropriately to support successful realization of ambition is an increasingly key capability in the post-Internet boom era. For organizations large and small, the timing of the necessary financial, strategic and tactical inputs from external expertise that have successfully made the IPR to IPO journey before is fast becoming a critical differentiator in the definition of the leaders for tomorrow.

The first step is always the business plan. Although often considered an academic exercise within large organizations, where creating attractive figures that push all the right budget buttons is a nominal prerequisite to gaining approval, when external funding is involved the business plan is the key means by which the critical initial yes/no investment decision can be taken. As such, it is no longer a side issue to be ticked off in a matter of minutes, but becomes the focus for all. Working in conjunction with external input, now more than ever, demonstrating the uniqueness of the proposition, its realistic potential and the key stages required to realize it are just the beginning. Today, ensuring that all legal frameworks covering ownership, intellectual property and deal structures are in place alongside the financial elements of valuation, determination of class of share, creation of options pools and the associated due diligence are all essential. If venture capital is involved, definition of lead investor in a syndicate, gaining acceptance from all other investors, agreeing respective amounts and gaining early access to key influencers in the financial markets are all vital. Having been bitten hard in the late 1990s, funding organizations are more vigilant than ever and so, even for relatively small investments, proving worth and credibility up front rather than later has been a fundamental shift in external and internal focus. This all helps to set the scene for future progression.

The next major point for investment integration comes when second-round funding is required. Usually occurring after all concepts have been proven in test markets with lead customers, and the scalability of the business or technology to address its claimed potential is the major question, this is the point where big investors get involved. Whereas a corporate based spin-off may have had some investment from the parent organization for initial development or a start-up may have benefited from initial angel investor input, this is where external money is critical. As such, if any of the elements associated with the former investment step have not been undertaken to a point where all key criteria have been met, the required financial input can now be very difficult to secure. Without it, bridging loans, usually in the form of convertible stock that converts to equity in subsequent funding rounds or market flotation, are increasingly required. Although practicable options, these are today more of a last resort for companies that are too late in trying to raise the necessary capital to continue apace.

The final step for typical investors is the exit point. For standard venture capitalists this is the focus of all their activities, and maximizing the return on exit is therefore what they steer the company towards. They try to make a venture as attractive as possible and put it in the best possible position with the financial markets. It is here where the earlier access to key point of influence makes the impact. Using leading corporate financiers, leveraging contacts discreetly, contacting potential purchasers and ensuring that the company has enough cash so that its development is confident throughout negotiations, is where a good network of expert input comes to the fore. Today, in a more suspicious and risk-averse market, where the guaranteed IPO is no longer the obvious route for investment realization and continued financing for new companies, the alternatives of trade sales, management buy-outs and reversals into existing floated companies are increasingly being used. If undertaken professionally, the exit of lead investors runs smoothly, provides increased financial stability for the company and sets it up for future growth. If the lead investors do not perform their roles adequately in this ever more demanding market, then the whole enterprise can be put in jeopardy as drawn-out decisions paralyse companies, negotiations are protracted and fail to deliver the goods, and key individuals lose focus as they try and fill the gaps. Insufficient technical understanding, poor communication, too great a focus on the pure financials and a lack of patience are, as ever, major barriers to success.

New approaches

To overcome and avoid such problems there are a number of companies emerging to the fore. Bringing together a combination of technological understanding, innovation prowess and financial expertise, several new firms are now increasingly becoming involved in these key investment decisions as organizations across the spectrum seek to exploit their ideas and technologies further. The escalating use of intellectual property is allowing the traditional value chain to become broken, and development and commercialization to become separate things, done by separate companies, with the patent acting as the formal transfer mechanism between the two. Traditionally this has been the preserve of the academic institutions, but now a new breed of companies has been able to generate considerable revenues through licensing and sales of the intellectual property that they have developed but someone else markets. Examples of such development companies include the Generics Group, Schipher, BTG and Accentus, all in the UK.

Generics

From its foundation as a technology consultancy in 1986, Cambridge-based Generics has gradually grown first into business consulting and then into technology development and product innovation. As it has done this it has increasingly invented new technologies, either for clients or internally. Recognizing the value that is associated with the intellectual property related to these, Generics has protected its innovations and used them as the basis for two avenues of income generation. Through traditional licensing of key technologies across multiple applications the company has already secured royalty revenue streams nearing £0.5 million, which underpin its investment in new research. In parallel with this it has also used internal and external investment to support the continued development of key technologies, incubating start-up ventures and then spinning these off as separate companies. Driven by integrated investment throughout the development of several technologies, it has created a number of spin-out opportunities. Recent successes include Quantumbeam and Imerge:

- Quantumbeam is built around 'point to multipoint' wireless communication, which is seen to play a major role in enabling the 'last mile' connection for non-urban broadband access. Having agreed relationships with a number of existing service providers, it already has an early stage valuation of £15 million.
- Imerge develops Next Generation Media Appliance Software and hard-disk based web-enabled home entertainment products. With second-round funding of £2.5 million in 2001, the company has licence agreements in place with six leading consumer electronics manufacturers.

Schipher

Schipher, by contrast, is a technology development and licensing company that grew out of the research laboratories of an existing company, EMI, the music and technology organization. Now the largest technology development company of its type in Europe, it is primarily focused on developing and licensing technologies invented within CRL, its own R&D facilities. Formed in 1996, the company focuses on six product areas comprising secure identification, displays, three-dimensional sound, broadcast monitoring, communications, and gas sensors. It has over 1000 patents, which generated revenues of nearly £15 million in 2001. Of Schipher's products, Sensura is a sound technology installed in over 50 million PCs and fitted as a standard feature on Microsoft's X Box, and its smart card secure identification is being used for bank passbooks in China and document protection in the USA. In addition, the company has a separate patent licensing business, QED, which increasingly creates value from the intellectual property held by external organizations. With over sixty-two patent families under management, including those of Toyota, QED is licensing patents for clients to organizations such as Samsung, Philips, Alcatel and Mitsubishi. Accentus, an IP exploitation business within AEA technology, is following a similar path by exploiting the company's 200 inventions and establishing itself as a technology development and exploitation channel for externally generated innovations.

BTG

The British Technology Group, BTG, is a successful pure commercialization firm. Listed in 1995, it has recently achieved notable successes in commercializing BeneFix, a drug for haemophiliacs that helps blood clotting, and MLC memory for expanding the capacity of flash memory. Ian Harvey, the Chief Executive of BTG, points to this being a UK phenomenon, and claims that 'there aren't many look-alikes in the US'. It is now a technology commercialization organization operating in the UK, North America and Japan. As a result, it has formed strong relationships with many of the world's leading research centres and major technology companies. Through its global reach, BTG has access to many sources of innovations around the world. It works with universities and companies to determine the value of their technology portfolios and identify ways in which they can leverage the value of their IP. Some companies prefer to initiate joint ventures and equity sharing arrangements, while others opt to assign their patented technologies to BTG for licensing. The company claims to do much more than simply protect IP, although this is still its core competence. Its ability to add real value comes from its expertise in analysing technological innovations to determine the steps in progressing towards product or service revenues. The company often brings together previously separate technologies to increase the potential of an existing portfolio. BTG looks for commercialization routes that create the greatest value, seeking out and sometimes creating new companies best able to bring the product to market.

Far Blue

Another new company that is further changing the investment approach for innovation by acting across the technology development/commercialization continuum is UK-based Far Blue (www.farblue.com). Unlike traditional venture capitalists who manage and invest funds with predetermined lifetimes of typically three to five years, Far Blue is a venture capital company investing off its own balance sheet. Rather than acting as an investor of other financial institutions' capital, it uses its own money to fund companies in their early stages of development. Focusing specifically on early stage technologies, Far Blue directly invests in them and helps to manage their growth. As such it does not have a very wide portfolio, but instead is involved with a few select companies.

Founded following recognition through experience that there were few early-stage funders who knew much about the technologies they were investing in, Far Blue has the internal capability to evaluate new technological opportunities. Rather than calling in expert consultants to undertake the technology assessment, the company can do this itself. As such, it is ideally placed both for undertaking investment and for providing active help during the early stages in managing the development of the technologies and the growth of the associated firms. It is one of the only early-stage funding organizations operating in the UK with full-time on-board technology skills to deploy as and where necessary. The benefit for the companies with which Far Blue is involved is that while it takes care of all the legal and financial issues required for the successful nurturing of start ups, the companies themselves can concentrate on developing the technology – something that is usually their forte. As well as providing the opportunity for rapid growth, the situation of these companies within a wider network of similarly positioned companies enables them to pull other technologies across from one to another, often creating partnerships for common areas of focus. Far Blue has already provided and arranged investment for several new leading-edge technology firms, including:

- IDS – a removable data storage development company
- Imerge – the home entertainment firm spun out of Generics
- mCentric – a mobile Internet application platform developer
- Polight – a Cambridge University spin-out with patents in holographic storage
- Polaris – an IP network security and building management system provider
- Voxar – a three-dimensional medical imaging company.

Together, these and similar companies emerging across the technology landscape are reinventing the way in which innovation is being financed. From up-front external investment in research, incubation of new ideas and enabling first-round venture capital funding through to managing IPO and similar value creation, they are playing an increasingly significant role in the innovation process.

References

Barrow, C. (2001). *Incubators: A Realist's Guide to the World's New Business Accelerators.* John Wiley & Sons.

Jones, A. (2001). Unilever may create fund for non-core ideas. *Financial Times*, 26 November.

Lewis, M. (1999). *The New New Thing: A Silicon Valley Story.* Hodder & Stoughton.

12

Virtual collaboration

Every organization collaborates as, in one way or another, they work with other parties to derive value. In everyday life we work with a group of people to get things done, and this is a key essence of innovation. As mentioned previously, the challenge is to collaborate effectively, focusing on quality and timely outputs, for in practice the standard of collaboration varies widely from one firm to another. In assessing how effectively an organization collaborates, it is important to consider all dimensions. These include the numbers and types of internal and external parties able to collaborate, the ease of connection, and the quantity and quality of output achieved. Some would argue that the most innovative organizations are also the most collaborative; whilst there is limited research to confirm this hypothesis the rationale makes sense. Innovative companies from 3M to Nortel tend to use temporary organizational structures and wide-ranging networks. Similar networks are increasingly being used by many organizations, and expert groups are progressively coming together to work on output-focused objectives – the key element behind effective collaboration.

Ingredients for collaboration

Whilst innovation has always utilized collaboration, the new challenge is to improve the effectiveness of, deliver consistent results from, and expand the network for *ad hoc* collaboration. In today's continuously changing and challenging business environment, the pressures are increasing. Revenue growth and cost reduction are now the key business drivers within any innovation programme. As such, they must be continually met, and ideally surpassed. At the same time, customers are demanding more complex or customized products and services faster, cheaper and better than ever before. Collaboration is key in making this happen, and has four critical ingredients:

1 Clear focus
2 Multiple connections between the right parties
3 Access to content
4 Working processes.

Focus

The starting point for any product and service development is increasingly focused on the potential customer and the associated set of needs. As highlighted in the earlier chapter on values recognition, although it is often difficult for customers to articulate their requirements clearly, they can provide critical knowledge that enables the creation of real 'value add' products and services. The use of customer collaboration in innovation can help firms to understand those needs fully and discover other unarticulated requirements that are simply not expressed. This provides the focus of the new product or service challenge.

Connections

To meet the challenges, companies often have to bring global expertise to bear on local problems. Increasingly, no single organization has the breadth of skills and knowledge to deliver the total solution, and hence partnerships, consortia and alliances are proving to be key to successful delivery. These need not only to be able to access global experts but also to work with them to create outputs and make decisions. In essence, successful organizations set up 'relational ecosystems' where, instead of 'one to one', 'many to many' collaboration is easy and also becomes the norm.

Content access

Once the connections are in place, the content has to be made readily available. This primarily consists of product specifications, industry news, operational parameters and, especially, codified expertise. To deliver the best ideas, companies need to be able to leverage their and others' previous experience more effectively and learn from past mistakes. They therefore require access to worldwide knowledge bases that incorporate this, and, more importantly, need to be able to find and manage appropriate information. Processing this information can then start to deliver value.

Working processes

In global organizations and most multinational projects, people are inevitably spread across multiple locations and time zones. Even if they may be mobile or home-based, it is essential that everyone can contribute effectively, in his or her own time and space. As businesses become more global in scope and reach, it is increasingly important to be able to work with people across the planet with effective communication but at limited cost. Synchronous face-to-face collaboration has always been preferred, but in today's climate this is often too expensive and simply takes too much time. The challenge is therefore to develop both synchronous and asynchronous approaches that reduce cost and process time whilst at the same time improving quality.

Enter the technology solution providers, who have seized the opportunity to create a wide range of increasingly virtual collaborative tools built specifically to provide support for different collaborative innovation interventions. At a helicopter view, three groupings of tools have emerged containing both synchronous and asynchronous solutions:

1 The first grouping majors on information discipline and sharing to cover issues such as product breakdown, bill of material structures and knowledge depositories
2 The second group looks at collaborating around the actual development process or programme – for example, collaborative portfolio tools, workflow for decision-making
3 Finally, the third group focuses on the actual content development and design activities such as collaborative engineering visualization tools and asynchronous design pads.

Whilst these are similar to tools used in everyday working, they require different technologies and applications when used for virtual collaboration. For example, although aeronautical engineers will typically use powerful CAD/CAM technology to perform their every day roles, to collaborate using the output from the tool is a different process entirely. The standard CAD files are therefore increasingly converted into 'lite' format files that require less memory and can work with simpler viewer-type software. These are then used for collaborative design activities such as virtual design reviews, with changes stored in the form of simple mark-up layers.

It is this technology development that has given rise to some of the latest buzzwords in innovation. Combining collaboration with technology has given rise to Collaborative Commerce, c-Commerce or, more commonly, Collaborative Product Commerce (CPC). It has started to enable the art of the previously impossible – high quality and timely collaboration is now within our reach, and traditional product development activities can at last really start to become Collaborative Product and Service Development (CPSD).

Collaborative product and service development

At its simplest, CPSD is the ability electronically to enable innovation process interactions within a working community to deliver benefits. Across the product development arena, it has been the usual early technology adopters of the aeronautical, automotive and medical industries that have been fast to catch on. CPSD can deliver significant advantage by using virtual collaborative approaches both intra- and inter-organizationally throughout the innovation process. It promises tangible benefits to the bottom line through process and actual product development cost reduction, significant quality improvements and reductions in warranty cost savings, as well as shorter time to market and development cycles. In many areas the approach and benefits are already being proven, with automotive and aerospace industries quoting up to 67 per cent time-to-market reductions, 3–5 per cent actual part cost reduction, and efficiency improvements of up to 30 per cent.

Ford has implemented web collaboration technology to share design changes and other information with engineers and suppliers in different locations during the design and manufacturing lifecycle stages of development. Their metrics indicate a near 100 per cent reduction in analysis time – three days to one minute – and 0.25–0.75 per cent reductions in development cost of one vehicle model, saving between $5 million and $15 million (*Computing*, 2001). Ford used web collaboration to develop its new Mondeo platform in 2000. This involved connecting engineers and suppliers in the USA, England, Germany and Japan, with the majority of the design stage being completed in the digital world and providing the end benefit of a 67 per cent reduction in development time from forty-eight to sixteen months (*Information Week*, 2000). GM quotes similar figures. This equally challenged firm installed a system to provide its worldwide product teams with simultaneous access to digital vehicle information. The result was a 43 per cent reduction in development time from forty-two to twenty-four months (*Design News*, 2000).

These evident advantages are being further backed up by softer benefits such as the ability to access information easily, as people can look through databases via web browsers any where in the world, at any time. Moreover, information access changes from a push to a pull mentality, with people retrieving the desired data when it fits into their own time plan. Version control becomes centralized and, rather than relying on one individual, entire teams can manage the process. There is 'one version of the truth' and, with check in and out facilities, people can update and build documents safely in serial fashion without the cumbersome administrative task of merging information. However, one of the most significant non-measurable benefits is proving to be improved and documented decision-making. The use of even simple workflow and routing allows decision-making processes to be made explicit, with information easily accessible and responses and dates clearly stated. This improves the quality of any decision by both providing easier access to the available data and the ability to acknowledge missing data, whilst the recording aspect also ensures that decisions tend to be considered better. In addition, this collaborative approach supports easier reporting and management control. Teams involved in development programmes can update their individual status, and many approaches now utilize dashboard-style information displays to give simple traffic-light summaries of overall programme progress.

Providing these hard and soft benefits also has an impact on the way that organizations work. Collaboration starts to break down traditional silos between functions such as development and procurement, whilst simultaneously extending the capability to involve other organizations. Using new tools broadens the range and number of partners that an organization can realistically work with – suppliers, customers, and competitors alike. There are in fact many other CPSD opportunity areas, including:

- Overall programme and project management
- Phase-gate management
- Portfolio management
- Collaborative and virtual design

- Collaborative engineering
- Engineering change management and engineering change notifications
- Product data management (PDM)
- Bill of materials creation and change management
- Collaborative requirements capture.

In all these cases, collaboration is about connecting people to people so they can work together to deliver higher quality output faster. However, whilst there are evident benefits to be had, learning how to collaborate and delivering the results requires significant time and effort.

Implementing collaborative product and service development

The most effective method for learning how to collaborate tends to follow a stepwise approach in process complexity. Organizations typically start with document sharing, then move on to process management and finally progress to more content-specific type tools. This is beneficial in handling the change management aspects of collaboration, as it allows for organizational learning and also delivers results incrementally. Implementing collaboration often requires a 'transformation map' type approach, collectively tackling organizational, process, technology and partner issues, and in practice can well become a three- to five-year programme. Clearly any CPSD approaches have to be aimed at delivering a desired output, and need to improve the current process. In short, for CPSD to be successful it must make it easier to collaborate with other people, and that changed interaction has to deliver some incremental improvement such as reduced process time, lower cost or increased quality. Given its potential complexity there are, unsurprisingly, several cases where CPSD has simply not worked, where it has been more complicated than it was thought to start with, and where there has been no apparent benefit. Current lessons learnt identify several key ingredients that are proving to be critical in ensuring successful collaboration. These include:

- Producing a strong rationale or reason for collaboration
- Ensuring evident willingness and organizational support
- Adopting the partners to collaborate with
- Presenting explicit understanding of how to collaborate
- Having an appropriate, accessible item to collaborate on
- Providing the technological and procedural means to collaborate.

Rationale and business case

Early pioneers of CPSD, such as Boeing, took a leap of faith in experimenting and proving the potential benefits. There were limited numbers and evidence to create business cases, and consequently they were largely driven by firms believing that there had to be opportunities to increase the effectiveness of multi-partner working and, thereby, to reduce time to market. Following some early successes, there was then enough evidence to build reasonable business cases that delivered measurable strategic benefits, reducing development and design costs whilst improving time to market. A top-down benefits analysis can often highlight the potential opportunity areas in the key innovation processes; however, many such analyses show opportunities that are difficult to quantify, thereby making it difficult to develop a compelling business case for virtual collaboration.

The understanding of the size of opportunity and how this fits with an organization's strategic objectives is imperative to adopt a virtual collaboration technology-supported approach. If it is to deliver success, stakeholders have to be unwavering in their support for such an approach. Virtual collaboration programmes are a long-term commitment – two to three years out is the minimum time perspective. They can require significant technology investment, and often demand a supported organizational change programme if they are to deliver the results. A successful collaboration programme therefore increasingly starts with key stakeholders and the organization having a clear understanding of, and commitment to, the benefits and strategic fit of the programme.

In many instances the usual approach is the top-down benefits case, utilizing collaborative benchmarks to both identify the size of the opportunity and define how it delivers against the organization's strategic direction. It is important to consider both internal and external metrics in identifying these opportunities – if collaboration could reduce an organization's time to market from ten to six months but the market leader delivers in three months, then the impact will be minimal. Prioritizing the benefits by ease of delivery and likelihood of success identifies several areas that could potentially gain from pilot approaches, and it is at this stage that key performance indicators can be applied. These can be used to understand and measure how successful an organization is at collaboration. In reality, collaboration will have an impact on an organization's targeted business innovation measures, and in virtual collaboration some specifics (such as number of external parties capable of collaborative working or design) are also good indicators of progress made.

An understanding of the benefits case is especially critical when successful partner adoption is a key driver in achieving results. For example, in the creation of vertical marketplaces offering collaborative working solutions, the key to success has been to build such a rationale collaboratively with all sponsors and partners alike. This evidently facilitates partner buy-in as they help identify the most beneficial scenarios.

Willingness and organizational support

It requires the usual trio of rational, political and emotional issues to be addressed at an organizational and an individual level for an organization to develop successful collaborative approaches. To facilitate effective collaboration requires classic change management techniques – stakeholder support, a strong value proposition, clear project management, good communication, appropriate training, and active involvement of the end users.

At an organizational level, the serious use of virtual collaboration creates 'collaboration networks'. These are unlike usual explicit organizational structures, as they have no boundaries and no paradigms in their own right and bring with them their own organizations' cultures and approaches. This means that there is no code for 'this is the way we do things round here'. In these cases, working together is extremely difficult and painful. As a result, collaboration either stops as collaborators find it too agonizing, or they persevere until some way of working has eventually been mutually arrived at. This is another reason to invest in working collaboratively from the beginning to identify how to collaborate, and also builds on top of a collaboratively agreed benefits case.

These organizational issues are further manifested by industry 'rules'. For example, as highlighted earlier, it is not uncommon now for competitors to be expected to collaborate, but it is a very different mindset that is needed when you work with someone rather than against them. In the construction industry, individual companies are still commonly tasked to compete against each other and face penalties for late delivery. These 'rules' actively discourage collaboration and therefore would need to be unpicked before a collaborative approach could have any significant chance of success.

Organizational learning is also critical in developing collaboration. Successful collaboration programmes often consist of a series of pilots, and reviewing lessons learnt is critical in ensuring that progress down the collaborative roadmap keeps moving forward. This approach helps to build trust, a key ingredient of collaboration, and as this grows people start to take more risks with each other and both the quality and quantity of collaboration correspondingly increases.

At an individual level, the key drivers of success are similar and also have to be in place. People need to see the benefit of collaborating – 'what's in it for me?' Hence the change must really make their job easier. They need to be willing to give collaboration a go. It must therefore be as much of a risk-free, non-threatening activity as possible. Moreover, individuals also need reassurance that it will help to move them forward and do things in a different way rather than perhaps do them out of a job. Finally, they need to know how to collaborate. Training and communication are therefore critical, as is instilling individual 'plan-do-review' learning loops.

Partner adoption

In practice, the internal issues associated with collaboration frequently also remove some of the effort from managing adoption of partners – who can be any other entity that an organization will need to collaborate with, ranging from suppliers and customers to competitors and knowledge experts. Partner adoption starts with selection, with defining who an organization should collaborate with, why, and what level of collaboration is required. The benefits available and how they fit with both organizations' strategic directions usually determine this. Typically, both partners fall into collaborating; however, formalizing the rationale, agreeing how to collaborate and answering any concerns also aid more managed collaborative programmes. Taking these issues seriously helps to establish the trust that is then further developed through fair and mutually rewarding collaboration. For CPSD, the specific area of intellectual property can create significant concerns and be a complete barrier to collaboration. It is therefore essential to have a predetermined agreement on how collaborating organizations will manage and agree IP ownership and any resulting benefits.

A further key consideration here is the application of technology. Virtual collaboration tools are e-tools, and different organizations have different levels of e-readiness and associated capability. Issues such as connectivity, security and access have to be assessed and agreed up front. In the current climate organizations are finding the need to use various collaborative tools due to the requirement to interact with different market places, and hence interoperability is becoming a prerequisite when partners are considering adoption.

Processes, collaborative scenarios and content

Collaboration in innovation can also be applied to most sub-processes. Here the real benefit is in identifying the key opportunities where collaboration can potentially solve many issues. The starting point is therefore to create a document of the process by which people can collaborate. This is usually highly iterative, involving many decision-making sub-processes, and hence can be better described as a 'collaborative scenario'. Effectively a series of facilitating processes with specified roles focusing on a clear output, this may, for example, be to agree engineering changes. This may consist of facilitating processes of virtual design reviews, decision-making and approvals, notification of change and document management.

Technology

Finally, there are hundreds of applications available to support virtual collaboration. These have all developed from different legacy backgrounds, such as ERP, PDM, Project Management, CAD/CAM and dotcoms. Market competitiveness ensures a high rate of innovation and development in the offerings themselves, but it is nevertheless important to note the range and types of collaborative activities that these tools support. There is core collaborative functionality, which covers content, process, access management and communication, and more specific collaboration functionality in a host of modules covering PDM, lifecycle management, programme and phase-gate management, requirements capture, virtual design tools, visualization and mark-up. Such current collaboration suites include:

- ERP providers – Oracle (oPDX), SAP (PLM)
- PDM providers – PTC Windchill, MatrixOne, EDS PLM
- CAD providers – EDS PLM, UGS/EAI
- Software providers – Microsoft, Sharepoint
- Marketplaces/dotcoms – eRooms.

In addition, key technology journals and trade magazines continually assess available offerings. Critical parameters in the selection of the most appropriate include visioning the capability of the provider to move the solution to meet future needs, ease of deployment and scalability, cost of ownership, ability to interface and integrate with legacy systems, and interoperability with other partners' collaborative technology. The latter is becoming increasingly important in ensuring that collaborative software actually delivers value. If information cannot be seamlessly integrated to other sources, then any subsequent effort-requiring manual links or uploads destroys collaborative value.

Covisint – automotive collaboration

The lead example of virtual collaboration in practice to date has been Covisint (www.covisint.com), a global automotive market-place that offers a range of solutions including collaborative tools to support new product development in the automotive industry. It was founded in 2000 by three major automotive OEMs (Original Equipment Manufacturers) – Ford, General Motors and Daimler Chrysler – to try and avoid multiple costly and complex marketplace solutions. Previously all OEMs had taken their own route in creating trade and collaborative exchanges, and if this had continued it would have led to increased industry costs rather than the reductions the companies required. Covisint's approach is to select strong technology providers and host these selected applications, hence providing value by being a cheap source of the best technology solutions.

Covisint became operational at the end of 2000, by which stage Renault and Nissan had also joined the investors, and many 'Tier One' suppliers, as well as the leading technology partners, had all voiced their support. Covisint offers several key marketplace solutions with focus on three key areas:

1 Product Development & Programme Management – enabling faster introduction of new products and providing for lifecycle sourcing
2 An Electronic Procurement Marketplace – connecting sellers and buyers globally, and offering on-line auctions and catalogue services
3 Supply Chain Collaboration/Synchronization – reducing inventory and cycle time, and enabling faster constraint visibility and resolution.

For virtual collaboration, Covisint focuses on three distinct offerings under the branding of Virtual Project Workspace (VPW). These include a base collaborative offering for content and core process collaboration, a collaborative procurement offering for supplier management and electronic requests for quotation, or 'eRFQ', and a dedicated product development programme management offering. In addition, Covisint manages user registration, deployment and training, and provides help-desk support covering tool use and troubleshooting. The business model relies on monthly subscription fees for initial use, with costs ranging from $30 to $300 a month per user depending on the level of functionality registered for.

Within the first few months, take up of the VPW range of services was most successful with the basic collaboration packages and eRFQ offering. For product development, the main utilization has been to support data and content sharing – synchronous through application sharing and asynchronous through file storage and management – and, by using the base collaboration offering and utilizing the eRFQ solution, to link product development with procurement organizations. All OEMs and several Tier One suppliers have actively pursued the virtual collaboration approach and tools, and applied them in pilots within the product development and procurement communities. The main benefits delivered have been process time-savings, along with the softer advantages of programme participants being able to communicate better and to find appropriate information. Within the product development arena, the use of application sharing conferencing has helped to avoid the need for face-to-face meetings, reduced travel costs and improved the quality of output between such events by providing an alternative method for synchronous collaboration. In practice, this has meant the real-time sharing of data and drawings in usual Microsoft formats such as Word documents and tif or pdf files.

In some aspects this uptake has followed the wider business experience of the uptake of collaborative solutions, starting with the basics, document management, and sharing and utilizing solutions where value can be easily identified such as with eRFQs. However, Covisint has had to handle the usual scepticism and concerns of a marketplace provision of collaboration tools. This has included functionality issues, end user ease of use, and speed, solution scalability and security, as well as the ability to integrate with current systems.

Customer feedback combined with company changes led Covisint to review its choice of initial collaboration technology partner. After assessment and customer consultation, Covisint decided to offer the MatrixOne suite for collaboration tools. This stressed some key lessons learned; to provide better-targeted solutions and collaborative offerings that had ongoing development plans. This was particularly pertinent for product development, where the offering was too generic easily to demonstrate and offer benefit to specific product development processes. The new approach continues to maintain the same target segments, but the new solution has also two offerings focused on meeting product development and programme management needs:

1 'Engineering Manager' focuses value on collaboratively creating and defining parts, building and managing the bill of materials, creating and managing engineering changes, and dynamic workflow creation. This offering collaboratively acts as the glue between OEM and supplier product data management systems. Specifically, it provides concurrency of information between engineering, procurement and the supply base for engineering changes and bill of materials. This can drastically reduce both engineering change time and issue management, as well as provide a bill of materials structure that can be built and managed collaboratively. In theory this could remove several manpower weeks and eliminate the rework time for the bill of materials validation that typically occurs several times throughout a new vehicle development programme, and can take a team of four to eight people up to six weeks to carry out. However, it needs to prove integration capabilities and have significant change management and deployment support in order to deliver this potential value.

2 'Programme Manager' provides collaborative project management, managing multiple project plans, merging timelines, providing issue tracking and status reporting. Again, the solution can be integrated into most conventional project management software. This has less of a visible business case, as most view this as a replacement for tools that currently exist, and hence its benefit comes in the integration with the other collaborative solutions.

Further solutions scheduled for 2002 release included a collaborative Advanced Product Quality Planning tool, a type of phase-gate approach focusing on ensuring quality deliverables by suppliers at the end of each development phase.

At the end of its first year of operation, Covisint had active collaboration programmes running with all main OEMs across the industry. The challenge was to develop these programmes, scale up to include more users, and develop the complexity of collaborative functionality being utilized from basic selected information sharing to collaboration on the core product development process. To achieve this there are three significant issues:

1 Convincing the OEMs of security and data protection by ensuring there are no risks to data stored outside their own firewalls.

2 Being able to build business cases within the product development communities to drive potential programmes going forward. For real benefit, product development collaboration must

sit at the heart of the business process, and this requires full integration into existing development systems.

3 Being able to change the way automotive product development works, and embracing the new opportunities collaboration brings.

Well on its way to achieving these by the middle of 2002, Covisint has become the largest, most prominent and arguably the most significant user of virtual collaboration to date. As such, it has proven that a concept that works at an inter-corporate level can also deliver benefits at an industry level, and is a model being repeated across other sectors.

c-Medica – medical collaboration

In June 2001, a new product development web site focused on improving speed to market for medical devices was launched. The first collaborative data management site dedicated to this sector, c-Medica (www.c-Medica.com), similarly provides OEMs and suppliers with a suite of on-line tools that seek to streamline the product development process. As with Covisint, through a secure workspace c-Medica users share CAD files and technical data, access extensive databases, conduct meetings, manage project milestones, and make use of work-plan processes aligned to the all important FDA deliverables. In addition, specific medical industry content such as industry news, discussion forums and procurement offerings provide extra functionality for users.

Initiated by Dow Plastics, a business unit of Dow Chemical, and the Medical Device Manufacturers Association, c-Medica became commercially active at the end of 2001, and, through the involvement of this industry body in particular, began to extend its reach across the sector. Like the automotive industry, the $150 billion medical devices arena has thousands of manufacturers and suppliers that need to coordinate new product development activities, but had previously been limited by traditional methods of information sharing and exchange. Especially in such a fragmented sector with over 30 000 new development projects initiated each year, bringing key players together had been difficult, and c-Medica was the first major opportunity for all to join in a centralized but, most significantly, neutral workspace.

Built around ProductSync data management software provided by Boston-based Conferos that focuses specifically on web-based tools for the plastics industry, this virtual collaboration marketplace is also focused on the key objectives of reducing costs, shortening development times, increasing efficiency and simplifying increasingly complex innovation programmes. Connecting designers, manufacturers and suppliers throughout and, particularly, early in the development process, like Covisint, c-Medica has again proved that, in the appropriate circumstances, the benefits that can be gained at corporate and industry levels from increasing virtual collaboration can be significant.

References

Computing (2001). 19 October.
Design News (2000). 13 November.
Information Week (2000). 2 October.

13

Brand exploitation

The emergence of the significance of the role of the brand in innovation throughout the early and mid-1990s, highlighted in Part 1, was fundamentally linked to an ever-increasing inter-relationship between the company, its products and the brand(s) that it used to both promote and represent these. In the vast majority of cases this was underpinned by interaction between the brand values or propositions and the products or services that the company itself delivered into the markets. The increasing promi-nence of the brand and the associated rise in brand value for companies as diverse as Microsoft, Coca Cola, IBM, Citibank, Mercedes and even Intel, highlighted by their relative positioning in Interbrand's annual brand survey, were all largely driven by, and linked to, the software, drinks, servers, financial services, cars and microchips that they respectively provided. As new arrivals in the brand value leaders, such as Starbucks, Amazon and Cisco, grew through delivering innovative new products and services, maximizing corporate value was, in an ever-increasingly promi-nent manner, significantly influenced by how they created, developed, nurtured and deployed their brands to support their products and *vice versa*. At this time there was, however, limited exploitation of brand equity outside companies' core product portfolios.

By and large, over the past decade extension of a brand into a new areas has largely been linked to new products or services that a company is directly involved in delivering, in one way or another. Benetton achieved a cross-over from fashion to Formula 1 by financing its own team; Nike extended from footwear to clothing, equipment and eyewear; Samsung moved from the manufacture of TVs to fax machines, microwaves and laptops; the *Financial Times* grew from newspapers into book publishing and Internet services; Amazon increased its product offering from books to CDs, videos and consumer electronics; and, in its own way, American Express extended its brand and product portfolio from charge cards to credit cards, insurance and travel services. All these were successful extensions of organizations' fields of operation achieved through the firms themselves delivering new products into both new and existing markets, and all have ensured innovative growth to revenues and brand value.

An alternative approach to brand extension has recently become prominent. Building and exploiting brand value through partnerships with others outside the company's core area of activities has become a key new way to create revenue. Using the values represented by a brand and the associated customer base to leverage new opportunities via external alliances has become a new item on the agenda of marketing and business development directors in many major organizations. By 'lending' a brand to either a partner or joint venture activity to support a new product's proposition, appeal or delivery, several companies are now realizing significant benefits. Rather than create and deliver new products and services internally, more and more firms are beginning to identify and exploit new opportunities with other organizations from the start. Whereas in the past external alliances were secondary to the core proposition as companies sought to transfer technology, improve supplier integration and even collaborate with competitors to define common standards, today partnerships are also increasingly being viewed more as a win–win opportunity for organizations collectively to address new markets, offer new products and redefine some of their customer relationships. Though requiring coherent management of the three key dimensions of risk, individual exposure and revenue share, working with leading players in a new field allows a company to move confidently into both new products and new markets whilst not extending, or being distracted from, its core business. At the same time, for existing or even new players in a market, partnering with an established brand linked to other products can provide the benefits of building the customer base and reducing operating costs, thereby supporting both revenue and margin growth.

Virgin everything

Without doubt, Virgin, the UK-based consumer services group, has to be credited with pioneering this approach. Starting from a minority position in the music business, owner and leader Richard Branson has successfully earned a reputation as one of the world's greatest entrepreneurs by leveraging the Virgin name into retailing, travel, financial services, consumer goods and property. In recent years these have nearly all been through joint ventures, where Virgin has been the initiator and in some cases the steward of the new product or service and its partners have been responsible for delivery. By 2002 the Virgin brand had grown from a single mail-order record business to exploit a plethora of arenas, including:

- Virgin Active – a UK and South African heath and leisure club operator
- Virgin Atlantic – a leading long distance airline
- Virgin Balloons – a hot-air balloon trip provider
- Virgin Bikes – an on-line motorbike and scooter retailer
- Virgin Blue – an Australian low-cost airline
- Virgin Books – a publisher and on-line retailer
- Virgin Bride – a bridal emporium
- Virgin Cars – an on-line car retailer
- Virgin Cosmetics – skin-care products sold through independent Virgin Vie consultants
- Virgin Direct – a UK financial service provider
- Virgin Drinks – a global soft drinks company
- Virgin Energy – a UK gas and electricity supplier
- Virgin Express – a Brussels-based low-cost airline
- Virgin Holidays – a tour operator specializing in long-haul holidays
- Virgin Limobike – a London-based motorbike chauffeur
- Virgin Limousines – a California-based chauffeur service
- Virgin Megastores – over eighty entertainment stores in Europe, Japan and the USA
- Virgin Mobile – the largest virtual mobile telephone network
- Virgin Money – an on-line share dealing and investment site
- Virgin Net – a leading UK-based Internet service provider
- Virgin One – a banking and mortgage provider
- Virgin Radio – a UK FM and Internet music station
- Virgin Space – Internet cafes
- Virgin Sun – a Mediterranean holiday company
- Virgin Trains – a UK train operator
- Virgin Travelstore – an on-line travel agency
- Virgin Wine – the world's largest on-line wine retailer
- V. Shops – high street retailers of music, movies and mobile phones
- V2 – a music label that includes the Stereophonics, Tom Jones and Moby among its clients.

In addition, Virgin has either full ownership or interests in a number of other joint ventures operating outside, but frequently still supporting, the Virgin brand. These include:

- Arcadia – an in-flight entertainment production company
- London Broncos – a professional rugby league club
- Rapido TV – a leading independent UK production company
- Storm – a model agency that manages, among others, Kate Moss, Elle MacPherson and Kylie Bax
- The Trainline – a leading UK train-ticket booking service
- UGC Cinemas – a major UK and French cinema group, formerly Virgin Cinemas.

In all cases, the majority of the Virgin group's investment has been in the form of its overall brand equity and not in capital. Although revenues are typically shared fifty–fifty with partners, as with the company's highly successful Megastores in Japan, which started out from conception in 1994 as a joint venture with Marui (an existing but innovative Japanese retailer) and where the Virgin actual financial contribution was less than 5 per cent, the company has consistently used this mechanism in its approach to brand exploitation. The external partnerships now increasingly utilized for its different businesses, both real and virtual, demonstrate that this approach has not only been successful for Virgin itself, but also sufficiently attractive for its partners, even though they often provide the majority of the investment and take most of the financial risk:

- Virgin Atlantic is now a partnership with Singapore Airlines
- Virgin Direct is delivered by CGNU
- Virgin Drinks is managed and operated by Canadian soft drinks company Coots
- Virgin Energy is supplied and serviced by France's EDF, who have 25 per cent of the equity
- Virgin Mobile is delivered by T-Mobil in Europe, Sprint in the USA and SingTel in Asia
- Virgin Money is a joint venture with Australia's AMP
- Virgin One is operated by the Royal Bank of Scotland
- Virgin Radio is owned and operated by Scottish Media Group
- Virgin Trains is operated by partner Stagecoach
- The Trainline is outsourced to IT company CGEY.

In many areas, the only risk to Virgin is indeed to its brand. The onus and challenge is therefore for the company to be selective about where, when and how it allows its brand to be used, and to ensure that, in every case, the net result is positive in the long term. Whereas the foray into trains was initially seen by analysts to be damaging the Virgin brand, as performance and customer service have gradually improved and new rolling stock has been introduced, many would now argue that even here the overall brand is gaining value. Indeed, through the multiple alliances that are being used to provide new products and services under its name, the larger Virgin brand has certainly grown in recognition and delivered value to the joint ventures, external partners and the parent organization.

However, despite the visibility of this, given the complexities of the internal financing within the Virgin group of companies, it is almost impossible to determine how successful each individual brand exploitation partnership has actually been. *The Economist* for one has questioned the individual profitability of some of the Virgin businesses and the level of cross-business subsidy and support that is provided by the various offshore Virgin investment and holding companies to subsidize new ventures in their early stages and existing ones in hard times. Nevertheless, given its continued and more widespread application by Virgin in the first few years of the twenty-first century, this external partner approach for brand exploitation has clearly worked for the company. A number of other organizations are now also successfully exploiting their own brands through imaginative partnerships across a wide range of innovative products and services.

Calvin Klein, for example, has gained in terms of both revenue and market awareness through the creation and delivery of ck One, the most profitable range of perfumes and fragrances on the market. This has not been done by Calvin Klein investing in or even subcontracting manufacture, but rather through a partnership with Unilever, the Anglo-Dutch FMCG multinational. With an extensive, efficient and flexible global perfume manufacturing and delivery capability used for its multiple personal care brands such as Axe/Lynx and Rexona/Sure, Unilever was an ideal partner for Calvin Klein as the fashion company sought to grow and exploit its customer base through new product introduction. Although Unilever's arch rival Procter & Gamble has the Hugo Boss brand and leverages it across the fragrance market, Unilever did not have a premium brand in this area. Working together the revenue sharing is benefiting both partners, and whilst Unilever adds another brand to its fragrance portfolio and increases volumes in its production facilities (thereby reducing average product costs across its whole personal care range), Calvin Klein has moved its brand from fashion store to pharmacist, supermarket and airport duty-free outlets. This has delivered a massive increase in brand awareness that it would have taken years to achieve solely within the clothes business and would have cost the company a fortune to achieve through increased advertising and promotion alone.

Similarly, the *Financial Times* mobile phone services are being provided in partnership with European retailer the Carphone Warehouse, and in the financial services sector American Express is providing global stock investment management through a partnership with Sharepeople and the Bank of Scotland. In the UK, Centrica, formerly British Gas, has a successful credit card business, Goldfish, delivered by HFC Bank, and is also introducing additional products such as ISAs, loans, mortgages and share dealing in conjunction with Lloyds TSB, using the same brand. In addition, to maximize revenue from its customer base, the AA (which Centrica bought for £1.1 billion in 1999) has also moved its brand from roadside assistance and travel information to exploit higher-margin financial services, including insurance and loans, through partnerships with the Bank of Scotland; car repair via established UK auto-parts retailer Halfords; on-line car dealing through autobytel.com, and even on-line cheap petrol supply location in conjunction with pricebusters.com! However, by far the most successful and prominent example of consistent brand exploitation through external alliances and partnerships so far in terms of profitability, reach and diversity is the English Premier League football club Manchester United.

Manchester United – playing the field

Although it was the world's first football institution, by the 1980s most of the English football league was composed of loss-making clubs that operated as quasi-social rather than commercial institutions. Privately owned by locally based, wealthy and often indulgent benefactors motivated by a desire for prestige in the local community, nearly all of the eighty-plus clubs comprising the four English football divisions were in trouble. Average attendances had declined from a peak of 41 million in 1948 to only 18 million in 1983, and only eighteen clubs had assets in excess of liabilities.

Since the formation of the Premier League in 1991 and, particularly, the freeing up of TV rights, the English football industry has undergone a massive transformation. Many of the larger clubs have become highly profitable enterprises providing a host of leisure products to an ever-increasing number of spectators across an expanding range of income groups. Largely as a result of the 1990 Taylor report, which both provided a significant public subsidy through the Football Trust and laid the ground for increased TV income into the sport, clubs quickly turned themselves into businesses – and ones with a unique market at that. Unlike all other sectors, conventional economic analysis did not apply, as the clubs were each effectively local monopolies with significant allegiances and customer relationships that were based on emotion, not economics. Fuelled by growing capital investment, attendances grew and profits increased, and, led by London-based Tottenham Hotspur, clubs began to move onto the stock market. However, whilst many of the leading clubs, including Liverpool, Arsenal and Newcastle United, have all achieved significant growth, none have matched what has now become the world's richest club – one that in 2000 became the first sports 'business' to have a market value in excess of £1 billion. That club is Manchester United, a football team that, largely through world-leading brand exploitation, has now become one of the most admired companies listed on the London Stock Exchange.

Formed as Newton Heath in 1878 before changing its name to Manchester United in 1902, the club has had a long history in and out of the select few of English football. An ever-present name in domestic sport throughout the twentieth century, Manchester United first gained global recognition in 1958 when twenty-three people, including eight players, were killed in an air crash in Munich. Ten years later a rebuilt team won the European Cup, and throughout the 1970s achieved increasing notoriety for its players' performances both on and off the field. Dominating the English Premier League during the 1990s, winning six out of ten titles, and crowned European Champions again in 1999, by 2000 Manchester United had 200 official supporters' clubs in more than 25 countries and registered members in over 120 countries, featured prominently in fixtures broadcast weekly to over 133 countries, and marketed its products in over 40 countries. With 50 million fans worldwide, it has grown from a football club to a diverse business with interests ranging from media and retail to licensing, hospitality and financial services. The Old Trafford Experience is increasingly emulating Disney as it provides a museum, themed restaurants, megastores, banqueting suites, hotel accommodation, a web site, a dedicated TV channel, Internet portal and credit cards, as well as a football stadium with a Premiership-leading capacity of 67 500.

IPO and BskyB

Under the guidance of chairman Professor Ronald Smith, an ex-director of British Aerospace, Manchester United went for its IPO in May 1991. Although having an arguably poor start as a business, with only 46 per cent of the 2.6 million shares offered being initially taken up and the rest having to be bought by the flotation underwriters, at a price of 385 p each this nevertheless provided valuable income for growth and development of the football club into a major multinational business. With his big company background, extensive network of contacts throughout corporate and financial institutions, and at heart being a long-standing fan of the club, over his eleven years as chairman, Ronald Smith was the navigator of the business. Although at times having to fight against the rest of the board over such issues as increasing stadium capacity, his view has largely prevailed and, as in this instance, where after following his advice the club subsequently generated more match-day gate revenue than any of its competitors, he has consistently been shown to be the driver of the overall vision. He has been behind the implementation of a strategy delivering constant growth, but, unlike some of its European rivals like Real Madrid, most of the time with costs such as player wages kept well under control. Supported by new board recruits including Peter Kenyon, from sports equipment manu-facturer and club supplier Umbro, and (highly significantly) Roy Gardner, chief executive of another leading UK brand-builder Centrica and from 2002 Chairman of Manchester United, Ronald Smith steered the business from a football club to a multifaceted empire at the forefront of popular culture.

In the early years of Ronald Smith tenure, the strategy of the business was very much focused on maximizing the benefits available from media rights. The emergence of satellite TV had a major impact on the whole football industry, and especially on Manchester United. Led by BSkyB's desire to provide attractive and, in many ways, purchase-decision driving content for their growing customer base, the exploitation of football TV rights and innovative marketing techniques that have accompanied it enabled football as a whole to make the cross-over into mainstream popular culture. As BSkyB first acquired the TV rights for Premiership football from the BBC with its near £200 million five-year contract in 1992, Rupert Murdoch's leading business moved into an influential and arguably controlling position in English football.

As satellite and cable audiences grew both nationally and globally, BSkyB and Manchester United formed ever-closer links, with the media company gradually building up a significant share ownership in the club. BSkyB became the preferred conduit through which club news was released, and, as on-the-pitch performance remained high through the mid-1990s, Manchester United in turn gained prominence in the programming schedules. With a second £670 million deal for exclusive rights to the English Premier League for the three seasons from 1997–2001 also awarded to BSkyB for live games and the BBC for highlights, the continued promotion of the league champions was guaranteed. However, things did not continue to go quite as smoothly as planned, for in 1999 the UK government's Department of Trade and Industry blocked a £632 million bid by BSkyB for Manchester United. Determining that the full takeover of a major football club by a media company would operate against the public interest and damage the quality of English football, the DTI rejected the takeover. This decision was underpinned by concerns of an unfair advantage for BSkyB over other media companies, an acceleration of the large-scale introduction of pay-per-view services, and the potential for excessive rescheduling of matches to maximize advertising revenues, all of which had, with hindsight, started to occur anyway. With the resulting judgment also limiting other media companies such as Carlton, Granada and NTL to maximum investment of 10 per cent in any single UK football club, the future relationship between the clubs and the media companies was secure but, other than the future opportunities from pay-per-view, additional revenue was, for a time, limited. Further growth would have to come from other arenas.

Sponsorship and merchandising

From 1983 to 2000, Sharp, the Japanese consumer electronics company, was the major sponsor of Manchester United. This was a prominent and successful relationship for both parties: Sharp's brand awareness and recognition increased substantially and the club gained a steady revenue of £2 million a year for nearly two decades, which was largely profit. Together with additional second-tier sponsorships with suppliers such as Umbro and Carling, sponsorship became firmly established in the clubs P&L figures.

In parallel with incomes generated from TV and sponsorship, another early success for Manchester United was in its merchandising business. Starting with a small retail outlet at Old Trafford, demand for replica shirts, posters, mugs, scarves, wallpaper, duvet covers and toothbrushes took off and provided additional highly profitable revenues. A larger megastore was subsequently built at Old Trafford and a satellite store was opened in Manchester city centre. Moreover, as a first step in providing additional products to its fans through partnerships, in 1998 the ManUtd credit card was launched in conjunction with specialist supplier MBNA, providing fans with a competitive interest rate and balance transfers and the club with a good slice of the profits. This was quickly followed by a MUFC-branded savings account made available to UK fans through the Britannia Building Society, a long-established UK financial service company.

Fan base

Football fans are a unique market. Their loyalty to one particular organization is unwavering. The relationship between a team and its supporters is exceptional in the sense that the majority of customers do not require success to stay loyal. It is desirable but not essential, and hence is not a condition for their continued support. A key aspect of football supporters is that they do not brand switch; 99 per cent of fans stay with the same team for life, irrespective of performance. However, if a team is more successful fans buy more replica shirts as well as other merchandise as they seek to associate themselves with their heroes' success and express solidarity with their fellow supporters. There is even an emerging concept of 'fan equity' to describe the unique relationship that sports teams have with their customer base and the associated ability to create and deliver revenue growth from merchandising, information and access to games. It was this fan equity that the board of Manchester United identified as a rich vein for future growth, especially as its 50 million fans extend across multiple geographies and thus provide multiple opportunities. This is especially so in Asia. As an indication of the size of its fan base in this region, in 2000, 10 million Thais entered a competition to win tickets to Old Trafford! In fact an Asian tour at the end of each season now forms part of an ongoing effort to develop the international fan base. Especially in China, where there are dual aims of promoting the brand and increasing interest in football, linking this in to satellite broadcasting of matches from TV companies in Beijing, Shanghai and Guangdong now brings Manchester United to over 200 million potentially extra fans.

However, despite the global reach, maintaining a good relationship with local supporters has also been seen as key to maintaining the company's brand value. As the Dallas Cowboys American football team had successfully positioned itself as representing the state of Texas, Manchester United has done so within its own geography. Despite the presence of long-term local rivals Manchester City as well as other regionally-based teams Liverpool, Everton and to a lesser extent Blackburn Rovers, alongside Boddingtons beer and a series of pop groups from New Order and Simply Red to M People and Oasis, Manchester United is seeking to become the face of Manchester, the country's second city, of the North West, and even, on the international stage, of England.

Global licensing

With the early UK merchandising success of its megastore and credit card, in 1998 the club set out to identify additional opportunities to exploit its brand across its huge potential marketplace.

> *The board firmly believe that the most effective method of delivering top-line growth is through the formation of innovative external partnerships with global companies that combine the brand strength of Manchester United, its huge fan base and their individual expertise in their specialist product areas and market areas.*

The first and most immediate effect of the desire to expand the brand was to extend the already profitable merchandising business outside the UK as, in 1998, the company invested £150 million in setting up a global merchandising operation – but it was keen to learn from others' earlier experiences:

> *Internationally, we have pursued a relatively low-risk strategy. There are lots of examples of British retailers doing badly overseas, so we've been careful.*

The doors opened on the first overseas Manchester United club shop in October 1998 as Dublin Airport unveiled a branch. Outside the UK and Ireland this has, however, meant working with local partners with brand-building experience, including FJ Benjamin in Singapore and MMI in Dubai. Under the deals agreed, Manchester United has controlled the brand, the design and retail concept, while its partners have been responsible for the actual shops – from finding the best locations for them to fitting them out. The club takes a wholesale margin, while the partner gets a retail return. As it opened its first Manchester United hotel in the UK during 1999, agreements were also signed to take the club shops as far away as Japan, Malaysia and Australia, where the team had also become massively popular – the pre-season tours to the Far East and Australasia merely enhanced that standing.

By January 2001 the company was seeking licensing partners to accelerate the expansion of its brand globally, and decided to transfer responsibility for its overseas stores to regional partners with expertise in local markets. With existing outlets in Ireland, South Africa, Singapore, Bangkok and Kuala Lumpur, it started to look for more local partners to control marketing, distribution and sales activities and to exploit the opportunities available by opening others in Scandinavia, Hong Kong, Mainland China, South Korea and the USA. Within the UK, additional retailing growth was being secured through in-store franchise agreements with high street brands Debenhams and AllSports.

To support its global merchandising business further, in February 2000 Manchester United formed a marketing alliance with the New York Yankees baseball club. Winners of three of the last four world series of the 1990s, access to the Yankees' formidable fan base was a significant inroad for the company into its emergent US market. Moreover, although in principle a fifty–fifty deal for pooling marketing resources and sharing any combined sponsorship deals, the greater demand for football in the USA, especially for women, than for baseball in the UK meant that Manchester United were clearly the team with most to gain. This was further enhanced in 2002 by a switch of 'official beer sponsor' from UK-based Carling to US-based Budweiser, the major name in US sports sponsorship.

Alex Ferguson and David Beckham

Alongside Ronald Smith's leadership of the board, the second key managerial element that has driven Manchester United's renaissance as a football club and rise as a commercial organization over recent years has been Alex Ferguson. Recruited from Aberdeen in 1986, his period as manager of the team has been one of the most successful in football. Besides the six Premier League championships and the 1999 European Champions League, Ferguson has achieved a pivotal position in the world of football. Revered by his peers, adored by his players and knighted by the country, he has become increasingly influential across the sport and is today in many ways an ambassador and advocate of the Manchester United brand across the world. As he extended his contract for another three years in 2002 his track record is indeed impressive, and his impact on both the club and the company has already been significant.

In addition, leveraging its football stars has also been a key part of the Manchester United brand exploitation strategy. Following on from Eric Cantona, and alongside colleagues such as Ryan Giggs, the exemplar of this has been the way in which England national captain David Beckham has been marketed in mutual support of the club. Undeniably talented on the field and well promoted off it, David Beckham has risen to prominence as the most famous footballer in England and one of the most recognized sports personalities globally. Being married to Posh Spice and therefore part of one of the world's most famous couples in the eyes of the media has certainly helped, but in the varied non-football related sponsorships from sunglasses to hair gel that have come his way, reference has always been made to Manchester United and his position at the heart of the team. Having learned lessons (both positive and negative) from the way in which George

Best, the first Manchester United footballer to cross over into popular culture, was first idolized and then satirized by the media in the 1970s and 1980s, the promotion of Manchester United as a brand now fully leverages, and in many way supports, David Beckham's fame, which in turn reflects well on the club. As far as the company is concerned, translating a fan of Beckham into an extra fan of Manchester United and hence a potential customer is a positive outcome, irrespective of the manner of achievement.

Moving on up

It is, however, in the last few years that the exploitation of the Manchester United brand has moved to a higher level. From being 'best in class' in the UK, the club's brand has made a major jump, redefining sports' commercial relationships and fundamentally changing expectations of potential revenue streams. The first step was a new sponsorship deal.

After negotiating with several potential partners, including British Airways, Emirates and Amazon.com, in 1997 Vodafone was selected to replace Sharp as the main sponsor of Manchester United, providing £30 million (or £7.5 million per year) additional revenue for the club through to 2002. For Vodafone, the world's largest mobile service provider and already the £12.5 million sponsor of English cricket, the link to the world's leading football team was seen as a major opportunity to address the significant fan base and gain access to the jewel in the crown of sports coverage for its developing content provision businesses. Not only did Vodafone gain from being promoted by what it saw as 'one of the best sporting brands in the world supported by millions of fans of all ages', but it was also given an opportunity to woo that loyal fan base to its own network of Internet services. This was more than just another sponsorship deal. Linked to it was not only the usual high profile on-shirt and in-stadium logo positioning, but also the launch of a series of mobile communication and wireless Internet services for Manchester United fans. In the modern media age the Vodafone/Manchester United relationship was described as 'a classic example of marrying content with distribution', and has prompted a number of new ventures:

● Launched in 2000, ManUmobile is a private label mobile phone service running on the Vodafone network. In addition to a branded voice service, fans worldwide also benefit from a wealth of information available direct to their mobile via SMS text messaging, including text alerts detailing team news flashes, match information, goals and other incidents on the pitch, albeit at a heavy premium – currently twice that of a competitive offering from rival network Orange. In addition, Manchester United ring-tones featuring all the favourite terrace chants can be downloaded at £1.50 per minute – a 1000 per cent margin for ManUmobile. Alongside the introduction of GPRS and 3G mobile technologies, the range of services being offered to fans is now increasing to include personalized video, audio and multimedia clips, all of which are becoming available to download, obviously at a premium.

- Launched in 1999 as a joint venture with both major investor BSkyB and regional media group Granada, MUTV is a dedicated TV channel in which the club has a 33 per cent stake and hence share of revenues. Providing coverage of Manchester United games, pre- and post-match analysis, and interviews with Alex Ferguson, David Beckham and the rest of the team, MUTV also includes regular team profiles, fan phone-ins, repeats of famous victories, and documentaries in its increasing schedule. It is available on cable and satellite globally and, as the only place where fans can see the whole of every match rather than just highlights, is now building up a significant customer base. In China, MUTV is available to over 60 million subscribers of CCTV5, the government-owned sports cable channel; in the USA, Yes, the sports channel owned by the New York Yankees, relays over five hours of MUTV programming a week; and discussions are also ongoing with several Arabic television networks. This has been a low-risk investment for the club. While Manchester United invested just £1 million in the venture its two partners put in £4.5 million each, and although it lost £0.3 million in its first year of operation, as live screening of matches came on-line in the 2001–2002 season MUTV quickly delivered additional profitable revenue growth, even in the midst of a media downturn.

- ManUtd.com, the official website of Manchester United, now averages nearly 10 million page impressions per month, and is one of the most successful sporting sites worldwide. Launched as a joint venture with TWI, this has most recently become linked to the ManUtd financial services products, enabling them to be accessed through what has become an increasingly significant portal. In addition, through an alliance with Eurobet, an on-line betting company, links were established between ManUtd.com and Eurobet.com in return for a share of the growing proportion of gambling revenues derived from users originating from the club's site. ManUtd.com was revamped in 2002 as a multilingual site including several Asian languages as a key mechanism to access the millions of fans outside the UK, and provides a sales channel for both the merchandising and, particularly for China, the on-line gambling.

- Last in this roll call of new media services is a UK-based ISP, Manufree.net, which provides free Internet access for fans both in the UK and abroad. Although at one level this can be considered as a loss leader focused on building a significant independent Internet community, by charging 50 p per minute for customer support and commanding high margin advertising revenues from the start, it has also become an additional revenue stream for the company.

Nike

Although the Vodafone sponsorship was groundbreaking in Europe, it was a deal in November 2000 that really redefined the global sports sponsorship market. Scheduled to take over when the Vodafone contract expired in 2002, a massive £303 million deal with Nike broke all records. The most lucrative sponsorship in football, it dwarfed Nike's ten-year, £138 million deal to sponsor the Brazilian national team. More significant than the size of the deal is its scope. In return for the £303 million, of which £133 million occurs over the first six years (at which time Nike has the option to terminate the agreement), as well as sporting the famous swoosh on its shirts Manchester United has made Nike sole supplier not only of the official kit but also of replica kit, footwear, apparel and equipment. Moreover, through the creation of a wholly owned subsidiary to control them, Nike also gets to operate Manchester United's global retail outlets. Net profits from merchandise sales in these outlets are split fifty–fifty between the two companies if the club performs to expectation. If, however, Manchester United fails to finish in the top half of the Premier League or the team does not compete in Europe, then the club's share falls accordingly. This linkage of revenue to performance was an innovation that the club has since also used in other areas.

Lastly, from a social responsibility perspective, the Nike deal also included the promise for the two companies jointly to launch a 'grass roots' football programme to support youth participation and skills development. This is clearly good both for the country and for PR; it is especially good for Manchester United, as it is a programme that is being fully funded by Nike alone.

And on and on . . .

In September 2001, Manchester United announced a rebranded and significantly extended MU Finance. Joining existing partners MBNA and the Britannia Building Society were the Bank of Scotland and Zurich Financial Services. The Bank of Scotland is now providing Manchester United branded loans and current accounts, while ZFS delivers similarly configured insurance policies to fans. In addition, at the same time the Britannia added mortgages to its existing MU deposit accounts. In a unique and potentially highly controversial move, as with the Nike deal, interest rates across all these products are linked to the club's performance on the football field. When Manchester United wins, interest rates go down; if it fails to deliver, then rates go up. Either way, overall revenue for the company is secured.

By October 2001, Manchester United plc was providing over 100 branded products and services, from toothbrushes to mortgages, to its growing customer base of fans. Turnover for 2000–2001 was up another 12 per cent at £130 million, £46 million of which came from gate receipts alone. Despite spending £50 million to strengthen its squad over the summer by buying just three players, including records of £19 million on striker Ruud van Nistelrooy from PSV Eindoven and £28 million on Juan Sebastian Veron from Lazio, with TV income increasing to £31 million and sponsorship revenue from an increasing number of second-tier partners (including Pepsi, Western Union, Sun, Lotus and even biscuit producer, McVities) collectively running at over £20 million per annum, the company beat analysts' expectations, with pre-tax profits of nearly £22 million. Moreover, as a business it is unique in that 80 per cent of its annual profits come up front in the form of sponsorships and advanced purchase of season tickets.

The huge fan base has become the world's most profitable. However, with only 1 in 100 of its 50 million existing 'customers' considered by the company to be active in terms of buying tickets, services or merchandise, there is clearly a way to go and, for many analysts, there is a belief that the brand is still not yet fully exploited. Manchester United is not only the world's richest sports club but it is also Europe's most valuable sports brand, beating both rival football clubs (including Spain's Real Madrid and Italy's Juventus) and Formula 1 racing teams Ferrari and McLaren Mercedes. Although marginally number two in the world, just behind the Dallas Cowboys, if all investments are considered, it is unlikely to remain there for much longer. Now worth over seven times its nearest rival, as football continues to grow globally, even in the USA, and the football industry becomes internationally recognized as a major money spinner, especially through its industry-leading exploitation of its brand via external alliances and partnerships, Manchester United has moved from being one of several major clubs into a position where, despite imitation from the likes of German champions Bayern Munich, it is both literally and metaphorically in a league of its own.

14

The next wave

Market-breaking strategies, increasing personalization of products and services, and up-front recognition of underlying consumer values and behaviour are all coming on stream now. Increased sharing of intellectual property, more effective integration of external investment, virtual collaboration and wider brand exploitation partnerships are similarly becoming established in the core of innovation practice today. These are the new approaches that are being proven to deliver benefit and that will therefore, just like their predecessors in the earlier waves of overall innovation capability evolution, migrate across most sectors.

For some, such as personalization and brand exploitation, this transfer will inevitably be quicker than for others. Because these are more immediately directly applicable across many sectors with little specific adaptation, they will be the first to enter the mainstream of corporate innovation. These are conceptually easier for other organizations to understand and so will subsequently be easier to integrate. Values recognition and sharing intellectual property will by contrast take more time, as the applications are more specific. Although the principles are generic and can therefore be used in many different sectors, the individual implementations are more dedicated to the specific challenges present. As with R&D integration and launch management in the previous wave of innovation evolution, these will transfer into other sectors, but, owing to the necessary tailoring of approach to suit the circumstances present, they will just not be so quick to permeate through.

On the other hand, whilst improved external investment and virtual collaboration are certainly sufficiently generic in scope and therefore application, the individual circumstances that prompt their adoption are currently evident in only a few sectors. Migration of these as common approaches will consequently take a while longer to occur. Of the seven approaches described in Chapters 7–13, it is breaking the market that will be most ambiguous in its roll-out across industry. The desire to achieve this and successfully emulate the likes of Smint and Egg is undeniably there, and is correspondingly raising the concept on the corporate agenda. However, implementation is more complex. It is such a compelling idea that whilst many may seek to achieve it, only a few can succeed. Any individual sector can, by implication, only be reinvented sequentially. Whereas in a programme to improve performance all players across an industry can implement approaches such as core competencies and R&D integration, although it may be a common aim, successfully breaking a market will be a less frequently observed result. It will nevertheless occur.

As these latest approaches are being transferred and the benefits from their successful implementation duly achieved, the big question for those organizations seeking to gain a further strategic advantage going forward is evidently focused on what will be next. What will the fifth wave of innovation include? Where will it occur? Who will be at the leading edge this time? The answers to these questions are clearly largely a matter of educated guesswork, as the candidates are multiple and the probabilities of their individual fruition widely variable. Moreover, without the benefit of hindsight, predicting the leading approaches for the next wave of innovation capability is plainly a bit of a gamble. However, from the challenges that are being faced, the new ideas that are being promoted and the trends that have developed across many of the leading sectors, it is apparent that there are already several candidates already emerging. Although there are clearly no guarantees, the leading innovators in the future may well be adopting one or more of several new approaches:

- *Value-chain reconfiguration (strategic impetus).* Fuelled by the success of the market breakers but finding it difficult to individually redefine their respective marketplaces, companies are now looking for partnership opportunities where together they can create new types of value. In a desire to change the value-chains across industries, materials suppliers, brand owners and key intermediaries are developing new strategic approaches where they can collectively use innovation across the board to provide new, differentiated, unique and previously undeliverable propositions to their customers.

- *Attitude exploitation (market focus).* Building upon the greater understanding of customer values gained from recently introduced needs-based discovery techniques, product personalization is evolving into exploiting consumer attitudes. Equipped with the capability to recognize underlying values, innovators are becoming more focused on matching new products and services with what people think, what they believe and how they want to be seen, more than simply with who they are, where they live and what they do.

- *Lifetime lease (product attributes).* As initiated by the car manufacturers in the late 1990s and PC retailers in 2000, organizations are progressively looking to increase the opportunities for enabling customers to lease rather than buy products and services. Like several service-dependent products, mobile phones are no longer bought by the user but are in reality loaned as part of an open, or sometimes hidden, inclusive deal. Similarly, consumer products, domestic appliances, furniture and even clothes are becoming candidates for lifetime leases, where at the end of their use they are returned to the original provider for recycling and upgrade. This implies a fundamental change in the ways in which many are both configured and promoted.

- *Increased creativity (activity effectiveness).* As innovation exploitation and delivery processes are becoming ever more effective and companies across the world are able to achieve similar levels of execution performance, the need for the really novel core idea is becoming increasingly important. As products and services have become ever more uniform, firms are paying greater attention to improving the ideas that they are accessing in the first place. Either through the adoption of a wider range of techniques for internal idea generation and selection or through the use of external facilitation or provision, organizations across several sectors are already increasing their focus on creativity.

- *Equity management (development process).* As intellectual property, external investment and the growing levels of corporate partnership become more widespread, firms are starting to manage creatively the associated equity that they each control. Driven by the need for greater transparency of ownership, clarity of revenue streams, leverage of capability and maximization of brand equity, as well as the management of resource and capital injection, management of the changing equity stakes throughout and across joint ventures is also becoming an integral part of the innovation process.

- *Permanent networks (enabling organization).* Firms, especially in the professional services arena, are beginning to operate as networks from the start. Several groups that rely on a partnership between varied organizations with differing capabilities collectively to deliver services that individually none can perform are emerging. Rather than being temporary expert networks that come together to solve an industry issue, set a standard or even just to collaborate on specific projects, these are more permanent links that, although individual firms may transfer in or out of them over a period of time, will endure and be seen to be the entity that delivers the product to the market.
- *Information brokers (external alliances).* In the increasingly complex networks that are correspondingly evolving between companies, there is the emergent role of catalyst for the interactions between parties. Facilitating the introduction and defining the operating principles between external partners are the information brokers. Positioned as centres of expert information input in an ever-expanding web of firms operating throughout and across industry value chains, these intermediaries are fast becoming the hub of new innovation creation and exploitation activities.

Whichever (if any) of these turn out in practice to be the new approaches that prove to be most effective and thereby deliver the greatest benefits, they will again be largely additional rather than substitutional. Earlier skills and capabilities from the previous waves of innovation will still be required, and most often have to be mastered, before the evolved concepts can be suitably introduced and implemented. Most, but not necessarily all, will be additional layers of innovation capability that can be built upon existing strengths. To succeed, some may well demand a redefinition of earlier strategic ambitions, processes or even organizational structures, but even these will use and build upon earlier themes, experience and learning. Whatever and whoever is innovating at the edge in the future will undoubtedly demonstrate evident evolution, and maybe even revolution. As with all the earlier advances, the key challenge for most companies will, however, still be how to adopt and adapt successfully whichever is the most appropriate approach and embed it within the heart of their organizations.

Part 3

Focus and integration

15

Embedding innovation

Embedding innovation is focused on integrating the most appropriate new tools, techniques or changes required for improved innovation performance into the heart of the organization. It is no easy task. It is not simply a matter of picking up a new toolbox of techniques and going off and using it. Innovation is a complex and multi-faceted capability that has an impact on all levels and areas of an organization. It is not particularly straightforward, and certainly cannot be thought of as a plug-and-play module for corporate success. However, despite this it is something that many organizations have already successfully achieved and benefited from, and hence it is something that, with the appropriate interventions, any firm can accomplish. Although maybe initially appearing to be a major challenge full of multiple barriers, the hurdles and pitfalls have usually all been previously encountered and overcome elsewhere. As such, achieving a defined and sustainable improvement in innovation performance is something that, with clear understanding of the scope and scale of the challenge ahead coupled with access to the required insights, can be undertaken in each and every company. While specific implementation may vary from firm to firm and sector to sector, the overall approach to embedding innovation successfully is actually largely generic. Similar techniques have been proven to be transferable and, most importantly, to work across different industries. The core mechanisms for successful implementation are broadly similar, irrespective of company size, market or position in the value chain.

Like any change process, successfully embedding innovation in any group, from a small team to a large organization, requires a coherent approach using a number of different interventions throughout a series of identifiable stages. Anyone familiar with major transformational programmes will recognize key elements for facilitating sustainable change in an organization, from refining strategic intent to modifying individual attitudes and behaviours. Moreover, the critical success factors of having an identified leader, defined scope, senior management support and resource availability coupled with a real desire to move forward will also all be recognized. Other high-level similarities with 'traditional' major change programmes include:

- Focusing on a combination of short- and long-term outcomes
- Linking change to a high-level business objective
- Cascading the improvement to an individual's benefit
- Training identified change agents to act as pioneers
- Engaging lead groups to pilot new approaches
- Clarifying individual and group roles and responsibilities
- Ensuring effective communication of focus and progress
- Accommodating varied reactions from different groups
- Introducing key metrics to highlight improvements
- Ensuring roll-out of proven concepts to schedule
- Having defined review points to evaluate progress.

However, there are also a number of fundamental differences. For example, transformational change programmes that can typically focus on reducing overheads, improving manufacturing efficiency, enhancing customer service or adding a new sales channel can all be one-off step changes where there are unambiguous before and after states of being that can be clearly differentiated, hopefully by some recognized improvement. Embedding innovation is, by contrast, rarely a step change. It is more gradual. It is something that is both continuous and evolutionary. As such, improvements can often come drip fed as the enhancements introduced take effect on, say, the next round of new products and services launched into the marketplace. Organizations that take innovation to their core can produce dramatic and industry-changing results, but these effects are rarely instantaneous. They may appear to be so from the outside, but internally aligning the required capabilities to affect such a shift takes time. Because innovation frequently relies on successful delivery and exploitation of new ideas across a company, its customers and its partners, the associated interplay between strategy, process and organization can often take time to permeate. As such, patience is clearly a virtue, and managing expectations both internally and externally around this can be a major driver to ensuring long-term success. Short, sharp, 'quick-win' initiatives, such as introducing new idea generation techniques or slimming down a product portfolio, can produce immediate and visible results of more ideas or less projects to support, but the deeper, more subtle and usually more sustainable elements can take some time to bear fruit. An upfront awareness of this in any programme to improve innovation performance is therefore vital.

Key steps

As mentioned above, although embedding innovation varies in implementation from one company, sector or team to another, there is a generic similarity of approach that works across the board. There are distinct and hence definable stages to enabling a systematic change in innovation performance and, whilst different organizations may apply different labels to these steps, in successful firms there is always a high level of commonality of approach. Embedding innovation is a continuous five-stage cycle encompassing:

1 *Evaluation* – understanding current company and industry performance, identifying opportunities and assessing benefits
2 *Focus* – prioritizing action against corporate reality and defining the scope of the desired improvements, the targets and success criteria
3 *Design* – defining the changes that need to be introduced to deliver the defined improvements in the strategy, process and organizational arenas
4 *Implementation* – piloting, evaluating and rolling out defined changes across the organization and its partners to realize the improvements
5 *Review* – assessing progress against the defined targets and criteria, evaluating both success and failure, and capturing key learning and insights.

Whereas the evaluation stage defines where you are and where you could be, the focus stage concentrates more specifically on where you want to be. The design stage determines how you are going to get there, what needs doing in which order during the implementation stage, and who does what by when with whom. Implementation is where everything should come together, and finally, post-implementation, the review stage assesses how far you have come, what worked, what didn't work, where and what else needs to be done, thus feeding back into the first evaluation stage of a second cycle. Every step is essential, and each pass through the cycle improves performance by introducing key changes and building sustainable innovation capability. Embedding innovation is very much a continuous journey, where each cycle round both raises performance and also improves awareness of what else can be done (Figure 15.1).

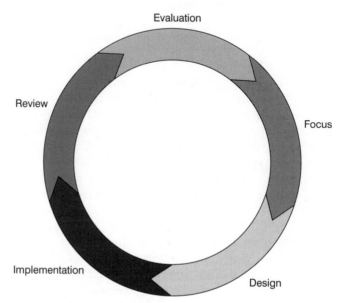

Figure 15.1 Embedding implementation cycle.

If you want a metaphor, then think of the process of embedding innovation as being like ascending the spiral staircase of a castle tower. Each step forward gives more understanding of what is ahead, whereas each cycle round raises your potential and simultaneously affords you a better view of the world and the opportunities available for improved performance. Getting to the top takes time, and may well take several separate rounds of improvements, but with each step forward you are making progress. There is unfortunately no express elevator, although there is certainly a fireman's pole! Through clear focus, defined steps and a determination to move forward, the rewards from achieving higher and higher innovation performance are all there for the taking.

The following chapters address some of the key issues in each stage, and provide a number of insights from a range of organizations where new innovation capability has been successfully embedded and where the associated improvements in team, group and corporate performance have duly been delivered. The same examples have been used throughout to provide continuity of theme and linkage from one stage to the next. Although each one may not appear in every one of the following five chapters, they do recur from one to another. None of these examples is unique in either scope of improvement or implementation of associated change, and they can all therefore be taken as reliable and relevant models for practice.

16

Evaluation – finding the start point

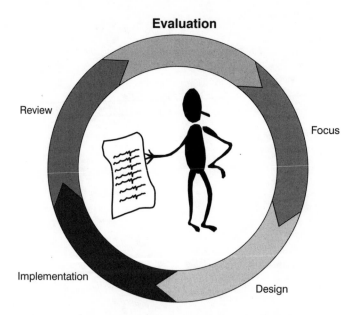

Many organizations can easily highlight the problems they may have had in innovating successfully. Talk to colleagues, managers, team members or the receptionist, and they will all have an opinion on what is wrong and what needs to change. They can, with some conviction, identify where any individual organization is under-performing:

- Not enough ideas
- Too many projects

- Too long a development period
- Too short a product life
- Not enough management support
- Too much interference
- Not enough budget
- Too few resources
- Not enough innovation
- Too much innovation.

Depending on who you talk to and what they do in a company, these and a host of similar diagnoses of the core problems to be solved will be forthcoming. Whilst some may well be true, they are unfortunately largely subjective, are certainly influenced by individual attitudes, and are frequently symptoms and not the cause. Despite the temptation, using such existing perceptions as the starting point for any attempt to improve performance through embedding innovation is always a false start. Prioritization of focus is impossible. Measurement of progress is difficult to say the least. Moreover, the chances of significant short-term (never mind any lasting) improvement are slight. No matter how strong the conviction, how urgent the need or how politically expedient the action, diving straight into designing and implementing any change is potentially disastrous. Up-front objectivity, clarity of true status and clarification of the real, not the imagined, issues present is paramount. Without these, no realizable benefit can ever be delivered.

Where to start?

For steady-state activities, such as an automated assembly line, a customer support call centre or a sales order process, measurement of performance is relatively easy. The number of defects per shift, the number of calls handled or the number of invoices paid are all easily identifiable metrics that directly relate to the activity. Moving an organization from 80 per cent to 90 per cent performance is a visible, measurable and, most importantly, executable task. For innovation it is different. For a start, innovation performance is such a collective issue that it has traditionally been difficult to summarize in one single number, percentage or ratio that really means anything. Number of ideas generated, time to market, resource utilization, increased revenue, number of hours spent in a lab, service profitability and the like are all involved, but overall innovation performance is a combination of these. As such, how these interact and how their interplay affects company performance has to be fully understood before any focus is applied on one or another arena. Furthermore, innovation is not an immediate product of any single change. The very interdependency of issues and complexity of the collective output means that the outcome of any change takes time to flow through the process and the organization. If it takes six months for cause and effect to be linked, then there are few firms that can afford the luxury of tinkering around in different areas on the off chance that one will be the magic button. Companies are continually moving organisms, and not machines. If left alone they do not stand still; they change and adapt themselves. Improving performance implies having to embed innovation in a continually changing host. As such, any intervention that is made to improve performance has to be taken in this light.

For a successful outcome, before anything is done to change an organization you must have an accurate, although not necessarily fully detailed, picture of where, in terms of overall innovation capability evolution, the company is at the start. Moreover, this has to be an insight in the context of the industry sector in which the company exists, the markets in which it operates and the overall state of its evolution. There are five different levels of initial assessment that can be undertaken. The approach for companies will vary; sometimes some but not necessarily all of them are used, and often only those that are felt to be most relevant. Largely depending on the specific circumstances, the time and resources available, as well as the initial scope, some are looked at first and the rest later as part of a second cycle of improvement. There are also two major risks in selecting the initial assessment approach, both of which can have detrimental impact. Looking at too few means that you end up still guessing and making stabs in the dark over missing information, whereas looking at too many at once can overwhelm both the company and the evaluation team. Either way, these five levels of assessment are key to providing the initial data points from which current status can be reliably determined, changes can be introduced and progress can be measured. They are:

1 Overall corporate performance in an industry context
2 Innovation activity performance across the organization
3 Firm and sector evolution in terms of current and leading practice
4 Opportunity identification, clarification and validation
5 Skills, structure and culture to support innovation.

Each has a different mechanism for evaluation, and each provides a different insight. However, when taken in combination, and of course ideally all together, they provide a unique view of where an organization is and more specifically where, given the appropriate enhancements underpinned by an understanding of industry context, it could be.

Overall corporate performance – king of the castle?

For quite understandable reasons, firms, and particularly their executives and investors, like to know where they stand in relation to their peers. Growth in share price, market capitalization and P/E ratios are all recognized means of comparing one company with another, but, as these can all include an element of M&A activity, sales performance, market conditions and other elements such as analyst sentiment, unfortunately none give a reliable indication of real corporate growth derived from innovation.

Effectively measuring how innovative a company is has been something that many have been grappling with for some time. In a bid to provide meaningful insights and, particularly, to understand relative performance, identify the leaders and hence question what it is that they do that makes them so innovative, a variety of approaches have been taken over recent years. Perhaps the most well known and the most indicative metric so far adopted has been 3M's internal target of generating 30 per cent of revenue from products launched in the previous four years, a goal recently increased to 35 per cent. Taken in combination with the company's more short-term driver of 10 per cent sales from products introduced in only the last year, again recently increased to 15 per cent, as mentioned in Part 1, this has certainly proven to provide both a very good motivation for that particular organization and an accurate representation of 3M's collective innovation performance. However, unfortunately few other organizations actually track and even less publicly declare their performance against this or a similar measure. Thus although arguably an ideal metric, it cannot, without consistent inside information on every competitor, be used for any credible cross-industry comparison.

From the available public information there have been two main approaches, each with differing philosophies that have therefore been used for assessment of comparative corporate innovation performance. Especially in the USA, and increasingly across the high-tech arena, there has been a focus on innovative output which, given the broad range of end products, components and services delivered by business, has tended towards a league table based on the number of US patents granted to organizations in any one year. By using data from the US Patent and Trademarks Office, the definitive intellectual property registry today, consultants, academics, journalists and even companies themselves have all been able to produce rankings that, by implication, correlate a higher number of patents granted with better innovation performance. Hence, as a consequence, large multinationals tend to dominate. Alternative output measures, such as the number of new products launched in any one period, do not include any innovation threshold, and there is therefore no distinction between an enhancement and a wholly new product. Although potentially more representative, this cannot therefore be seen as a reliable indicator. However, by implication, a patent is only granted if it relates to something that is both original and new and thereby provides a suitable common measure. In addition, although some may argue that patents granted elsewhere by the UK or European patent offices should also be included, given both the predominance of the USPTO as the place to file intellectual property and the fact that most companies submit multiple applications across several regions, the number of US patents granted is the most appropriate. MIT's *Technology Review* uses an extra level of refinement in its annual patent scorecard by also taking into account how often a patent is cited as prior art in other applications as a means of trying to determine the worth of patent portfolios. The results, however, are largely the same as straight patents granted rankings, and are thus dominated by large firms and also open to subjective interpretation. Consequently, as a reliable and indicative innovation output metric, the number of US patents granted per annum, although not perfect, is one of the best available. As an illustration of its insight (Table 16.1), the

Table 16.1 Pharmaceutical industry patent ranking 2000 (source: USPTO/Innovaro Analysis)

Rank 2000	Rank 1999	Company	Country	US patents 2000	US patents 1999	% change 1999/2000
1	18, 1	GlaxoSmithKline	UK	374	346	8.1
2	2	Johnson & Johnson	USA	238	237	0.4
3	5	Merck	USA	230	195	17.9
4	11	Pfizer	USA	175	209	−16.3
5	8	Novartis	Switzerland	172	166	3.6
6	7	Roche	Switzerland	166	166	0.0
7	4	Eli Lilly	USA	165	206	−19.9
8	6	Novo Nordisk	Denmark	157	183	−14.2
9	13	Pharmacia	USA	132	105	25.7
10	3	Incyte Genomics	USA	130	234	−44.4

2000 data for the pharmaceutical industry provides a ranking headed by GlaxoSmithKline, Johnson & Johnson and Merck.

The other major approach, championed in the UK by the DTI-sponsored annual R&D Scoreboard and also widely recognized, has been to measure innovation input, most commonly seen as annual R&D expenditure. Again ultimately biased to larger organizations, drawing from company annual reports, this provides a separate ranking of innovation performance. In a bid to represent input more accurately, the same R&D scoreboard also includes a measure of 'R&D intensity' or, more simply, the percentage of annual revenue invested in R&D. Although better in terms of providing a relative rather than absolute metric, and thus being far more reliable for benchmarking purposes, this does nevertheless suffer from a sector bias. Pharmaceutical companies, by the very nature of their business, invest more of their revenue in R&D than in their electronics and automotive counterparts. Thus they inevitably score higher. Moreover, as shown by 2000 pharmaceutical data, within the sector ranking varies widely (Table 16.2). By pure R&D investment, Pfizer, GlaxoSmithKline and Johnson & Johnson predominate. However, by R&D intensity, it is all change with Millennium Pharmaceuticals, Incyte Genomics and Chiron in the lead (Table 16.3). Although a step forward but clearly not perfect, this measure is also still only tracking input rather than output. Depending on which perspective you take, Millennium Pharmaceuticals could be considered to be the 'most innovative'

Table 16.2 Pharmaceutical industry R&D investment ranking 2000 (source: DTI/Innovaro Analysis)

Rank 2000	Rank 1999	Company	Country	R&D spend 2000 £m	R&D spend 1999 £m	% change 1999/2000
1	2	Pfizer	USA	2 968 938	1 722 405	72.4
2	7, 11	GlaxoSmithKline	UK	2 526 000	2 287 000	10.5
3	4	Johnson & Johnson	USA	1 958 763	1 613 203	21.4
4	1	AstraZeneca	UK	1 936 672	1 813 613	6.8
5	3	Novartis	Switzerland	1 923 824	1 645 800	16.9
6	12	Pharmacia	USA	1 842 951	889 744	107.1
7	5	Roche	Switzerland	1 631 759	1 465 948	11.3
8	6	Merck	USA	1 569 019	1 283 303	22.3
9	9	Eli Lilly	USA	1 351 252	1 106 658	22.1
10	8	Bristol-Myers Squibb	USA	1 298 032	1 143 513	13.5

Table 16.3 Pharmaceutical industry R&D intensity ranking 2000 (source: DTI/Innovaro Analysis)

Rank 2000	Rank 1999	Company	Country	R&D as % sales 2000	R&D as % sales 1999	% change 1999/2000
1	2	Millennium Pharmaceuticals	USA	137.1	86.9	57.8
2	1	Incyte Genomics	USA	99.3	93.5	6.2
3	3	Chiron	USA	46.7	60.1	−22.3
4	4	Biogen	USA	32.7	27.9	17.2
5	5	Genentech	USA	28.2	26.2	7.6
6	7	Elan	Ireland	23.4	22.8	2.6
7	6	Amgen	USA	23.3	24.6	−5.3
8	8	Serono	Switzerland	21.2	21	1.0
9	9	Chugai Pharmaceutical	Japan	20.4	19.8	3.0
10	13	Eli Lilly	USA	18.6	17.8	4.5

whereas, judging by relative positions, companies such as Merck, Eli Lilly and Pfizer, who rank at number 21, are all poorer performers.

By implication, neither of these two approaches therefore provides a fully reliable indication of how well an organization actually uses its available resources. An innovative company is one that delivers more from less, and hence, to measure innovation performance, organizations should clearly take some account of the linkage between output and input. The most effective high-level measure for innovation performance is therefore to provide a ratio that represents this linkage. To be useful to as many organizations as possible, this has to be independent not only of company size, but also of revenue. Moreover, as far as possible, it also has to provide a reliable indication of relative performance between firms.

The approach that has been shown to be most effective has been to take the key reliable metrics for innovation output and input in combination. A measure of the ratio of output/input is more valid, and for this, output can be considered to be the average number of patents granted per employee and input to be the percentage of revenue invested in R&D. This provides a score, the innovation index, which successfully takes into account company size (number of employees) and revenue as well as the R&D investment and hard innovation output. Thus smaller companies are considered on a level field with larger ones. Moreover, as a ratio it gives a more accurate indication of relative performance. If one company has an innovation index twice that of another, then it can reliably be considered to be twice as effective at delivering innovation. Again using the pharmaceutical industry as an example, 2000 performance analysis shows a rather different picture to previous rankings (Table 16.4). Despite their lower actual investment in R&D, with none in the top ten, and their mixed positioning by R&D intensity and number of actual patents filed, Incyte Genomics, Novo Nordisk and Genentech are the top three in terms of overall innovation performance. Of the top ten leading major investors in R&D, only Merck, consistently recognized within the sector as a leader, is ranked as one of the top ten innovation performers.

Although not perfect and, as with the US favoured patent approach, more applicable to products than services, the innovation index metric does provide a more reliable and consistent overall measure for comparative use. It is not necessarily the ideal top level metric for a firm's balanced scorecard, but it does provide cross-industry insight and is therefore highly useful for setting one organization in the context of the rest of the sector in which it exists. It gives an idea of where top-level performance should eventually be if a firm is to be either up with the pack or leading its sector. When taken in combination with other internal assessments, it also gives a long-term target to aim for.

Table 16.4 Pharmaceutical industry innovation index 2000 (source: Innovaro Analysis/Reuters)

Rank 2000	Rank 1999	Company	Country	Innovation index 2000	Innovation index 1999	% change 1999/2000
1	1	Incyte Genomics	USA	9.9	18.9	−47.6
2	2	Novo Nordisk	Denmark	7.6	7.6	0.0
3	5	Genentech	USA	6.2	5.7	8.8
4	6	Takeda Chemical	Japan	5.9	5	18.0
5	7	Merck	USA	5.7	5	14.0
6	11	Chiron	USA	4.8	3.8	26.3
7	10	Sankyo	Japan	4.4	4.2	4.8
8	3	Millennium Pharmaceuticals	USA	4.2	6.3	−33.3
9	14	E Merck	Germany	3.9	3.2	21.9
10	15	Daiichi Pharmaceutical	Japan	3.7	3.1	19.4

Innovation activity performance – doing what matters

Within any organization there are a host of measures that can be used to assess performance of the component activities that impact and influence innovation and growth. These cover a broad range in scope, from input to output, as well as in level, from business unit to individual task. This spread in itself makes the selection of the most appropriate indicator a challenge. However, to make matters worse, measures also vary from sector to sector and market to market. Potential candidates include:

- Number of new product launches
- Percentage of revenue from new products
- Market share
- Customer base growth
- Time to market
- Time to profit
- Average time between launches
- Average launch delay
- Change in product profitability
- Return on sales
- Market penetration
- Market ranking
- Installation time
- Number of employee suggestions
- Number of patents filed
- Number of patents granted
- Number of licences awarded
- Number of design awards won
- Percentage of projects killed
- Number of business cases evaluated
- Average improvement in service delivery
- Customer satisfaction
- Customer churn rate
- Resource utilization to plan
- Budget utilization to plan
- Employee satisfaction
- Average number of training days per employee
- Employee retention.

All are, in principle, relevant. However, measuring each one would turn into a logistical nightmare, take forever, most likely lead to information overload, and certainly delay the introduction of any improvement. Far more effective is to choose a few that are most relevant to the organization, its sector and its market, and for which reliable external data of either industry average or best practice are available. This means that an effective and pertinent view of current performance can be obtained in as short a time as possible.

For a consumer product company operating in four major markets, the internal metrics assessed for innovation performance were therefore agreed to be:

- Return on sales
- Number of successful new product launches
- Average time to market
- Market share in each core segment.

For a high-tech firm developing and licensing new instrumentation technology into the medical sector, the corresponding metrics were:

- Number of patents granted per annum
- Number of successful licences per annum
- Average time to royalty income
- Overall five-year return on innovation.

By contrast, for a financial services organization providing traditional and on-line banking to a consumer retail market within one region, the best measures were found to be:

- Number of new services introduced
- Customer churn
- Annual increase in operating margin
- Sector market share.

Lastly, for a data communications company providing high-speed connectivity to the global business market, the most appropriate innovation measures for evaluation were:

- Billed revenue from new services
- Average installation time
- Average launch delay
- Market share by sector.

Each organization clearly had different scope and therefore different core activities that contributed to its ability to create and deliver real innovation to its customers. As such, each set of these different measures was the most appropriate for gaining the necessary insight into individual performance. A consumer product company should be competent at quickly launching new products that increase market share, whereas a financial services organization should be effective at growing its customer base through the delivery of higher value services. These aims are different, and hence the specific capabilities required to achieve them can also be somewhat dissimilar. However, comparing like with like enables quick and effective identification of where any individual firm is, and is not, performing the applicable innovation activities to, or even above, industry and market expectations.

Firm and sector evolution – where on the scale?

One of the easiest but also one of the most insightful assessments of any organization is to look at where it, its competitors and the sector as a whole are in the overall evolution of innovation capability. Using the key steps in the evolution of innovation practice outlined in Parts 1 and 2, we can create a summary of all the elements that can contribute to the capability of an organization to innovate in terms of strategic, product, market, organizational and process focus (Figure 16.1).

Key areas	Initial phase (1980–86)	Second phase (1987–93)	Third phase (1994–99)	Fourth phase (2000+)
Innovation strategy	Product strategy	Core competencies	Integrated R&D	Market breakers
Market focus	Regional products	Global/customer	Mass customization	Personalization
Product attributes	Quality	Brand significance	Innovation integration	Values recognition
Activity effectiveness	Project selection	Speed to market	Launch management	Patent pooling
Development process	Stage gates	Fuzzy gates	Continuous	Investment integration
Enabling organization	Product champions	Matrix organizations	Knowledge management	Virtual collaboration
External alliances	Technology transfer	Supplier partnerships	Competitor collaboration	Brand exploitation

Figure 16.1 Innovation capability evolution framework.

Any one firm is unlikely to be at the forefront of innovation practice across all the seven identified elements, but by investigating the current status of a company its position within an overall innovation context can be determined through a combination of observation and questioning. Moreover, frequently through a combination of secondary research and existing in-house understanding of competitor as well as industry activities, these can be mapped alongside the specific company in question. This gives a useful representation not only of where an organization is generally but also of the arenas in which it is ahead or behind the competition and sector best practice.

For a financial services organization perceived internally to be class leading at innovation, the assessment showed that although it was ahead of the sector average in many areas, the movement of its lead competitor into personalization as apposed to mass customization of new products could be a major source of differentiation going forward. Similarly, in an IT services company, it was clear that the company in question was operating at an early stage of innovation capability evolution in all but two areas, the fact that this is largely typical of the sector as a whole indicated that, at the time, no major competitive advantage was either being gained or lost by any of the players. The consequence of this is that, if the company itself did not make an appropriate step forward, its competition could well do so. Whilst, for example, a move solely from using a stage-gate to a fuzzy-gate process may not deliver immediate competitive advantage by itself, taken in combination with an organizational change to introducing matrix-based teams and increasing involvement of key suppliers in the heart of the innovation process, the impact on its ability to launch more and better products more frequently could prove pivotal. However, the fact that a lead competitor was seen to be more advanced in terms of its capability in leveraging the significance of its brand did indicate a specific opportunity and threat that would have to be addressed going forward. This simple analysis therefore both highlights current status and identifies clear opportunities for improved performance.

Opportunity identification – asking the right questions

The fourth key area for innovation assessment goes back to the initial perceptions offered by individuals across the organization. Whilst these are often highly subjective, influenced by personal circumstances, relationships and attitudes, and frequently symptomatic of under-performance, they may nevertheless provide accurate self-diagnosis. They therefore need to be captured and understood, but at the same time questioned and, if necessary, investigated. This is a lost cause if driven by the statements themselves, for, to be effective in terms of objective evaluation, any such clarification and validation of perspectives internal to the organization has to occur within a consistent framework. Undertaking a combination of individual one-on-one interviews and team-based focus group type workshops is often the most effective and efficient approach for this.

Handing out questionnaires to be filled in by a sample selection of the organization is always an obvious route, but one that rarely delivers any specific insight. As with countless employee and customer satisfaction questionnaires, unless specifically focused on one or two fields for detailed and statistically reliable analysis, the survey approach to asking questions rarely provides an organization with anything other than the answers it is expecting. A combination of closed questions, lack of opportunity to express opinions and fear of follow-up all combine to make the results from this type of approach largely superficial and predictable. Far more effective is the use of confidential interviews and open group based discussions facilitated by an objective and ideally independent moderator. The former provides the opportunity for more in depth exploration of issues relevant to the individual and the associated areas of input. Although requiring a willingness from the interviewee to talk openly and often taking an hour or so for each session, the insights gained from such an approach are often the most relevant in determining key areas that need to be addressed to improve performance. By contrast, group-based discussions enable the working of issues and opinions towards a common and agreed perspective. Often through the discussion of recent examples of success and failure to provide focus and relevance, a typical two-hour workshop where individuals from across the organization are encouraged to provide their perspectives has multiple benefits. As well as enabling more collective insights to the challenges and opportunities ahead, through effective facilitation, such group discussions can be pivotal in creating the basis for cross-disciplinary cooperation, providing stimulus for change and engaging key sources of influence.

In an FMCG packaging company where successfully delivering new products into an increasingly competitive market place was an acknowledged core problem, such questioning validated a number of initial perspectives, including:

- Ideas primarily reactive to competition
- Unwillingness to take risks
- Difficulty in terminating projects
- Little success in commercializing projects
- Poor communication across new product development
- Poor interaction between R&D and marketing
- Confusion over roles in projects
- Late application of commercial perspective.

It also identified a number of 'new' issues, including:

- No clear innovation strategy
- No clear ownership of product development

- No clear project selection procedure
- No idea collation across the organization
- Haphazard idea generation
- Little engagement of the organization in innovation
- Poor and absent decision-making
- Too much political influence.

At the same time several initial perceptions expressed by some were shown to be unsubstantiated, including:

- No process being used for innovation
- Functional isolation and protection
- Insufficient manufacturing input
- Limited internal testing and evaluation
- Localized innovation within R&D
- No clear launch responsibility.

Together these provided a good start in identifying what key issues had to be addressed within the organization. In addition, the parallel use of a short, reliable diagnostic questionnaire focused specifically on the single subject of the management of ideas across the company provided effective supportive information (Figure 16.2). Through a controlled survey of perceptions within a defined population, a collective view of current company performance was obtained that, as well as confirming points from interviews and workshops, could also be used at an executive level to summarize the main issues.

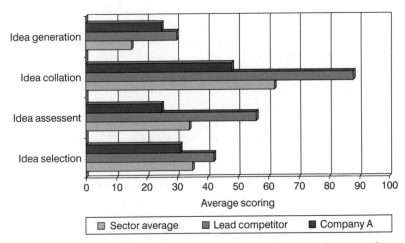

Figure 16.2 Internal perspectives of idea management performance for packaging company, 2000.

Skills, structure and culture – the raw materials

Last, but by no means least, is the issue of the environment within which innovation takes place. Although some aspects of this can be highlighted by many of the preceding elements of assessment, there is always the option of taking a more in-depth look. Requiring greater up-front investment in time, a detailed evaluation of the skills, structure and culture of a defined group using a combination of techniques can provide highly useful contextual information in advance of the introduction of any change. More than just an indication of how a firm is performing at a moment in time, this can also highlight the potentially greater, as yet under-utilized, capacity of the organization to innovate.

The three areas of individual skills, group structure and corporate culture are mutually dependent elements. At the heart of the organization, the available skill-set is most directly associated with the process of undertaking innovation activities, but the organization's structure and the prevailing culture both provide compound influence:

- The available skill-set provides the core means by which innovation can occur. The interaction between individuals and groups of different disciplines and levels of development is the fundamental element underpinning the core processes and the interdisciplinary working that promotes innovation within an organization.
- The structure within which the skill set operates directly affects the means by which the skill set can interact both inside and outside the organization. The more decentralized and informal the structure and the fewer the number of structural barriers the greater individual and group autonomy, but at the same time, maintenance of corporate coherence to an overall innovation strategy is potentially more difficult.
- The culture in which both the structure and skills exist determines how people behave, how they relate and therefore how they interact. It is the culture that characterizes a significant aspect of an organization's capacity to innovate, as it helps to define the organization's style as well as its values and practices (Hofstede, 1991).

Whereas the proficiency of an organization in performing innovation activities and maintaining core processes and linking mechanisms can be assessed through analysis of commonly available numeric data, measuring this softer side of an organization's ability is less straightforward, for it is influenced by such issues as group dynamics as well as individual and corporate comfort zones.

However, through using a selection of techniques including skill mapping, process modelling, psychometric profiling, layout analysis and culture diagnostics, the attributes of the innovation environment within an organization can also be evaluated (Cooke and Lafferty, 1983; Xenikou and Furnham, 1996).

Such an evaluation provides a measure of the mix and level of skills, the form of organizational structure, and the type of culture present. In determining the attributes of the individual elements, a means by which the full capacity of the organization to innovate can be assessed and made available. Through defining the parameters of the innovation environment, the opportunity to identify, facilitate and measure change in areas other than just activity performance becomes available. Opportunities to redefine governance, change physical layouts and even modify influencing aspects of the corporate culture are revealed. This type of assessment also provides a normalized configuration of information by which the environmental characteristics of a wide range of different organizations operating across varied sectors can be both determined and related to their individual and collective innovation performance. The resulting output allows this facet of an organization also to be compared with and suitably benchmarked against global, national or strategic group averages, or industry best practice.

In a multifunctional business services organization, this assessment was used to investigate the status of one of its interdisciplinary groups focused on leading technology innovation. As well as contributing to the diverse range of projects within the company as a whole, this group had the key role in creating new technologies to enable such projects to be initiated. This core group was considered to be the heart of innovation within the company, and, although integrated within the larger organization, was therefore assessed as a self-contained centre of innovation (Figure 16.3).

Skills

The group was comprised of a mix of technology literate personnel, most of whom had postgraduate qualifications or previous industry experience. Some were specialists, but most could be considered as generalists, able to apply their skills across a diverse range of fields. Within the constraints of its focus on technology innovation, the group had a high level of functional integration and interdisciplinarity. Psychometric profiling revealed the majority of the group to be creative, self-motivated, intuitive and independent thinkers. They usually focused on the big picture and were largely future-orientated, taking an objective perspective of problems and frequently adopting cause-and-effect reasoning. Although possessing the capabilities to take innovations forward, as a group most

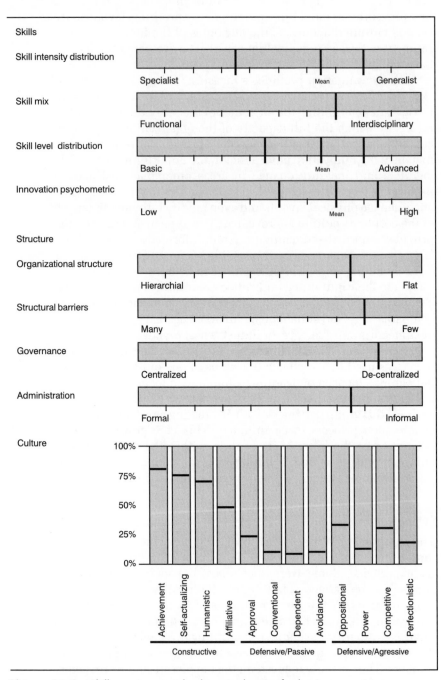

Figure 16.3 Skills, structure and culture evaluation for business services organization.

members could be considered to be initiators, often relying on other personnel or groups within the organization to complete projects, developing and exploiting their innovations. There was evidently a highly skilled and innovative selection of individuals within the group.

Structure

As a whole, the company sought to achieve an open, people-focused structure, where the independence of the individual is both respected and enabled. Although an unacknowledged hierarchy, influenced by personal relationships and cross-organizational politics, was perceived to exist and control power within the group, the organizational structure was almost perfectly flat. Whilst there was an identifiable leader representing the group within the organization, decisions were largely based on consensus, with high levels of intra-group consultation and discussion. Physical co-location of personnel within a single open-plan office environment, with open access to on-site development laboratories and testing facilities, resulted in few structural barriers between group members. Moreover, a high level of mutual trust and appreciation of each other's skills and capabilities led to close working relationships. Together with the ability of individuals to take their ideas forward on their own initiative with good resource support, this provided highly decentralized governance within the group. Lastly, although formal process-based techniques were adopted elsewhere within the organization, within the group projects relied more on individual and group experience and intuition with considerable flexibility and informality in approach. Although unconventional in make up, the group was very adept at moving things forward in its own way.

Culture

The culture of the group could be summarized as being highly constructive. Overall it was very focused on achievement, with enthusiastic pursuit of challenging but realistic goals seen as a key. In addition it was felt to be self-actualizing, nurturing creativity and encouraging individuals to enjoy their work. It was both reasonably humanistic and people-centred, with participation encouraged and ideas openly shared. Moreover, it was moderately affiliative, with good levels of sensitivity, loyalty and cooperation. However, the group scored very low in the defensive areas. Both approval and avoidance were seen as minor issues – individuals were not expected to comply with the *status quo*, and failure was tolerated, with mistakes not punished and blame not given. The group was in no way seen as either conventional or dependent, and nor was power in terms of position and authority or a desire for perfectionist detail felt to occur. Lastly, there were relatively low scores in oppositional and competitive areas. Confrontational decision-making was not felt to exist, nor were group members seeking to out-do one another. In short, from a purely cultural perspective, the group could be seen as an ideal place to work.

Together with some, if not all, of the other levels of assessment, this type of more in-depth look at the organization itself completes the portfolio of evaluation approaches. With these insights, a firm has a realistic view of its current state as well as a greater understanding of where improvements in its ability to innovate can be made. Moreover, the benefits from achieving such improvements are also made more evident.

Summary

Using a combination of these five types of evaluation provides a unique insight into the existing state of innovation performance. As well as identifying overall relative corporate innovation effectiveness within a sector, the use of the more detailed internal assessments points to where the key challenges and hence opportunities for improved performance may lie. Interviews and workshops are where the real insights from within the innovation organization are obtained that often confirm some of the possibilities identified elsewhere and always raise new perspectives. Lastly, if there is the time and the scope, the in-depth look at skills, structure and culture helps not only to highlight current status but also to identify where additional capability within the firm may be most effectively built.

References

Cooke, R. A. and Lafferty, J. C. (1983). *Organizational Culture Inventory*. Human Synergistics.

Hofstede, G. (1991). *Cultures and Organisations: Software of the Mind*. McGraw-Hill.

Innovaro Analysis/Reuters (2002). *Innovation Leadership*. Reuters Business Insight.

Xenikou, A. and Furnham A. (1996). A correlation and factor analytic study of four questionnaire measures of organizational culture. *Human Relations*, **49(3)**, 349–71.

17

Focus

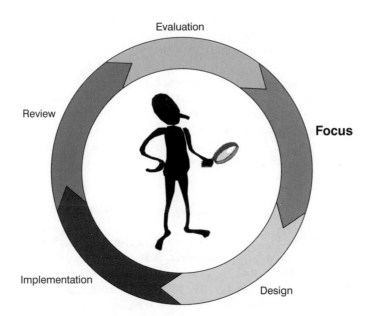

Equipped with a coherent and validated overview of current corporate performance and the opportunities for improvement, the next step is to prioritize the possible areas for action. Having determined where an organization is and where it can potentially move to, succinctly defining where it wants to be is a critical element in improving innovation performance.

Strategy

Fundamental to this is the clarification of what strategic position an organization wants to take within its sector. Going back to the fundamentals of product strategy that emerged in the early 1980s:

- Does it want to be a market-breaking innovator, introducing new products and services that have the potential to change the dynamics of the sector?
- Does it want to be a close follower of another company, focused less on creating the pioneering change and more on providing an incremental improvement in any of the key dimensions of customer service, value or performance?
- Does it want to be the imitator of others, preferring to compete on the basis of price, reach, speed to market or cost of ownership?

As an illustrative example, does it essentially want to be the Sony, Matsushita or Goodmans of its sector? Such a core perspective is key not only to determining the innovation approach taken but also to the overall business strategy itself. This should therefore be clear. It may not necessarily be articulated as such in any mission statement, PR campaign or internal communication, but the desire to be one of these three types of innovator is usually evident within the board. If it is not, then there may be more fundamental change necessary in the leadership and direction of the firm.

While it is easy for organizations to jump towards an ambition of taking the first option, it is pertinent both to realize the risks within its particular sector and to gain an insight of overall business statistics:

- Whilst the rewards to be reaped from being the market breaker are significant, so are the risks of failure. There are many, such as Boo.com, Rabbit and Chemdex, who fail in the attempt, but for some, such as Dyson, eBay and Sony, it is clearly possible. The more conservative close-follower approach is often less risky, but at the same time unless, like Dell in the 1990s, this is used as an interim stage towards being a lead innovator, the rewards can also be reduced. Lastly, although the third, imitator option is the route of minimal risk, unless there is a key technological or cost of provision advantage available, it is also the one of lowest margin.
- In the overall context, over the years there has been little variation in the 'types' of innovation strategy pursued by companies across industry (Griffin, 1997). Two studies conducted thirteen years apart in the manufacturing and consumer

products industries (Booz Allen and Hamilton, 1982; Group EFO, 1995), showed that only one in ten innovations were actually 'new to the world' and only two in ten could be considered as 'new to the firm' (Figure 17.1). Over 50 per cent of innovations introduced were either improvements or simply additions to existing lines, whilst the rest were either focused on market repositioning or on cost reductions. This complements the perspectives of risk and reward. Only a few organizations go wholly for breakthrough innovation strategies.

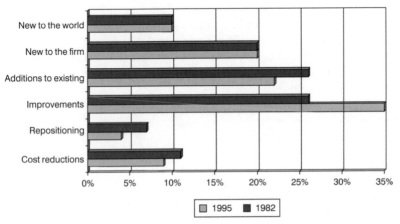

Figure 17.1 Product innovations by type 1982–1995 (source: Griffin, 1997).

The determination of which single approach, or which combination of approaches, is to be taken by the company itself can also be facilitated by recognition of current industry best practice and lead competitor strategy. Using the assessment of both overall corporate innovation performance and comparative innovation capability evolution, a good understanding of what realistic opportunities exist for innovation in a sector can be attained. Whilst this does not necessarily imply that these two should act as guides, they are at least terms of reference in this all-important corporate decision.

In the FMCG packaging company mentioned in Chapter 16, the outcome of this decision was to focus the organization on two main areas for new innovation. In parallel with the ongoing maintenance of existing products being delivered to the current customer base in a largely reactive stance, the key focus for proactive new product and market development was defined to be on a combination of 50 per cent new-to-the-world and 50 per cent new-to-the-firm innovation.

Tactics

With an overall strategy suitably defining the ambition of what the company wants to be, determining how it is to get there is a critical linked activity. Only by determining the specific focus for action can any progression be made possible. This primarily involves selecting the areas of company activity that require attention – in essence, defining what improvements will have greatest effect for the firm in moving its innovation performance forward to realize its strategic intent. The analysis undertaken during the evaluation stage provides a wealth of insight and opportunities for intervention. The key challenge is determining which opportunity or weakness is going to have the most impact if addressed. To do this, identified issues are often best split against several dimensions. These help to group the areas for potential attention by type, scope and benefit. Typical dimensions used by firms here include:

- Barriers vs opportunities
- High impact vs low impact
- Process vs organization
- Essential vs optional.

For a European telecommunications company where delivery of new services was being delayed and, when it happened, product introduction and market penetration were both failing to meet projections, these classifications helped to identify which of the issues were to be the priority going forward (Tables 17.1, 17.2).

Table 17.1 Impact assessment – European telecommunications company

	Low impact	*High impact*
Barriers	• Inconsistent documentation	• Poor cross-business communication • Too many projects • Too much political influence
Opportunities	• Too long sales training • Low quality marketing material	• No prioritization of projects • No clear launch approval • Poor handover of sales to operations

Table 17.2 Scope assessment – European telecommunications company

	Optional	*Essential*
Process	• Different approaches across portfolio • Varying terminology • Services developed as favours	• No clear accountability • No metrics to measure progress • Inaccurate sales forecasts
Organization	• Geographically dispersed team • Ineffective use of pan-European staff	• Limited involvement of sales force • Poor cross-country alignment

Whilst all issues were ones that needed to be addressed at some point, the priority was clearly on those on the right-hand side of these matrices. Problems with documentation, training schedules and marketing material were things that would be nice to have solved, whereas having too many projects and too much political influence coupled with no prioritization, no clear launch approval and poor handover from sales to operations all had to be addressed. Similarly, solving problems with the process, such as the lack of accountability, no supporting metrics and inaccurate sales forecasting, were considered more imperative than the fact that differing approaches using varied terminology were being taken during projects. Furthermore, the fact that many tasks were being performed as personal favours was also seen as less immediate. Likewise, from an organizational perspective, addressing the limited involvement of the sales force in new service development and poor alignment of product offerings across all the markets was deemed more of a priority than dealing with under-utilized and geographically dispersed resource.

This is not to say that all issues were not important, but in order to make any significant progress, there was clearly priority. Moreover, of the priority issues to be addressed there was also clear sequence in terms of both the ability to improve practice and the resulting impact on the company (Table 17.3). Solving the issues of having too many projects and a lack of prioritization was something that was both quick to improve and would have immediate impact, as would improving cross-business communication. By contrast, although defining accountability and metrics throughout development, introducing an appropriate launch approval process and improving the accuracy of sales forecasting were quick to improve, their impact would be more

Table 17.3 Impact/implementation summary – European telecommunications company

	Immediate impact	Longer-term impact
Quick to improve	• Too many projects • No prioritization of projects • Poor cross-business communication	• No clear accountability • No clear launch approval • No metrics to measure progress • Inaccurate sales forecasts
Longer to improve		• Limited involvement of sales force • Poor cross-country alignment • Poor handover of sales to operations • Too much political influence

long term. Gaining greater integration of the sales force across development and launch activities, aligning cross-country input and reducing political influence were, however, all issues that would take a while to improve and deliver tangible benefits.

Thus, improving innovation performance in this organization required three differing types of change to be introduced:

1 'Quick wins' that could be undertaken in a short time and would have immediate benefit
2 Improvements that could be made quickly but would take longer to demonstrate benefits
3 Long-term changes that would take a while both to implement and to provide results.

Each of these is different in approach as well as in schedule. As such, each demanded different interventions to be successful, but ones that had to address all the issues in a collective manner. In addition, wherever possible, any opportunity simultaneously to fix some of the identified low impact, optional issues also needed to be taken, as long as this did not distract from the main priorities.

Targets

Underpinning the selection of the desired strategy, and the prioritization of the most appropriate arenas for attention to realize it, is the definition of applicable targets. As well as providing clarification of the corporate ambition, these also enable progress towards it to be measured and reviewed. Hard and soft metrics provide focus for design and implementation steps and set the expectation for the degree of improvement to be achieved. Again, as with the differing evaluation of internal innovation activity performance, this is highly company and sector dependent. However, since the insight on current performance is to hand and, in many instances, qualified through either numeric or evolutionary assessment, realistic targets for progression can be determined.

For a financial services organization, the outline innovation targets defined at this point were to:

- Double the number of services offered to customers
- Reduce the average time to market by 20 per cent
- Halve customer churn
- Increase the operating margin by 10 per cent
- Maintain existing sector market shares
- Increase average customer deposits by 30 per cent
- Triple the level of internal cross-selling
- Achieve top-five consumer rankings for innovation and customer service.

In an oil company with a need to improve innovation effectiveness across its business, the comparable targets were to:

- Decrease upstream costs by 10 per cent
- Double the profitability of retail sites
- Increase the annual market share by three per cent
- Reduce the time to market for new product introduction by 20 per cent
- Double renewable energy revenues over three years.

As this initial target setting most commonly uses a combination of different levels of performance criteria, it is best undertaken as a pre-emptive forecast of what may be subsequently developed and implemented through the creation and population of an innovation balanced scorecard in the next stages.

Summary

Such decisions and techniques help to define the precise areas that an organization is best to focus on. The definition of strategic intent sets the direction and overall schedule, while the tactical determination of opportunities and the selection of the most appropriate clarify the specific issues that are to be addressed going forward. Lastly, the choice of appropriate measures and targets brings these together, helping both to cement focus and to provide a mechanism for tracking of progress during the sub-sequent stages as the innovation improvements are duly embedded.

References

Griffin, A. (1997). PDMA research on new product development practices. *J. Product Innov. Management*, **14(4)**, 429–58.

Booz Allen and Hamilton (1982). *New Products Management for the 1980s*. Booz Allen and Hamilton.

Group EFO (1995). *1995 Innovation Survey: Report on New Products*. Group EFO Ltd.

18

Design – planning action

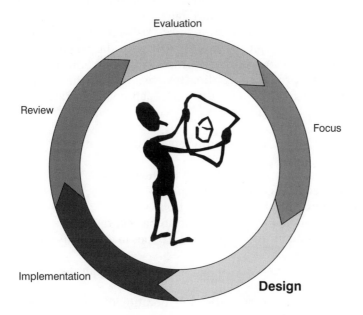

In the pharmaceutical industry, patents protecting the key molecules that are the essential ingredients in the development and manufacture of the drugs are the fundamental currency. In a leading US pharmaceutical company, an identified gap in the future product pipeline between drugs already in clinical trials and those still in discovery prompted the need to acquire additional molecules that were in development external to the firm. A number of recent failures of prospective new products in testing had culminated in this break in the pipeline. Only by filling a gap that corresponded to about two or three years of the typical ten-year development cycle would the company be able to maintain the continued and constant release of major new drugs into the marketplace, something that it, its customers, its investors and the markets all expected. The fact that previous successes and failures during the early discovery stages of new drug development had coincided to produce such a lengthy gap could not have been predicted up front. However, once it had occurred and had consequently been identified as a key area for action, some means of solving the problem had to be defined. For this, the analysis of options available, ranging from full-scale merger with a competitor with a complementary pipeline through to the acquisition of a number of smaller players with the sought-after molecules at the right stage of development, had in the end pointed at a combination of in-licensing and partnered cross-selling as the most appropriate solution. This would provide both additional molecules that could progress through the company's own clinical trials and product launch processes, as well as approved drugs that could be strategically co-branded with the respective manufacturers so that a stream of new products would continue to enter the company's product portfolio. However, despite this clear strategic intent and focus, before this approach could be implemented it had first to be designed:

- Candidate companies and appropriate molecules had to be clarified
- The in-licensing process itself had to be developed
- Due diligence activities had to be planned
- Regulatory approval procedures had to be verified
- The necessary financial resources had to be secured
- The required human resources had to be made ready for deployment
- Individual projects needed to be scoped and team leaders identified
- Overall strategic options and considerations had to be reviewed
- Applicable metrics and reviews to monitor progress had to be established.

Such a major programme, involving significant sums of money but hopefully having a major bearing on the company's future, as well as potentially impacting the industry dynamics, had to be carefully crafted. Successful execution was paramount, and so, although time was an issue, clear up-front definition and scheduling of all the component elements, as well as the necessary contingencies to overcome any unexpected barriers, were critical to success. To evolve the company's innovation capability into sharing intellectual property and partnering with competitors to plug the gap in its pipeline, designing the necessary implementation was an essential step.

This is true for all interventions, large or small. Without such preparation, once a focus for action has been determined, organizations can easily rush headlong into the challenge only to find themselves later either bogged down in a never-ending cycle of greyness with no clear idea of progress or heading off in an entirely inappropriate direction, using the wrong approaches to realize the ambition. Although many find it frustrating to hold off immediate action, just as with the development of any new product or service, time after time successful implementers of innovation change identify clear up-front planning as a key success factor.

With clear focus on what overall changes must be achieved, what improvements must be introduced and what capabilities must be built, the design stage of embedding innovation is concentrated on how best to achieve this. With prioritization of issues and an outline definition of targets for the short, medium and even long term provided from earlier stages, this is where the specific actions that are required to facilitate the chosen improvements to an organization, its strategy, its processes and even its structure are selected and their respective introduction scheduled. Such a level of planning often requires a schedule itself. The design stage of embedding innovation can take from a few weeks to a couple of months to undertake fully, and, owing to the interdependencies that are often present between the different issues being tackled, there is frequently related order to the corresponding selection and scheduling of the applicable approaches. Two different procedures for such a task are commonly used:

1 The 'designing the design' approach, where an intensive, cross-business, short, sharp review and approach definition leading to full-scale implementation of changes is followed.
2 The 'designing a pilot' approach, which is used when time is less pressing, limited resources are available or a new concept has to be first proven to get the necessary buy-in. This enables new ideas and tools to be used on a live project, refined to fit the organizational issues present, and shown to deliver results prior to roll-out across the company.

The procedures are equally effective, and the choice of which to adopt is largely down to individual circumstances.

Designing the design approach

In the example of the European telecommunications company, where the prioritized issues to be addressed included too many projects with little prioritization, no clear accountability, no evident approval nor metrics within the process, poor interaction and involvement of the development organization with sales and operational areas and poor cross-country alignment, there were clearly actions required in all three areas of strategy, process and organization. Moreover, given the size of the company and the geographical dispersion of the individuals and functions involved across twenty different countries and cultures, effective communication and consultation with as wide a group as possible throughout the design stage would be essential. To facilitate this in the most effective manner, the design approach for embedding improved innovation practice was therefore split into four parallel but inter-related streams of activity (Figure 18.1). Time was an imperative for the firm, and so short, sharp, high-value, active participation of all key parties was critical. The design stage was therefore undertaken over a one-month period and used a number of half-day workshops where senior representation from all areas involved could participate and define the key means for delivering the new approaches across the four streams of activity:

1 The *strategy* stream first reviewed the existing product portfolio against a combination of market impact, revenue generation and quality of service delivery, and as a result defined the

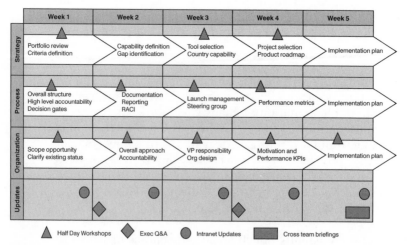

Figure 18.1 Design stage schedule in telecommunications company.

criteria by which future projects could be prioritized. Using this information, the capabilities required to deliver existing products were clarified and gaps in both resource and the product portfolio identified. Equipped with this insight, the third week focused on selecting the most appropriate tools that could be used to help with strategic project selection and identifying available skills and resources that existed in other countries that could be used to help both develop and deliver new services. This then enabled the approaches for new project selection and the development of associated product roadmaps to be selected and drafted.

2 The *process* stream began with a review of the overall structure and definition of high-level accountabilities for the key development phases and activities before using the criteria from the parallel strategy stream as the basis for defining revised key decision gates. Modifications to existing documentation and reporting mechanisms were determined the following week, together with a more detailed definition of individual roles and responsibilities. Week three focused on identifying and defining an improved approach for launch management and gaining the agreement to create a new high-level product steering group to oversee cross-business product strategy and approve project progression. The last element within this stream concerned the selection of the most appropriate performance metrics that could be used across all projects to measure and review progress.

3 The *organization* stream was designed to address any changes required to the structure of the development organization to enable the desired improvements to be achieved. The first workshop scoped out the opportunities available for change and clarified the existing state of transition of varied parts of the company resulting from a recent rationalization programme. Equipped with input from the first two streams, a new overall structure for a more product-focused organization was then determined, together with clarification of the associated accountabilities. Individual VP responsibilities within the new organization were determined and detailed cross-team support structures defined. Lastly, the respective motivation and performance metrics were reviewed to ensure alignment with the new strategic and process approaches.

4 Finally, the *update* stream was primarily focused on using weekly intranet updates to communicate key outcomes from the half-day workshops to an extended team across multiple geographies and to gain feedback and input. In addition, two executive team 'question and answer' sessions were used to ensure that the leadership team gained understanding of the

revised approach being developed, as well as having the opportunity to supply guiding input. Lastly, two full day cross-team briefings provided the opportunity to involve the whole development organization in the process, give an overview of the selected new approaches, enable input into the proposed revised process and share the outline implementation plans that had been co-developed across the three other streams of activity.

Together these four streams provided the definition of an effective, inclusive and consistent new approach for improved service development that could then be implemented across the organization. By being undertaken in parallel with a high-profile team drawn from across the organization with executive input and support, not only was the priority for improvement emphasized and communicated to all but also, through achieving such high levels of engagement, the motivation for change was created. This led to the immediate adoption of the new strategic tools to cull several projects and refocus resources on those that would deliver optimal value. The revised process was appropriately introduced across all development programmes, and, through the engagement and involvement of the wider sales and operations areas of the company, the foundations for future improved introduction and delivery of subsequent new services were also laid.

Designing a pilot

In the packaging company, where the outcome of the overall strategic decision for future innovation had been to pursue a dual approach of concentrating on new product development for a combination of new-to-the-world and new-to-the-firm innovation, several areas were chosen as focuses to enable this to happen. Of the multiple issues identified in the first evaluation stage, four had been prioritized for initial attention during the subsequent assessment. The associated areas for focus were to:

- Improve the idea management process, capturing ideas from across the whole organization
- Implement a more coherent development process for all projects, with clearer decision-making
- Restructure technical and market development activities into a single multifunctional unit
- Introduce a new approach to partnered product launch focused on key lead customers.

It would involve significant effort to implement each of these inter-related improvements successfully, and all had identified indicative targets against which success could be judged and the associated progress measured. These formed the innovation ambition for the company, and were, respectively:

- A 300 per cent increase in ideas assessed, with an average of five new development projects initiated per annum
- A reduction in the average development cycle from thirty-six to eighteen months, coupled with at least 50 per cent launch success
- Better interaction to enable the 50 per cent reduction in cycle time and launch of five new products
- Entry into two new market segments with resulting market share in excess of 10 per cent within three years.

The design phase here was built around a different line of attack for determining the new innovation approach. Because there was a small group involved and geographical dispersion was not a barrier, as many of the key functions were largely co-located, bringing all the decision-makers together to determine the improved innovation focus was more easily achievable on a regular weekly basis for a reasonably long duration. As the key players were also actively involved in ongoing development and launch activities, an ongoing 'learning by doing' approach could be used. Rather than redefining all key aspects of the process and organizational elements simultaneously ready for parallel implementation, in this company one key market was chosen for use as a pilot for introducing new approaches into the organization. This focused on the full conception to realization process, but with particular attention paid to two specific aspects – the front-end idea management and the market introduction launch activities. In designing this pilot programme, the key elements that had to be considered were:

- Which project to use
- What aspects of the existing approach to maintain
- Which specific changes to introduce
- How to manage and evaluate these introductions
- The timescales for realization
- How to transfer successes across the rest of the company.

Given the position of the company in the middle of the value chain of an increasingly competitive marketplace, selecting a project for the pilot that was sufficiently insulated from dramatic external influence but at the same time was not so isolated that it was unrepresentative was a major factor. With the awareness of the specific problems in the front-end activities that had been identified from the evaluation stage, a project where new ideas would implicitly be required was also fundamental in being able to address as many issues as possible. Introducing improved approaches to idea generation and idea selection would be a core part of the pilot. In addition, an area that could involve a lead customer (and ideally several end users) would also help to test out new tools and techniques for enhancing interaction and integration of these external perspectives throughout development, from conception through to launch. In an ideal scenario, conducting two separate parallel pilots – one focused on trialling front-end improvements and the other addressing the product launch issues – would have been preferred in terms of accelerating the ability to transfer improvements fully across the organization. However, in this company, due to a combination of limited resource availability and some residual scepticism that needed to be overcome through proven demonstration of defined benefits, focusing full attention on only one pilot was the chosen route. Although this meant that improvements to launch activities would not be introduced for over a year, it did nevertheless enable better and fuller evaluation of the improvements introduced.

The fact that the evaluation stage had determined that a core innovation process did exist within the organization, with cross-business input during development, testing and evaluation, indicated that these parts of the existing approach could be largely maintained as they were, with only minor changes in task accountability. Changing everything would have involved introducing so many new approaches that achieving buy-in from all and being able to recognize any specific improvements demonstrated would have been difficult to realize. The implication of this meant that although only one pilot was being used, since the main areas for improvement were front end and back end, there would be no need to wait until the project was complete to begin to migrate improved front-end practice across the company. Once the project had a defined concept entering the familiar core development process, learning from the idea management approaches could be transferred to other projects, with the experiences from improved product launch similarly moving across as and when available. As a result, whilst the project itself would take around eighteen months to complete, full-scale roll-out of some of the early improvements could occur within four months of pilot initiation (Figure 18.2).

It was anticipated that as it would take between six and eighteen months, from the start of implementation of the pilot

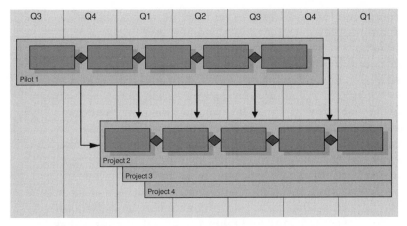

Figure 18.2 Piloting approach in packaging company.

programme, fully to introduce the improvements across the company, the outline targets would begin to be met within two years and full achievement within four years would be credible. The outline targets therefore gave the long-term ambition.

Although the implementation plans for improved idea management, reduction in cycle time, restructuring of market and technical development activities and introduction of a new launch approach would all differ in scope, schedule and resource, up front the focus and coherence of all four improvements of the company had to be put into a structured framework. To aid cross-business integration and visibility of these benefits deriving from the improvements, all the varied changes being introduced to the organization across its innovation activities had to be brought together in a clear and all-embracing perspective. The preferred approach, and the one taken by this organization, was to create an innovation balanced scorecard.

Innovation balanced scorecard

Whilst Robert Kaplan's approach for developing a balanced scorecard to evaluate current performance and target future ambitions is now commonplace across multiple sectors, its specific use within the field of innovation is less prominent. Either because some organizations prefer to maintain a balanced scorecard only at the highest level and therefore do not cascade it down with the associated key performance indicators into the full range of corporate activities, or because others do not consider that innovation can be managed using the same approach, less than 10 per cent of major firms are yet to gain from its successful implementation. However, for those that have used this approach, the benefits both in clarity of progression of the firm and success ratios for new products have been significant.

As with the development of any balanced scorecard, the fundamental issue in creating one for innovation is to cover all four key perspectives of financial, internal/business, external/customer, and learning and growth, and to define both lead and lag measures and targets for each. Moreover, to be effective these metrics have to be relevant to the organization and its marketplace, as well as being of similar levels in a cascaded KPI hierarchy. In addition, to promote integration they needed to be mutually supportive. The resulting innovation balanced scorecard for the packaging company (Table 18.1) used measures that were similar, but not identical, to the targets previously defined in outline during the earlier focus stage but supplemented by other metrics.

- External measures focused on customer perceptions were a combination of repeat customer orders, for which the target was 85 per cent, and the number of design, innovation, quality and customer service industry awards received, with four per year being the aim.

Table 18.1 Innovation balanced scorecard for example packaging company

External (customer)		Internal (business)	
Lead	Lag	Lead	Lag
Repeat customer orders (85%)	No. of industry awards p.a. (4)	New product launches p.a. (5)	Average development cycle (18 months)
Financial		Growth	
Lead	Lag	Lead	Lag
Forecast two-year revenue from new products ($26m)	Overall return on innovation (250%)	No. of ideas submitted for assessment p.a. (200)	No. of market segments with >10% share (4)

- Internal measures within the business were a mix of the traditional number of new product launches achieved per annum and the average development cycle time, for which the targets were five and eighteen months respectively.
- Financial indicators chosen by the company included a forward-looking two-year forecast of additional revenue generated from new products, and a retrospective calculation of overall return on innovation achieved. Targets of $26 million and 250 per cent were set for these.
- Growth indicators looked at the future potential in terms of the number of new ideas being submitted for assessment per annum, with a target of 200. To encourage increased diversification and movement away from a dependency on only one market, ongoing performance as related to the number of new market segments within which the company achieved greater than 10 per cent market share was also selected. The target here was four.

Developed over a three-week period, this provided the leaders of the firm and the implementation teams alike with an appropriate and validated means by which the impacts on the business of the progress of the innovation improvements being introduced could be successfully judged and monitored. Together with the pilot activities, this provided clear strategic and operational foci for the implementation of innovation performance improving change across the organization.

Summary

The two different approaches of an all-at-once redefinition of strategy, process and organization and the use of a pilot to trial new ideas are two ends of the spectrum. Both have benefits; equally, both present challenges. For the all-at-once approach, gaining sufficient input and focus can certainly get things moving across the firm, but it can also raise expectations of improvement delivery too early. Conversely, the slower prove by doing a pilot approach requires a smaller team but, owing to timescales, it can be difficult to keep momentum going and ensure continued interest by the organization. The choice of which to adopt is clearly a matter of context, but, although each can be modified slightly in focus and time, it is generally better to go for one or the other and not to fall into the middle ground. As with innovation itself, high-level breakthrough change and incremental improvements are both more effective at delivering the results than a middle-of-the-road hybrid.

19

Implementation – concepts are not solutions

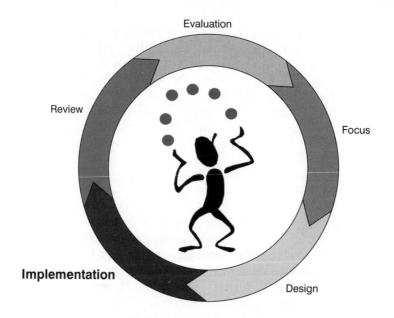

Evaluation

Review

Focus

Implementation

Design

It is easy to believe that once a new approach has been defined, discussed, approved and shared, actually applying it is straight-forward. Unfortunately this is a fallacy. Any designer will tell you that a concept is never the same as the finished production item, whether a product, a service, a corporate identity or a web site. Whatever is created in theory is rarely the same in practice. Concepts are not solutions. This is particularly true for the introduction of an improvement to the innovation approach within a company. Especially here, with the ever-changing organization, individual behaviours and attitudes, and corporate strategy (never mind the competitive landscape) to accommodate, it is hoped that the final solution will bear similarities with the design concept, but the two will never be exactly the same.

In theory, the implementation of a new approach could be logical, ordered and timely. It should occur to schedule, with full and timely support of all involved and enthusiasm from the leaders. The introduction of a well-planned and appropriate enhancement to an organization should be a clean process. Unfortunately, no matter how effective the evaluation, how clear the focus and how proficient the design, in practice things just don't always turn out as expected and often, when they do, for many companies it is more from luck than judgment. Implementation is frequently revised to accommodate slippages, barriers are encountered that are larger than expected, sometimes expected barriers do not appear, and often resistance to change emanates from unexpected directions. Despite the opportunities to express perspectives in the evaluation and design stages, for personal reasons and agendas individuals inside the firm may well keep doubts hidden. Alternatively, market changes may result in reduced commitment and support from external partners. All of these require flexibility of approach and an early awareness of the likelihood of their occurrence.

This fact of life has to be understood up front, not just by the initiators and leaders of any change but also by all stakeholders involved, from senior management to analysts and from suppliers to customers. If the evaluation, focus and design stages have been performed efficiently and implementation is undertaken with these in mind, then the results delivered and the benefits achieved by or for the organization may well be greater than expected, but the method of their realization can sometimes be very different. There is a fundamental difference between knowing what to do and actually doing it in practice.

Critical success factors

In many cases, the barriers to implementation can be predicted. Across sectors there are common issues that frequently arise and, within specific industries, sizes of organization or generic corporate focus, there are usually early signs of problems that, as long as they are watched for and noticed, can all be suitably accommodated. As with innovation itself, there are a number of issues that impact effective delivery which, if understood, anticipated and catered for, can become drivers of success rather than of failure. Time and time again, efficiently embedding innovation is influenced by a number of critical success factors. These include:

- Superior, differentiated improvements with unique benefits
- Strong business orientation throughout
- Sharp, clear definition of scope
- Enthusiastic executive support
- An appropriate role for senior management
- Quality execution of activities
- Multifunctional motivated and empowered teams
- Appropriate team structure and governance
- Well-planned and resourced interventions
- A multistage and disciplined game plan
- Clear decision-making and progress reviews
- Validated and shared interim milestones
- Rewards for achievement and delivery
- Continuous and appropriate communication of progress.

These are unfortunately not mutually exclusive, and to be successful in delivering the benefits to be gained from improved innovation performance, all must be accommodated appropriately. Failures in one area can, if not set right, undermine all the achievements in the others. Only by understanding why these issues are critical to success, how they impact on organizations, how they can influence implementation and how to rectify any problems can successful delivery of the desired benefits be forthcoming. The following examples provide some illustrations of these in practice.

Pharmaceutical firm

In the US pharmaceutical company seeking to plug a gap in its product pipeline through a combination of in-licensing of molecules and strategic marketing alliances, a vital component of successful implementation was initially to keep these two new corporate activities separate from the established business operations. The vast majority of the organization was focused on the core discovery to market processes that continued to be the powerhouse of the company, the driver of its revenue streams and the provider of much of its future product portfolio. The two additional elements required for fixing the gap were additional and not substitutional to these core activities. The firm was not intending to switch to in-licensing as its primary vehicle for new product development; nor was it moving towards joint marketing of products with competitors as a default approach. These were new capabilities that needed to be added to existing skills both to fix the short-term problem and to provide a future strategic option that could be deployed where and when necessary.

Consequently, dedicated teams with specific project focus and scope were the preferred implementation approach. One, drawn mainly from a combination of resources from the scientific and business development groups within the organization but supported by legal and financial expertise, concentrated on the in-licensing opportunities, and the other, comprising of a mixture of global marketing and sales executives again supported by legal and financial expertise, focused on developing strategic marketing alliances. The approach, the targets and the scope for each had been defined during the design stage, and so the respective remits were clear. With direct reporting to the executive board, the two teams were fully empowered to address the problems and implement the most appropriate solutions for the business. Moreover, if they needed additional resource from the manufacturing or regulatory areas of the business to support key activities, they were guaranteed to receive it. The problems being addressed were of such strategic importance to the company that internal cross-functional disputes over such issues as resource availability could not be allowed to become barriers. In addition, the teams were empowered not only to determine the most appropriate companies to work with, but also to undertake and agree all associated negotiations. Executive support was there to be called upon to facilitate overcoming any major obstacles that were faced, but it was not there to interfere with or to influence any of the decisions being taken by the cross-functional teams.

Within twelve months of initiation, five new molecules had been licensed into the organization and three different marketing alliances had been agreed. Together these effectively plugged the gap and solved the fundamental problems. In addition, the lessons learnt and the capabilities developed by the organization in these two areas were such that, as both quickly became key strategic options for the company, they were introduced as standard practice across different geographies. Once the optimal approach for accommodating an externally sourced molecule into the internal development process had been determined and proven to work, the financial benefits seen to be gained from using this as a core means of extending the product portfolio were such that four years later nearly 30 per cent of the firm's product pipeline comprised of in-licensed molecules. Similarly, as the costs of marketing new drug launches continued to rise across the sector, strategic marketing alliances between competitors became a more widely deployed approach as companies sought to maximize the effectiveness of their sales forces. As a consequence, the company now uses this approach for around 20 per cent of its new product launches. What had started out as a short-term problem of the two- to three-year gap in the product pipeline had, through effective definition of approach and successful implementation, become a core capability for the company as it sought to increase its innovation performance.

Industrial b2b business

In a diversified industrial conglomerate that wanted to improve performance through embracing the opportunities from developing and exploiting b2b e-businesses, appropriate leadership of the group tasked with achieving this was a key issue for implementation. As well as several cross-business proposals that would require inter-group cooperation for delivery, the candidate new business ideas originally floated at board level included a combination of discrete opportunities that were linked into individual areas of the business and that hence could, in theory, largely be undertaken independently. However, to aid learning and the creation of a centre of excellence within the organization, the company wanted all projects to be undertaken collectively by the same core team. The organization had a divisional structure with each business unit headed by competent senior managers, any of whom had the capabilities to lead such an initiative, but none of whom had any specific e-business experience that could be used. Given the high profile of the initiative, both internally and especially externally, there were two core issues to be addressed up front that would impact implementation. External e-business expertise would evidently be required throughout the programme for design, implementation and even operation, and the leader had to be highly competent, enthusiastic, objective, able to influence and, most significantly, non-aligned to any specific business unit but well regarded by all. Whichever of the original ideas actually came out top in the early evaluation and focus stages, the figurehead for this new area of activity of the business had to be the right person to lead implementation, no matter which divisions of the overall group were ultimately involved.

In addition, content-rich cross-business resources had to be made available when and where required and full executive team support throughout was also deemed critical. While the executive would be the review committee tasked with endorsing the selection of the preferred idea, reviewing progress and providing financial backing, again, as with the pharmaceutical company, they could not be allowed to interfere or to bring any personal, divisional or political influence to bear. The candidate chosen for the role was a relatively recent addition to the company's management who, although younger than most of his colleagues, was ambitious, enthusiastic, and had previously completed the successful introduction of an intranet-based cross-business idea management initiative that had identified a wealth of new opportunities across the company. In turn, this project leader was supported by a number of recent graduates who had joined the firm and made good early impact on the company. They were equally enthusiastic to continue to make their mark and deliver an innovative growth opportunity for the company, and very much became the powerhouse for the project as it progressed from concept through to launch.

As ten proposed candidates were evaluated, strategies assessed and relative returns validated over a three-month timeframe, one stood out as offering a combination of financial benefit to the organization together with the building of new capabilities around existing markets and customers. To fulfil the expectations placed on it, it did however require major input from a range of external organizations – software solutions providers, systems integrators and telecommunication equipment suppliers and network operators. Along with the definition of a clear, unique and superior value proposition that could be delivered reliably across multiple geographies, the other key success factors for the implementation of this chosen opportunity were therefore managing the network of external partners, understanding their differing capabilities and inputs, sharing value and accountability accordingly, and ensuring objective and realistic governance. As the project moved from business plan to full-scale launch during the following year some of these partnerships were modified, but they largely remained focused on the original scope. In addition, the varied business units affected by the new business were continuously supportive, providing required inputs and resources whenever required. Perhaps most significantly, alongside the project lead, three of the initial business concept team (two of whom were internal resources) stuck with the project throughout the eighteen-month design and implementation. Without this level of continuity of insight and focus, many on the team considered that the successful launch and the subsequent integration across the business would not have occurred.

Packaging company

In the packaging company, early success of piloting improved idea management to validate the new approach was vital. Not only would this demonstrate clear output; it would also increase buy-in for increased support for the pilot project as it progressed. Internal resistance to change was still present in several areas and, although senior management support was strong, changing market conditions similarly required an early success. With a core team of five drawn from across the organization, an improved idea management process was duly introduced. (Figure 19.1). Focused on the pilot project, a number of different stimuli for new ideas were introduced – R&D, marketing and manufacturing personnel were encouraged to put forward ideas through a dedicated suggestion scheme, customers were consulted by the sales force, and a facilitated off-site cross-functional focused idea generation workshop was arranged with expert external technical and market input to complement internal capabilities.

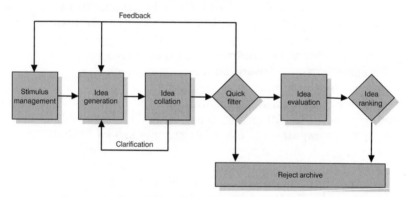

Figure 19.1 Pilot idea management approach in packaging company.

All ideas were collated centrally, and within a week feedback (either in the form of acknowledgement of receipt or requests for clarification on the suggested idea and its areas of application) was provided. This ensured that all contributors understood where their own ideas were in the process, and that similar levels of information were available across all proposals. The following week, all generated ideas were evaluated against killer criteria contained within a new 'quick filter' being used for the first time by the organization. Based on the approach implemented to great effect by Siemens Medical, this effectively used ten key questions to weed out only those candidates that met the company's product, market, financial and operational desires and capabilities. Following feedback to idea originators on success or failure regarding passing the quick filter and the associated reasons for this, the five-man team undertook more in-depth evaluation of the remaining opportunities over the following three weeks. With members providing input from their own technical, commercial, business or manufacturing perspectives, short four-page summaries of idea opportunities, barriers, issues to be resolved, assessment of ability to deliver, outline market and financial potential were all prepared for each. From these, the ideas were ranked according to a new scoring system weighted by the strategic objectives of undertaking 'new to the world' and 'new to the company' developments, and delivery and launch plans drawn up for the top opportunities.

In an organization where no central idea collation had previously occurred and new projects had been a rarity, within two months of pilot kick-off 280 new ideas had been generated, of which 32 successfully passed through the new quick filter. Of theses, five passed the more rigorous assessment of opportunity and two were selected for progression (Figure 19.2). Of these, one was used for the first pilot and another was prepared for top priority roll-out as part of the subsequent implementation, which with capture and sharing of learning from the new idea management approach all completed within two weeks of passing the first review gate, was ready for initiation less than 6 months after the pilot. Within 18 months the pilot was complete and a world-first new product was launched to market acclaim in partnership with a leading consumer brand. The new approach to innovation was duly rolled out across the company.

Over the following year more new products were introduced that both pioneered fundamental changes to the packaging sector

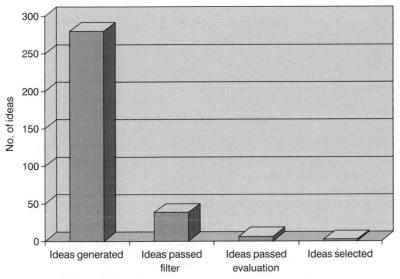

Figure 19.2 Pilot idea management approach in packaging company.

and, through the adoption of new techniques from partner companies and business units, provided higher performing, lighter and lower-cost materials for the industry.

New drug delivery

In a medical device manufacturer that, although expert in several key technological areas, was primarily a subcontractor to several large multinational pharmaceutical firms, there was a strategic objective to move up the value chain by adding an up-front concept development capability and an 'own-label' product sales activity. Recognized across the sector for its longstanding expertise in drug delivery system design and production, the firm already had an excellent supplier relationship with its primary customers but suffered from being reactive in the market space. When a new drug was developed that required a new delivery system, the respective pharmaceutical company and, frequently, external design consultants would typically define this conceptually before passing it over to the medical device manufacturer for detailed design and production. The firm had both the market and technological insights proactively to create the next generation of drug delivery devices, but to date had not fully exploited them. The main challenge was therefore to build and integrate a full concept development capability that would match seamlessly with its existing design and production capability, and could also interface well with pharmaceutical customers' product specification processes. By contrast, a mix of training and recruitment could largely achieve the secondary issue of widening the scope and expertise of the sales force to sell the own-label devices.

After successful evaluation of the opportunity and design of the new concept development approach, a cross-business desire to extend the whole company up the value chain was fundamental to effective implementation. This included senior management, marketing and sales, as well as the more conservative design and production areas of the company. To be successful, buy-in and support from all was considered essential and proved so to be. As part of a three-phase implementation plan, the first focused on using existing market and technological understanding to build the industry view of the future 'road map' for new drug delivery device introductions. This provided detailed context for anticipated developments, as well as a summary of the likely requirements that would have to be met and thus defined a clear scope for internally generated new concepts to follow. Phase two involved increased interaction with several key customers' development activities to increase awareness of the new product concepts that were being developed proactively, and to gain direct input into how these could be best configured to meet the emerging requirements from the pharmaceutical companies themselves. This enabled concepts to be refined to known partner needs and therefore to become candidates for future products. Lastly, improved integration of CADCAM equipment between the concept, design and production capabilities increased the firm's ability quickly and efficiently to take concepts through to manufacture with minimal delay and rework. Within twelve months three internally initiated products were being produced for customers as the primary delivery devices for new drug applications.

Summary

In each of these examples, the implementation approaches taken were clearly different. What worked in one would not have necessarily worked in another. Each had its own specific problems and opportunities, and therefore each had its own solutions. The most important factors were: the selection of the most appropriate implementation route as determined by the issues being addressed; the levels of additional innovation capability being introduced to the firm; the industry, market and organizational dynamics present; the resources available; and the timescales for realization of benefits. Implementation is where most organizations fail to deliver the benefits anticipated from the expectations raised during the evaluation, focus and design stages. This is partly because many fail to pay sufficient attention to the disparate needs, and partly because the desire for immediate results often forces interventions to be accelerated and key capabilities introduced too quickly with insufficient learning. As these examples illustrate, above all else successful implementation demands defined scope, schedule and targets, a clear but flexible approach for realization, and a motivated, empowered, capable and well-resourced team.

20

Review – how did it go?

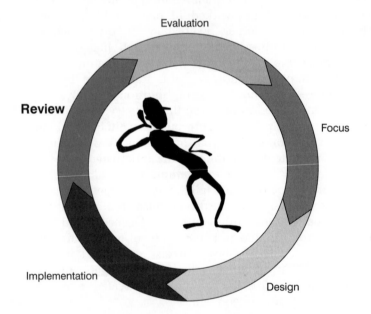

The fifth, final and potentially most influential stage for embedding innovation to improve performance is the review stage. Often forgotten, this is for many organizations the point where the greatest long-term benefits are actually put in place. This is where the sustainability of approach is discussed, new opportunities are highlighted and necessary improvements are first identified. It is the point where the component activities undertaken and the decisions made throughout the other four stages are reviewed and, especially for design and implementation, where the respective approaches taken are investigated. Although the final stage, this is also a precursor to the next round of enhancements. As it ends one cycle, so the review stage begins the next. It is the vital link in an ongoing programme of continuous improvement focused on constantly raising performance by improving how the firm addresses the challenges it faces through leveraging innovation. It is therefore vital that it is not forgotten.

It is, however, all too easy for any firm to skip this stage. Once the benefits are evident to all and momentum has built up, stopping to pause and reflect on how this has been achieved can appear to be a distraction. If everything is working so well, then why waste time looking back when the important issue appears to be continuing to move forward? Similarly, if for any reason delivery of the anticipated improvements failed to meet expectations, it is only natural for a firm to push everything under the carpet and hide mistakes. Although people are sometimes happy to discuss success they rarely enjoy examining the causes of failure, and hence avoid taking stock of what went wrong. Both perspectives are erroneous. If success was down to a new approach, then surely it needs to be captured and diffused across the business? If it was down to luck, then should not this too be recognized? Similarly, if failure is a symptom of poor planning or inappropriate execution, then, if it is to avoid falling into the same trap again, a firm owes it to itself and its employees to identify the causes and determine how to overcome them in the future.

Success or failure, the opportunities that stand to be gained from capturing the experiences and lessons learnt and then sharing them across the organization are multiple. If successful, a new internal standard is defined. Best practice can become the norm and, through conducting a post-implementation review, the new things that worked can be identified and the experiences captured. Similarly, if there is a failure in any aspect, a *post-mortem* helps identify what went wrong and provides the focus for identifying how to avoid the same issues in the future.

When undertaking such a review, it is vital that it takes place in a constructive and objective environment and not one where praise and self-congratulation or blame and criticism dominate. Although usually initially focused on the process and the procedures adopted for designing, introducing and implementing a change and identifying the key leanings from this, it is often in the inter-relationships and cross-functional interfaces that the real insights are found. What makes this work and differentiates between success and failure here is the interaction between the various parties throughout the process. Dealing with aspects such as frequency of communication, detail of information, level of trust and respect are often the softer elements in a successful project that come out in a post-launch review. It is these people-based skills and capabilities that need to be fed back into the rest of the organization and integrated into working practice to ensure future success and continued improvement.

As a primary focus, how well overall ambitions and especially milestone targets were met is always a key starting point. If implemented, a balanced scorecard will have provided indication of high-level progress during monthly or quarterly interim reviews, but for detailed analysis a more granular breakdown of what was achieved against each target is more appropriate. Likewise, if for some reason an innovation balanced scorecard was not used, then a rigorous examination of whatever performance criteria were adopted is certainly demanded. However, although the investigation of hard deliverables and targets is important, it does not give a company the whole picture. More often than not, the real reasons for either success or failure lie in the highlighted softer issues of how people worked together, how ideas were communicated, how teams were motivated, and how well organizational learning was enabled. These are where the differentiation occurs, and, although harder to determine, it is here that the true insights are usually to be found.

The approaches that can be used for undertaking and facilitating this review stage are varied. From off-site meetings to in-company presentations, from taking a day to a week, and from using informal experience sharing to executive panel reviews, companies often adopt a combination of different approaches – usually dictated by the topic being tackled, the number of people involved and the outcome of the implementation. Whichever is most appropriate to the circumstances, the fundamental issue is to ensure that the review goes beyond the superficial and gets under the surface, in deep where necessary, to highlight the true causes of success or failure and not to focus on the symptoms.

Telecommunications company

Following implementation of approaches aimed at improved interaction between sales and development activities in the telecommunications company, a two-day off-site workshop was used as the major review session. Bringing product managers from across Europe together with key development personnel involved with all relevant products, this was led by a newly introduced product launch manager whose responsibilities included acting as a communication channel between all key parties. As such, he was seen as an independent facilitator with no legacy or personal prejudices.

The two days were split fifty–fifty. Day one focused on what had happened, both positively and negatively, during the introduction of the new approach, and day two looked forward to how things could be further improved in the future. With the intermediary evening providing an opportunity for reflection, this timetable was designed to maximize input, minimize distractions and maintain a clear focus.

During the first day, attention was focused on four themes:

1 What went well, how, and under what circumstances
2 What did not turn out as planned, with examples
3 Why things that went well did so
4 Why things did not happen as planned.

Including examination of both hard and soft issues, these aspects were aimed at first getting the facts out for all to see before moving into explanation of why. Only by ensuring that all the key elements were captured and plastered on the wall in the morning could the afternoon of contemplation and detailed investigation be effective. To have jumped into suggesting reasons for outcomes before all were satisfied that everything was out in the open would have led to individuals using unarticulated facts as excuses for either behavioural or procedural success and failure. The outcome of this first day was thereby a comprehensive list of all key elements that had occurred during the implementation of the improved sales and development interaction approaches, alongside initial suggestions for rationale. Particularly when differing functional perspectives were rife, maintaining focus on the rational and avoiding the emotional and political was key.

Day two took the results further, first by grouping and prioritizing around common themes and then by identifying actions for the future. Of the varied topics that had been raised the preceding day, there were three generic areas seen as major contributors to success:

1 Detailed planning
2 Cross-company support and executive buy-in
3 Enthusiastic and motivated leadership.

Conversely, there were four common themes that were seen as having presented barriers to implementation:

1 Low frequency and level of communication
2 Lack of availability of and access to information

3 Unclarified roles and responsibilities at a detailed level
4 Under-utilization of opportunities for joint sales and development customer visits.

Although the metrics had demonstrated that the target improvements of decreasing the number of non-standard installations, increasing the accuracy of sales order processing and improving cross-company awareness of new service introductions had all been achieved, it was evident that even greater performance could have occurred if the issues underpinning these four themes had been better accommodated.

The resulting actions from day two not only defined how to ensure that the positive outcomes could be repeated through concise best practice capture and dissemination, but also provided alternative approaches that could overcome the identified barriers in the future. In a short, sharp, two-day session, over forty lead players within the company had shared their individual perspectives on the implementation, collectively addressed the arising issues, further improved their group identity, and reaffirmed their intent for the future as they sought to take the organization the next step forward.

Pharmaceutical company

Following initial implementation of the new in-licensing approach within the pharmaceutical company and the successful introduction of three new molecules into the firm's development pipeline, an executive review session was used to evaluate progress six months down the line. With key representatives from the implementation team presenting an overview of the outcomes to the executive board of the company, this was a formal high-level afternoon review. Following on from a week-long team offsite meeting that had examined each in-licensing deal attempted in detail before drawing cross-portfolio conclusions, this was the point at which executive acknowledgement of success would be interwoven with the opportunity to extend the approach wider. Although established as an interim solution to a relatively short-term gap in the product pipeline, the successes that had been achieved from in-licensing were such that it was apparent that, with appropriate endorsement and support, the team could maintain and grow this into a core corporate capability for the future.

The afternoon meeting therefore comprised of a two-hour overview followed by a Q&A session from the executive. This overview covered seven main areas:

1 The context for the initiative
2 The strategic options pursued
3 The high-level approach taken
4 The companies investigated
5 The molecules acquired
6 The learning gained, both positive and negative
7 The proposed next steps for the company.

With such a tight schedule, it was key for the team to get across a consistent and valid perspective, pitched at the right level, and positioned to enable subsequent approval for increased adoption and migration of the approach, albeit in a slightly modified form.

The preceding offsite team meeting had concluded that although the identification of candidate molecules and the associated due diligence approach had both worked well, accurate forecasting of future revenues was not as confident as with fully internally developed drugs and the learning was largely confined to a relatively small group. As such, there were clearly opportunities going forward for wider involvement of the market research group in future in-licensing, albeit under the constraints of confidentiality agreements, and the secondment of additional lead resource from both the scientific and business development areas. These were the desired outcomes of the review from the team's perspectives and, with sufficient preparation, prior briefing of key decision-makers and validation of the implications for continued development with the lead business units, were thus achievable.

The fundamental issues present here were that, from its off-site session, the team as a whole had a clear view on what had worked, why and where, and knew specifically what was required going forward; and, through effective involvement and positioning of the executive, the decision to progress and kick-off of a second level of development stood a good chance of being taken without excessive debate and hesitation. Without the preparation, a sound viewpoint or a clear agenda, the executive review could just as easily turned into an uninformed speculation of 'what if' scenarios that could have suspended – or even terminated – what was clearly a successful improvement for the company.

Packaging company

Lastly, in the packaging company a full week of design and implementation reviews were undertaken five months after completion of the pilot project. Bringing all the team together in a single location, each day they addressed a different aspect of the new innovation approach, examining what had worked, where expectations had been met, and where all areas of the improvement programme could have been further enhanced. Over the course of the week, all relevant areas were addressed:

- The new idea management process used for the pilot
- Migration of the idea management approach to other projects
- The refined core development process used for the pilot
- The integrated launch management approach as used in the pilot
- The innovation balanced scorecard application.

From this intensive review, a wealth of information and insights on the new processes was collated and much of the improvements were clarified in terms of both direct and indirect implications on how the company now managed its innovation activities. A number of specific improvements for the future were also identified, including:

- Revising the criteria used for the filtering of initial ideas to allow more non-core product concepts to be developed
- Amending the scoring systems used for detailed idea assessment better to reflect updated strategy for improved margins
- Modifying some group-level accountabilities during development for ongoing updating of market forecasts and in-customer trials
- Redefining some of the targets, but not the measures, contained within the innovation balanced scorecard to promote greater focus on increasing revenue in existing markets
- More direct involvement of end customers in the front-end concept evaluation process, as well as in lead piloting and testing of new materials
- Increasing engagement of the influential design specification community, both through improved communication of new products and involvement in market research activities.

These were all included in a second round of improvements, which were kicked off over the following twelve months in a bid to cement the achievements already gained by the company and raise its innovation performance another step forward.

Summary

Although again, as with the previous stages, the specific approach taken for the review stage has to vary from firm to firm in order to accommodate individual issues and requirements, it is nevertheless fully evident that it is a vital component of the five-stage cycle for embedding innovation. Without it, companies easily fail either to capitalize on the benefits achieved or to qualify where and why implementation failed to deliver. With it, organizations large and small provide the opportunity for objective reflection on what worked and how to take the next steps forward in developing their individual and collective innovation capability. As highlighted by these examples, embedding innovation is not an instantaneous activity, but clearly takes time to allow gradual building and exploitation of capabilities. As the pivotal point between one cycle and the next, the review stage is key in assessing how things went and also in laying the foundation for the next round of improvement. It is where the assessments undertaken during the evaluation stage, the decisions made during the focus stage, the planning done during the design stage and the changes introduced during the implementation stage are all questioned and the benefits gained determined.

As the end of one cycle of innovation improvement and the potential starting point for the next, the review stage is fundamental to enabling continued and successful adoption, integration and embedding of new approaches to raise innovation performance further. Together the five stages outlined here provide a generic, proven approach for enabling such improvements to be successfully delivered time and time again.

Conclusion and resources

21

Conclusion

Throughout this book we have seen how innovation practice has evolved over the most active period of industrial change yet to have occurred. From the earliest formulation of distinctive product strategies by Sony, the development of quality principles by Toyota and the use of product champions by Honda to the increasingly mass customization being achieved by Dell and Nike, cross-company exploitation in 3M and the collaboration between Nokia and Ericsson on the development of WAP, we have traced the gradual development of the ways in which leading firms have innovated during the past twenty years. As the first three waves of innovation capability have emerged and become integrated in standard practice across sectors, it is clear that, like innovation itself, the range of abilities needed to undertake it successfully is also a continuously moving and developing arena.

The most recent wave of innovation practice has highlighted the issues, techniques, methods and approaches that are coming to the fore today. From the market-breaking activities of Egg and Smint and the increasingly higher levels of product personalization being delivered by Nokia and digital TV to the more sophisticated use of intellectual property and management of investments being undertaken for DVD and Bluetooth development and the world-leading partnered brand exploitation being achieved by Manchester United, we can already see the latest ideas delivering the results in practice. As this, the current edge of innovation capability evolution, migrates across industry, so the identified additional new crop of approaches may well then emerge.

In Part 3, core aspects of how to embed innovation in the organization have been highlighted. Using a generically applicable approach that has been proven to deliver the results across multiple sectors, the cases used have shown how and where the varied elements have been introduced in a number of major organizations. From undertaking up-front evaluation of issues and gaining clear focus and priority through the design and implementation of dedicated improvements and on to the eventual review of approach and benefits gained, an indication of how to improve innovation performance through integrating a higher level of innovation capability within your organization has been provided.

The intent of this book was to 'inform, enthuse and guide those who will lead the next wave of innovation practice'. Hopefully this has been achieved. In a world where innovation is playing an ever-greater role in the creation and sharing of value to underpin and enhance corporate performance, understanding what some have achieved in the past and what others are doing today is a vital context within which those who will take innovation to the heart of organizations can execute their role. As real, not incremental, innovation is recognized as a key differentiator in good times and bad, and the effects that it can have on the organization as well the environment within which it exists are more widely revealed, it is hoped that this has provided a coherent and insightful overview.

What is certain is that in this ever more complex world, where more, newer, faster, quicker, cheaper and better are all at the forefront of every customers' requirements, innovation is the key means of enabling this. Innovation is something that is not a fad, it is not just another word for improved efficiency, and it is definitely here to stay. Moreover, rather than opposing innovation myths, I hope that *Innovating at the Edge* will have provided you with the insights and understanding to enable the demonstration of ten innovation truths:

- Truth 1: Innovation does impact the bottom line
- Truth 2: Innovation applies equally to products and services
- Truth 3: Innovation is relevant to all industries
- Truth 4: Innovation does not require high investment in new technology
- Truth 5: Innovation can occur in all areas of the organization
- Truth 6: Innovation is a capability that everyone can exploit
- Truth 7: Companies, large and small, can all innovate
- Truth 8: Innovation stimulates the organization
- Truth 9: Innovation can be managed
- Truth 10: Innovation can be measured.

22

Resources

There is a wealth of organizations and publications that provide data, information, insights and expertise that can support innovation across the arena. Some of these are national and some global in scope and reach; some are linked to academia and others focus purely on the business world. Fourteen varied key resources that can provide useful input to your organization as you seek to drive innovation forward can be recommended:

- Two of these, the PDMA and the DMI, are US-based international non-profit professional bodies
- Three, the Design Council, the Chartered Institute of Marketing, and the CBI, are UK-based organizations
- One, CORDIS, is a European Union funded service
- Three, the Center for Innovation in Product Development, the Center for Creative Leadership, and the London Business School Innovation Forum, are academically related groups
- Two, the Strategos Institute, and the Cap Gemini Ernst and Young Center for Business Innovation, are linked to consultancies
- Three, the *Journal of Product Innovation Management*, *Technology Review* and *Red Herring*, are international publications.

Product Development and Management Association

Founded in 1976, the Product Development and Management Association (PDMA) is a volunteer-driven, non-profit organization. About 80 per cent of its members are corporate practitioners of new product development, with the remaining 20 per cent split evenly between academics and service providers. The organization is based in the USA but has activities worldwide, including a growing major presence in the UK.

The PDMA's mission is to improve the effectiveness of people engaged in developing and managing new products – both manufactured goods and services. This mission includes facilitating the generation of new information, helping to convert this information into knowledge that is in a usable format, and making this new knowledge broadly available to those who might benefit from it. A basic tenet of the PDMA is that enhanced product innovation represents a desirable and necessary economic goal for firms that wish to achieve and retain a profitable competitive advantage in the long term.

The PDMA actively supports several knowledge-generating activities. It sponsors a yearly research competition, and rewards up to three proposals with financial support and research access to PDMA members. PDMA has sponsored a yearly PhD Proposal Competition since 1991 to encourage young academics to engage in new product development research. Finally, PDMA has also directly supported three streams of research over the last eight years, resulting in several papers and many presentations of the finding: Profiles and compensation of new product professionals (Feldman, 1991, 1996); Measuring product development success (Griffin and Page, 1993, 1996); and Trends and best practices in the practice of managing new product development (Page, 1993; Griffin, 1997).

Knowledge-disseminating activities include annual international conferences in both the USA and the UK on the general subjects of innovation and new product development. The PDMA publishes the highly rated *Journal of Product Innovation Management* six times a year. In addition to this a newsletter, *Visions*, is published quarterly and distributed to all PDMA members. It has also published *The PDMA Handbook of New Product Development* (John Wiley & Sons, 1996), which comprehensively covers the latest developments and insights in new product development from a managerial point of view.

Links

www.pdma.org
www.pdma.org.uk

Design Management Institute

Another non-profit organization, the Design Management Institute (DMI), was founded in Boston in 1975. It is dedicated to demonstrating and promoting the strategic importance of design in business. In addition, the organization seeks to improve the management and utilization of design. The Institute's programmes aid design managers in becoming leaders in their professions, as well as in educating and fostering interaction among design professionals, organizational managers, public policy makers and academics.

The DMI has several ongoing activities that support and facilitate improved design in all aspects of life from new products and services to government activities and education:

- A case study programme is focused on developing teaching case studies in the classic Harvard Business School format – 35 are available, and are used in 200 business schools worldwide
- The International Forum on Design Management Research and Education is an annual conference designed to facilitate improved communication and collaboration between education and design practice
- The *DMI Academic Review* is a major journal that disseminates the latest ideas and concepts across both business and academic arenas.

Links

www.dmi.org

The Design Council

The Design Council is a UK-based non-profit organization that identifies, develops and promotes best use of design to improve competitiveness and fuel economic growth and British success. Founded in 1944, it has for over fifty years been striving to promote the effective use of design and design thinking in business, in education and in government. The Design Council is independent of the government, and is run as an autonomous, non-profit public body funded by the Department of Trade and Industry. The organization enhances the interaction between design professionals and the cross-sharing of expertise through the series of lectures on a wide-ranging field of topics running through the year. These are often aimed at provoking debate and thus adding to the thinking and development of knowledge. In addition to these seminars, the Design Council also runs and develops events, exhibitions, TV programmes, publications and research.

The Design Council aims to help UK businesses to understand and use design as a central part of their business strategies to drive competitiveness and, in doing so, works with a number of partners from the industry.

Links

www.design-council.org.co.uk

Chartered Institute of Marketing

The Chartered Institute of Marketing (CIM) provides leadership and expertise for those involved in the marketing arena. As the world's largest marketing association, the CIM works closely with the marketing profession, government, industry and commerce to develop greater understanding of what and how marketing contributes to UK and international business.

The CIM has expanded to include six international branches and four member groups, in addition to its fifty-eight branches and market interest groups in the UK. All in all, the CIM has some 60 000 members. The association provides professional qualifications up to postgraduate level through some 350 colleges and universities worldwide. Furthermore, it provides marketing professionals with residential training courses, designed to be flexible in meeting different corporate needs. The CIM also operates a consultancy arm and a comprehensive information service.

Links

www.cim.co.uk

Confederation of British Industry

The Confederation of British Industry (CBI) is the UK's leading independent business organization, and exists so that the government of the day, the European Commission and the wider community understand both the needs of British business and the contribution it makes to the well-being of UK society. As well as providing a forum for the exchange of ideas and representation of UK business interests, the CBI also publishes a number of reports. The CBI's *Innovation Trends* survey was initiated in 1989 to gauge companies' perceptions of and attitude towards innovation. The survey is now undertaken and updated annually in cooperation with industry sponsors, and provides a wealth of information for both business representatives and academics.

Links

www.cbi.org.uk

Community Research and Development Information Service

The Community Research and Development Information Service (CORDIS) is a free service provided by the European Commission's Innovation SME programme. It offers access to a wide range of information on EU research and innovation development activities. Its comprehensive coverage of community R&D helps companies to:

- Find information about participation in, and benefit from, the European Commission's R&D framework programme
- Keep up-to-date on current research findings and strategic directions
- Identify various funding sources for R&D
- Find partners to cooperate in R&D activities and share expertise.

The Innovation and SME Programme itself stands at the cross-roads of the Community's policies on Research, Innovation and SMEs. It promotes innovation at community level, and encourages SME participation. The programme supports European businesses to innovate, to develop, market and integrate new technology, and to manage change more effectively. It also aims to contribute to a more innovation-friendly environment in Europe, improved conditions for the creation and development of new companies, the diffusion of new technologies, the emergence of new economic activities, and foster an innovation culture across Europe.

The EU Innovation Scoreboard is an assessment of innovation performance in the individual Member States of the European Union. To measure innovation performance a set of seventeen qualitative indicators are used, based on available statistics covering human resources, knowledge creation, the application of knowledge and innovation finance. The scoreboard is a bench-marking tool that highlights both strengths and weaknesses. For comparison, it also includes equivalent figures from the USA and Japan, and shows the EU average. It is designed to stimulate debate between members of the business, research and policy-making communities, as well as to provide a starting point for policy improvement.

Links

www.cordis.lu/innovation-smes

Center for Innovation in Product Development

The Center for Innovation in Product Development (CIPD) is one of the key research centres in the USA. Based at MIT, it seeks to unite representatives from academia, industry, and government who share its vision of the future of product development. Its mission is to lay the conceptual groundwork for, and contribute core components to, a product development infrastructure that helps companies to succeed in the services marketplace we envision.

Links

http://me.mit.edu/groups/cipd

Center for Creative Leadership

The Center for Creative Leadership (CCL) is a recognized, non-profit educational institution that acts as a resource for enhancing the understanding of the leadership capabilities of individuals and organizations alike. The Center believes that leadership development is a cornerstone of organizational effectiveness, and addresses the leadership components of both organizational and business challenges.

The Center has been in operation for more than thirty years, and has during this time created programmes and services blending relevant models, research, assessment tools and expertise with proven tools and techniques aimed at enhancing learning. The CCL provides executive education in a number of fields, ranging from fostering innovation and merging cultures to working globally. In addition, the Center also has a wealth of information and materials that, together with the other services, provide a source of knowledge within the field of leadership.

Links

www.ccl.org

London Business School Innovation Exchange

The London Business School Innovation Exchange is a UK-based organization, linked to the London Business School, where members are able to engage in discussions, exchange ideas and information, and seek advice on issues related to innovation. Experts are brought in to contribute to leading edge debate and ensure that latest management thinking and developments are brought into the Innovation Exchange. The Innovation Exchange has been designed in response to feedback from the practising managers and chief executives committed to innovation in their businesses. It provides a place in which to be imaginative and creative; a place that offers access to comprehensive and regularly updated resources; and a place to gain access to practical help.

It is a forum for sharing ideas through informal liaison and peer group discussions, and offers an extensive range of resource material that is constantly updated. The Exchange addresses emerging innovation issues on behalf of its members, and can represent its members' interests through a wide network of contacts and associations. In addition to the resources available remotely and on site, it also runs seminars and workshops for its members on a range of themes relating to innovation to encourage peer group review and informal exchange of ideas and experiences.

Links

www.lbs.ac.uk

The Strategos Institute

Linked to the Strategos consultancy, the Strategos Institute is a consortium of successful companies who are addressing the business challenge of how to embed a deep, systemic capacity for innovation in large companies. During its first two years, representatives from about twenty companies have worked both as a group, and in intensive sub-teams, to pioneer new ways of inventing, testing, scaling and leveraging innovative, wealth-creating strategies. They were guided and supported by the Institute's own staff and by a Research Advisory Board comprised of leading business innovators and professors from the world's premier business schools. The consortium has created a blueprint for strategy innovation that encompasses the tools, metrics, processes and climate that must be put in place to drive strategy innovation and new wealth creation in an increasingly uncertain and complex world. This blueprint includes:

- A framework for understanding the role of strategy innovation in the creation of new wealth
- Tools for assessing the decay of an existing business strategy and the threats to its profit stream
- New ways to think about industries and competitive domains that identify potential threats and white space opportunities
- Insights into the organizational preconditions that must be created for innovation to flourish
- A diagnostic for pinpointing the impediments to strategy innovation in any organization
- A set of practical levers that management can use to stimulate new thinking, test new business models, and scale them up so that they become major revenue and profit contributors
- New performance measures designed to monitor a company's success in creating and capturing new wealth faster than its competitors.

Links

http://institute.strategosnet.com

Cap Gemini Ernst & Young Center for Business Innovation

The Cap Gemini Ernst & Young Center for Business Innovation discovers and develops innovations in strategy, organization and technology to deliver high value. The group collaborates with leading thinkers in business, academia and other research institutions. The research is used to aid the development of new strategic consulting services aimed at a general business audience. Based in Boston, more than 500 business executives visit the Center for Business Innovation annually, to participate in research and to share information and experience. The Center for Business Innovation also publishes a variety of research and consulting methods that benefit a wide audience.

Links

www.cbi.cgey.com

Journal of Product Innovation Management

The *Journal of Product Innovation Management* is the leading academic journal in the area, and is dedicated to the advancement of management practice in all of the functions involved in the total process of product innovation. Its purpose is to bring to managers and students of product innovation the theoretical structures and the practical techniques that will enable them to operate at the cutting edge of effective management practice. The scope is broad, taking account of those issues that are crucial to successful product innovation in the organization's external as well as internal environment. The intent is to be informative, thought provoking, and intellectually challenging, and thereby to contribute to the development of better managers.

The *Journal* takes a multifunctional, multidisciplinary, international approach to the issues facing those for whom product innovation is an important concern. It presents the research, experiences, and insights of academics, consultants, practising managers, economists, scientists, lawyers, sociologists, and thoughtful contributors from other professions and disciplines. Since approaches to product innovation often differ in different economies and cultures, the *Journal* draws on the work of authors from all over the world. Articles are based on empirical research, observations of management experience, and state-of-the-art reviews of important issues as well as conceptual and theoretical developments.

Links

www.jpim-online.com

Technology Review

Published by MIT, the *Technology Review* is a leading magazine providing insights into new technologies and emerging applications. With regular contributions from leading scientists as well as major business personalities, the *Technology Review* provides a clear, objective and authoritative point of view on issues that will affect future ideas.

Links

www.technologyreview.com

Red Herring

Launched in 1993, *Red Herring* magazine provides a forward-thinking, analytical look at technology companies and industries, and evaluates technology as a strategic asset. *Red Herring* magazine's content seeks to be timely, analytical and sceptical. It aims to tell its readers 'what's first, what's new, and, most importantly, what matters'.

Links

www.redherring.com

Index

PUFFIN BOOKS

HI I'M ROWLEY JEFFERSON.

HERE ARE SOME BOOKS MY BEST FRIEND GREG HEFFLEY WROTE.

THE DIARY OF A WIMPY KID SERIES

1 Diary of a Wimpy Kid

2 Rodrick Rules

3 The Last Straw

4 Dog Days

5 The Ugly Truth

6 Cabin Fever

7 The Third Wheel

8 Hard Luck

9 The Long Haul

10 Old School

11 Double Down

12 The Getaway

13 The Meltdown

14 Wrecking Ball

YEAH AND THEN YOU TOTALLY STOLE MY IDEA!

by Jeff Kinney

PUFFIN

PUFFIN BOOKS

UK | USA | Canada | Ireland | Australia
India | New Zealand | South Africa

Puffin Books is part of the Penguin Random House group of companies whose
addresses can be found at global.penguinrandomhouse.com.

www.penguin.co.uk www.puffin.co.uk www.ladybird.co.uk

Penguin
Random House
UK

First published in the USA in the English language in 2019
by Amulet Books, an imprint of ABRAMS
(All rights reserved in all countries by Harry N. Abrams, Inc.)
Published simultaneously in Great Britain by Puffin Books 2019
This edition published 2020

002

Cover design by Jeff Kinney, Lora Grisafi and Chad W. Beckerman
Book design by Jeff Kinney

Printed and bound in Great Britain by Clays Ltd, Elcograf S.p.A

A CIP catalogue record for this book is available from the British Library

ISBN: 978-0-241-40571-0

All correspondence to:
Puffin Books, Penguin Random House Children's
80 Strand, London WC2R 0RL

HERE'S SOME
BORING STUFF
THEY MADE ME
PUT IN HERE.

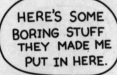

<u>My First Entry</u>
<u>Hi I'm Rowley Jefferson and this is my</u>
<u>diary. I hope you like it so far.</u>

<u>I decided to start a journal because my</u>
<u>best friend Greg Heffley has one and we</u>
<u>usually do the same stuff. Oh yeah I should</u>
<u>mention that me and Greg are</u>

<u>I'm sure you're probably like "Well tell me</u>
<u>more about this Greg guy." But my book</u>
<u>isn't about HIM, it's about ME.</u>

The reason I called my book "Diary of an Awesome Friendly Kid" is because that's what my dad is always saying about me.

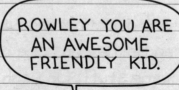

ROWLEY YOU ARE AN AWESOME FRIENDLY KID.

Like I mentioned already, Greg is my best friend which makes my dad my SECOND best friend. But I don't tell him that because I don't want to hurt his feelings.

WE ARE BEST FRIENDS RIGHT SON?

PAT PAT

GULP.

Now that I brought up my dad I should
mention he doesn't seem to like Greg
all that much. And the reason I get
that feeling is because my dad is always
saying it.

I DO NOT
LIKE GREG.

But that's only because my dad doesn't
really get Greg's sense of humour.

Right now you're probably thinking "Hey Rowley I thought this book was supposed to be about YOU." Well you're right so from now on I promise there's gonna be a lot more Rowley in here.

The first thing you need to know about me is that I live with my mom and dad in a house at the top of Surrey Street, which is the same street my best friend Greg lives on.

I already talked about my dad but my mom is pretty great too because she feeds me healthy food and helps me keep my body clean.

SCRUB
SCRUB

Every morning I walk to school with my friend Greg. We usually have a total blast when we're together but sometimes I do things that annoy him.

But what REALLY gets on Greg's nerves is when I copy him. So I'm probably not gonna let him know about this journal because it's just gonna make him mad.

Anyway writing in this book is a lot of work so that's all I'm gonna do for today. But tomorrow I'll put a little more Greg in here because like I said we're best friends.

My Second Entry

OK so bad news: Greg found out about my diary.

I guess I felt kind of proud that I had my own journal and I wanted to show him. But just like I predicted it made him MAD.

Greg said I totally ripped him off and that he was gonna sue me for stealing his idea. I said well go ahead and TRY because you're not the FIRST person to write in a diary.

Then Greg said it's a JOURNAL not a diary and then he whapped me with my own book.

WHAP

I told Greg if he was gonna be a jerk then I wouldn't say nice things about him in my journal. Then I showed him what I wrote so far.

At first he seemed annoyed because I always forget to draw noses on people. But then he said my book gave him an IDEA.

Greg said one day he's gonna be rich and famous and everyone will want to know his whole life's story. And he said I could be the one to WRITE it.

I said I thought that's what your JOURNAL is for and he said that's his AUTObiography but my book could be his BIOGRAPHY.

Greg said there are gonna be a LOT of biographies about him one day but he'd give me the chance to write the first one.

I thought that sounded like a good idea because I'm Greg's best friend and no one knows him better than ME.

So I'm gonna start this book again with a new title and now the main character is gonna be Greg instead of me. But don't worry I'm still gonna be in it a lot too.

DIARY

OF **GREG**

HEFFLEY

by Greg Heffley's Best Friend

Rowley Jefferson →

<u>EARLY LIFE</u>

Most biographies about presidents and famous people start with a chapter called "Early Life". Well the problem is that I didn't meet Greg until the fourth grade so I don't know a lot about what happened to him before then.

I've seen a few photos hanging on the walls in Greg's house and from what I can tell he was a regular baby. And if he did anything important when he was little you can't really tell from the pictures.

Anyway fast-forward to right before
the start of fourth grade and now this
biography is gonna get a lot more detailed.

We used to live in a whole different state
but then my dad got a job and we had to
move. My family bought a new house at
the top of Surrey Street and we moved
in over the summer.

The first few days I didn't leave the
house because I was scared about being in
a new place.

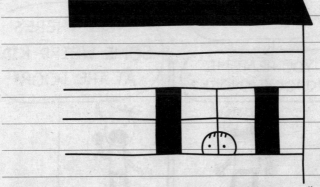

I know you are probably wondering "Well
when is he going to meet Greg?" but just
wait because I am getting to that part.

My mom said maybe I should try to make some friends and she even bought me a book called "How to Make Friends in New Places" to help me do it.

The book had all kinds of things like knock-knock jokes to help a kid like me meet new people. But the tricks in the book didn't really work on Greg.

Luckily me and Greg became friends anyway.

I told Greg I lived in the new house at the top of the hill and he said that was kind of bad news for me because when our lot was empty he planted a flag there so now he owned my house plus everything in it.

But later on my dad told me that wasn't true and then he went to Greg's house to get my bike back.

I'm pretty sure that's the first time my dad told me what he thought about Greg.

I DO NOT LIKE GREG.

But I like Greg a LOT. He is always doing hilarious things like making me laugh right after I take a big gulp of milk.

BWAHAHAHA!

Plus Greg is always playing wacky pranks on me and they usually make me laugh pretty hard too.

So I'll bet you can tell why me and Greg have been best friends since fourth grade. I even got us a locket to make it official but Greg says those things are for girls and that's why he won't wear his half.

BEST FRIENDS

Well I could probably fill up a whole book with all the zany things me and Greg do but since this is his biography I should probably write some stuff about his family.

Greg has a mom and dad just like I do but they are pretty regular parents so I don't have a lot to say about them.

But Greg isn't an only child like me. He's got an older brother named Rodrick who has a rock band called Loded Diper.

Some of their songs have swears in them so my mom and dad won't let me be at the Heffleys' house when Rodrick has practice.

Greg also has a little brother named Manny who is only three. And don't ask me why but the first time I went to Greg's for a playdate Manny randomly pulled down his pants and showed me his bum.

Now every time I see Manny he acts like we have this big secret or something which makes me feel uncomfortable.

Anyway I guess that wraps up the first chapter of Greg's biography. And if you're thinking "Rowley when are we gonna get to the exciting parts?" then just WAIT.

THE TIME I HAD MY FIRST
SLEEPOVER AT GREG'S

After me and Greg met we had a few playdates at MY house and a few playdates at HIS house. Oh yeah I forgot, Greg doesn't like it when I call them "playdates" so I will have to change that in the next draft or else I'm gonna get whapped again.

Anyway me and Greg "hung out" a lot at each other's houses but then one day he invited me to his house for a SLEEPOVER.

I was pretty worried because I'd never slept away from home before. In fact I wasn't even sleeping in my OWN bed yet because I was scared.

I told my mom I was too nervous to stay at Greg's but I got a little LESS nervous when she said I could take Carrots with me.

When I got to Greg's we played in his room for a while but at 9:00 Mrs Heffley said it was time to go to bed. And she said we had to sleep in the BASEMENT. Well now I was SUPER nervous because I think basements are really creepy.

As soon as Mrs Heffley turned the lights off, Greg said he needed to tell me something important. He told me there's a half man, half goat that lives in the woods in our neighbourhood so I probably shouldn't go outside alone at night.

Well I was NOT happy to hear that news and I really wished someone told my parents about this goat guy before we moved into the neighbourhood.

Anyway the goat thing got me TOTALLY spooked so I hid under the covers. But I think Greg got pretty spooked too because he crawled under them WITH me.

Then all of a sudden there was this crazy
noise right outside the window and it
sounded exactly how a half man, half goat
would sound.

Me and Greg didn't wanna get eaten by
this goat guy so we got out of there as
fast as we could.

21

But we almost died anyway because we trampled each other running up the stairs.

We locked ourselves in the laundry room so the goat man couldn't get us. But that's when we found out it wasn't the goat guy at ALL, it was just Greg's brother Rodrick playing a trick on us.

RAP
RAP

OK this next part is embarrassing but since it's a biography I've gotta tell the whole truth. I wet my pants when we were in the basement and heard those noises outside.

Mrs Heffley gave me an extra pair of Greg's underwear but they were too small. So my dad had to come get me and bring me home in the middle of the night.

It was a long time before I was allowed to go to Greg's for another sleepover, but that's a MUCH longer story and I'm not even sure there's room for that one in this book.

THE TIME I SAVED GREG FROM
TEVIN LARKIN'S BIRTHDAY PARTY

There is a kid named Tevin Larkin who lives over on Speen Street and last summer his mom invited me and Greg to Tevin's birthday party. We didn't wanna go because Tevin is hyper but both our moms said we HAD to.

It turned out that me and Greg were the ONLY kids invited to Tevin's party but we didn't know that until we got there.

After we gave Tevin his presents his mom said it was time for party activities.

The first activity was to watch this movie about a guy who could turn into a bear and an eagle and a bunch of other animals.

When the movie was over Tevin wanted to watch it AGAIN. But me and Greg told Tevin's mom we didn't wanna watch the movie a second time so she said we could move on to the other activities like pin the tail on the donkey.

Well that just made Tevin MAD.

He got all wound up and started acting
like the guy in the movie who could turn
into animals.

I guess Tevin's mom was used to this sort
of thing but me and Greg didn't know
what we were supposed to do. We asked
Mrs Larkin if she could take us home but
she said there were still two hours to go
in the party.

So we went out of the back door and
waited in the yard for Tevin to calm
down.

But eventually Tevin found us and now he was acting TOTALLY nuts.

I took a few steps back to get out of Tevin's way but that's when I fell into a giant ditch. Luckily the ditch wasn't TOO deep or I probably would've broke some bones. But when I got to my feet I heard this buzzing noise all around me.

It turned out there was a HORNETS' NEST at the bottom of the ditch and they were all stirred up.

I got stung twelve times and two of the
stings were inside my MOUTH.

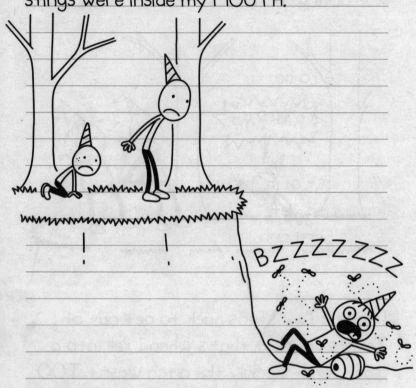

BZZZZZZZ

Mrs Larkin drove me home early and Greg
hitched a ride too.

Anyway Greg is always saying he "owes
me" for getting him out of that party
and I put it in this book in case I ever need
to remind him.

28

GREG'S ACCOMPLISHMENTS

Every biography I've ever read for school has a chapter called "Accomplishments" so I figure I'd better add that in here before I forget.

The problem is that Greg is only a kid and most of his accomplishments haven't happened yet. So I'll leave some blank space here and I can fill it in later on.

1.
2.
3.
4.
5.
6.
7.
8.
9.
10.

THE TIME ME AND GREG DISTURBED
AN ANCIENT BURIAL GROUND

If you were spooked out by that goat
man story from before then you might
want to skip this one. OK if you are still
reading, remember I warned you.

One time me and Greg were playing vikings
and ninjas in the woods and then some
teenagers came by and ruined our fun.

BUT THAT'S NOT EVEN THE SCARY
PART YET so keep reading.

Me and Greg went further back in the woods to get away from those teens. Greg said we should build a fort so if they came looking for us we could protect ourselves.

So we spent the rest of the afternoon making a fort out of sticks and logs.

Greg said we should put some rocks in our fort in case things got REALLY bad, but it was starting to get dark and there weren't a lot of rocks lying around in the woods anyway.

But then I tripped over something and guess what? It was a big ROCK.

I told Greg I thought I sprained my ankle but he was a lot more worried about that rock than my injury.

Greg said it wasn't a rock, it was a GRAVESTONE and we'd just disturbed an ANCIENT BURIAL GROUND.

I guess you already knew that was coming because it was in the title of this chapter. I'll probably change it later on so I don't give the surprise away.

Anyway me and Greg were TOTALLY spooked out by this ancient burial ground thing and by now it was REALLY dark out so we were extra scared. But Greg must've totally forgot about my ankle because he took off and I couldn't keep up.

I kept waiting for Greg to come back but he never did.

Luckily my parents called Greg's house to ask where I was and that helped him remember I was still out there.

And just to show you what a great pal Greg is, he let my parents borrow his flashlight and pointed them in the right direction.

DRAG

AN EVEN MORE SCARY STORY

OK while I'm on the topic of scary stuff I want to share a story about something that happened a couple of years ago.

One time I was at my grandpa's log cabin with my dad for the weekend and we took a hike and I got kind of dirty. Well technically it's my DAD'S cabin now because my grandpa died the year before.

I called my grandpa "Bampy", and the reason I called him that is because when I was two I couldn't say "Grampa".

BAMPY!

But when I got older and I COULD say
"Grampa", nobody would let me change it.
And when my grandpa got older it's the
only word he really said.

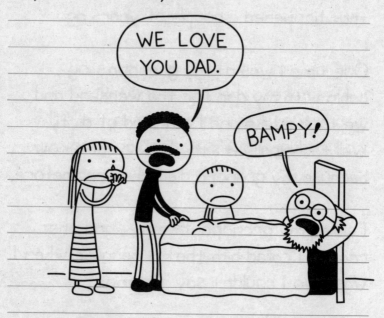

WE LOVE
YOU DAD.

BAMPY!

So anyway back to the story. After I got
dirty from that hike my dad said I had to
take a shower.

But Bampy's cabin is really old and it
doesn't HAVE a shower, it just has one
of those creepy old-fashioned tubs.

After I filled up the tub with water and got in, here's what happened NEXT. I heard footsteps coming down the hall and I thought it was my dad bringing me a towel or something.

Then the door opened real slow, but
guess what? NO ONE WAS EVEN THERE.

I jumped out of the tub and ran around
the house looking everywhere for my dad.

And if you're thinking "Oh Rowley the
door thing was your dad playing a trick
on you," well guess what? It WASN'T.

My dad was getting some milk at the
store and he didn't come back until like a
half hour later.

I told my dad what happened with the door
and he said it was probably just the "wind".

But I know what it was: the GHOST OF
BAMPY.

39

THE TIME GREG PLAYED A HILARIOUS PRANK ON ME

OK I know the last chapter didn't have a lot of Greg in it but I wanted to mention that story real quick because the Bampy thing totally FREAKED ME OUT.

If you like scary stuff then you're in luck because this one is pretty scary too.

One day me and Greg were hanging out at my house and Greg told me he saw on the news that there was a burglar going around breaking into people's homes.

Then he said he had to go home for dinner, and once he left I started getting scared because my parents weren't around.

But here's the thing: I found out later that Greg just PRETENDED to leave. He shut the front door but then stayed inside my house.

SLAM

He took off his shoes and walked up the stairs super quiet so I couldn't hear him.

Then he started stomping around real loud upstairs. At first I thought it was the ghost of Bampy all over again.

Then I realized it was probably that
BURGLAR Greg told me about and I
almost peed my pants for the second
time in this biography.

I heard footsteps coming down the
stairs and I ran into the garage to hide
from the burglar.

It was PITCH BLACK in the garage but
I didn't want to make a move until I was
sure that guy was gone.

Then all of a sudden the door to the
garage opened real slow and I knew the
burglar was gonna get me if I didn't do
something. So I whacked him in the face
with my dad's tennis racket and made a
run for it.

WHACK—

Then I ran out of the front door and
went to Mrs Monroe's house next door
to tell her to call the COPS.

But then Greg came out of my house and that's when I found out the whole thing was just one of his hilarious pranks.

Greg was mad at me for two whole weeks and he said I should've known from the way the footsteps sounded that it was HIM and not a burglar.

I guess he's got a pretty good point about that since he is always playing wacky pranks on me. So I feel kind of bad about whacking him with a tennis racket.

but not really

ANOTHER TIME GREG
GOT MAD AT ME

OK that last story made me remember another time Greg got mad at me.

Me and Greg were walking home from school a few months ago and there were slugs everywhere because it just rained the night before. And whenever there are slugs lying around, Greg chases me with one.

I guess it's pretty funny if you think about it but it's never that funny when it's happening.

Luckily I am really fast when someone is chasing me with a slug so I got away from Greg by climbing up on the big rock in Mr Yee's front yard.

Greg tried to get me to climb down but I stayed right where I was.

Greg tried to fling the slug at me but he lost his balance and almost fell in a giant puddle in front of the rock. He was stuck and I felt bad for him because he is my best friend after all.

I got down from the rock and tried to help Greg. He told me to pull him back up to his feet but I guess I heard him wrong.

I grabbed him BY his feet and that turned out to be a pretty dumb move.

I didn't know WHAT Greg was gonna do
once he got out of that puddle but I didn't
wanna stick around to find out. So I ran
to my house and locked myself in my room
and didn't come out until Greg got called
home for dinner.

The next day Greg said he was gonna
get me back when I "least expect it". I
just hope Greg forgets because when
it comes to paybacks he's got a good
imagination.

THE TIME WHEN GREG CREATED
A SPECIAL AWARD JUST FOR ME

OK the last two chapters were about
times Greg got mad at me but this
chapter is the total OPPOSITE.

This one's about the time when I did
something Greg thought was really
awesome so then he did something really
awesome for ME.

Anyway this one Saturday last autumn me
and Greg were supposed to hang out at my
house but he said he couldn't because he
had to clean his garage. Then he said if I
came and helped him we'd be done TWICE
as quick. But I said no thanks I'll wait.

Then Greg said if I helped him he'd give me
HALF of his Halloween candy.

Well that was a really big deal to me
because my parents went through all my
candy on Halloween night and they barely
let me keep ANYTHING.

But I knew Greg still had a TON of candy
because his parents don't make him throw
out ANYTHING. So I told him OK I'll be
right over.

Cleaning Greg's garage was hard work and
it took like three hours.

After we were done Greg said OK now let's go hang out at your place.

I said hey what about that CANDY and Greg said oh yeah I forgot. But I knew that was gonna happen because whenever Greg owes me stuff he forgets.

We went up to Greg's room and he got his bag of candy out of the wardrobe.

But when he emptied out the bag it was almost all WRAPPERS.

The only things LEFT were three gobstoppers and a little box of raisins. I told Greg he promised me a TON of candy and he said he only promised HALF. Then he said a deal's a deal and he gave me a gobstopper and the box of raisins.

I told Greg I was gonna tell his MOM. And then Greg got real worried because he said his mom would be mad at him if she found out he ate all his Halloween candy already.

Greg said he was gonna give me something WAY better than candy, and he got out a piece of paper and a pencil and started drawing at his desk.

When Greg was done he handed me the
piece of paper and here's what was on it.

Greg said Good Boy awards are SUPER
rare and you have to do something really
AWESOME to get one.

He said I was EXTRA lucky because this
was the first ever Good Boy award he'd
ever given out and it was gonna be worth
a lot of money.

Well I knew Greg was just trying to get out of giving me the candy he owed me so I tried to act like I thought this Good Boy award thing was dumb. But somehow Greg could tell I thought it was kind of COOL.

Well that was only the FIRST Good Boy award but I got a lot MORE. For the next few weeks Greg made me one every time I did something awesome for him.

After a while I had a TON of Good Boy awards. And I kept them in a binder in clear plastic sheets so they wouldn't get messed up.

But then I started to feel like maybe my Good Boy awards weren't that rare any more since I had so MANY of them. Plus Greg was making the new ones a lot quicker than he made that first one and they didn't seem all that special.

So one time when Greg called and asked me to come down and help him rake his yard I told him I couldn't because I had homework.

And Greg said that's too bad because he came up with a totally new kind of Good Boy award and he was sad I wasn't gonna get to see it.

I was like well at least TELL me about it, and Greg said he COULDN'T because it was top secret and he didn't wanna ruin the surprise.

Then he said he was gonna call Scotty Douglas and see if HE wanted to help rake the yard and I said OK I'll be right over.

Well I wish I knew we had to rake the front yard AND the back because it was a lot of work. Plus I had to do it MYSELF because Greg was busy making that new award.

When I was finally done Greg gave me my award and I've gotta say it was even more awesome than I THOUGHT it would be.

This new one was called a SUPER Good Boy award. Greg said one Super Good Boy award was worth FIFTY regular Good Boy awards and I could totally see WHY.

In the next few weeks I earned a BUNCH of Super Good Boy awards but after a while even THOSE didn't seem all that special.

Besides I was spending a lot of time doing stuff for Greg and I wasn't getting my OWN chores done.

But every time I told Greg I didn't need any more Good Boy awards he'd come up with something NEW and then I'd have to have THAT.

After a while I had so many awards that my binder was STUFFED and I couldn't fit new ones in. So I told Greg I wasn't gonna try to earn any more no matter WHAT.

But Greg said that's OK because he made up a whole NEW system and I should probably just recycle my old awards.

I was pretty mad because I worked HARD for those awards and now Greg said they were totally WORTHLESS.

But I was still curious about this new system so I asked him about it. Greg said the new idea was called "Li'l Goodies" and it was a POINTS system and there wasn't any paper involved.

Greg said that every time I did something NICE for him I'd get a Li'l Goodie point. And once I got fifty Li'l Goodies I'd get a Fantastic Prize.

61

I was like OK what's the prize? And Greg said he couldn't tell me but it was under a sheet in his bedroom.

Well I couldn't figure out what was under that sheet but I could GUESS. And a LOT of my guesses were things I really wanted.

So I spent about a month doing lots of things for Greg and he gave me a Li'l Goodie point each time, like he promised.

Eventually I got to fifty Li'l Goodies. And I told Greg I was ready to turn them in for that Fantastic Prize.

But Greg told me that since it was the first day of the month my Li'l Goodie total got reset back to ZERO. And I said well you never told me about that rule and he said well you never ASKED.

I was really MAD and I yanked the sheet off the Fantastic Prize so I could see what it was.

But guess what? It was a LAUNDRY BASKET filled with dirty clothes.

I told Greg he was a crummy friend for making me do all that work for a phoney prize. But he said the laundry thing was just a TEST to see if I'd peek and that I failed the test.

Then he said the REAL prize was locked in the basement and that now I was gonna have to earn a HUNDRED Li'l Goodies to get it.

All I can say is I'm not a FOOL. I'm gonna take my TIME earning those Li'l Goodies, so if Greg thinks I'm in a rush to get that Fantastic Prize he's gonna be disappointed.

THE TIME I FOUND OUT GREG IS A LOUSY STUDY PARTNER

OK I know this is Greg's official biography and I don't want to put any negative stuff about him in here. But Greg if you are reading this I just need to say you are a TERRIBLE study partner. I hope that doesn't hurt your feelings but somebody has to tell you the truth.

Most of the time I don't really need to study for tests because I pay attention in class and I do my homework. Plus Mom always says it's important to get a good night's sleep so on school nights I go to bed extra early.

But this one time we had a really hard chapter in maths and I had trouble paying attention in class that week. That's mostly because Greg moved to the seat right behind me.

The night before the test I knew I was gonna have to go over the chapter and do some practice problems at home. But when I told Greg my plan he said we should study TOGETHER.

I wasn't sure that was such a good idea because when it comes to school stuff sometimes it's hard for Greg to focus.

But Greg said we're best friends and best friends should study together so I guess that made sense to me.

Well the FIRST thing we had to do was find a place to study. Greg said we couldn't be at HIS house because his brother Rodrick was having band practice.

And Greg was banned from MY house because he played a practical joke where he put cling film over our toilet bowl and he got my dad pretty good.

Greg said we should go to the LIBRARY because it was quiet there and nobody would bug us. So Mrs Heffley gave us a ride to the library after dinner and we found a table where we could do our work.

We got out our books and I said maybe we should do practice problems to see what we needed to work on. But Greg said he hadn't even READ the chapter yet so we needed to start from the BEGINNING.

Well that was kind of a waste of time for me so I told Greg he could read the chapter on his OWN to catch up. But Greg said I was being a bad study partner and that we were supposed to do everything TOGETHER.

I said OK fine let's start from the beginning of the chapter and go through the whole thing. But Greg said before we got started we needed to plan our study breaks so we didn't get too stressed out.

Then he said we should START with a break so we'd get off on the right foot. And that's what we did even though it seemed like a bad idea to me.

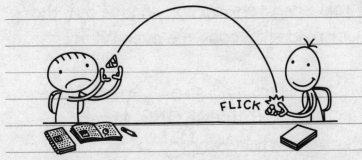

FLICK

After like ten minutes I said we need to get to work because it's a long chapter and we have a lot to go through.

Well don't ask me why but Greg pinched his nose with his fingers and said the exact same thing I said but with a really annoying voice.

I told Greg to stop copying me but that just made him copy me even MORE.

Finally I got smart and started reading the chapter out loud.

ANGLES IN A TRIANGLE ADD UP TO 180 DEGREES.

A RIGHT ANGLE IS 90 DEGREES.

ANGLES IN A TRIANGLE ADD UP TO 180 DEGREES.

A RIGHT ANGLE IS 90 DEGREES.

After a while Greg figured out what I was doing and he stopped copying me.

I told him maybe it would be better if we both just read the chapter quietly, but Greg said that wasn't his "learning style" and he needed to make things FUN so they would stick.

I said what do you mean? And Greg said he knew a way to make learning maths into a GAME.

First he balled up a piece of notebook paper. He said we should take turns reading a few words from the chapter and toss the paper ball back and forth each time. So we tried it and it worked for a little while, I guess.

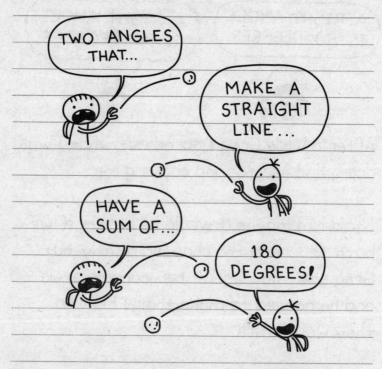

But whenever someone DROPPED the paper ball Greg said we had to start the whole page AGAIN.

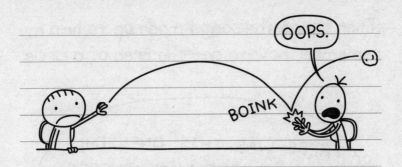

And sometimes I think Greg was trying to make me drop the ball on PURPOSE.

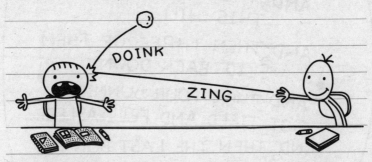

I told Greg we were wasting too much time and we needed to do this another way. And Greg said he didn't care HOW we studied as long as it was FUN.

So I told Greg a trick my dad taught ME. He said that whenever I had trouble remembering something I should make up a SONG to make it easier.

Then I sang the song I made up to help me remember how to get the area of a circle.

Greg said that was the dumbest thing he ever heard and I said well if it's so dumb then why do I have 95 in maths and you only have 72?

I guess Greg didn't have a good answer to that and he said it was time for another break. So we played video games on the library computer until some grown-up reported us to the librarian for making too much noise.

When we got back to the table Greg said
we weren't studying the right way and
that he had an idea of how we could do
it BETTER. He said he'd read the FIRST
half of the chapter and I'd read the
LAST half and then we could team up
during the test.

I said well you're not allowed to TALK
during the test so I didn't see how that
was gonna work. Then Greg told me
about these monks who can transmit
their thoughts through the air if they
concentrate real hard.

So we tried doing it but I guess I couldn't concentrate good enough to make it work.

Greg said we needed to figure out a DIFFERENT way to communicate during the test.

I said if we just studied the chapter we wouldn't NEED to communicate, but once Greg gets something in his head he doesn't let it go.

He made up this whole system of sneezes and coughs and stuff so we could talk to each other during the test without our teacher Ms Beck noticing. But there was a lot to remember so I wrote it all down.

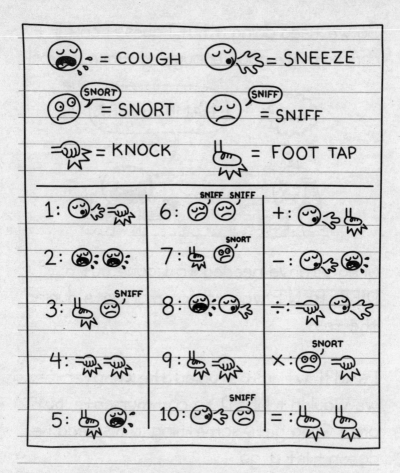

I said well what if one of us needs to ask the other guy a QUESTION and Greg said you just put a question mark at the end. And I said well we don't have a signal for a question mark and Greg said it could be a fart.

I told Greg I didn't think I could fart if I didn't really NEED to and Greg told me to try anyway and I did but nothing came out.

So Greg told me some different foods I could eat for breakfast that would make it easier to do a question mark.

But that idea made me nervous because
the last time I went to Greg's we drank
a lot of soda and tried to burp the
alphabet, and I got sick on the letter "B"
and had to go home early.

Greg said OK if I couldn't fart for REAL
then it would be OK to make a fake fart
noise under my arm.

That's when I told Greg I thought this was a bad idea and it was CHEATING to send each other signals during the test.

Greg said I was being a goody-two-shoes and that the only reason I wanted to get a good grade in maths was because I was a teacher's pet and I was in love with Ms Beck.

I said I was NOT in love with Ms Beck but that I just like her personality and the way she smells.

So Greg said that PROVES I'm in love with Ms Beck and then he sang that song about two people sitting in a tree.

I knew Greg was trying to make me mad but for some reason the song didn't really bother me that much.

I guess Greg got mad that he wasn't making ME mad so he started singing even MORE.

I tried to tune him out but he just got louder and louder.

Then I went into the bathroom and tried to study in THERE but Greg followed me.

But I guess somebody else complained
because the librarian came in and told us
we both had to get out of there.

Then she said if we made any more noise
she was gonna have to call our parents and
have them come get us. Well that sounded
great to ME but I don't think Greg was
ready to go home so he promised we'd
quieten down.

I really didn't wanna sit at the same table
as Greg any more so I moved to one of
those desks with dividers between them.
But Greg sat right across from me.

I was starting to get some work done but then Greg slid a note under the divider.

He had a maths question so I answered him and passed the note back.

Hey Rowley
what do the
angles in a
quadrilateral
add up to?
    -Greg

360
degrees.
    -R

And then Greg asked me ANOTHER question. But I didn't really mind because this was a MILLION times better than the way we were doing things before.

But then Greg slid the note back and it had another question on it that didn't have anything to do with maths at ALL.

Check one. I am embarrassed I wet the bed last night.

☐ YES
☐ NO

Well I checked the NO box because I DIDN'T wet the bed. I slid the note to Greg but then he wrote something on it and slid it BACK.

☐ YES
☒ NO

Ha ha ha you're not embarrassed you wet the bed.

That made me kind of mad because that's
not what I MEANT. But I didn't wanna
spend a lot of time explaining myself
because I really needed to get back to
studying.

So Greg wrote ANOTHER note and slid it
under the divider.

Truth or Dare?

☐ TRUTH   ☐ DARE

I didn't wanna take a dare from Greg
so I picked TRUTH. But I didn't like the
question Greg came up with.

☒ TRUTH   ☐ DARE

Are you in love
with Ms Beck?

OK I switch
to Dare.

87

Then Greg dared me to get him a drink from the vending machine. I didn't know that was the way truth or dare WORKED but I was just glad Greg didn't make me answer that question.

After I got Greg his drink I did a little more studying but then he started up with the notes again.

Hey Rowley
THAT'S YOU

Well I didn't like THAT so I sent back a drawing of my OWN.

And then Greg drew another picture of ME and I drew another one of HIM.

After a while we filled up two whole PAGES with drawings.

Greg tried to start a NEW page of drawings but I just ignored him. And I guess he didn't like that because he kept trying to get my attention.

I decided to move to a new spot that wasn't so close to Greg. I was glad I could finally get some peace and quiet but THAT didn't last long.

If you're wondering what that "bang" was all about, well here's what happened. When I got up and moved to another desk some grown-up took my spot. And I guess Greg thought it was still ME and he tied the guy's shoes together.

Then when the guy stood up he fell backwards.

After that happened Greg got out of there as fast as he could. I figured I'd better get out of there TOO because I didn't want that guy to think I was the one who tied his shoes together.

I followed Greg into the children's section where there was an empty table. He put his stuff at one end and I sat down at the other so I didn't have to be too close to him.

Greg said we should take another study break but I said I was gonna keep working. Then Greg balled up a piece of paper and tried to throw it in the trash can across the room.

He missed but he kept shooting balled-up
pieces of paper which made it hard for me
to concentrate.

Then Greg finally got one in and he said
he bet I couldn't make the same shot as
him. But when I told him I really needed to
study he said I was too scared to try and
then he started acting like a CHICKEN.

I tried to ignore him but it wasn't so easy, ESPECIALLY when he got up on the table.

Then all of a sudden Greg sat down on the table and started making grunting noises. At first I thought he might be having a bathroom emergency. But when he got up there was an EGG.

Well I didn't want Greg to lay another egg so I balled up a piece of paper and tossed it at the trash can. And I wasn't looking to see if it went in but I guess it DID.

Greg said my shot was total LUCK and there was no WAY I could make it again even if I tried a thousand times. But I decided I wasn't GONNA try again.

Greg said I COULDN'T retire but I said yeah I COULD. And it was his own fault for giving me the idea anyway.

One time I had my birthday party at the bowling alley and Greg hit a strike with his first ball. Then he retired and it ruined the game for everyone else.

When Greg couldn't get me to UN-retire he tried making a backwards shot HIMSELF. But he went through like a million pieces of notebook paper and he couldn't even come CLOSE. I was just glad he was leaving me alone because I was getting a lot of work done.

I finished the practice test and then I was
gonna go over my notes from class. But
that's when I found out Greg was getting
all his paper from MY NOTEBOOK.

Well that made me really mad because
Ms Beck said we were allowed to look at
our notes during the TEST.

So I got down on the floor and started picking up all the balled-up pieces of paper. I figured maybe I could smooth the pages out when I got home and then tape them back into my notebook.

But Greg just kept SHOOTING and he finally got one in by bouncing it off my HEAD.

Well that made me really mad and I started chasing Greg with that egg he laid.

But I guess we were making too much noise and that got us in trouble with the librarian again.

She made me call my parents to come get us and that was fine with ME.

I had to stay up for two more hours uncrinkling my notes and taping them into my notebook and was up ANOTHER half hour researching stuff on my dad's computer.

THE TIME I MADE THE BIGGEST MISTAKE OF MY LIFE

OK this is just part two of that last chapter but I got so mad writing it I kind of had to take a break. But I've gotta take some deep breaths because this chapter is gonna be even HARDER to write.

The next day during the maths test I tried to use my notes to help but they were all out of order.

Plus it was hard to concentrate because Greg kept trying to ask me questions.

Some of the OTHER kids were getting stressed out about the test too because Timothy Lautner got dizzy and Ms Beck had to take him to the nurse's office.

Well as soon as Ms Beck left the room Greg scooted his chair real close to mine and looked over my shoulder.

SCOOT
SCOOT

I whispered to Greg to go away because he was trying to CHEAT. But Greg said it's not cheating since we were study partners and we both had the exact same information in our brains.

I guess he had a point but I still didn't feel GOOD about it.

Then Greg said he already FINISHED his
test and was only trying to make sure
I got the right answers. And that made
me feel kind of nervous because I wasn't
positive about a few of them.

So I let Greg check my test, and believe
me if I could do everything over again I
wouldn't have LET him.

After a minute I started thinking maybe
Greg wasn't just looking over my test
to check my answers but that he was
COPYING me.

And it was too late to STOP him so I
tried to pretend it wasn't happening.

Greg pushed his chair back to its normal
spot right before Ms Beck came back.
And when the bell rang for the end of
class she went around and collected all
our papers.

The next day Ms Beck gave us our tests back and I got 89. I was kind of disappointed in myself because I usually do a lot better. But Greg got 89 too which was a really good grade for HIM.

But if you think this chapter has a happy ending, well guess what? It DOESN'T.

When class ended everyone got up to leave but Ms Beck told me and Greg to stay in our seats.

After everyone left Ms Beck told us she wanted to talk to us about our tests. She said she noticed we got the same grade and we got the same answers right.

But Greg said that made SENSE because we were study partners and we knew all the same stuff.

I felt pretty glad Greg was my friend because he's real good at explaining stuff like that to grown-ups.

I thought Ms Beck was gonna let us leave but she DIDN'T. She said it seemed a little suspicious that our tests were IDENTICAL and she put them side by side to show us what she meant.

Well that's when I found out Greg copied EVERYTHING on my test, even my NAME.

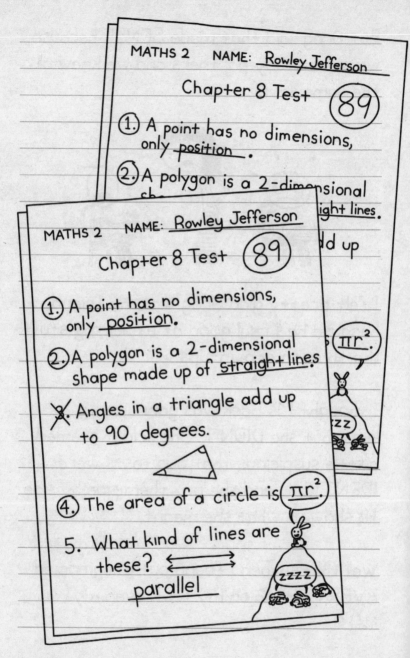

MATHS 2   NAME: Rowley Jefferson

Chapter 8 Test   (89)

1. A point has no dimensions, only _position_.

2. A polygon is a 2-dimensional shape made up of _straight lines_.

3. Angles in a triangle add up to _90_ degrees.

4. The area of a circle is πr^2.

5. What kind of lines are these? ⟷
   parallel

Ms Beck said it was obvious that Greg copied my paper so he was gonna have to do three days of detention PLUS he had to take the test again.

I thought Ms Beck was gonna give me detention too but she DIDN'T. But what she said was WORSE than detention.

ROWLEY I AM DISAPPOINTED IN YOU.

Ms Beck said she wanted us to learn a lesson from this and we both swore it would never happen again. Ms Beck said well that's good because once people know you're a CHEAT it follows you wherever you go.

Then Ms Beck said we were free to go. Greg got up and left but I gave Ms Beck a hug to show her I was sorry. But I think maybe I hugged her for too long.

On the way home from school all I kept thinking about was what Ms Beck said about being a cheat.

Well I learned MY lesson but I'm not so sure about Greg.

The next day Ms Beck made Greg sit at the back of the class and retake the test. But Greg was asking me questions pretty much the whole time and I had to pretend I couldn't hear him.

And if you're like "Rowley why are you still friends with Greg?" well my answer is that Greg's still a good FRIEND, he's just a bad study partner.

Plus he's the only person I know who can lay an egg.

THE TIME GREG TOTALLY
HAD MY BACK

OK Greg if you're still reading this then sorry if I made you look bad in the last two chapters. But don't worry because in this one you're gonna come out looking pretty good.

So last year our science teacher was Mrs Modi, but when she had a baby the school got this guy named Mr Hardy to fill in for her.

I think Mr Hardy used to teach at the school a long time ago and now they bring him back whenever they need a long-term sub.

Mr
Hardy

I thought Mr Hardy was just going to do things the same way as Mrs Modi but I was WRONG. All Mr Hardy did every day was write our assignment on the board and then read at his desk for the rest of class.

After like the third day, kids started goofing off during class. And Mr Hardy didn't even CARE.

One time a couple of kids tried to kill a bug
by dropping their textbooks on it. Luckily
the bug got away but even with all the
noise Mr Hardy never looked UP.

THUMP   WHOMP

Well maybe Mr Hardy wasn't bothered but
I couldn't concentrate on my assignments
with all that craziness going on every day.

Greg told me I was wasting my time doing the daily assignments because Mr Hardy was never gonna even LOOK at them. Greg said I should just live it up with everyone ELSE until Mrs Modi returned and things went back to normal.

Well guess what? Mrs Modi DIDN'T come back. She decided she wanted to be a full-time mom and that meant Mr Hardy was our teacher for the rest of the YEAR.

Now that Mr Hardy was our official science teacher I thought things would get better. But they got WORSE.

Then on the last day of school Mr Hardy announced he was gonna give everyone their GRADES. Well that freaked out most of the kids in my class because just about everyone in there deserved an "F".

Mr Hardy started going down the aisles and whispering each kid's grade in their ear. But Mr Hardy doesn't have a whispering voice so everybody else could hear what he was saying.

The first kid to get his grade was Dennis Diterlizzi and he got a "C". But Mr Hardy talks real slow so it sounded more like this:

CEEEEEEEE

The next kid got a "C" too and so did
every kid after that. Even Greg got a "C"
and he didn't hand in a single assignment.
And he was real happy about it because
he didn't wanna go to summer school.

So then it was MY turn and I was kind
of crossing my fingers hoping I'd get a
GOOD grade. But I got the same grade as
everyone ELSE.

So I guess Greg was right that Mr Hardy never looked at those assignments.

Mr Hardy moved on to the next kid but all of a sudden Greg stood up and argued with Mr Hardy. Greg told him I was the only kid who did any work and that he's a terrible teacher and that someone should report him to the PRINCIPAL.

I was pretty shocked because Greg never stood up for me like that before. For a second I thought Mr Hardy was gonna send GREG to the principal.

But after a minute Mr Hardy whispered the NEW grade in my ear.

On the walk home I told Greg he was a great pal for doing that for me. And I said now we were even for that time I saved him from Tevin Larkin's birthday party.

But Greg said what he did for me was WAY better than getting him out of Tevin's party. He said by getting me that "B" he probably just saved me from getting some crummy job later on in life.

So I said OK how much more do I have to do until we're EVEN? And then he drew a chart to show me.

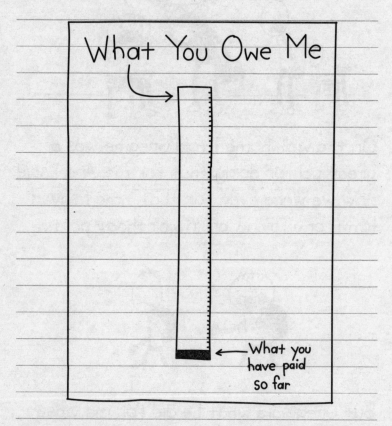

What You Owe Me

What you have paid so far

I guess that means I've got a long way to go. But that's OK because me and Greg are gonna be friends for a long time and I'll get a lot of chances to pay him back.

THE TIME I REALIZED MAYBE GREG DOESN'T ALWAYS TELL THE TRUTH

So after that time me and Greg were study partners I asked him how the heck he laid that egg and he told me he can lay any kind of egg he WANTS.

And I said OK then lay an OSTRICH egg, and he said for that he'd need to eat a lot of crisps and then he took some of mine.

MUNCH
MUNCH

But a few days later when I stopped by Greg's house to pick him up for school his mom gave him an egg for his lunch. And then I remembered Greg ALWAYS has a hard-boiled egg for lunch and so he must've had one in his coat pocket the night we studied together.

Well that made me start to wonder if some OTHER stuff I know about Greg isn't true. We've been friends a long time and he's told me a BUNCH of things that seemed a little shaky so now I'm kind of thinking not everything he's told me is a hundred per cent accurate.

Here are a few things I'm starting to wonder about.

1. Greg says he is dating a supermodel but they have to keep it a secret since her career would get ruined if people found out she was dating a middle-school kid.

Greg said whenever she goes on TV she sends him secret messages by blinking.

2. Greg says that one time he threw a frisbee and the wind took it so far that it went all the way around the world and hit him in the back of the head so that's why he won't play sports any more.

3. Greg says that the "star" on the keypad of a phone is really a SNOWFLAKE and it's a direct line to the North Pole. So whenever I do something Greg doesn't like he tells me he's gonna report me to Santa.

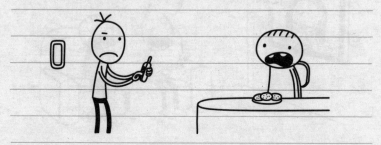

4. Greg says that when he was a baby his mom brought him to a modelling agency and they took some pictures for diaper cream ads.

Greg said the ads never ran in the United States but that if he went to China he'd get totally MOBBED.

5. Greg says that he came up with the "DE-FENCE" chant at basketball games and every time a crowd says it he gets one hundred dollars sent to his bank account.

6. Greg says he's 500 years old but he doesn't age and he has to move every few years so no one will figure it out. He says he knew Abraham Lincoln in middle school and he was kind of a jerk.

7. Greg says there's a form you can fill in at the town hall to legally adopt any kid you want, and that he adopted me so now I have to do whatever he tells me.

8. Greg says that he can turn into any form of water whenever he wants, but when I asked him to turn into a glass of water he said the LAST time he did that Rodrick drank him and it took two days to get back to human form.

9. Greg says he only uses five per cent of his brain, and if he WANTED to he could levitate a building with his mind. I said maybe I could levitate a building too but he said probably not because I'm already using one hundred per cent of my brain.

10. Speaking of BRAINS, Greg says he's got ESP and he always knows what I'm gonna do before I do it.

That one might actually be true because I've seen him do it a bunch of times.

Anyway I'm guessing at least HALF this stuff is made up but I'm just writing it down here in case it ISN'T.

And for the record Greg's been eating a LOT of my crisps over the last three weeks and there's still no ostrich egg.

THE TIME ME AND GREG CAME UP
WITH OUR OWN SUPERHERO

OK this is probably gonna be the best
chapter in this book because it's the only
one that's got superheroes in it. And I
hope I didn't spoil the surprise but even if
I did, trust me it's still gonna be a pretty
good chapter.

This one day it was raining so me and
Greg couldn't go outside. And Greg wasn't
allowed to play video games because he
lost his temper playing Twisted Wizard.

Mrs Heffley said kids our age spend too much time in front of screens anyway and it was good for us to take a break.

Then she gave us some markers and a sketchbook and told us we should use our imaginations and make up our own comics like we USED to.

Well the LAST time me and Greg made some comics together it didn't turn out so good for me. And if you don't know the whole story then I'll give you the short version.

In our first year of middle school me and Greg worked on a comic together called "Zoo-Wee Mama".

But then Greg got bored of it and said I should do it by MYSELF.

And then my comic got in the school paper and Greg was mad at me even though he's the one who TOLD me I should do it.

Then we got in a big fight in front of the whole school and some teenagers came out of NOWHERE and they caught me and Greg.

Then they made me eat a piece of _____ that was on the basketball court.

CHEW
CHEW

I still can't eat pizza or mozzarella sticks or anything else with _____ in it but Greg says I need to "get over it" because that happened a long time ago.

So anyway when I opened that sketchbook Mrs Heffley gave us, there were a bunch of Zoo-Wee Mamas in there that we never handed in to the school paper.

Greg said I should put them in here because they were gonna be worth a lot of money when he gets famous.

I told Greg maybe we should write some MORE Zoo-Wee Mamas but he said that joke is stale and we need to come up with something NEW.

And then Greg had an AWESOME idea. He said we should create our own SUPERHERO. Well I liked that idea a lot because it sounded FUN. But Greg said that he didn't care about having fun, he just cared about the MONEY.

Greg said that if you come up with a superhero then you can sell the movie rights and sit back and wait for the money to roll in.

Then we started talking about what we'd do with all the money we were gonna make from our superhero idea. I said I'd go to the toy aisle at the store and I'd fill up a shopping trolley with as many toys as I could fit.

But Greg said I wasn't thinking BIG enough. He said he'd buy the whole STORE and wear a different pair of sneakers every day and he'd live in the snacks aisle.

Then I said I'd buy a fancy sports car and I'd give Ms Beck a ride to school every morning.

Greg said we were gonna be so rich we could buy the whole SCHOOL and fire all the teachers and have epic paintball fights in the hallways.

I said maybe we shouldn't fire ALL the teachers because Ms Beck is really nice and she's good at teaching maths.

Greg said we'd be so rich we wouldn't NEED to learn maths any more but we could keep Ms Beck around because we'd need someone to count our money for us. And I guess that made me feel a little better.

Greg said we had PLENTY of time to figure out what we were gonna do with all our money LATER ON but right now it was time to get serious about this superhero idea.

Greg said the FIRST thing we needed to do was figure out what kind of POWERS our superhero should have.

I said maybe he could fly or have super strength but Greg said both those ideas were dumb because they've been done a million times before.

Then I said maybe our superhero could have X-ray vision but Greg said that wasn't a good superpower because once he accidentally saw his grandpa naked and he wishes he HADN'T.

Greg said we needed to do something ORIGINAL so we started coming up with ideas that no one had ever THOUGHT of before. And the ideas we came up with were OK but not great.

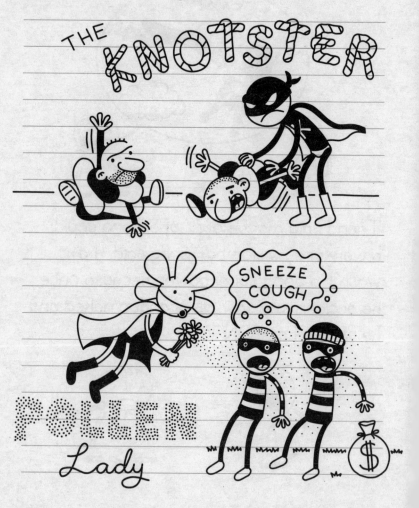

DIAPER WHIP

SQUISH

KRUNCHER

CRUNCH!

THE SQUISHER

The one we liked the best was this guy called the Chuckster who could throw his own HEAD like a football.

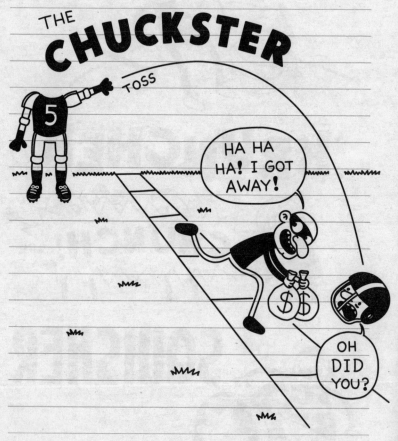

But Greg said the Chuckster wouldn't work as an action figure because the head would be a choking hazard for little kids.

Then we tried to come up with some characters that WOULD be OK if a kid accidentally swallowed them but most of our ideas weren't that good.

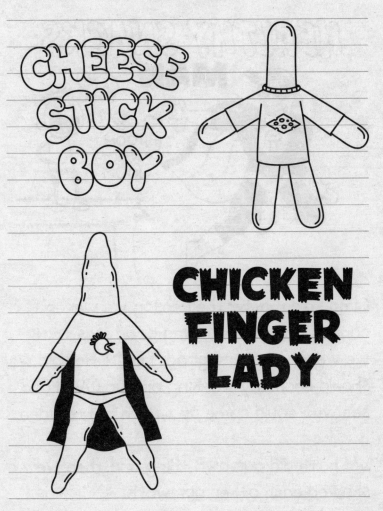

CHEESE STICK BOY

CHICKEN FINGER LADY

Greg said moms are usually the ones who buy their kids toys so we should come up with something THEY'D like. But we weren't happy with that idea either.

Greg said maybe the reason we weren't coming up with anything good was that we weren't a very good TEAM. He said we should each try working on our OWN and see who could come up with a better idea.

We both did our own thing and then we showed each other our work.

Greg's superhero was a guy from space who had a different kind of power in each fingertip which was actually a pretty awesome idea.

I told Greg his idea was cool and we should go with THAT.

Then Greg said well what's YOUR idea? But I didn't wanna tell him because I knew he'd laugh. And then he promised he WOULDN'T laugh so I showed him my character.

Greg asked what Amazing Guy's superpower was and I said it was KINDNESS. And that made Greg break his promise about not laughing.

Greg said a superhero should be EDGY and it would be cool if Amazing Guy had knives coming out of his knuckles and wore a black leather jacket and said swears when he fights the bad guys.

But I said I wanted Amazing Guy to be a role model for children, and that made Greg break his promise a second time.

POUND
POUND

I told Greg if he didn't like my character that was fine but I wasn't giving him any money if I sold the MOVIE rights. And all of a sudden Greg got real interested in Amazing Guy and said if I get rich I owe him half the money because I used his markers and paper.

I said that wasn't true and Greg said he'd call his lawyer to find out. Then Greg dialled a number on the phone and I listened in on his half of the conversation.

MM HMM. YEP, THEY'RE MY MARKERS. FIFTY PER CENT? OK THAT'S WHAT I THOUGHT.

Then Greg hung up the phone. I told him to call his lawyer BACK because I wanted to ask him a few questions.

But Greg said I couldn't AFFORD his lawyer and I had to get my own.

Greg said since we were gonna split things 50-50 then we were equal partners and we needed to work TOGETHER. I said fine but I still don't want Amazing Guy to say swears and Greg said OK we'll talk about that later.

Greg said the FIRST thing we needed to do was give Amazing Guy an "origin story" to show how he got his powers. Then he told me how OTHER superheroes got their powers.

I said Amazing Guy just had good parents
who raised him to be a nice person and
that's why he decided when he grew up
he'd fight for people who needed his help.

But Greg said that's a TERRIBLE origin
story. He said something EXCITING
needed to happen, like Amazing Guy gets
hit by a meteor or gets bitten by a
radioactive bug or something like that.

And I said OK fine then Amazing Guy gets
hit by a double rainbow and THAT'S how
he gets his powers.

Greg said that didn't make SENSE but
he didn't feel like getting into a dumb
argument about rainbows so we'd come
back to the origin story later on too.

Greg said every good superhero has a
secret identity so we needed to come up
with one for Amazing Guy.

I said he could be a nurse at an emergency
care clinic and when he gets off work at
6:00 p.m. he becomes Amazing Guy and
then helps people until his bedtime.

And no one knows his secret identity, not even Nurse Beck who works with him at the emergency care place.

Greg said I got that name from Ms Beck our maths teacher but I said nope it's just a coincidence.

Greg said we were wasting too much time talking about stupid stuff and we needed to design Amazing Guy's SUIT.

I said I liked the suit I came up with just FINE but Greg said it was stupid because everyone could tell who he was if they saw him walking around in regular life.

Greg said Amazing Guy needed a mask, so he drew one that looked pretty awesome. And he added a cape too.

Then Greg said if Amazing Guy doesn't have any real powers then maybe his SUIT could have powers. But I said Amazing Guy has the power of KINDNESS and his gloves are padded so he doesn't hurt the bad guys too much.

I said I wanted to do all the drawings and Greg said that's fine but he'd do the WRITING. So I drew this awesome scene where Amazing Guy has to leave work early to fight some bad guys and I left space for Greg to fill in the words.

I told Greg he totally messed up my comic
and that from now on I'd do the drawing
AND the writing. Then Greg said he was
gonna call his lawyer again and I said go
right AHEAD. And even when he said he
was gonna call SANTA I wouldn't budge.

Greg said he didn't want to write for
my stupid comic anyway because my
superhero was terrible and he said he was
just gonna write Intergalactic Man comics
and I said fine because my character was
BETTER.

Then Greg said if Intergalactic Man got
in a fight with Amazing Guy he'd wipe him
out in like five seconds. And I said oh yeah
let's see about THAT. So then we drew
this battle and he drew HIS superhero
and I drew MINE.

I guess I got a little carried away with that last drawing because after I drew it Greg said it was probably time for me to go home.

Maybe next time I won't have Amazing Guy use his FULL powers on his enemies. Because I wouldn't want his parents or Nurse Beck to be disappointed in him.

THE TIME ME AND GREG HAD A TWO-NIGHT SLEEPOVER

OK you already know this from the title of the chapter, but this one time me and Greg had a TWO-NIGHT SLEEPOVER. And I bet you think we had a total blast and you want to read about all the wacky stuff we did, but guess what? It was not that fun at ALL.

The reason this sleepover happened was because my Nana got sick and me and my parents were gonna go visit her but then Mrs Heffley said:

WHY DON'T YOU TWO GO AND WE'LL WATCH ROWLEY FOR THE WEEKEND?

When my mom said OK to that idea, me and Greg were HYPED because we never had a two-night sleepover before. But I guess we should've waited until later to celebrate because of the whole Nana thing.

On Friday my mom packed my bag for the weekend and she put in an extra pair of underwear "just in case".

Plus she packed a picture of her and my dad so I could look at it if I missed them too much while they were gone.

Like I said before, the sleepover wasn't a lot of fun but it started off pretty good. We played video games in Greg's basement and ate snacks. Then we prank-called Scotty Douglas and he blew the whistle he keeps right by his phone for when we do that.

EXCUSE ME SIR YOUR REFRIGERATOR IS RUNNING SO MAYBE YOU SHOULD GO CATCH IT.

TWEET

But then Mrs Douglas called Mrs Heffley
to tell on us for prank-calling Scotty.
Then Mrs Heffley told us we were
"bullying" and that made me feel ashamed.

At 9:00 Mrs Heffley said it was time for
bed and she went back upstairs.

I was pretty tired but Greg said he had an
idea. There is this kid on our street named
Joseph O'Rourke who has a trampoline
but he never lets anyone use it. Greg said
we should sneak out and jump on the
trampoline while Joe was asleep.

Well I wasn't so crazy about this
sneaking-out idea but Greg said if I was
going to be a baby I should go up to
Manny's room and sleep in THERE.

I said I wasn't a baby and he said "Yuh-huh"
and I said "Nuh-uh." Then he said "Yuh-
huh times INFINITY" but I was ready
for that and I said "Nuh-uh times infinity
SQUARED." And I thought I had Greg beat
with that one, but he got me anyway
when he said "Yuh-huh times infinity
squared plus ONE."

So we snuck out of the back door and I
followed Greg up to Joe's. It was really
cold outside and all I had on were my
jammies, but I didn't wanna complain
because then Greg might call me a baby
again.

Sure enough all the lights at the O'Rourkes'
house were off so this was our big chance
to use Joe's trampoline. Greg said we
couldn't make any noise and then he
climbed up and did a bunch of jumps but he
was real quiet.

Then it was MY turn. This was my first
time on a trampoline and it was REALLY
fun, and I guess that's why I forgot we
were being sneaky.

The lights came on inside the O'Rourkes' house and their dog started barking and Greg took off without me. I wanted to run TOO but it's not so easy to stop bouncing when you're on a trampoline.

Once I finally stopped I ran to the Heffleys' house and went around to the back door.

But I guess Greg wanted to teach me a lesson for making too much noise at the O'Rourkes' because he wouldn't let me in.

I tried to show Greg that I was freezing but I don't think he really got what I was trying to tell him.

I thought he was gonna make me stay out there all NIGHT so I ran around the house to see if the front door was unlocked.

But it WASN'T and I kind of freaked out a little.

The good news is that someone came to the door pretty quick but the bad news is that it was Mr Heffley.

Mr Heffley told us to get our stuff from the basement because we were gonna have to stay in Greg's room so he could keep an eye on us.

Then Mrs Heffley came into Greg's room and said she was disappointed in us for sneaking out and that made me feel ashamed all over again. But I think Greg gets in trouble a LOT because he didn't seem that ashamed.

As soon as Mrs Heffley went to bed, Greg said I was dumb for making all that noise at the O'Rourkes' and EXTRA dumb for ringing the doorbell. I said I was sorry for saying "wheeee" on the trampoline but the doorbell thing was all his fault.

Then Greg whapped me with his pillow and I whapped him BACK but I guess we made too much noise and that's why I had to see Mr Heffley in his underwear for the second time in one night.

Mr Heffley told Greg he had to sleep in
Manny's room and all I could think was,
who's the baby NOW?

The next day Mrs Heffley woke me up
and said breakfast was ready downstairs.

Greg was in the bathroom brushing his
teeth and he said he hoped I brought my
own toothpaste because if I wanted to
use his I was gonna have to pay for it
since it was his house.

I told him I DID have my own toothpaste
and then he said I was gonna have to pay
for the water I used to brush my teeth.

I said I wasn't gonna pay for the water because I was the guest and guests are supposed to get treated SPECIAL.

So he said if I wasn't gonna pay what I owed I couldn't eat breakfast or any other meals either.

I was like yeah RIGHT and then he said I was using his electricity and he shut the light off on me.

When I got downstairs I told Mrs Heffley about all the stuff Greg said upstairs and she said I was RIGHT about guests being special.

Then she let me pick which pancakes I wanted before Greg got to pick.

After breakfast Mrs Heffley said we had too much screen time the day before and that we had to figure out something to do until lunch.

Greg was in a grumpy mood so I decided to cheer him up with a knock-knock joke. But he wouldn't do the "who's there" part no matter how many times I tried.

I told Greg I was gonna go upstairs and tell his mom he wasn't saying "who's there". And that finally made him do it.

WHO'S THERE?

I said what do elephants do at night? But Greg said you're not supposed to ask a question in that part of a knock-knock joke and I said yes you are.

Then he told me I was dumb and I said I was gonna tell on him for THAT. And Greg said go right ahead and so I DID.

So Mrs Heffley came down and told Greg he wasn't allowed to call me dumb or stupid or any other bad names either.

But then when she left, Greg said he had a new nickname for me. At first I thought it sounded cool but then I figured out what he MEANT.

I told Greg I was gonna tell on him AGAIN but then Greg said that it was Opposite Day and everything meant the opposite of what it was supposed to.

Well I knew what he MEANT so I went and told Mrs Heffley. But at first she didn't get mad because she didn't know it was Opposite Day.

I explained it to Mrs Heffley and she made Greg apologize. But I think he might've been being opposite.

Mrs Heffley told us that sometimes friends get on each other's nerves but we needed to figure things out since we had a whole day to go on our sleepover.

She said maybe we should spend some time apart and I thought that sounded like a GREAT idea. So I hung out with Manny in his room for a while.

Even though I was having fun with Manny, I missed my mom and dad and I looked at their picture whenever I got the chance.

WHIMPER

The next time I saw Greg was when we had lunch. Mrs Heffley made peanut butter and jam sandwiches and she even remembered to cut the crusts off mine.

After we finished our sandwiches she gave us chocolate-chip cookies for dessert. She gave Greg one but she gave me TWO because she said I was the guest and guests are SPECIAL.

I ate one of my cookies but I made a shield around the other cookie with my arms so Greg couldn't get it. Sometimes if I have something Greg wants he will lick it so I won't want it any more.

That's what he did last Halloween when I got more candy than he did.

LICK

But Greg said he was full and didn't even WANT my cookie. He said that while I was playing with Manny he was reading a book about magic and he wanted to show me a trick. I really like magic so I said OK.

First Greg told me to put my fingers on the edge of the table so they were close together like this:

Then Greg took my glass of milk and put it on top of my fingers.

I asked him when the magic part was gonna happen and he said it was ALREADY happening because I couldn't move. Well he was right because if I did, the glass of milk would tip over and spill. And Mr Heffley gets mad when I spill stuff in his house.

But then Greg said here's the REAL magic part and he took my cookie and ate it up.

GOBBLE
GOBBLE

After that, Greg went upstairs but I was
stuck at the kitchen table. And I was still
there a half hour later when Mrs Heffley
came back to the kitchen.

I told her what Greg did and boy was she
mad but it wasn't because of the magic
trick. She was mad that Greg took
something that belonged to me without
asking.

189

We went up to Greg's room and then
Mrs Heffley told me I could pick out one
of Greg's things to take home with me so
we'd be even.

Well Greg had a BUNCH of cool toys that
he never let me play with so it was really
hard to pick. But every time I got close
to one of his favourites he kind of let me
know I shouldn't pick that one.

I picked an action figure that was a knight with a missing arm and Greg seemed OK with that.

But as soon as Mrs Heffley left the room Greg said I could play with my lame action figure because he was gonna play with all his cool stuff by himself.

It kind of bugged me and I wanted to bug Greg BACK. So I pretended I was having a total blast with my toy.

Well it WORKED and Greg said I had to hand over his toy. I said no way and he said he was just gonna wait for me to fall asleep and he'd take it back HIMSELF.

I told him I was gonna put the action figure down my underwear so he couldn't get it and he didn't like that idea.

Then Greg said he'd TRADE me for the action figure and I asked him what he'd give me for it. Greg said he'd give me ninety-nine cents for the knight and I said OK to that.

But then Greg took a dirty sock out of his hamper and tried to get me to smell it.

And I was like what was that for? And Greg said that was my first "scent".

I said I wanted ninety-nine CENTS not ninety-nine SCENTS. But Greg said a deal's a deal and then he tried to get me to smell another sock as my second scent.

When I told Greg I was gonna go tell on him again, he said he'd trade me his Lego dragon for my knight and I said YES because that dragon is way better than a knight with no arm.

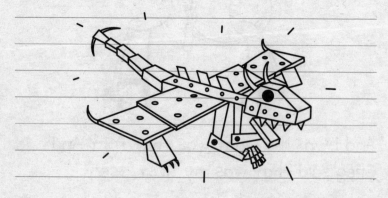

But then when I gave Greg my knight he wouldn't give me the dragon because he said I should've remembered it was still Opposite Day.

Well that was the last straw for me and I tried to grab the dragon from Greg. But it kind of slipped out of my hands and hit the floor and broke apart.

CLATTER   CLATTER

I guess we were making a lot of noise because the next thing we knew Greg's mom was back in the room. She said she was gonna have to separate us for the rest of the night which was fine with ME.

Mrs Heffley said that we each had one half of the bedroom and that we had to stay on our own side. So she asked me which side I wanted and I picked the side with the BED which made Greg mad.

When Mrs Heffley went back to her room, Greg said he was turning on an invisible force field between our two sides.

Then he said if someone crossed over they'd get zapped.

Greg said he was fine with me having the bed because he could sleep on an air mattress and plus all the fun stuff was on HIS side of the room. And when I reached over to Greg's side for my action figure, sure enough I got zapped.

197

I opened the drawer in the table next to Greg's bed to see if he had any comics I could read. Well there weren't any comics but one of Greg's old handheld video games was in there.

So I played it and Greg couldn't do anything because of the force field.

But Greg said I could play video games by myself like a nerd because he was having a wild party on HIS side of the room and I wasn't invited. And I got kind of jealous because his party looked pretty fun.

I said well I'm having a party on MY side and it was even more wild than HIS party and I had really good music. Greg said I couldn't even come up with an original idea but I still think he was jealous of my party.

Then Greg said the plug to my party speakers was on HIS side of the room so he pulled it out to shut off my music.

Greg got back to his party and I tried to tell him to plug my speakers back in but Greg couldn't hear me because the music at his party was too loud.

But this time MR Heffley came into the room and Greg didn't notice him standing in the doorway.

Mr Heffley said he didn't want one more peep out of us and then he left the room. We were both quiet for a long time but then Greg tried to get me to laugh and I almost did.

I was kind of glad we had to be quiet
because I was getting pretty sleepy
anyway and I wanted to go to bed.

I told Greg I needed to brush my teeth
and he said too bad because the force
field was still on and I was trapped in my
half of the room for the whole night.

So I asked if he could just turn off the
force field for a little while so I could brush
my teeth but he said once the force field
is turned on it stays on until the morning.

And then Greg went to the bathroom to
brush HIS teeth and came back to the
room after he was done.

That's when I remembered I need to use the bathroom before I go to bed every night so I don't have any accidents.

But Greg said I was just gonna have to hold it until the morning. I said I couldn't MAKE it all the way to morning and Greg said that wasn't his problem.

I said if Greg didn't shut off the force field I was gonna have to pee into the Chewbacca mug on the table next to Greg's bed. Then he told me he had a special invisible knife that could cut through the force field.

Greg showed me how the knife worked by cutting a square in the force field right next to the table where the mug was.

Then he reached through the hole and grabbed the mug.

I asked Greg to cut a Rowley-sized hole in the force field so I could get through it to use the bathroom.

But Greg said the knife ran on invisible batteries and they got used up when he made HIS hole so I was out of luck.

Then Greg started talking about all sorts of things that made me feel like I really needed to use the bathroom.

Finally Greg got tired and he fell asleep. I thought about trying to sneak past him but I was worried he was just faking it and I was gonna get zapped.

After a while I fell asleep too. But I woke up around six in the morning feeling like I was gonna BURST.

I didn't care about the force field any more but I was worried that if I used the bathroom I might wake up Mr Heffley. But I should've just used the bathroom anyway because Mr Heffley was already up for the day.

Luckily Mr Heffley didn't look up in time to see me at the window and when he got to Greg's room I was already back in bed.

I fell back asleep after a while and got up when Mrs Heffley said it was time for breakfast.

After we ate, I went to get my knight action figure from Greg's room but I couldn't find the toy ANYWHERE.

Greg said he didn't know what happened to it, but Mrs Heffley said he had to help me look for it.

So the two of us searched Greg's room but to be honest he wasn't all that helpful.

I guess Mrs Heffley thought Greg was hiding the action figure from me because she said if he didn't hand it over in two minutes then he was gonna be in big trouble.

Greg said he needed to use the bathroom but he'd keep looking for my action figure after he was done. But I noticed he had something in his hand when he went in there.

Greg locked the bathroom door and
Mrs Heffley told him to come out right
this instant. But then the toilet flushed
and when Greg opened the door there
wasn't anything in his hand any more.

Mrs Heffley made Greg give me THREE
toys and this time I picked out ones that
WEREN'T broken.

My mom and dad came and got me just
before lunch and boy was I glad to see
them. And P.S. if you wanted to know
the answer to that knock-knock joke, it's
"Elephants watch elevision."

THE ADVENTURES OF
GREG AND ROWLEY

I'm pretty much up to date on Greg's life so today I showed Greg what I wrote so far. I thought he would like it but he was MAD.

Greg said this book was supposed to be about HIM and not about ME. I told him it was hard to write about just HIM because most of the time we do stuff TOGETHER.

He said I need to go back through the book and take out all the stuff with me in it. I told him that would be dumb because then the book would only be like one page long.

I said maybe we should change the title to "THE ADVENTURES OF GREG AND ROWLEY" and it could be OUR biography.

Then I said since there's a lot of scary stuff in this book we could make it into a spooky series where these two pals solve mysteries. We could make a lot of money and we'd BOTH be rich and famous.

Greg said that was the stupidest idea he ever heard.

He said this book is about HIS life and if he wants to he can change the name of Greg's best friend to "Rupert" and then he wouldn't owe me ANYTHING. Plus he said he'd make Rupert really dumb and drooling all the time.

Then Greg told me the book smelled funny anyway and when I brought it up to my nose to sniff it he closed the book on my face.

So I said hey what was THAT for? And
Greg said that's what I got for dropping
him in the puddle.

Then he said he got me back when I least
expected it and I guess he was right
about THAT.

But I was pretty mad and I whapped him
with his own biography.

WHAP

Well I guess Greg wasn't expecting THAT
because he lost his balance and fell in a
big puddle.

Anyway I am up in my room now and I
am hoping Greg's mom calls him home
for bedtime soon because he already
skipped dinner.

I'm glad all that stuff happened today
because it gave me a whole new chapter in
our biography. I'm sure we'll be pals again
tomorrow and we'll have a bunch of new
adventures that I can put in here.

And I'll bet if we go with my idea about
the scary stuff it'll sell a million copies.

But if Greg changes my name to Rupert I
just want to say for the record that he
wet his pants at that first sleepover too.

OK Now Back to This Being About Me

Well if Greg's not happy with his biography then I can go back to using this journal to write about MYSELF.

So now I'm officially the main character of this book again. And from now on this thing is just gonna be about me and my mom and my dad and I might mention Ms Beck one more time if there's enough room.

Speaking of my mom and dad, after my last fight with Greg they came to my room to talk about it.

ROWLEY MAYBE IT'S TIME TO FIND SOME NEW FRIENDS.

But I don't really think I can add any new friends because Greg takes up so much of my time.

I know me and Greg don't always get along but like Mrs Heffley said, sometimes friends get on each other's nerves.

Well me and Greg get on each other's nerves a LOT so I guess that just proves that we're

I TOLD YOU IT WAS GONNA BE BAD!

Feeling sneaky?

Check out this **EXCLUSIVE EXTRACT** from

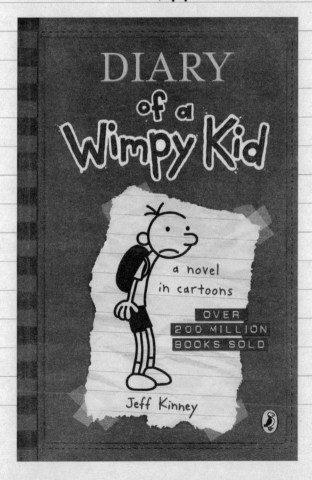

SEPTEMBER

<u>Tuesday</u>

First of all, let me get something straight: this is a JOURNAL, not a diary. I know what it says on the cover, but when Mom went out to buy this thing I SPECIFICALLY told her to get one that didn't say "diary" on it.

Great. All I need is for some jerk to catch me carrying this book around and get the wrong idea.

The other thing I want to clear up right away is that this was MOM's idea, not mine.

But if she thinks I'm going to write down my "feelings" in here or whatever, she's crazy. So just don't expect me to be all "Dear Diary" this and "Dear Diary" that.

The only reason I agreed to do this at all is because I figure later on when I'm rich and famous, I'll have better things to do than answer people's stupid questions all day long. So this book is gonna come in handy.

Like I said, I'll be famous one day, but for now I'm stuck in middle school with a bunch of morons.

Let me just say for the record that I think middle school is the dumbest idea ever invented. You've got kids like me who haven't hit their growth spurt yet mixed in with these gorillas who need to shave twice a day.

And then they wonder why bullying is such a big problem in middle school.

If it was up to me, grade levels would be based on height, not age. But then again, I guess that would mean kids like Chirag Gupta would still be in the first grade.

Today is the first day of school, and right now we're just waiting around for the teacher to hurry up and finish the seating chart. So I figured I might as well write in this book to pass the time.

By the way, let me give you some good advice. On the first day of school, you've got to be real careful where you sit. You walk into the classroom and just plunk your stuff down on any old desk and the next thing you know the teacher is saying –

So in this class, I got stuck with Chris Hosey in front of me and Lionel James at the back of me.

Jason Brill came in late and almost sat to my right, but luckily I stopped that from happening at the last second.

Next period, I should just sit in the middle of a bunch of hot girls as soon as I step in the room. But I guess if I do that, it just proves I didn't learn anything from last year.

Man, I don't know WHAT is up with girls these days. It used to be a whole lot simpler back in elementary school. The deal was, if you were the fastest runner in your class, you got all the girls.

And in the fifth grade, the fastest runner was Ronnie McCoy.

Nowadays, it's a whole lot more complicated. Now it's about the kind of clothes you wear or how rich you are or if you have a cute butt or whatever. And kids like Ronnie McCoy are scratching their heads wondering what the heck happened.

The most popular boy in my grade is Bryce Anderson. The thing that really stinks is that I have ALWAYS been into girls, but kids like Bryce have only come around in the last couple of years.

I remember how Bryce used to act back in elementary school.

But of course now I don't get any credit for sticking with the girls all this time.

Like I said, Bryce is the most popular kid in our grade, so that leaves all the rest of us guys scrambling for the other spots.

The best I can figure is that I'm somewhere around 52nd or 53rd most popular this year. But the good news is that I'm about to move up one spot because Charlie Davies is above me, and he's getting his braces next week.

I try to explain all this popularity stuff to my friend Rowley (who is probably hovering right around the 150 mark, by the way), but I think it just goes in one ear and out the other with him.

Wednesday

Today we had Phys Ed, so the first thing I did when I got outside was sneak off to the basketball court to see if the Cheese was still there. And sure enough, it was.

That piece of Cheese has been sitting on the court since last spring. I guess it must've dropped out of someone's sandwich or something. After a couple of days, the Cheese started getting all mouldy and nasty. Nobody would play basketball on the court where the Cheese was, even though that was the only court that had a hoop with a net.

Then one day, this kid named Darren Walsh touched the Cheese with his finger, and that's what started this thing called the Cheese Touch. It's basically like the Cooties. If you get the Cheese Touch, you're stuck with it until you pass it on to someone else.

The only way to protect yourself from the Cheese Touch is to cross your fingers.

But it's not that easy remembering to keep your fingers crossed every moment of the day. I ended up taping mine together so they'd stay crossed all the time. I got a D in handwriting, but it was totally worth it.

This one kid named Abe Hall got the Cheese Touch in April, and nobody would even come near him for the rest of the year. This summer Abe moved away to California and took the Cheese Touch with him.

I just hope someone doesn't start the Cheese Touch up again, because I don't need that kind of stress in my life any more.

WANT MORE
Wimpy Kid?

Go to
www.wimpykidclub.co.uk/audio

to listen to extracts from the
Wimpy Kid audio series.

Available on CD and digital download.

www.wimpykidclub.co.uk

- Watch TONS of cool videos

- Enter AWESOME competitions

- Take the WIMP WARS challenge!

- Read EXTRACTS from the books

- Download must-have FREEBIES!

Sign up to the newsletter to get ALL the latest **Wimpy Kid** gossip FIRST!

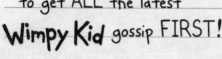

YOU ARE
Awesome

Just like Rowley, spread some awesome friendliness and celebrate the great people you know! Share these awesome award stickers with your family, friends and teachers.

Teacher

Brother

Sister

Friend

Parent

Pet